Katherine Anne Porter

Katherine Anne Porter

THE LIFE OF AN ARTIST

DARLENE HARBOUR UNRUE

University Press of Mississippi / Jackson

A Mary Jayne G. Whittington Book in the Arts

www.upress.state.ms.us

The University Press of Mississippi is a member
of the Association of American University Presses.

First edition 2005

Library of Congress Cataloging-in-Publication Data

Unrue, Darlene Harbour.
   Katherine Anne Porter : the life of an artist / Darlene Harbour Unrue. —
1st ed.
      p. cm. — (Willie Morris books in memoir and biography)
   Includes bibliographical references and index.
   ISBN 1-57806-777-4 (alk. paper)
   1. Porter, Katherine Anne, 1890–1980. 2. Authors, American—20th
century—Biography. 3. Women and literature—United States—History—
20th century. I. Title. II. Series.
   PS3531.O752Z828   2005
   813'.52—dc22   2005001791

British Library Cataloging-in-Publication Data available

For John

CONTENTS

PREFACE

I saw Katherine Anne Porter for the first time in 1961 in Huntington, West Virginia, one of her stops on a cross-country reading tour of college campuses. She impressed me then with her eloquence and drama as she read her beautifully crafted "The Jilting of Granny Weatherall," but I thought little about her for the next fifteen years, while I married, had children, completed master's and doctoral degrees, and began my professional work of teaching and writing. I arrived maturely at Katherine Anne Porter's fiction through Henry James when I saw a similarity in their classical techniques and learned he was one of her masters. In 1976 I met her in Brownwood, Texas, during her final visit to her homeland, and it was then that I turned to an earnest study of her and her work.

In the beginning I had no intention of writing her biography. I was writing critical essays and books about her fiction and editing her uncollected works, and I trusted that the biographical record existing then was dependable and sufficient. When I discovered serious errors and omissions in the published accounts of her life, however, I decided to write what I had come to see as a necessary, new biography of Porter. And although my initial intention was simply to correct mistakes and fill in gaps, as I undertook the task I saw an equally important opportunity to re-envision the themes of her life. Despite her foibles and lapses of judgment, I found myself sympathetically drawn to her, and I developed an abiding passion for my venture.

In 1993 I assumed I was several years away from beginning the actual writing of the biography. I had another book-length Porter project underway, and I wanted to be clear-headed and unencumbered when I began the work of reconstructing her life. In early December, however, my husband and I were having dinner with the critic and scholar Cleanth Brooks, who was in town to present a lecture at the University of Nevada. Questioning me about my then-current task (a textual study of *Ship of Fools*), he said, "I think you should set that aside and begin the biography. And I think you and your husband should come to New Haven and spend a week with me reading through my forty years of letters from Katherine Anne Porter and letting me tell you all that I know about her."

It was a terrible time to take a trip. I was in the middle of final exams and soon expecting a houseful of holiday guests, but we did go. Underlying the present book is the memory of that week: sitting in Cleanth's dining room for hours reading through the hundreds of letters Katherine Anne Porter had written to him and his late wife, walking through the New Haven snow to his favorite restaurants and pubs, listening to his reedy southern voice as he talked about the woman whose biography I was going to write. Five months later he was dead at age eighty-seven from cancer.

By 1993 I already had spent more than a decade in the major and minor repositories of Porter's papers and interviewed a great many people who had known her in the United States and Mexico. For the next several years I continued to track down and speak with members of her family, close friends, and acquaintances, to examine related archives, and to retrace her wanderings throughout the United States, Europe, and Mexico. I visited again her birthplace at Indian Creek, Texas, and the small house in Kyle in which she spent her second through eleventh years. I traipsed through cemeteries and copied tombstone engravings. I found her exact houses, apartment buildings, and hotels (or where they had once stood) in such places as San Antonio, Greenwich Village, Santa Monica, Georgetown, Saratoga Springs, New Orleans, Salem, Reno, Guadalajara, Bermuda, and Mexico City. Mindful of the great changes that had taken place in the years since she was in Europe, I located the boardinghouse in Berlin in which she had lived in the dark, early winter of 1931, her hotel in Basel on the banks of the Rhine in the summer of 1932, her Paris apartments from 1932 to 1936, the inn in Brittany where she spent important months in the 1950s, and the hotel in Rome to which she escaped during the celebrity of *Ship of Fools.* Following her footsteps was impressionistic investigation, to be sure, but the kind that contributed to my sense of *place* in Porter's long, nomadic life. By the time I began the writing I had clearly in my mind a rich and complex portrait of one of the twentieth century's most important and enduring modernist writers and one of its most fascinating women.

Katherine Anne Porter found offensive the labels "nouvelle" or "novella" and insisted that she wrote "short stories," "long stories," "short novels," and one "long novel." Throughout this work I have respected her designated categories. I have placed in quotation marks story titles as well as titles of her unpublished works and works-in-progress, and I have italicized the titles of her novels, both short and long. In quoting her words I have corrected obvious typographical errors, but I have let stand misspellings (including omissions of diacritical marks in foreign words and names) and preserved her sometimes unconventional punctuation with one exception: because she had a habit of inserting a running series of periods within or between sentences, to avoid confusion with ellipses I have changed that mechanical peculiarity to five periods.

ACKNOWLEDGMENTS

During the years of researching and writing this biography, I have become indebted to many people. I owe thanks, first of all, to six persons whose contributions to this biography have been extraordinary: Harrison Paul Porter Jr., Katherine Anne Porter's nephew, who shared with me memories, photographs, taped recordings of his conversations with his aunt, and vital background information and who was always willing to answer my questions in numerous e-mails and telephone conversations; Barbara Thompson Davis, trustee of the Katherine Anne Porter Literary Estate as well as longtime friend of Porter, who, in addition to giving her full support to the biography, also read the manuscript with conscientious attention and discussed with me hours on end, always with rare insight, various elements of Porter's life; Beth Alvarez, archivist at the University of Maryland in charge of the Katherine Anne Porter Papers, who promptly supplied materials I requested, responded to my many questions, meticulously read the manuscript, and offered valuable suggestions based on her own extensive knowledge of Porter's history; Charles East, editor, historian, and writer, who discovered Porter's sworn statement in the Baton Rouge Parish records and, thus, the identity of her third husband, Carl von Pless, and who also by reading the manuscript with care and sensitivity helped make the biography more accurate in both spirit and fact; George Hendrick, whose own work on Porter in the 1960s set the standard for meticulous Porter scholarship and who turned over to me his valuable and extensive files; and finally my husband, John Unrue, who lived the adventure with me, tirelessly read the manuscript at all its numerous stages, and offered wise and thoughtful critical comments as well as continuous encouragement. It is he to whom this book is dedicated.

I am also particularly grateful to other persons who read the manuscript from their specialized perspectives and made helpful suggestions and corrections: Charleen Gagliardi, who examined the story of

Porter's life with a poet's eye; and Sarah H. Smith, MD, who read the manuscript for medical accuracy. I want to sincerely thank, too, David Locher, Porter's student and friend who made important observations in the five chapters that followed the recounting of his meeting of Porter at the University of Michigan, talked with me many times on the phone, and provided me with mementos from her.

I would like to express my appreciation to the University of Nevada, Las Vegas, for various kinds of assistance, including sabbaticals, released time, and grants, and I want to thank especially former president Robert C. Maxson, who enhanced an important segment of my study with contributions from his faculty research fund. I have also valued the support of English Department chairs Christopher Hudgins, John Irsfeld, and Joseph McCullough and former Arts and Letters College dean Guy Bailey.

Other persons at the University of Nevada, Las Vegas, have kindly aided my research: Margaret Wells, who helped with genealogical investigation; Richard Harp, who contributed to my knowledge of *Ship of Fools* analogs; Karen Haggar, who directed me to important information about Yvor Winters; and graduate student assistants Joyce Ahn, Elaine Bunker, Cheryl Cunningham Emerson, Lynette Curtis, Mary Dengler, John Kerrigan, Cynthia McCoy, Jeff McIntyre-Strasburg, Karenmary Penn, Daniel Sievek, Greg Wright, and Gigi Yoshida.

My debt to the staffs of the James Morrow and Lied Libraries at the University of Nevada, Las Vegas, is extensive, and I owe special thanks to former humanities librarian Susan Biery, who investigated an important aspect of Porter's Kentucky ancestry.

Librarians and archivists at other institutions have also provided valuable help. I thank Cathy Henderson of the Harry Ransom Humanities Research Center at the University of Texas at Austin; Patricia Willis at the Beinecke Library, Yale; Howard Gotlieb at the Mugar Memorial Library, Boston University; Carol Turley and Dennis Bitterlich at the University Research Library, University of California, Los Angeles; Nancy Baird and Connie Mills at the Kentucky Museum and Library, Western Kentucky University; Charles Spurlin at the Victoria, Texas, Library; Vicky Marlette and Sr. Maria Carolina Flores at Our Lady of the Lake University; Robert Matuozzi at Washington State University Libraries; Kathryn Talalay at the Academy of Arts and Letters; Sharon Abbey at the Green Library, Stanford University; Sally Gross at the University of Texas at Arlington Library; Christopher Coleman at the Jean and Alexander Heard Library, Vanderbilt University; Vicky Jones, at the University of Oregon Libraries; Jennifer King at the American Heritage Center, University of Wyoming; Charles W. Mann at the Pattee Library, Pennsylvania State University; Alice V. Clark at the Princeton University Libraries; Sigrid Perry at the Northwestern University Library; L. Rebecca Johnson Melvin at the University of Delaware Library; Heather Munro at the Lilly Library, Indiana University; and special collections staffs at the Mississippi Department of Archives and History; the History Center at the University of Texas at Austin; the New York Public Library; the Houghton Library, Harvard; Butler Library, Columbia University; the Central Dallas Public Library; the Newberry Library; Syracuse University Library; the State University of New York at Buffalo Libraries; Amherst College Library; University of Nevada, Reno, Library; Middlebury College Library; Miller Library, Colby College; the Carl A. Kroch Library, Cornell University; the Schlesinger Library, Radcliffe College; University of Washington Libraries; the University of California, Davis, Library; Sweet Briar College Library; the Gelman Library at George Washington University; the Kenneth Spencer Research Library at the University of Kansas; the University of Illinois at Urbana-Champaign Library; the Dartmouth College Library; the Virginia Polytechnic Institute Library; the Church of Latter Day Saints Family History Center in Las Vegas; and the Library of Congress.

My Texas research would not have yielded nearly so much without the help of Bette Irsfeld, Mary Sue Fairchild, Lon Drushel Jr., Jay Moore of the Historical Society of San Antonio, Lou Rodenberg, Sylvia Grider, Yana and David Bland, Breckenridge Porter Sr., Amola James, Evelyn Franke, and Bill Crider. I am especially grateful to Tony Hilfer, of the University of Texas at Austin, and Jane Hilfer, former director of Community Relations in the Texas Department of Mental Health and Mental Retardation, who traced for me the history of the Southwestern Lunatic Asylum; Paula Allen, of the *San Antonio Express News*, who supplied me with the history of the Thomas School and ran a fruitful column requesting information about Electric Park; Walter Robertson, who gave me legal documents about Indian Creek and the Jones, Russell, and Porter families and confirmed the identity of his aunt Callie Jo Russell; R. J. Koch, Callie's son, who sent me photographs of Callie Jo Russell; and Charlotte Laughlin, who first brought Callie Jo Russell to my attention, provided me a transcript of

Porter's 1976 talk at Howard Payne University, and otherwise filled in gaps in Porter's Brown County connections. Rita Johns gave me a copy of the autobiography of her mother-in-law, Erna Schlemmer Johns; and Roger L. Brooks, former president of Howard Payne University, made possible my 1976 private introduction to Katherine Anne Porter.

I am greatly indebted to other persons who gave me vital information: Catherine L. Mason, of the Buffalo and Erie County (New York) Historical Society, who located the obituary of Carl von Pless; and Ruth and Howard Pless, who directed me to genealogical information about the Pless family. Horton Foote recalled his meeting with Porter and time they spent together at a New York theater; Fred Barkey increased my understanding of the socialist movement in Texas; Bobbye Miller gave me photographs and a copy of the unpublished autobiography of her grandmother Laredo (Lady) Bunton Humphris, Porter's first cousin; Lynne Hazen discovered an important Delmore Schwartz letter that illuminated an important period in Porter's life; John Edward Hardy shared his memory of Katherine Anne Porter at Louisiana State University when he was a student there; Suzanne Marrs made possible my long interview with Eudora Welty, who recalled for me illuminating details about her forty years of friendship with Porter; Richard Pope helped with my genealogical investigation in Connecticut; Sally Reeves answered my many questions about parochial schools in New Orleans; Herbert Steiner gave me a verbal portrait of Porter in the Stanford classroom; Michael Sundell was an accommodating host during my visit to Yaddo. My attempts to secure Katherine Anne Porter's FBI file were facilitated by J. R Kirkland and especially the office of Nevada Senator Harry Reid.

Outside of the United States my research was strengthened significantly by persons I interviewed in Mexico City with the help of Thomas C. Wright of the University of Nevada, Las Vegas (UNLV), History Department: Kathryn Skidmore Blair and her father, Edgar Skidmore; Winifred Hill; Joe Neal of the *Mexico City News*; Señora Soledad Guzmán (whose mother was Porter's landlady in the early 1920s); Carol Reynosa; Felipe García Beraza, director of the Instituto Mexicano-Norteamericano de Relaciones Culturales; Paul O'Higgins; and Juan O'Gorman. In Paris, Catherine Bachet, André Cointreau, and Patrick Martin of Le Cordon Bleu L'Art Culinaire helped me determine Porter's likely course of study at the school. In Berlin, Hart Wegner, my colleague from the Foreign Languages Department at UNLV, helped me find Rosa Reichl's boardinghouse and retrace

Porter's wanderings in the city and located the record of the *Werra*. In Basel, Fredy Gröbli and Martin Steinmann at the Öffentliche Bibliothek der Universität Basel showed me the Erasmus manuscripts Porter consulted, and Christophe Weder of the Kunstmuseum pointed out the paintings Porter studied in 1932. I particularly appreciate the hospitality of my Belgium hosts, Jerry and Joan Pierson. I thank, too, the Sébilleau family at Le Moulin de Rosmadec in Pont-Aven, France.

I am grateful to the other persons who consented to give me interviews (and often photographs and copies of letters) that yielded important details about specific periods of Porter's life: E. Barrett Prettyman Jr., William and Fern Wilkins, Marcella Winslow, John and Catherine Prince, Toni Willison, Donald Heintze, Richard Scowcroft, and Janet Winters. I especially thank Rosanna Warren, who generously shared with me her memories of her godmother and made it possible for me to spend beneficial hours with her mother, Eleanor Clark.

I appreciate the generous help of biographers Virginia Spencer Carr, Jackson Benson, Jeffrey Myers, Hubert McAlexander, and, especially, Matthew J. Bruccoli, who provided memories of Porter and Albert Erskine and of Porter at the University of Virginia. Other persons who significantly facilitated my research include Blanche Ebeling Koning, Andrew Burke, Carl Griffin, Lisa Botshon, Tom Crouch, Anita and Cecil Wagner, Barbara and Phil Brown, William Hamilton, Porter's godson Daniyál Mueenuddin, and Tamur Mueenuddin, MD.

I wish, finally, to express my sincere gratitude to my agent, Owen Laster, of the William Morris Agency, for his support and encouragement over the years; to Seetha Srinivasan, director of the University Press of Mississippi, for her continuous interest in this biography as well as her wise advice; and to all other persons involved in the conscientious production of this book, particularly Anne Stascavage, editor, Walter Biggins, assistant editor, and Karen Johnson, freelance editor.

Introduction: Katherine Anne Porter and the Honest Biography

Don't be afraid of giving yourself away, . . . for if you write, you must. And if you can't face that, better not write.

On the evening of 10 May 1976, Katherine Anne Porter made a dramatic entrance into a banquet hall on the campus of Howard Payne University in Brownwood, Texas, about twenty-five miles from Indian Creek, where she was born in 1890. Tiny, white-haired, elegant, bejeweled with pearls, diamonds, and emeralds, and dressed in a Mexican wedding gown, she glided to the center of the dais. "I've always had a sort of feeling of homelessness," she told her audience. "I never had a home, except here, this one. And I've been away." She, in fact, had been gone from her native state most of her eighty-six years, and her homecoming seemed to her an apotheosis as she approached the end of her long life.

That "incredible" life, as she once described it, had intrigued the public for more than half a century, but she had revealed only the scantest details of it. Terrified, moreover, that someone else would lay her life bare, she had employed deception, misdirection, and dissuasion to keep her secrets. In 1924 she put forth a lie about her age that (in addition to a measure of vanity) was intended to obscure her most painful and humiliating experiences, and in the late 1920s she retrieved as many of her indiscreet letters as she could in order to destroy them. When Edward Schwartz, a young scholar who corresponded with her while he was writing a doctoral dissertation on her fiction, asked her permission in the mid-1950s to write her biography, she vigorously advised him against the enterprise. "You haven't got a notion of what you are asking for," she warned. Ultimately denying his request ("I think the blood pressure of your interest is not high enough for a biography"), she laid out for him a task she

thought would discourage anyone, describing bushel baskets and filing cabinets stuffed with papers, notebooks, unfinished manuscripts,
and thousands and thousands of letters and pointing out a vast collection of books with her marginalia. "Think of the chronology!" she
reminded him. "And the places I have lived or visited and the *reasons* [her emphasis] for my being there. Friendships, love affairs, marriages . . . ideas of a life time, varying and changing and coming
around again! And the genesis of stories and how related to my experience . . . This and a lot more"—so she ended her peroration—"is
what you undertake in an honest biography."

She had already decided she would outflank would-be biographers
by writing an autobiography in which she could select and shade her
experiences. Over the years, however, she wrote only a few dozen pages
and the year after her appearance at Howard Payne gave up the task
altogether. Her heart was never really in it. She told Schwartz, "Nobody
will be able to see what my life meant until it is ended. How can we
write a story until we know the end?" Quoting the motto Mary Queen
of Scots embroidered on her cloth of estate while confined to prison
awaiting her beheading, Katherine Anne Porter concluded, "In a special
and almost literal way, *In my end is my beginning.*"

When in the 1960s she accepted the inevitability of her biography,
she made letters and papers available and granted interviews. But
there still was a point beyond which she would not go. "There are
dozens of things that might be entertaining," she said, "but I have no
intention of telling them, because they are nobody's business; . . . endless little gossipy incidents that might entertain indulgent friends for
a minute . . . in print . . . look as silly as they really are. Then, there
are the tremendous, unmistakable, life-and-death crises, the scalding,
the bone-breaking events, the lightnings that shatter the landscape of
the soul—who would write that by request?"

Both the public record of Katherine Anne Porter's life and her inner
biography, which she called her "real life," have been hard to assemble not only because of her deceptions and omissions and buried or
missing records but also because biographers, critics, and journalists
have contributed to the construction of a false history by outright
errors, mistakes of interpretation, or simply reiteration of inaccurate
information. One source of a flawed impression is found in a 1961
interview in the *Paris Review* that has been cited over and over, out
of context, as an example of her blatant lying. Commenting on the
importance of the South in her fiction, Katherine Anne had said, "I'm

a Southerner by tradition and inheritance, and, . . . of course, I belong to the guilt-ridden white-pillar crowd myself." Although claim of a plantation upbringing might seem a bold lie in light of the modest bungalow in Texas in which she grew up, if we bear in mind that Katherine Anne Porter's grandmother who reared her was a skilled storyteller who entertained her children and grandchildren with long accounts of her slave-holding family's prosperous life in antebellum Kentucky and Virginia, her answer is not a fiction. In fact, Katherine Anne pointed out that the "white-pillar crowd" had existed decades before her birth: "[The guilt] just didn't rub off on me," she explained. "Maybe I'm just not Jewish enough, or Puritan enough, to feel that the sins of the father are visited on the third and fourth generations." In other instances she described her fin de siècle youth clearly: "We had no money and no prospects of any, and were land-poor in the most typical way."

A common error, on the other hand, is found in the prevailing account of her marriages. Porter had mentioned to a few friends an early marriage to an Englishman, and some believed that British husband to have been discovered in Ernest Stock, a former Royal Air Force pilot and apprentice artist with whom she lived in the summer of 1926. The assumption seemed strengthened in light of Josephine Herbst's having based a fictional couple on Stock and Porter in her story "Man of Steel" and of Porter's modeling the married pair in her own "Spivvleton Mystery" on herself and Stock. Although the identification was understandable, it was a leap to an inaccurate conclusion propelled by the faulty logic she once warned a young scholar against: "The search for factual material in a work of literature is a complete perversion of the whole aim of reading."

Impressions of Katherine Anne Porter's personality and character have been as contradictory as the record of her life. Many persons fell under the spell of her considerable charm, which began with her husky soprano voice. "Sweet," Glenway Wescott called it. "Girlish" and "breathless," said an interviewer. Like "someone talking to a bird, or coquetting with an old beau—light and feathery, with a slight flutter," said another. In the lecture hall or for professional recordings she spoke in an eloquent, clear tone, her inflection softened by her native Texas. In private conversation with family and friends, her voice was more deeply southern: she spoke rapidly and merrily, slipping into regional pronunciation (the *t*'s hard and rounded at the same time) and colloquialisms, rhythmically inserting *Don't you know*'s and *Honey*'s. Her laugh was part of the effect. One interviewer described it as "a soda-water syphon which has just learned to talk and is utterly delighted by the knack."

Her voice and laugh enhanced her widely acknowledged beauty. Small and well-formed, she had curly black hair that was prematurely white from the age of twenty-eight, classic cheekbones, and eyes that were large and violet (or gray or blue, depending on the light). From adolescence on, she had a fashion sense, and she learned to move with a dancer's grace. When beauty united with her desire to please others, or to entertain—a compulsion throughout her life—she enchanted many people. In private conversation or in a letter she made her guest or correspondent feel as though he or she were the only person in the world in whom she was interested.

She succeeded in conveying that message also to large audiences. James Ruoff described her eyes "that flared like blown coals" and "the firm eloquence" and "strange music" of her voice that fell on faculty and students at the University of Wichita in 1961. "There was candid affection in her eyes and voice," he recalled, "and every word seemed to arrange itself behind the other with compelling force and accuracy." It was that charismatic Katherine Anne Porter who was exalted in poems and plays and received numerous literary dedications and tributes. Thirteen children claimed her as godmother, and a half dozen little girls were named for her.

On the other side were persons who found no delight at all in her presence or in their association with her. A former friend who lost money in a real estate transaction because of her capriciousness could hardly bear to hear her name spoken, and one editor could think only of the word *bitch* when he recalled his experience with her. She also could be exasperating even to close friends and family, especially during her last years, when fatigue and illness encouraged irascibility and paranoia. Throughout her life she was temperamental and subject to hysterical weeping on occasions of only minor frustration. She was notorious for her failure to keep appointments and meet deadlines (and for her disingenuous excuses). Her friend Eleanor Clark conceded that despite all her charm Katherine Anne might have been "hell to live with for very long."

Especially cruel perceptions of Katherine Anne Porter began forming after the publication in 1962 of *Ship of Fools* and a few vitriolic reviews, most of them in German newspapers, where she was accused of vileness, but an especially brutal and surprising one in an American journal in which she was labeled "morally vicious." Such castigations hardened into caricatures of her that became the foundation for classifying phrases that proliferated and became more personal after her death. Over the course of more than forty years, even while Katherine Anne Porter was being praised as the First Lady of American Letters (a title she abhorred as patronizing sexism), she also was summed up as an FBI informant, a poseur, an alcoholic, a racist, and a hate-filled monster. Her life has been portrayed as one of deception and betrayal as well as artistic success, and she has been painted as a brilliant writer but a class-conscious, compulsive liar who was capricious, vain, and disloyal to friends and political ideals.

Robert Penn Warren, Eleanor Clark, Isabel Bayley, Cleanth Brooks, Seymour Lawrence, Eudora Welty, and Tillie Olsen were particularly outspoken in their indignation against such judgments. Warren, in fact, asked his biographer to present in his own life's story the Katherine Anne Porter who was his and his wife's loving friend for more than a half century and godmother to their only daughter, Rosanna. Welty spoke often about Katherine Anne's generosity to younger writers and her capacity for deep friendship, and Bayley spent more than a decade editing Katherine Anne's letters in order to disclose the mind and spirit of a friend to whom she was devoted. Brooks and Lawrence sought biographers who would perceive Katherine Anne Porter's life as closer to the way they saw it: "tragic," said Brooks, largely because of her "flightiness of judgment." Tillie Olsen passionately defended the woman and artist she held up as an example in *Silences*.

Dutiful biographers setting about their work of pursuing facts and winnowing out fabrications must try to answer the question of whether Katherine Anne Porter was anything, nothing, or everything persons perceived her to be. They must also decide when to stop in the search for truth. Does it finally matter whether she had the three husbands she acknowledged or the five that can be documented? Are their identities and histories significant? Does it matter whether she lost babies? And whether to miscarriage, abortion, or stillbirth? Does it matter that her maternal grandmother was institutionalized in a "lunatic asylum"? She would say that "simple decency" limited "baleful curiosity," any perceived "duty" to society, or the "search for truth" (she credited Henry James with determining these barriers, and she agreed with him). The proof against her argument, however, lies in her fiction and a return to her 1956 statement that the genesis of her stories was related to her experience. Deaths ordered her life. Insanity and exile were her lifelong hidden fears. She was disillusioned by her unfulfilled expectations of marriage, and she grieved over her failure at motherhood. Encapsulated in themes of betrayal and disillusionment, all these subjects are treated in her fiction. Her life and her art were thus "all one thing," as she said of her fiction and nonfiction, and all aspects of her life are the legitimate concern of biographers, who must also remain sensitive to the points of departure between her personal experience and her art.

Katherine Anne Porter described her recollection of her own history as the means by which she, as an artist, tried to "wangle the sprawling mess of our existence in this bloody world into some kind of shape," and she issued a warning that "utter confusion" would result if one could not "take hold firmly, and draw the exact line between what really happened" and what "since" has been "imagined." Although the fusion of her personal experience and her fictional versions is often seamless, sometimes the line between "what really happened" and her imaginative rendering is plainly visible. On a single page she might have begun to record the facts of a personal experience, but at a certain point the tone shifted, names were altered, and details were added—the fiction writer had taken over. The process was apparent, too, in conversation. On one occasion she was speaking on the telephone with her nephew Paul, who had asked her a question about her early life. As she began to describe a trip she and her sister Gay made to New Orleans when they were adolescents, she became carried away with the adventure of the telling, adding subplots, events, and characters that had not existed in reality but were created spontaneously in her mind during the reminiscence. Each new fantasy, more outrageous than the last, was marked by a whooping, hearty laugh, followed by the transition, "And then, Honey, don't you know . . . !" She was engaging Paul in an adventure they both understood, or, as her quixotic character Rosaleen in "The Cracked Looking-Glass" says, "He wanted a story, so I gave him a good one."

In 1976 Katherine Anne Porter urged the banquet audience at Howard Payne University to embrace the artistic life and "just jump in." "Everything can happen," she said, by way of introducing a summary of her history that was her contribution to her "honest biography." Although her life as she told it seemed glamorous in many ways, in truth it was often grim and lonely, marked with illness, poverty, and depression. She nevertheless had adventure and deep experience at the same time, and living as she did through the greater part of the twentieth century, she observed or participated in most of the major events in the Western Hemisphere during the epoch that circumscribed her life and formed her art. She reached maturity shortly after Queen Victoria died, witnessed the upheaval of World War I, survived tuberculosis and the 1918 influenza epidemic, migrated to Greenwich Village when it was a hotbed of radical politics and experimental art, traveled back and forth to Mexico during the cultural revolution of the 1920s, watched, from the close vantage point of Europe, the rise of Nazism between the wars, bore witness to the cold war in the United States, and finally enjoyed wide critical acclaim and the wealth of best-sellerdom. The woman who was thirteen years old when she first rode in an automobile and saw an airplane was invited in the last decade of her life to observe and write about the launching of the twentieth-century's last Apollo spaceship to the moon.

The story of Katherine Anne Porter's life actually has two beginnings, her birth at Indian Creek and her ancestral history. While that might be said about anybody, in her case it was particularly true, for in that two-pronged foundation lie crucial events that directed the course of her life and shaped her artistic vision: her mother's death before she was two years old and a childhood spent with her eloquent, yarn-spinning paternal grandmother, who provided raw materials for a crucial segment of her fictional canon. She ceaselessly searched for *home*, grounded in fanciful images of a bountiful, secure sanctuary presided over by her saintly dead mother, and for unconditional and pure *love*, offered by members of her family as well as lovers and husbands. Her idealistic view of love and her sympathy and longing for the luxurious past and domestic values of her ancestors clashed with the rationalism at the core of her intellect and provided the greatest tension in her fiction. Other beads of personal experience, "life's treasures" that she strung on the "unbreakable cord" of her life, as she described it, accumulated while she traveled "down all sorts of by-paths and up strange stairs." In the tangle of her life, in all the "fury," "destruction," and "so much just the pervasively trivial, stupid, or malignant-dwarfish tricks," those beads became the "marrow" of her bones, where her blood was renewed and where her art was created.

She never succeeded in her quest for the perfect lover. Neither did she find her Utopian home. Instead of a perfect place she had to reconcile herself to rented houses and apartments in cities far from her birthplace, and instead of husband and children she had to settle for a devoted nephew and niece, a phalanx of loving friends, and a lustrous critical reputation. Religion, despite her mild claims at the end of her life, had not provided either solace or compensation for her failures. But art, which became her real religion, had. She told her Howard Payne audience that when all was said and done, after religion, politics, and "the domestic roof," what remained was *art*. Like the statement she had often made throughout her life—"I am an artist"—it was her affirmation of deliverance and glory.

Katherine Anne Porter

CHAPTER ONE

Indian Creek

1890–1892

The sound of . . . mourning doves in the leafless trees . . . always makes me frightfully homesick for something I never knew and cannot describe, or a place very far off or that maybe does not exist at all.

"I was born on the other side of airplanes"—so Katherine Anne Porter loosely observed in one of her aborted attempts at autobiography. She was, in fact, born on the other side also of automobiles and radios, when American women were thirty years away from suffrage and Native American resistance to white settlement was still a fact in some parts of the United States. Her birth year—1890—was notable also, however, as an emblem of advancement and change. If it was a year of oil lamps and horse-drawn wagons, it was also a year of electricity, railroads, a new advertising industry, and the manufacturing of everything from steel to pancake flour.

Katherine Anne Porter eventually saw her very life a reflection of the Janus faces of 1890: "I was bred to nineteenth century standards and belong by nature to a generation still later than my own," she wrote. She meant that her manners and some of her tastes conformed to those of the mid-nineteenth century but that her artistic vision and philosophy belonged to the twentieth. She was pointing out also that she was modern in her distaste for conventions that restricted women and as young (in attitude, at least) as some of her lovers and husbands. She had limned her lifelong conflict between Victorian values and modernist revolt.

In 1890 Benjamin Harrison was president of the United States. Presbyterian deacon and former Union general, he nurtured the genteel in manners and art and a post–Civil War spirit of commerce in the urban centers of the manufacturing Northeast. He and his Republican

Congress, however, seemed unable to do much to alleviate the poverty in the region south of the Ohio-Potomac line and west of the Mississippi River where many farmers and ranchers had fallen back on tenant farming and sharecropping to make a bare living. It was into the impoverished farm area of central Texas and among such economically reduced people that Katherine Anne Porter was born at Indian Creek, in Brown County, 15 May 1890, the fourth child of Harrison Boone Porter and Mary Alice Jones Porter.

Harrison and Alice Porter were themselves children of prosperous, literate pioneers who had moved from the Upper South before the Civil War and had brought to the rough frontier of the Texas prairies a refined Puritanism and Old South culture. Katherine Anne described her parents as members of the "somehow gay and spirited and lively and attractive generation" who still had "tradition" and "land." There was some truth in her generalization.

Harrison Porter was handsome—dark haired and fair skinned—and debonair. Described by a cousin as the Beau Brummel of the community, he was known for the spirited horses he rode. He was also well read, especially in history and philosophy, having been educated at the Texas Military Institute, at College Station. In 1874 he had joined the Travis Rifles, a home guard company organized for the purpose of helping rid the region of carpetbaggers believed to be corrupting the state government. When his father died in 1879, he returned to the family farm in Hays County to help his mother. Soon he began courting Alice Jones, whom he met shortly before the wedding of his sister Louellah and Alice's brother George.

Everyone who knew Alice said she was pretty and charming, describing her as tall and slender with perfect teeth, copper-colored hair, and smooth white skin. She was also musically talented, sincerely religious, and well educated for her time and place. She had graduated as valedictorian from the Coronal Institute, a coeducational boarding and day school in San Marcos. The school's association with the Methodist Church and its general doctrinal base ensured a religious emphasis compatible with Alice's values, as they were reflected in her valedictory address, "Does the Bible Teach the Doctrine of an Everlasting Life?" Alice concluded that it unquestionably does.

Alice and Harrison's courtship and engagement lasted three years, during which they were frequently apart while Alice taught school in Mountain City and Harrison lived away from Hays County working on the railroad. In their letters they discreetly addressed each other as

"Friend" and were careful to avoid any language that could be construed as intimate. Alice was inclined to moralizing and poetic excess, and Harrison's own florid letters reveal a streak of melancholy and fretful self-pity that beset him even as a young man. Although Katherine Anne satirized the kind of overblown and didactic sentimentality found in their correspondence, she never expressly associated it with her parents and even told her father that she inherited her "literary bent" from him.

Alice broke their engagement near the end of 1882 when she became convinced Harrison was overly fond of hard liquor. "Almost everyone approves indulging in 'egg-nog' at Christmas," she wrote. "I do not. I think the day is only celebrated as it should be." Katherine Anne preferred to believe that her mother was not one of the prim and stern-faced Calvinists she derided in such stories as "He" and "That Tree" and her short novel *Noon Wine*. She told an interviewer that family members had reported Alice's talent for mimicry, an "impish quality" that delighted those who heard her tell stories, while others mentioned her kindliness and romantic sensibility. In fact, Alice did seem to have a streak of idealistic impracticality. In the "egg-nog" letter she described herself as a wanderer who would not be content until she found an "El Dorado."

In the spring of 1883, Alice and Harrison reconciled and planned a wedding for the summer. The timing was prompted not by Alice's discovery of an ideal place but by her new and unpleasant feeling of homelessness. Her father, John Newton Jones, had sold the family farm in Seguin, in Guadalupe County, where Alice had grown up, and he and her two brothers were moving 127 miles northwest to Indian Creek, where he had bought 640 acres of farmland. The uprooting was made even more painful for her because her mother, Caroline Lee Frost Jones, recently had been declared insane, and Alice's father was placing her in a private home for the mentally ill near Seguin.

Not much is known about Caroline Jones. Harrison told Katherine Anne that he believed she had grown up with foster parents in Tennessee. Others mentioned her beauty and air of good breeding. Neither is much known about her mental illness. Katherine Anne speculatively called it "melancholia," but at the age of forty-eight, Caroline might have been suffering nervous symptoms associated with menopause, "uterine problems" being one of the recognized causes of "lunacy" at the time.

John Jones, widely respected and admired (Harrison called him "the best man I ever knew"), made no effort to hide Caroline or her illness from his new community. Her name is listed among the founding members of Indian Creek's Oswalt Methodist Episcopal Church, and, apparently, when her nervous strength permitted, she visited with the family. She was probably not present, however, at Alice and Harrison's wedding that summer in the Jones home, where the ceremony was conducted by the Reverend Noah Byars, a Baptist circuit preacher well known throughout Brown County.

The first two years of their marriage Alice and Harrison lived in Hays County on Harrison's mother's farm, where their first child, a daughter, was born. They named her Anna Gay for Harrison's favorite sister and called her Gay. Although Harrison was earning their meager living by farming his mother's land, he hoped to resume his work for the railroad. He resigned himself to be a farmer, however, when John Jones offered him and Alice a free tenancy on his Indian Creek farm. Late in 1885 they moved to Indian Creek, joining Alice's father, her older brother, T. A. (Lon), and his wife, Sallie, and Alice's younger brother, George, and his wife, Louellah, Harrison's sister.

Indian Creek was a primitive frontier community lying at the southern edge of Brown County. Inhabited by several dozen farm families who lived in sod or log houses, the area was flat, with native grasses growing in profusion and mesquite and cottonwood trees edging the banks of the east-and-west-running creek. Within the unincorporated town were a general store and post office, a blacksmith shop, a cotton gin, a school in one farmer's pasture, and several churches.

Near the carriage road on the north bank of the creek Harrison and Alice built an L-shaped, two-room log house and fenced it in the Kentucky paddock style. They purchased a "modern" stove and filled their house with some fine pieces of furniture, such as a rolltop desk and spindle beds, that Harrison's parents had carried from Kentucky thirty years earlier. Within this small house Alice and Harrison began to increase their family, and by 1887 two-year-old Gay had a brother, whom they named Harry Ray.

Because Gay was the only one of Alice and Harrison's children to remember details of the family's years at Indian Creek, Katherine Anne would rely on her to give life to her fantasies about her own beginnings. Gay told her about the vineyards, roses, and chinaberry trees, Alice's baking corn cakes, and Harrison's playing the violin. She also remembered attending the Oswalt Methodist Episcopal Church, where Harrison, no doubt in deference to Alice, was superintendent of the Sunday school and where Alice sat in the church, wearing a black lace hat and a blue-and-white dress of gingham, and sang "Jesus Is a Rock in a Weary Land."

Alice and Harrison's years at Indian Creek were indeed spent in a weary land. For three disastrous years of severe drought Harrison had to struggle to save their livestock and crops and provide food for the family. Alice grew so frail that Harrison referred to her as his "invalid wife." Childbearing depleted her strength, as did an increasing burden of grief in an accumulation of family deaths. In March of 1885 Louellah and George Jones lost an infant son. In March Harrison's sister Anna Gay died, and in September Louellah died of typhus. Fifteen days later her two-and-a-half-year-old son also died. But still more tragedy was to come. In 1888 Alice's father, John Jones, died unexpectedly at the age of fifty-five. A year later Alice gave birth to a son she and Harrison named Johnnie in memory of her father, but Johnnie died, probably of influenza, soon after his first birthday. Gay described their mother as dry-eyed with grief, sitting at the head of Johnnie's grave, already pregnant with her fourth child, Katherine Anne.

Katherine Anne Porter was born on a sunny Thursday that in later life she imagined as festooned with flowers. When Gay and three-year-old Harry Ray were taken into their mother's room, Alice smiled, turned back a cover, and said, "Do you want to see my little Tad?" "And there you were," Gay told Katherine Anne, "like a new born little black puppy, your little black curls stuck to your head in damp waves." Alice named the baby Callie Russell Porter in honor of the twelve-year-old daughter of the Porters' Indian Creek neighbors William and Marinda Russell.

William and Marinda—she was known by the more common name "Miranda" in Indian Creek and remembered there as Miranda afterward—were twenty years older than Harrison and Alice. They had been in Indian Creek since 1875 and were well regarded in the community. Alice must have looked to Marinda Russell for help and advice in the absence of her mother, just as Harrison depended on William, especially after John Jones's death. The youngest of the Russells' seven children, Callie Jo might have stayed with Alice to help with household chores and manage Gay and Harry Ray during the late months of Alice's last three pregnancies.

Katherine Anne eventually convinced herself that "Callie" was a shortened form of the more elegant "Callista," and she identified her namesake as a close friend of her mother's. It is hard to imagine that she had not asked Harrison explicitly about this "friend" and had not known that Callie Jo was twelve years old in 1890, especially since she regularly plied Harrison with questions about her mother: "Was she beautiful? Did she ever spank my sister? How did she meet [you]? And how did she wear her hair? I had to know everything," she said. She must have known the names of Callie's parents because even after Harrison left Indian Creek he kept in touch with William and Marinda. The role of the Russell family in Katherine Anne Porter's infancy and naming presents intriguing possibilities for the reasons she chose "Miranda" for the most autobiographical of her fictional characters.

After Katherine Anne's birth Alice was more noticeably unwell. She nevertheless became pregnant again in April of 1891. Katherine Anne later pointed out that "birth control (assuming they had known about it) would have been the last thing in the world they would have practiced. It would have been considered indecent to trifle with nature." On 24 January 1892, Alice gave birth to another daughter. But this time she was weakened beyond recovery. She died two months later.

Alice's death was devastating to Harrison. He refused to let anyone else touch her body, and he himself performed all the ministrations before he allowed it to be placed in a coffin and buried beside Johnnie's in the Lamar Churchyard at Indian Creek. He attached Alice's glass-encased photograph to her tombstone, on which he had a tribute engraved:

> *Dearest loved one*
> *We have laid thee*
> *In the Peaceful*
> *Grave's embrace*
> *But thy memory*
> *Will we cherish*
> *Till we see thy*
> *Heavenly face.*

Within a few weeks Harrison named the infant "Mary Alice" to commemorate her mother, but she would always, even in adulthood, be called "Baby" by the family. Then Harrison began the mourning that would last his lifetime.

Katherine Anne in later years blamed her father for her mother's death, and she never quite forgave Baby for having been born. "Five children in eight years!" she exclaimed in rage directed at Harrison.

"No wonder our mother died of pneumonia after the exposure of childbirth in January in that house!" she told Gay. Writing to Baby on her birthday in 1942, she began, "Dear Baby: It is half past three in the morning of your birthday, very nearly the hour you were born . . . Our mother began her long dying on this day fifty years ago."

Harrison fought against feeling responsible for Alice's early death and shifted the blame to Alice and the children. "If your mother had listened to me," he told his children during their childhood, "none of you would have been born!" This statement made it easy for Katherine Anne to conclude that she and her sisters and brothers had been born because their mother had wanted them and loved them. "She lost her life on this point of faith," Katherine Anne said.

As soon as Alice died, Harrison's widowed mother, Catharine Ann Skaggs Porter, went to Indian Creek to help him with his motherless children and to convince him to move to Hays County to live with her. He felt that he had no choice since alone he could not manage the farm and his four small children. Neither did he have any heart, according to Indian Creek neighbors, for staying on in the house he had shared with Alice. Fifty years later one of his neighbors, who had been a child at the time, could still call up the scene of the family's departure: "There was an auction. They sold all their things. I was there, I remember. We bought the churn. Somebody bought the high chair. With the baby sitting in it . . . Katherine Anne was a little girl. Pretty little girl, I remember, running around all over everywhere, with little black curls." Once they left, Harrison and his children returned to Indian Creek only twice during the remainder of their lives.

After Harrison left with the children, Cora Posey, a young unmarried friend of Alice's, went to their vacant house to mourn for her friend and discovered Alice's mother, Caroline Jones, looking through the windows and "weeping like a soul in torment." Caroline's elder son, Alice's brother Lon, had died that same summer, and she was living with Lon's widow, Sallie, who refused to continue paying for her private care at Seguin while also resenting having to keep her. Soon after Cora Posey's encounter with Caroline Jones, Sallie had her unwanted mother-in-law committed to the recently completed Southwestern Lunatic Asylum in San Antonio, where she spent the rest of her life.

Caroline Jones never again saw any of her grandchildren or her only surviving son, George Melton Jones. Harrison, who secretly called upon her at the asylum in 1893, told his children later that their grandmother Jones had lost her mind out of grief (a deception, since she had been declared insane before the string of family deaths began). Katherine Anne eventually learned that she had died in an unspecified lunatic asylum and that Aunt Sallie Jones had played a role in her incarceration, but she did not know that the dark, gloomy complex of gabled buildings she often passed on the outskirts of San Antonio was the institution that housed Caroline Jones until her death in 1914.

Katherine Anne's morbid impressions of the nineteenth-century madhouse were gleaned from sensational Gothic romances and the horror stories of local gossip. In 1894 the *San Antonio Express* published an article—"Retreat for the Demented"—by an unidentified staff reporter who had been taken on a tour by the new hospital's superintendent, providing a contemporaneous view of life inside the Southwestern Lunatic Asylum at the time Caroline Jones was confined there. She almost certainly was one of the incarcerated women the reporter saw congregated in corridors or slumped lethargically in a large open room. Wearing simply long calico slips, the women were allowed to eat only with spoons. An occasional outburst of maniacal laughter reminded the reporter he was in a madhouse. The superintendent told him proudly that the assistants were so thoroughly trained in curbing violence that they had not had to put a strait jacket on a "lunatic" for six months.

Years later Katherine Anne said the story of "[my] mother's mother" was "the most tragically, frighteningly moving thing of its kind I ever heard, and it is not altogether because I am so near to it, to the women in it, but the whole desolation of all human loss and loneliness is in it." The family secret of Caroline Jones and the painful ostracizing of a "defective" family member inspired two of Katherine Anne's most powerful stories, "He" and "Holiday," and was an important subject in *Noon Wine.* She would, by her own account, represent her grandmother's "jailer," Aunt Sallie, as "fanged and clawed" in her short novel *Old Mortality.* But awareness of this grandmother and the mystery of her insanity affected Katherine Anne in other ways, feeding her anxiety about her own mental and emotional stability and leading her to seek understanding in books on psychoanalysis.

Harrison Porter's evasiveness about Caroline Jones's whereabouts was motivated in part by his desire to protect Alice's image. His Poe-like devotion to what Katherine Anne called "the cult he built around our mother's memory" remained unshakable. Forty years later she told him, "I wish you might have found some intelligent, pleasant woman you could have cared for, and who would have made a live-able life for you . . . But I suppose it is not really possible to love truly more than once, and if one dies young, the other is simply left." She long before had absorbed his romantic idea of love, just as she had accepted his view of a saintly Alice.

Katherine Anne had no conscious memory of either her mother or Indian Creek. With Alice's letters and schoolgirl essays, a few photo-graphs, and other persons' recollections, however, she created in her waking dreams both her mother and her birthplace, associating them with images of sun and bounty, making them symbols of *love* and *home*. She revisited them in her imagination—and thus also in her art—time and time again.

CHAPTER TWO

Catharine Ann Skaggs Porter

1892

Grandmother was by nature lavish, she loved leisure and calm, she loved luxury, she loved dress and adornment, she loved to sit and talk with friends or listen to music; she did not in the least like pinching or saving and mending and making things do . . . But the evil turn of fortune in her life tapped the bottomless reserves of her character, and her life was truly heroic.

Katherine Anne Porter said that "the real story" ended with her mother's death and the family's departure from Indian Creek. But if one story ended, another began. She was to spend the next nine years with her paternal grandmother, Catharine Ann Skaggs Porter, whom she ultimately credited with forging her character. Her grandmother's other contribution, however, was equally important: as a nexus to the old order of the feudal South and the Civil War past, she was Katherine Anne's conduit to an ancestry she personally embraced and later mythologized in her fiction.

Catharine Ann Skaggs—called "Cat" by her family and friends— was born into a colorful and prominent Kentucky family on 18 March 1827. Her great-grandfather Henry Skaggs had led the first white men to the portion of the Kentucky territory later designated Warren County. The subject of several historical novels set in the Kentucky territory, he became a folk hero in his own right and also a supporting player in the legends that accrued to Daniel Boone's name. Skaggs Creek and a Lincoln County hunting trail called Skaggs Trace are named for him.

Henry Skaggs's son James, Katherine Anne's great-great grandfather, who served under Washington in the Revolutionary War, accumulated substantial wealth as he and his wife, Susannah, moved from eastern Virginia to Tennessee before finally settling with other family members in Warren County, the nucleus by then of a modest Skaggs dynasty. His sons Daniel and Joseph were Baptist leaders in the region, and his sons Abraham and James owned and operated the prosperous Skaggs Mill.

Abraham Skaggs fought in the War of 1812, and in 1815 he married Rhoda Boone Smith, whose mother, Keziah Boone, was the granddaughter of Jonathan Boone, brother to Daniel. Through this great-grandmother Katherine Anne traced her antecedents to seventeenth-century England and the Boone family's migration to the New World. She studied the family daguerreotypes of Rhoda and Abraham and pronounced them "high-nosed old aristocrats of the South."

Abraham and Rhoda's large brick home, built in the area's characteristic Federal style, sat near a main road a few miles outside of Bowling Green. It comfortably accommodated their twelve children, two adult slaves (one male and one female), and two slave children. Warren County was a productive community of small and middle-sized farms, whose major commodity was livestock, especially horses, with which Cat early on developed an expertise. There were no public schools in Warren County until 1881, but in such a family as the Skaggses the daughters and very young sons would have been taught by their literate parents, boarding tutors or governesses, and teachers who set up private schools, such as the one in the basement of the Presbyterian Church on State Street. Cat, whose family were members of the Cumberland Presbyterian Church, might well have attended that school. She obviously was instructed in deportment and elocution as well as the liberal and domestic arts.

On 8 August 1849, twenty-two-year-old Catharine Ann Skaggs was united in marriage with her prosperous, thirty-five-year-old second cousin Asbury Duval Porter. Two years later they left Kentucky with their small son and a female slave and settled first in Louisiana, where Asbury had wealthy Duval relatives, and then in Texas, where several members of both their families lived. In 1857 they bought 384 acres of land on Plum Creek, in Hays County, and by 1860 they and their six children were thriving, active participants in the nearby communities of Mountain City and Science Hall.

Clouds of war, however, had gathered over the country, and the Porters girded themselves for the civil war that would erupt in 1861. Like most Texas settlers at the time, they had grown up with slavery and considered it not only normal but biblically sanctioned and central to states rights and the agrarian economy of Texas. Cat and Asbury passionately supported Texas's 1861 secession from the Union and entrance into the Confederacy.

Katherine Anne later thought that her grandmother's stories about the Civil War were the "merest surface ripples over limitless deeps of bitterest memories." Like many others, the Porters suffered hardship and pain almost from the moment war started. The Texas government required stiff tithes of all Texans, and the men went off to war, even Asbury himself in 1865, when the conscription law was expanded to include men fifty years old. Women such as Cat raised livestock and crops for the army, made blankets and clothes for the soldiers, and found substitutes for medicine and food for their children, who in Cat's case by 1864 numbered eight. When the war finally ended, many Texas farmers had been killed, as had one of Asbury's brothers and his cousin, or disabled, as was Asbury, who had been wounded in the leg during the final months and invalided out. Many farm buildings had been destroyed, and by the time victorious Union soldiers occupied the state, virtually every farmer in Texas was poor. "I am the grand-child of a lost war," Katherine Anne later wrote, "and I have blood knowledge of what life can be in a defeated country on the bare bones of privation."

In 1865 land in Texas quickly fell in value to an average of one-fifth its 1860 value, and mortgage foreclosures were widespread. With shrewd sales and purchases between 1866 and 1871 Cat and Asbury nevertheless recovered most of their losses, with the exception of their slaves (a thirty-some-years-old woman and two children), enhanced their holdings, produced their last child (a son they named for Asbury), and actually prospered again.

In the late 1870s Cat and Asbury's three beautiful daughters, Isabel, Louellah, and Anna, had many suitors and busy social lives, a cousin describing them as the "social belles of the community." Isabel was the first to marry, and marrying into the prominent Bunton family ("sho 'nuff honest to God aristocrats," Katherine Anne would say), she made the only match of which her mother approved. Anna, whose beauty was legendary in the family and whose early death might have been the result of suicide, consumption, a botched abortion, or all three, caused Cat the most sorrow. It was Anna's story that Katherine Anne would draw upon for *Old Mortality*.

Asbury Porter was away from home much of the time, and relatively little is known about him personally. Harrison recalled his father's many books, and Alice remarked in a letter that Harrison's father had given him "excellent advice." When he died in 1879 at the age of sixty-six, his death brought about finally by the war wound, the settlement of his estate revealed that he had been a careful investor and competent provider during a time of poverty and privation for many other Southerners.

Cat, who was fifty-two when Asbury died, stayed on at the Hays County farm for a couple of years, raising livestock and crops with the help of her sons and hired hands. The family was beginning to break up, however, with Harrison away working on the railroad and others of her children marrying and moving off. She soon decided to relocate in nearby Kyle, and at an auction held in the fall of 1880 she purchased a quarter-acre lot and hired men to build a house on it. She continued to slice off pieces of the farmland as gifts to her children, and she allotted some of the land as well as the livestock to tenant farmers. She retained a small portion of the farm to be used as a retreat from town life, but long after she moved into Kyle, the section of Plum Creek on whose banks the farm lay was called "the Cat Porter Branch."

She had become something of a legend in the region, where two generations of more than one hundred nieces and nephews called her "Aunt Cat" and other persons completely unrelated by either blood or marriage called her that as well. It was a name of affection and respect. She was known throughout the south-central area of Texas for her hospitality (her genius for cooking was noted even in her funeral elegies) and her aristocratic bearing. "Aunt Cat was too exquisite not to mark herself in my mind forever," said one of her grand-nieces. "Lovely," said Cora Posey, "just the kind of mother you would expect Mr. Harrison Porter to have."

While Cat's dedication to certain religious principles and specific aspects of Victorian manners was considered exemplary, she no doubt shocked the more conventional women in her community. Until the year she died she could ride a horse at a dead gallop (side saddle, as she had in her Kentucky girlhood), she smoked medicated cigars (for her throat, she said), and she enjoyed an occasional sip of good bourbon. It was a measure of her complexity and will that she was able to subsume her independence in her piety. She was summed up most frequently by her neighbors as "a devout lady of many good works."

Cat took pride in her independence, but she in no way considered herself a feminist. She was opposed to women's suffrage and detested the so-called new women. In times of tribulation she had simply drawn upon her innate willpower, which she attributed to the superior moral constitution of her father's family. "Skaggs pride," she called it, but it actually was to be found only in Skaggs women. She described the Skaggs men as gamblers, romantics, and weak-kneed fools. Two of her brothers had committed suicide, and an uncle had died from a wound received in a duel, all three suffering from a genetic melancholia (to which Harrison was inclined as well). Her attitude toward men, however, went well beyond the Skaggs line. She dismissed her late husband by claiming falsely that the Texas land had been a gift from her father and by refusing to acknowledge Asbury's prominent Louisiana relatives. She mentioned him hardly at all.

Cat's discounting of Asbury had the effect of assigning her husband to an obscure role in family legends, similar to a technique of omission she applied to family members of whom she disapproved, usually in-laws. When her daughter Louellah died at Indian Creek in the fall of 1885, it was Cat instead of the widower, Alice's brother George Jones, who erected the tombstone. Rather than have it read "Wife of George M. Jones," as would have been conventional, Cat had inscribed, "Louellah Jones, Daughter of A. D. and C. A. Porter," symbolically restoring Louellah to the Porter family, a triumph of her original opposition to the marriage and an expression of her disdain for George Jones as well as the whole Jones family. Her determined hand is likewise evident in the epitaph for one of the children buried with Louellah, which reads, "Lucius D. Jones . . . Is With His Mother's God," again ignoring George Jones (a person she wished had never existed) and revising history to her satisfaction. It was the technique of a natural storyteller.

When Katherine Anne mentioned the "great" storytellers in her family, she was referring most of all to Cat Porter, who was "articulate" and whose stories "had shape and meaning and point." Although Katherine Anne never credited her grandmother directly with the fictional techniques she developed, she obviously learned from her the value of telling a story before writing it down, the function of memory in crafting fiction, and the satisfaction that came from altering historical facts for both psychological contentment and artistic focus. As Cat unfolded her tales about life in antebellum Kentucky and the hard times during the Civil War and its aftermath, Katherine Anne acquired a consoling belief in her ancestors' prominence and wealth, a belief that offset the material and emotional deprivations of her Texas childhood. "I was fed from birth" she later wrote, "on myth and legend . . . and a conviction of natural superiority bestowed by birth and tradition." She reinforced her tie to her strong grandmother by identifying herself as a grandchild of her grandmother's generation rather than the child of her parents' age. The attachment is understandable also in that her grandmother was more forcefully present in her childhood, taking up where her dead mother and her often-absent and ever-grieving father left off.

CHAPTER THREE

The Fiery Furnace

Autumn 1892–Autumn 1902

*I have not much interest in anyone's personal history after the tenth
year, not even my own. Whatever one was going to be was all prepared for before that. The rest is merely confirmation, extension,
development.*

*Our sainted grandmother—I don't know what would have become
of me if it hadn't been for her . . . She was taken away from me when
I was eleven years old, but the seed had been planted.*

Folding in her twenty-five months in Indian Creek, Katherine Anne
rounded off childhood to ten years and described it as "the fiery furnace" in which she had been "melted down to essentials and that
essential shaped for good." While it is true that her grandmother
presided over the crucible, other people, events, and circumstances
in Hays County contributed significantly to her intellectual and
emotional development in the formative period of her life.

Kyle had grown to about five hundred residents by the summer of
1892, when Harrison and his children moved in with Cat. The town
had hotels, saloons, and churches, a drugstore, Thiele's meat market, a
grocery, a saddlery, Schlemmer's Mercantile Establishment, a lumber-
yard, a livery stable, a public school, and a one-cell jail. Printers, physicians, dentists, and lawyers also had settled there. In spite of Kyle's
development, however, it remained a raw, nineteenth-century frontier
town with no indoor plumbing and with livestock ranging freely
through the unpaved streets and unfenced yards. It was farm country,
rather than ranch country, and the Old South reverberated in antebellum mansions in nearby Austin, San Antonio, and San Marcos.

Having no intention of marrying again, Harrison expected to
assume the position of head of his mother's household. Cat, however,

let him know immediately that he had deceived himself. She was entrenched in the rank she long had held, that of "an old matriarch," Katherine Anne said, who "held the reins to everything." Harrison had no choice but bow to her authority and turn his children over to her. Katherine Anne observed that her father "became an elder child" in her grandmother's house, "and all of us felt this very early."

Cat considered it her duty to see that her grandchildren were inculcated with her Protestant religion and that they had good morals and proper manners. While she retained her membership in the Cumberland Presbyterian Church in Mountain City, she was weary enough to let the children attend the Methodist church that sat diagonally across the street from the Porters' house. Protestant beliefs in general, with emphases on right and wrong, sin and redemption, were a sufficient backdrop for what Katherine Anne called her more "effective" teaching at home when she "systematically ground the fear of God . . . into our tender bones before we were formed enough to protest."

Katherine Anne described her grandmother's brand of religion as "supernaturalism" founded on a system of "wrath," but she also placed her among the "liberal-minded moralists" in the family. A particular event in 1897 illustrated her point: The Kyle Methodist Church was holding a two-week-long revival meeting to which people from all around came for the social occasion and to hear visiting preachers well known for their effective oratory. When poor Roman Catholic Mexicans began to show up for the daylong meetings, however, the white Protestant congregation became so uneasy that the preacher asked the Mexicans to leave, citing membership in the Kyle church as a requirement for attending the revival. Cat knew this was a lie. She signaled to Harrison, who nodded to his children, and the family rose as a group to indignantly fall in line behind the silent and bowed huddle of departing Mexicans.

Cat remained within the boundary of convention when it came to instructing her grandchildren in manners, which in her view were nearly the same as morals. Katherine Anne explained her grandmother's logic: "Inappropriate conduct was bad manners, bad manners were bad morals, and bad morals led to bad manners, and there you were, ringed with fire and no way out." Cat insisted that her granddaughters sit without touching the backs of their chairs, refrain from speaking unless spoken to, and never, never cross their knees. There were words she did not allow them to use, including ordinary slang, and subjects she did not allow them to broach.

She also had rules of dress. From the time of Asbury's death in 1879 Cat wore mourning gowns of black silk and crape veils that fell over her face in front and to the hem of her skirt in back. She believed that a lady should be always covered in the appropriate places and properly corseted, free from such constraint only in the privacy of her bedroom. She consequently dressed her granddaughters in modest, dowdy clothes that caused them embarrassment around their more fashionable friends. Cat's adherence to a bygone style was one source for Katherine Anne's craving of fashionable clothes all her life and regarding the corset as an emblem of women's slavery. But it was also her grandmother's stories about her affluent life in Kentucky that made her hunger for fine clothes and other comforts of wealth. In "The Grave" she explained Miranda's (and her own) yearning for the opulent life: "She had vague stirrings of desire for luxury and a grand way of living which could not take precise form in her imagination but were founded on family legend of past wealth and leisure."

Cat, who subscribed to the prevailing Victorian rule that "children should be seen and not heard," discouraged her grandchildren from expressing opinions or straying from the circumscribed realm of a disciplined child's world. "Who are you?" she would query, when any one of them ventured a bold assertion. She was backed up in all this by the Kyle public school Katherine Anne attended from the mid 1890s through the spring of 1902.

Katherine Anne had no interest in the arithmetic taught at school, but she liked the offerings in *McGuffey's Eclectic Primers* and *McGuffey's Readers*—short biographies, essays, poems, scripture, and brief fictional works—despite the fact that every selection illustrated a moral or religious principle: unquestioning obedience to authority is a virtue; virtue will always be rewarded; and sinfulness will always be punished. There were other, more subtle messages in the *Readers* and *Primers*: the sentimental was preferable to the "realistic"; the "older" literature was "best"; and only works that were instructive and edifying were worthy to be read. Although Katherine Anne always had a predilection for an older literature, she eventually rejected the sentimental and didactic in favor of the realistic.

Among the readings that fascinated her in grade school were accounts of Joan of Arc and Cotton Mather, who Gay told her was a man who "caused witches to be burned." In her mind Katherine Anne yoked together Mather the "witch-burner" (and persecutor of women) and Joan of Arc, falsely accused of being a witch and burned at the stake. Katherine Anne's choosing "Witch" as a childhood pseudonym for herself was a measure of her wish to be identified with the dramatic, saintly, and persecuted Joan more than it was proof of her acceptance of her grandmother's Calvinist belief in innate evil.

Cat supplemented her grandchildren's education by hiring tutors or governesses who lived in the house with the family. There were one Miss Babb, who routinely spanked a recalcitrant Katherine Anne, Miss Ella Mudd, a relative of one of Cat's daughters-in-law, and yet another young woman, "pale, gray-eyed," and "dyspeptic," who taught the children a scrambled program of calisthenics and rudimentary education. None had been a competent educator, but all, according to Katherine Anne, had been harsh disciplinarians.

Other persons on the premises by virtue of being elders also had a degree of authority over the children. Masella Daney, Cat's former slave, lived at the house most of the time, helping with the washing, ironing, cooking, and minding the children, who called her "Aunt Jane" (Harrison called her "Mammy Jane"—she had been his wet nurse). Her husband, Squire Bunton, the model for Uncle Jimbilly in *The Old Order*, lived nearby and often appeared at the Porter house on his mule Aunt Fanny. There were also hired hands such as one Miguel, who was addicted to morphine, and Old Man Ronk, who contributed to the character of Olaf Helton in *Noon Wine*, and what she recalled as "a long procession of dreadful old women, of a most awful gentility, who consented to act as a sort of upper house keeper and companion and general nuisance, who merely took it out by gritting their teeth at us and wishing, in low voices when no one else was by, that they could blister our skins for being such bad children." She thought her grandmother had taken them in and tided them over some wave of misfortune.

Katherine Anne, full of emotion and energy, sometimes became exhausted in the overcrowded house with its "accumulation of storied dust never allowed to settle in peace for one moment." At such times she longed for a retreat to stillness and seclusion. She could find that only in the quiet of mornings when she wakened before the others and the household was not yet "tangled together like badly cast fishing lines," as Miranda recalls in *Pale Horse, Pale Rider*. Katherine Anne's childhood wish for "silence," a word she later described as "having a special meaning for me of remoteness from the urgency of external experience," increased in importance in adulthood, when withdrawal from society was necessary for her creative art as well as her emotional health.

During her childhood, books offered mental escape. Although Cat forbade her grandchildren to read fairy tales (too pagan) and dime novels (no literary merit), there were plenty of other books in the house that met her standard. "If one pulled out a battered, spine-broken, gotch-eared book, from any shelf or secretary or old cedar chest," Katherine Anne remembered, "it was inevitably an early translation of Dante's complete works, or one of a half dozen volumes of Shakespeare's plays, or the sonnets with marginal notes in twenty different handwritings, or Marlowe's plays, or Erasmus' 'In Praise of Folly' or the Letters of Madame de Sevigne, or the poems of Alexander Pope, or Jane Austen's Mansfield Park or Boswell's Life of Johnson, or Gulliver's Travels . . . or the Essays of Montaigne, or novels, such as Tristram Shandy." The family had, too, Dr. Percy's *Reliques* and "every poem written by Edgar Allan Poe."

Unlike his mother, Harrison allowed his children to read anything they wanted. He read to them from the works of Mark Twain (at whom his mother looked askance), and he ignored their reading of fairy tales, every dime novel they could lay their hands on, and "trashy" romances. Katherine Anne read at least six novels by Ouida ("pronounced 'Weeda,' not a name one forgets in a hurry") and various works by a writer she knew only as "The Duchess," "whose heroines were made of alabaster and snow, yet strangely subject to temptation, the grosser the better."

Despite her restriction on books, Cat approved of certain concerts and plays, and she managed to find the few dollars required to take the family to hear the singer Adelina Patti or the pianist Ignace Paderewski or to see performances of Shakespeare or Schiller or Dumas when touring actors such as Ada Rehan or Madame Helena Modjeska appeared in San Antonio or Austin. Katherine Anne never forgot seeing *Hamlet*, an English adaptation of Schiller's *Maria Stuart*, and Sarah Bernhardt in *Camille*. She had trouble understanding the difference between reality and pretense, telling an interviewer later, "No one *acted* the part of Hamlet: he *was* Hamlet."

Reading and theater encouraged Katherine Anne's earliest expressions of creativity. "A precocious child full of miscellaneous talents and hellish energy," as she described herself, she experimented in all the art forms from the time she was a very young child. Gay recalled one event: "I remember you on a little foot stool showing off before Cousin David Porter (the old Baptist minister) singing your little made-up songs, and making your little speeches, and all the old

Methodists and Baptists and Presbyterians were fully convinced you were possessed of the devil and would come to no good end. And dear grandmother was so proud of you and always showed you off and did you love it." A neighbor also told of walking past Cat Porter's house many times when a play was being produced: "The yard would be full of children watching or participating in a drama directed by the grand-daughter Callie. Aunt Cat's bedspreads would be draped over goods' boxes to serve as properties for one of the earlier experiments in theater in the round. The porch was curtained off, not as a stage, but as a dressing room and cave of emergent wonders. Callie would invite the passers-by to come in and see the show. Once she charged admission and gave the proceeds to charity." Cat's pride and indulgence had a limit, however. She whipped Katherine Anne/Callie "awfully" and "ceremoniously" for telling the Reverend David Porter that she wanted to be an actress when she grew up. The message Cat sent her creative granddaughter about "art" was thus ambiguous.

Katherine Anne's best friend, Erna Schlemmer, strictly reared by her Old World parents, was fascinated by Katherine Anne's daring and imagination. "A flame burned bright within you always," Erna wrote in middle age, "I felt it even then, and nothing is so vivid in my recollection of those days as the scenes in which you played the lead." The "scenes" included their singing duets in the Methodist church, acting out the life and death of Joan of Arc (with Katherine Anne, of course, playing the tragic Joan), and performing circus stunts on patient mules in the Schlemmers' barn. It was Katherine Anne who assigned Erna the name "Fairy" as the counterpart to her own "Witch."

Katherine Anne believed that from the age of about three years, as soon as she could form letters on a page, she tried to write stories. The first of her fictional works she could recall with any detail was one she wrote around the age of six, a "nobbel" that she titled "The Hermit of Halifax Cave," inspired by a nearby place the family went for picnics or overnight camping. "And so I put an old man there," Katherine Anne told an interviewer, "and drew long whiskers on him and had him sitting at the entrance to this cave, you know, and I had him go down and catch a fish and fry his fish, and eat his fish, and then I couldn't think of another thing to do with him. So I had to stop, and I put 'to be continued,' and I sewed it together like a book." She gave it to her grandmother and her father, who handed it around to neighbors and relatives, and "they all laughed their heads off," she recalled. "Such were my beginnings in my predestined art." (She might also have equated her story writing with sinfulness because McGuffey used "storytelling" in its beginning reader as a synonym for lying. "Tell the truth; do not tell stories," the *Primer* admonished.)

Harrison and Cat might have agreed on Katherine Anne's "nobbel," but they agreed on little else, including religion. Harrison was a "natural skeptic," Katherine Anne said. "All organized religion seemed to him barbarous and illogical." When his mother went off to church on Sunday morning with the children, he stayed behind, sitting on the porch, typically and ostentatiously reading the *Dialogues* of Plato.

Her father and grandmother represented to Katherine Anne a disquieting opposition of two powerful forces that she described as "almost equal." "Between them," she said later, "I was almost torn in two." Besides religion, they lined up on opposing sides in their attitudes toward Alice and in their very different notions of female beauty. Cat, who had lost parents, husband, and children—among them all her daughters—was impatient with Harrison's pervasive and unrelenting grief over Alice's death. "She had no sympathy," Katherine Anne remembered, "for my father's feeling of resentment against the fact of having, somehow, been betrayed into a bargain that left him wifeless when he had wanted a wife, and a father when he did not want children." Cat also refused to idealize the dead Alice: "My grandmother was dry and cynical about her: she had had beautiful daughters of her own, and in some way we gathered that our mother was lackadaisical, not very spirited or energetic, in no way a good manager. I sometimes felt she wished to make it appear that even our mother's death was an act of carelessness."

Katherine Anne's curiosity about her mother, however, outweighed her grandmother's judgment. Harrison told his children beautiful and romantic stories about their mother, and he liked to show his daughters relics of her life: "We saw and touched her gloves, her curls of hair, her strange and charming dresses: he showed us bits of jewelry we should have when we grew up." Harrison told them that when Alice died, his "earthly hopes" went "down in an endless darkness" and left him only with "memories that not time nor death could take away."

In the face of such devotion, Katherine Anne feared that her father might not have any love left over for her. To prove otherwise, from early childhood on, she tried to elicit from him even a small measure of affection and approval. She became convinced when she was still very young that if she were pretty enough he would love her a little. Gay remembered that Katherine Anne read in a magazine that if she ate an onion every night she would be beautiful. "Since I was your bedfellow," Gay said, "I could have kicked you to Jericho."

Katherine Anne knew that her father thought only slender women, sylphs like her mother and grandmother, could be beauties. For nearly as long as he lived, she sent him flattering photographs of herself and reported her weight to him. She thought Harrison the handsomest of men, and she took for her own his preference for gray, which enhanced his fine gray hair and very black eyebrows. But she learned many times over that beauty fails, and by midlife she had concluded that beauty might even be a curse. In *Old Mortality* it is her grandmother's "small voice of axiomatic morality" that echoes in Miranda's mind: "Beauty goes, character stays."

The opposition between Cat and Harrison seemed to Katherine Anne to have a physical form. She considered the farm her father's domain, and the town, her grandmother's, and the farm seemed perfect as part of the "summer country" of her childhood that she idealized: "I remember all kinds of beautiful things: hound dogs panting under the china trees, and Negroes singing in the cotton field." This romantic view, however, was only one aspect of the farm, which was also a place marked by the "hoverings of buzzards in the high blue air," an ominous intimation of death.

At a young age Katherine Anne associated death with violence. The frontier region's vigilante law led occasionally to hangings, and murders were not uncommon in Kyle saloons on Saturday nights. The earliest murder she remembered took place near the farm around 1893: "It was late summer and near sunset, for the sky was a clear green-blue with long streaks of burning rose in it, and the air was full of the mournful sound of swooping bats. I was all alone in a wide grassy plain—it was the lawn on the east side of the house—and I was in that state of instinctive bliss which children only know, when there came like a blow of thunder echoing and rolling in that green sky, the explosion of a shotgun, not very far away, for it shook the air. There followed at once a high, thin, long-drawn scream, a sound I had never heard, but I knew what it was—it was the sound of death in the voice of a man. How did I know it was a shotgun? How should I not have known? How did I know it was death? We are born knowing death."

It would have been nearly impossible for her to remain ignorant of death. The whole family had been in continuous bereavement for Harrison's sister Anna, who died in 1885, and Harrison's unabated mourning for Alice made an even deeper impression. He also talked about the baby Johnnie, who had died shortly before Katherine Anne's birth. She imagined that the ghost of her little brother appeared to her in a dream when she was two-and-a-half years old, and she thought she was about three when she knew that her mother was dead. Throughout her childhood she acknowledged the deaths of all the baby animals that died at the farm by conducting funeral services for them that included burial in shoeboxes, a pivotal scene in her story "The Fig Tree."

The farm and the town together constituted the physical and social environment that provided the backdrop to her childhood. The physical space affected the way she saw the world as much as the social structures and conventions did. She wrote in her autobiographical entry for *Authors Today and Yesterday* (1933) that her physical eye was "unnaturally far-sighted." "I have no doubt," she said, "that this affects my temperament in some way. I have very little time sense and almost no sense of distance. I have no sense of direction and have seen a great deal of the world by getting completely lost and simply taking in the scenery as I roamed about getting my bearings." To understand this statement fully, we have to consider the area of Texas in which her visual perspective developed. The low, clear prospect of Kyle and the farm, the absence of mountains and great trees, rendered the horizons unobstructed. One could see far off without knowing how far, and there were few reference points in the homogenous landscape of dry prairie grasses, scrub pine, and wild flowers. This setting of her earliest perceptions determined her nonlinear way of looking at the past, and that habit of mind ultimately influenced her fictional techniques.

Following the nineteenth-century convention of making visits, usually to the homes of relatives, the family often took trips. Traveling was exciting to Katherine Anne, and the desire to roam occasionally took the form of running away. One summer she fled the farmhouse after an argument with Gay and Harry Ray and walked about three miles before Harrison caught up, chided her, and took her back home. Her grandmother asked her why she had done "such an ungrateful, cruel trick." Katherine Anne recalled struggling to explain that she wanted "something strange and wonderful and far-off."

Although Cat had called Katherine Anne's running away "cruel," she, in fact, understood the impulse. Feeling a deep need to get up and go somewhere, she would hitch up the family surrey or mount a favorite horse and take off at a gallop. She most often visited her sons, her sister Eliza Jane in Lockhart, or one of Eliza Jane's daughters, all of whom lived with their own large families within traveling distance of Kyle. She even might make the long trip to New Orleans, where a large group of Skaggs relatives lived.

When Cat took only one of her grandchildren with her, she inevitably chose Katherine Anne, seeing herself in this willful, imaginative granddaughter. The longest trip they made together was the nine-hundred-mile round-trip journey by train to Marfa to visit Cat's sons Azzie, Newell, and Bill, and they made it three times. Their last trip to Marfa in October of 1901 encased the greatest trauma of Katherine Anne's childhood, for while they were there Cat Porter died.

Not long after they arrived, Cat collapsed with what apparently was a severe stroke. She survived for three days, and Katherine Anne thought she saw her grandmother's last breath. Much of the experience was erased from her conscious memory, however, and for the rest of her life she never mentioned the train trip alone with the coffin back to Kyle, where Cat was buried on 4 October. In "The Fig Tree," however, she created a scene that may well be her memory of traveling home with her grandmother's corpse: "Miranda could never find out about anything until the last minute. She was always being surprised. Once she went to sleep in her bed with her kitten curled on the pillow purring, and woke up in a stuffy tight bed in a train, hugging a hot-water bottle; and there was Grandmother stretched out beside her in her McLeod tartan dressing-gown, her eyes wide open."

Katherine Anne imagined that for some of her grandmother's children, her death had been their release from her iron grip. For eleven-year-old Katherine Anne it was a painful end to another story, the closing of her childhood. That it coincided with the death of Queen Victoria and the inauguration of a new century seemed only to affirm the momentousness of the terminus.

Cat's death contributed heavily to Katherine Anne's dark memory of childhood. "I do not believe that childhood is a happy time," she wrote. "It is a time of desperate cureless bitter griefs and pains, of shattering disillusionments, when everything good and evil alike is happening for the first time, and there is no answer to any question." "Remembering childhood," she said, "is like swimming and floating in a sea without land anywhere in sight, with stormy weather now and then and a feeling of drowning." She often used the words "forlorn" and "lonely" to describe her early life.

Her loneliness before her grandmother's death grew out of her painful awareness of her mother's absence. When she later read in

Joseph Grasset's *The Semi-Insane and the Semi-Responsible* that "earliest impressions received at a time when [persons] were hardly able to talk, manifest themselves later in an obsessive fashion, although those impressions themselves are not consciously remembered," she wrote in the margin, "So my horror and pain here and now from that old terrible time." She believed that after her mother's death she had been "an awful child and the devil of a nuisance," but she feared she also had been not quite sane. She set off another passage in Grasset that described early manifestation of neurosis: "From childhood they draw attention to themselves by their precocity, their quickness in taking hold of everything and understanding it, and at the same time by their whims, their headstrong ways, their cruel instincts, their violent and convulsive attacks of anger." She queried in the margin, "Alas myself?" She believed that the emotional experiences of the neurasthenic child had been her own: "an incredible sense of smell, a feeling of mad presences, intuition of others' thoughts, mad agonies and disturbances without any cause." In the margin she wrote, "That's me, from my first memory . . . except I think I had cause."

She was suggesting here, as she did elsewhere from time to time, that her mother's death and the circumstances of her childhood and youth contributed to instability in her psychological makeup. But she also liked to think that her childhood suffering had a noble cause and a high purpose. "The extraordinary thing is," she observed, "that I grew up with a whole generation of girls brought up in the same identical way, and it seems to have made almost no impression on them— it did not prevent them from growing up normally and going the way of the world successfully." But this was the difference: "Not one of them," she said, "wanted to write." Looking back, she thought of herself as the infant-artist, preparing herself in the fiery furnace. I was "the cheil among 'em," she said, "taking notes."

CHAPTER FOUR

Adolescence

Autumn 1902–Spring 1906

I was self-conscious and vain and <u>mad for love</u>.

In the late autumn of 1901 Harrison Porter was living in his mother's Hays County houses, his future uncertain, faced with his four motherless children, whom he hardly knew how to handle. "Father was strange," Katherine Anne recalled, ["he alternated between impatient tenderness and terrifying bursts of desperate impatience, when he quite obviously could not bear the sight of us] It was impossible to remain in his good graces for long. His affection was always a little disconcerting to me, it was so incalculable, based on motives I could not understand, liable to change for reasons that could not be foreseen and averted." Although Harry Ray was the most "amenable" of the children ("he had a great deal of tenderness in him"), he became a scapegoat for the three girls instead of the "petted only son." "I think my father's treatment of my brother did a great deal to alienate me from him," she said later, "for very early I saw the injustice of his judgements, the unreasonableness of his punishments." Katherine Anne, Gay, and Harry Ray became closer than ever, while Baby continued to be moodily detached.

Harrison and his children went to the farm the following June for the last time. The once pleasurable sojourn had an unhappy edge to it in the summer of 1902, for the farm and the house in Kyle were to be sold and Katherine Anne faced an uprooting. She also became aware of other consequences to Cat's death. Like Miranda in "The Grave," she "knew . . . though she could not say how" that people were whispering that "the motherless family was running down, with the Grandmother not there to hold it together." They were to be "landless," a classification Katherine Anne always associated with a lower social rung. In *The Old Order* and *Old Mortality* she mythologized that summer as the changing of orders and made it the gateway to Miranda's adulthood, as it was to hers.

Cat directed in her will that her estate be apportioned equally among her six sons, with Harrison as executor. The land at the farm had dwindled to the few acres that surrounded the run-down house, nearly a half-century old, and the value of the six-room Kyle house and quarter-acre lot was not great, although much more than the ten dollar sale reported in county deed records, a token transaction to avoid taxes and fees and to equalize debts among the brothers, including Harrison's payment of rent for the year following Cat's death.

Harrison sold for a lump sum to a junk man most of his household furnishings before he and his children set forth, carrying with them their meager personal possessions and their few treasures. He hung on carefully to Alice's photographs, their courtship letters, and what he had salvaged of her clothing and jewelry. It was the beginning of a lifetime of wandering and instability for Katherine Anne, who had yearned, to be sure, for adventure and travel and occasionally escape from home. She had not bargained, however, for this forced displacement and the hardship that went with it. "We were poor," she recalled. "How do I know what happened to the money, except that the land was gone, the house in town was gone . . . and then real poverty with my father quite helpless."

The only plan Harrison seemed to have was to take his children to visit relatives throughout Texas and southern Louisiana while he picked up occasional work. For the most part he simply helped with household, farm, and ranch chores at whatever home he was visiting and took short-term paying jobs whenever he could. At one point he worked as a furniture salesman, and off and on he taught school, an occupation notoriously unremunerative in Texas at the time. Most often he stayed with his brother Alpha and his family at their home on Cadwallader Street in San Antonio, but he also had friendly relations with his female first cousins who were daughters of his Aunt Eliza Jane Myers. The widowed Ada Myers Bentley, who lived in Hays County and took in boarders, no doubt welcomed them for short visits when she had vacant rooms. They frequently stayed with Virginia Cahill, who lived with her family in a big house at 418 West Elmira Street in San Antonio, a house usually full of visiting cousins and in-laws. Occasionally, Harrison's children split up among relatives, and at least once Katherine Anne returned to Kyle to visit Erna Schlemmer.

Katherine Anne shoved out of her conscious memory almost all of her many unpleasant stopovers between 1902 and 1906, but one particular visit left an unusually strong impression on her. Shortly after they departed Kyle, Katherine Anne and her sisters were left with Harrison's first cousin Ellen Myers Thompson, her husband, Eugene, and their sons, twelve-year-old Herbert and nine-year-old Jesse, at the Thompson dairy farm, near Buda, while Harrison and Harry Ray moved along to visit other relatives. Katherine Anne never forgot her discomfort in the small house and the offensive teasing of Eugene Thompson and his sons. Three decades later she drew upon the Thompsons, their farm, and their hired man, William Helton, for the central characters and the setting of her short novel *Noon Wine*.

Books were still Katherine Anne's primary means of escape from unpleasant living conditions, but she also had a hunger for knowledge. She dated the beginning of her self-education 1902, when she read the rest of Shakespeare's plays and memorized all his sonnets. Between 1902 and 1904 she, in fact, absorbed a substantial body of literature, having long given up the light reading she had done in summers at the farm. Her favorite writers were the Russians, and she especially admired Dostoyevsky's "The House of the Dead" and Tolstoy's *Anna Karenina*.

Harrison's taste in literature ran to French and British works from the eighteenth and nineteenth centuries and earlier. Some of what he recommended, such as Thomas Paine's *Common Sense,* he hoped would nudge Katherine Anne in the direction of his leftist political sympathies that had solidified after the depression of the 1890s that had forced thousands of small farm owners throughout the South to relinquish their land and resort to tenant farming. Harrison supported the socialist Eugene Victor Debs, who, after his 1900 run for the presidency, had steadily multiplied his base in Texas. Katherine Anne went with Harrison to see Debs at a rally in San Antonio in 1902, long afterward recalling a "tall, pale colored thin man," who talked very "urgently but gently" and made "mild and reasonable statements."

In 1903 Harrison found a shabby little house to rent in a suburb of San Antonio and hired an old woman to cook. Within the next year he allowed Katherine Anne and Gay to make two trips to New Orleans with his brother Newell and Newell's pretty, young wife, Ione (pronounced Yon-ee), who always stopped at the dilapidated house on their way to Louisiana. The first trip, in March of 1903, was the occasion of Katherine Anne's first ride in an automobile and her first sight of an airplane. The second trip was made in the early months of 1904, and it was during this stay of several months that convent-educated Ione placed Katherine Anne and Gay in the St. Ann Street Ecole du Sacre Coeur, which was later absorbed in the St. Louis Cathedral Parish School. Katherine Anne and Gay slept in a long, chilly dormitory, where they were watched over by nuns, who insisted the girls stay at least six feet away from open windows when dressing and required them during nightly baths to wear bathing gowns that floated in the tub like lily pads. Katherine Anne probably tried to create some drama by thinking of herself as "immured" like a heroine in a Gothic novel, but she concluded that the experience in the convent school was finally only "dull."

Nuns at the Ecole du Sacre Coeur recognized the advanced level of Katherine Anne's reading and suggested works they thought might interest (or enlighten) her, such as selections by Saint Thomas Aquinas. She preferred Saint Augustine, however. In her copies of his *Confessions* she faithfully wrote out on the title page her favorite passage: "It doth make a difference whence cometh a man's joy." She also filled her copies with marginal lines and comments that illustrate the appeal Augustine held for her. His descriptions of his struggle with lust resonated with a thirteen-year-old girl in the early stages of puberty, as did his account of his loving and selfless mother, St. Monica.

The Porter girls attended as day students several convent schools in and around San Antonio under the sponsorship of Virginia Cahill and Alpha's wife, Lee. Wherever he lived or visited, Harrison tried to enroll his children in whatever schools were available. Not only did he give considerable importance to education, but he saw school as a way of ordering their lives. What could he have done with them otherwise? Schools in San Antonio, like New Orleans, were largely Catholic schools, especially convent schools, which appealed to him for their solid academic reputations and the fact that they adjusted or waived the tuition for Protestant students unable to pay. When much later one of Katherine Anne's friends suggested that Harrison had sent her to convent schools because they were free, Katherine Anne responded, "Nasty friend," but she did not deny it. The roving Porter girls, however, did not stay in any one school long enough to leave behind records of attendance or grades. With obvious accuracy, Katherine Anne said of her early education, "It was scant and fragmentary because I was a traveler from an early age."

Despite all the advantages of convent schools, Harrison preferred that his children not receive the religious instruction that was part of the curriculum. He consoled himself by countering that instruction the same way he had offset his mother's earlier Calvinist indoctrination of them. According to Katherine Anne, he stamped out of them every-thing religious by encouraging them to read a broad range of humanis-tic books, history, philosophy, and especially "rational"—that is, not romantic or sentimental—literature. Although the family books had disappeared with the sale of the Kyle house and Harrison had no money to buy more, books were readily available in public libraries. Katherine Anne recalled her father's taking her up to a long line of books in the San Antonio Public Library and telling her, "Why don't you read this? It'll knock some of the nonsense out of you." They were the forty-three volumes of the *Works of Voltaire*, with notes by Tobias Smollett. He also directed her to the six volumes of Edward Gibbon's *The Decline and Fall of the Roman Empire*.

At age fourteen Katherine Anne was intellectually sophisticated, and she felt grown up. To signal her exit from childhood she decided to change her childhood name, Callie Russell. She changed it in stages (the final stage would not take place for a decade), first choosing "K. R.," preserving her original phonetic initials. Then she began also to call herself "Katherine"—her grandmother's name with a change of two letters in the spelling. Her brother, Harry Ray, also chose to change his name at the same time. He became "Harrison Paul," to be known as "Paul."

Before September of 1904 Harrison decided to enroll his daughters and his son in private, non-Catholic schools. He had concluded that his children needed a more systematic education than they were receiving from his haphazard tutoring and their sporadic attendance at a variety of educational institutions. If Katherine Anne's fixing of 1904 as the date of an argument she had with Harrison over the concept of the virgin birth is accurate, he might also have feared that his daugh-ters were becoming even more indoctrinated in Catholicism than they earlier had been in his mother's Calvinism.

His decision was made after he learned about the newly estab-lished Thomas School, a boarding and day school founded in 1902 by Professor Asa A. Thomas and his wife in a three-story red brick build-ing near West End Lake in San Antonio. It accommodated girls in grades one through twelve as either boarding or day students, and, although they didn't advertise it, boys in the primary levels as day students. The Thomases employed first-class teachers specifically to train young ladies either "for the active duties of life" or entrance to colleges and universities for further education. Moral instruction and intellectual development were equally stressed.

Harrison believed he was taking a step that would have pleased Alice, who had admired Professor Asa Thomas when she was his student at the Coronal Institute in San Marcos in the late 1870s. To pay the tuition for Gay's, Katherine Anne's, and Baby's year as day students at the Thomas School and Paul's year as a boarding student at the nearby Peacock Military Academy, however, he was obliged to borrow money from some of his cousins, and to save streetcar fare he rented a house at West End Lake close to both schools. For the next year he and his daughters lived in a little two-room house that had no hot water. "I know that we were at the end of our resources," Katherine Anne wrote later, "living on the edge of real poverty, but I do not remember any hardship, or discomfort."

Her year at the Thomas School in 1904 and 1905 was the most coherent year of post-grammar-school education she would have. Although she remained a poor student in math, she was still a good student in history, French, and English, and her reading expanded to include literary classics she had missed earlier (she mentioned Chaucer in particular). The students, who wore uniforms of navy sailor dresses and flat-crowned navy caps, attended free concerts sponsored by a music club of local women, and for twenty-five cents they could attend shows, operas, and plays in San Antonio, then a stop for touring performers such as Edwin Booth and Lily Langtry. Katherine Anne also had private singing and violin lessons at the nearby Our Lady of the Lake convent, well known for the high quality of its music instruction, which it made available to outside students.

The Thomas School was under the wing of the Methodist Church, and Katherine Anne thus was not able to avoid religious training at the school, as Harrison would have preferred. Professor Thomas, however, who instructed the girls in religion and Bible history, made the experience more palatable than had Cat Porter or nuns at convent schools. Nevertheless, as counterpoise during the year, Katherine Anne read, no doubt at Harrison's suggestion, William James's pragmatic *Varieties of Religious Experience*.

Mrs. Thomas was a teacher of languages and bookkeeping at the school. Trying hard to provide for their students a balanced education that included a well-controlled social schedule, she instructed the girls in manners and deportment and arranged dances with suitable young men from the community. She taught the girls how to curtsy and how to maintain proper distance from their dancing partners, and she told them never to look a gentleman in the eyes for more than a second, but to look over his shoulder or at his necktie. (Katherine Anne thought that *then* it was acceptable to "flash the eyes up.") The girls drew the young men's names from a hat and were permitted to promenade on a balcony under the watchful eyes of chaperones.

Katherine Anne's adolescent interest in boys was in full flower. Ten years later she wrote "Brother Spoiled a Romance," a version of an experience she said occurred after a school dance, and the *Chicago Tribune* paid her one dollar to publish it in their column "How Did He Propose?"

> Dear Miss Blake: We were coming home from a dance on a brilliant moonlight night, picking our way very carefully along a narrow trail around a little lake near my home. He was a shy lad and I was a shy girl, so conversation languished until he mustered up enough courage to slip an arm around my waist and stammer some incoherent thing about loving me, asking me to marry him as soon as he graduated in June etc., when, without warning, a heavy hand seized him by the back of the collar and tossed him into the lake, which was pretty deep there.
>
> I turned with a squeal of fright to behold my very big and very proper brother, bristling with rage at what he termed the "impertinence" of any man who would dare embrace me.
>
> "Proposal!" snorted Brother, "you just wait until you're out of school before you think of proposals. Come right along home with me this minute." And he marched me away forthwith, leaving my discomfited gallant to flounder out of his predicament as well as he might. "He'll never come back," I wept loudly to any unsympathetic relative. And for a fact, he did not!

The account reveals her father's attitude, as well as her brother's, toward her interest in boys and romance at the ages of fourteen and fifteen. Her father, she thought, was too suspicious of her flirtations, and he questioned her rigorously when he could not account for each minute she spent outside his sight.

Reacting angrily to Harrison's old-fashioned paternalism that co-existed with his progressive political views, she later reconstructed a monologue by him that illustrates the conflict between them and affords as well a realistic glimpse of the family's life at the time: " 'Don't ever let me hear you talking any of that nonsense about the slavery of women,' said her father, 'I wish all you women who talk about slavery had to be turned into men for just one day . . . . . Then you'd know the meaning of slavery.' He wrapped his ragged old bathrobe around him and started down the hall. 'Just look at me with my elbows out trying to keep a houseful of women in fine under-clothes. Where are you going at this time of day, anyhow?'" Katherine Anne became committed to the cause of women's rights and later claimed to have published her first essay on the subject that year.

During the Easter holidays in 1905 Harrison took his daughters to New Orleans to visit relatives and attend a horse race in which Thomas Gay, once married to Harrison's late sister Anna, had entered one of his horses. Katherine Anne had formed a highly romantic image of her uncle Thomas based on the family stories about his devotion to the beautiful, capricious Anna. The loud, red-faced, fifty-year-old man she met, however, bore no resemblance to the handsome, griev-ing lover she had imagined. The disillusion was completed at his run-down boardinghouse in Elysian Fields, a side of New Orleans Katherine Anne had not seen before, one very different from the sec-tion of town in which she had gone to school. She would fictionalize the whole event in *Old Mortality* and make New Orleans the symbol of a romantic past and a decadent present.

As the school year of 1904–1905 approached its end, Harrison had to think about the future for himself and his daughters. Katherine Anne already had an idea about hers: during the year she had become increasingly beautiful, and she wanted to be an actress. At five feet two, with curly black hair and blue-gray eyes, she matched one of the age's two ideals of female beauty (the other was the taller, athletic Gibson Girl). A local photographer saw promise in her looks and asked her to sit for a photograph to be submitted to a contest (he won the prize). In the photograph she is affecting a pose that resembled her idol, Sarah Bernhardt. She also had worked hard to improve her acting skills. In a commencement program at the Thomas School, she recited the 107-line poem "Lasca," a wildly popular, sentimental ballad about a Texas cowboy and his Mexican sweetheart, Lasca, who dies by pro-tecting his body with hers when they are thrown off a horse during a cattle stampede "down by the Rio Grande." Apparently impressed, Katherine Anne's drama teacher, an elderly actress, urged her to con-sider joining a local summer stock company after she left school.

Harrison ignored the fact that his mother and wife would have objected strenuously to his encouraging Katherine Anne to go on the stage, and he gave both her and Gay permission to perform at the

Electric Summer Theater on West Evergreen Street in San Antonio. The outdoor theater was the first attraction to open in Electric Park, an amusement compound that eventually would include Ferris wheels, cafés, a penny arcade, and a chute ride. The premise of Electric Park was lights, the more the better—taking advantage of the turn-of-the-century public's fascination with the novelty of electricity. Hundreds of white lights were to line every structure and walkway of the park, and an early photograph reveals a light-strewn stage facing multiple rows of audience seats. A news story in the *San Antonio Express* promised that "the open-air theater" would be "as bright as day."

The Electric Theater opened 14 May 1905, the day before Katherine Anne's fifteenth birthday. She probably considered it a lucky omen. Four plays were produced there in June by the Albert C. Taylor Company, which advertised lavishly in the local papers and received in return front-page mention of its productions, which ran about a week each. Although the company boasted that its players were "professional," advertisements and news stories that summer did not include a cast list or a detailed review of the plays. The reviewers only called the productions "excellent" and generally praised the "modern" staging and the "facilely" acted parts. Two plays the company performed that summer were *Peaceful Valley* and *The Christian*, titles that suggest the kind of sentimental and moralistic fare the acting company thought respectable citizens of San Antonio might pay ten cents admission to see. Which parts Katherine Anne played in these dramas, or in two other unidentified ones, are unknown, but she later remarked that Gay always had the ingenue parts, while she relished the roles of "Peck's bad boy."

To get to and from the theater, Katherine Anne and Gay had to ride a trolley to downtown San Antonio and transfer to the line that ran to West Evergreen Street. After the performances they had to hurry to catch the last trolley, the "Owl Service." One night they became terrified when they suspected that a shadowy man had followed them from the theater and onto the trolley. Although they dashed home when the trolley stopped, the man walked doggedly behind them all the way to the door opened by Harrison. The stranger had accompanied the girls at a distance to protect them, he told Harrison, and he sternly rebuked Harrison for allowing his daughters out in the city unescorted late at night. Even though the summer acting had been Katherine Anne's idea, she later thought it more evidence of her father's failure to take care of his daughters.

When the 1905 summer theater season ended, Katherine Anne and Gay thought that they might be able to capitalize on their past year of education and theatrical training and convinced Harrison to move to Victoria, the center of a cotton-growing and ranching area about one hundred miles southeast of San Antonio. Katherine Anne imagined an air of prosperity in Victoria's wide streets, fine homes, opera house, and the well-stocked Brontë Public Library. Harrison settled the four of them into the Pridham House, a boarding establishment on Juan Linn Street, and he rented a room on nearby Santa Rosa Street where Katherine Anne and Gay could offer lessons in "music, physical culture and dramatic reading," as they advertised that fall in the *Victoria Advocate*.

As soon as Katherine Anne's brother, Paul, completed his academic year at the Peacock Military Academy, he joined the navy. From the outset he wrote letters to Katherine Anne, expanding her world by describing his experiences and the ports into which he sailed. A letter he wrote her in early December of 1905 from Guantanamo Bay, Cuba, is the earliest to survive: "Dear little sister," he wrote, recounting the voyage to Cuba and life aboard a ship. He asked whether she and Gay had any more pupils, and then he said, "Continue your stories for they are fine." It is the earliest independent confirmation of Katherine Anne as writer, and she was thrilled with his praise, tucking it away permanently in a corner of her mind to savor. She quoted it back to him a quarter of a century later when she inscribed a copy of her first book for him.

Katherine Anne received Paul's 1905 letter close to Christmas. That season was a fateful one for her, for it was at a holiday party she attended with Gay that she met nineteen-year-old John Henry Koontz, home for the holidays from Louisiana, where he worked as a clerk for the Pacific Railway Company. Katherine Anne recalled the crucial encounter: "When he saw me standing near an alcove he took me by the hand, pulled me toward him, and tried to kiss me, barely grazing my cheek as I twisted away."

Katherine Anne was a natural flirt, who knew how to exploit her sexual appeal when she danced with John Koontz. Although her lessons in deportment at the Thomas School had included directions for maintaining proper distance from a dancing partner, that very decorum intensified the interest. She pointed out many years later, "The fact that I was instructed to hold off this wild man gave him such importance. He was dangerous, don't you see, and it set him up no end." In this instance the "set up" was effective on both sides, and shortly after the Christmas party Katherine Anne was invited to the Koontz ranch at nearby Inez.

Not long after Katherine Anne met John Koontz, the advertisements in the *Victoria Advocate* by the "Misses Porter" stopped. Perhaps there had not been enough students, as Paul hinted in his December letter, or perhaps Gay and Katherine Anne thought better opportunities lay elsewhere for their "little academy," as Katherine Anne referred to their school. In the spring of 1906, they moved with Harrison and Baby to Lufkin. In addition to the fact that they had Myers cousins there with whom they could stay, Katherine Anne might have encouraged the selection of this town, which was about fifty miles from the Louisiana state line and considerably closer to Lafayette, where John Koontz worked.

Sexual magnetism was all Katherine Anne and John had in common. Religion was the first of many differences. Like all the rest of John's family, he was firmly Catholic; he also was pragmatic and unimaginative with no interest in literature or other arts. And although he had as much formal education as she had (he spent a year at St. Edward's School in Austin), he had none of the intellectual curiosity of the Porters. Katherine Anne, however, did not register as potential trouble the differences between them or the danger she perceived at the Christmas dance. The problems that seemed most serious to her were Harrison's near-poverty and her battles with him, which resulted in long silences that had to be mediated by Gay. John Koontz, who exuded self-confidence, seemed an attractive alternative to what she regarded as an unfair and domineering father, and his family's comfortable prosperity contrasted pleasantly with the financial straits in which she existed with her father.

CHAPTER FIVE

Marriage

Spring 1906–February 1914

*My own experience was this: I was given the kind of education and
the kind of upbringing that in no way prepared me for the world I
was to face. When I was ready to step out in the world supposedly
grown up, I was as ignorant of the world as it was possible to be.*

Soon after the Porters moved to Lufkin, Katherine Anne and John
Koontz began to plan a wedding despite the fact that they had the
approval of neither family. Katherine Anne was, after all, only fifteen
years old, and she was not Roman Catholic, as the Koontzes would
have preferred. Soon, however, in the face of youthful determination
Harrison as well as John's parents agreed to the engagement, with
Harrison insisting that they wait until Katherine Anne was sixteen
to get married.

Among Katherine Anne's autobiographical notes is a cryptic description of Mrs. Koontz sewing a dress. It was white organdy with "a mass
of little frills on the skirt and sleeves," and it no doubt was Katherine
Anne's wedding dress. The wedding took place 20 June 1906, only three
weeks after her sixteenth birthday. Gay had met and become engaged
to Thomas (T. H.) Holloway, and the sisters were married in a double
ceremony performed by Ira Bryce, a Methodist minister.

Nearly a half century later, Katherine Anne wrote, "The trouble
with me is—always was—that if you say 'marriage' to me, instantly
the word translates itself into 'love,' for only in such terms can I grasp
the idea at all, or make any sense of it. The two are hopelessly associated, or rather identified in my mind; that is to say, love is the only
excuse for marriage, if any excuse is necessary." For a few months in
1905 and 1906 Katherine Anne thought she was in love with John
Koontz, and she apparently felt a physical attraction to him. But she
was too inexperienced to realistically imagine the sexual expression

of that ardor. She entered the marriage with little idea of what to expect in the marriage bed.

Cat Porter's Victorian sense of duty to her granddaughters had included keeping them ignorant about sex. Harrison concurred with his mother and confused his daughters further by idealizing the carnality out of his marriage to their mother and teaching them to be wary of boys. His attitude was represented in a particular event in Katherine Anne's childhood, when on an idle day she had accompanied her brother, then called Harry Ray, who, having set out to hunt small creatures, killed a rabbit. As he skinned it, they discovered the rabbit was pregnant; multiple tiny embryos nestled in a sac inside the carcass. Despite her promise to her brother not to tell their father what she had seen, she promptly did, and Harrison whipped Harry Ray for unintentionally revealing to Katherine Anne a secret of procreation.

What scant information about sex Katherine Anne had at the time of her wedding (Gay, despite being five years older, was equally naive) had been picked up from Tante Ione, who seemed less reticent than other women in the family about speaking of conjugal intimacies to her young nieces. She advised Katherine Anne and Gay shortly before their wedding to get in the habit of sitting in cold water before going to bed with their husbands. "That makes you tight, harder to get into," she explained. "Men like that," she said.

John Koontz was indifferent to his wife's romantic expectations and inexperience. She told a close friend many years later that she had "held out" for forty-seven days before this marriage was consummated, implying that the experience had been tantamount to rape. Decades later, when she was writing *Ship of Fools*, she created a fictional portrait of John Koontz in the character of William Denny, a crude, insecure, bigoted young man who carries aboard ship the fully illustrated book *Recreational Aspects of Sex as Mental Prophylaxis: A Guide to True Happiness in Life.* He is observed disdainfully by Mrs. Treadwell, who like Katherine Anne had married "the wrong man" when she was "too young" and asks herself, "Was I really ever married to a man so jealous he beat me until I bled at the nose?" abused her

Some margin having been granted to the exaggeration of caricature in the novel, according to the legal documents of Katherine Anne and John Koontz's eventual divorce, the fictional portrait is close to Koontz as he was during their marriage. Nine years after the wedding he admitted that from the beginning of their union he was frequently guilty of adultery, extreme intoxication, vile name-calling, and physical attacks that resulted in Katherine Anne's broken bones and lacerations. At the age of sixteen—the age she fixed as the dividing line between naiveté and maturity—Katherine Anne was abruptly disillusioned about marriage and sex, or as she said later about John Koontz, "I saw through my monster very shortly." The monster was Koontz, of course, but it was also the institution of marriage, which she later called "the merciless revealer, the great white searchlight turned on the darkest places of human nature." It was as well that original "set up" at the Christmas dance, the sexual attraction she had assumed was love, "a phase only, which being passed is too often mistaken for the whole thing."

Katherine Anne habitually obscured unpleasant details of her private life, and it is doubtful that anyone in either the Koontz or Porter families knew the full truth about John Koontz's abuse. His family seemed especially oblivious to his tendencies toward violence. Although they were aware of constant tension and disagreements between him and Katherine Anne, they probably blamed the trouble on her flightiness and flirtatiousness and no doubt thought that motherhood would settle her down. In the first years of the marriage, however, there was no sign of a baby, and the Koontzes must have wondered whether Katherine Anne was in some way preventing pregnancy out of fear of childbirth or an unwillingness to assume the responsibility of rearing a child.

Katherine Anne was well aware of the dangers of childbearing. Her mother and at least two of her aunts had died from complications of pregnancy or childbirth, and Mrs. Koontz had raised the specter of death by childbirth by commenting on her soon-to-be-daughter-in-law's slight frame and worrying aloud that without "good broad hips" Katherine Anne would not be able to "stand what she was made for." Katherine Anne, however, identified with her paternal grandmother, who had been physically slender and remained hardy in spite of giving birth to eleven children. Katherine Anne was intuitively drawn to children, and she probably wanted a child, especially later in the marriage. John's sister Beatrice recalled Katherine Anne's fondness for her daughter Mary and her delight in being mistaken for the baby's mother. But even had Katherine Anne wanted to prevent a pregnancy, she would not have known how. She would have relied on Tante Ione's additional advice, to "douche with water as hot as you can stand it immediately after the performance if you do not want to have babies every year." Katherine Anne's fallowness in the first years of the marriage, if not the fault of her husband, was probably the result of stress and missed opportunities during fertile segments of her cycle.

During the early years of the marriage, she did not seriously consider leaving her husband. She had no parental home to which she could retreat as Harrison and Baby continued to wander among relatives. She merely tried to cope with her pain and unhappiness by falling back on the family habit of visiting friends or relatives, attending whatever local theatrical performances she could afford, and avid reading, which was still her most prized pastime. Without children to care for or a big house to manage, she had plenty of time for it, and all the towns she lived in during her marriage had good public libraries. She said that her life until 1915, the year she was divorced from John Koontz, was "one long orgy of reading," first "a grand sweep of all English and translated classics from the beginning until about 1800" and then steady movement through the nineteenth century into the twentieth. She read *Wuthering Heights* a dozen times before 1910, a turning point occurring when she came to prefer the "cold realism" of Flaubert to the Gothic realism of Brontë. She also went through her Nietzsche and Freud "jags" between 1906 and 1915.

Although her brother confirmed that she was writing stories in 1905, she dated the beginning of her "serious" writing 1906, the year of her marriage. "I practiced writing in every possible way that I could," she said, "I wrote a pastiche of other people, imitating Dr. Johnson and Laurence Sterne, and Petrarch and Shakespeare's sonnets, and then I tried writing my own way. I spent fifteen years learning to trust myself."

Her reading and writing provided daily and satisfying escapes from the unpleasantness of her contentious marriage. But there were also occasional respites from the conflict and temporary reconciliations. Usually the hiatus occurred with a change of location, such as that of 1908, when John was laid off by the Southern Pacific Railway and they moved from Lafayette to Houston, where he took a position as a stenographer with William D. Cleveland and Sons, a wholesale grocery and cotton-factoring company. Katherine Anne hoped that in Houston, where John's sister Beatrice Hasbrook and her husband lived, her marriage would improve. Her optimism was short-lived, however, for John's violence and infidelity continued. Soon after they moved into a boardinghouse at 1807 Crawford Street, he threw her down a stairway, breaking her right ankle and severely injuring her knee.

It was after this incident that Katherine Anne made a long journey to Marfa to visit her Uncle Asbury (Azzie) and Aunt May and her adored first cousin Anna Laredo (Lady) Bunton, who was living in Marfa with her fifty-four-year-old husband, their three-year-old son, Oren, and her husband's three children from his first marriage. Katherine Anne was returning to the scene of her grandmother's death, the most painful loss in her memory, but Marfa was a kind of family home. Azzie and May's three grown children and Lady's sisters and brothers also lived nearby with their families. It was a comforting circle of what Katherine Anne called "consanguinity and affinity."

Azzie and May evidently sensed something of the marital strife that drove her more than four hundred miles away from her husband, and Azzie, a prosperous rancher and civic leader in the community, offered her a little arts-and-crafts-style cabin he owned as a place for her to live. It must have been appealing to Katherine Anne, but she did not know how to negotiate even a modified separation from her husband and to support herself afterward. She was also afraid he would come after her, since he threatened to kill either her or himself if she ever left him. She saw no alternative to returning to Houston and John Koontz.

Soon another lull in the marital warfare took place when John's father, Henry Clay Koontz Jr., died. Although Katherine Anne was afraid of her husband and antagonistic toward him, she willingly spent weekends in Inez with him and his grieving family. The benefit of being in Inez was that she was spared John's drunken abuse, and she enjoyed the spread of the large ranch, where she could ride horses and wander at will. The unpleasant part of being there was that, with the exception of John's younger sister Mildred, she did not much like John's family, especially his mother, whom she thought opinionated and provincial. "Oh, that narrow-minded family I stumbled into," she told an interviewer in a hushed voice sixty years later.

At the beginning of 1909 the troubled marriage reached a new crisis when John beat her unconscious with a hairbrush. She later said, "Between 1908 and 1910 I was battling for my life." She began to consider separation, at least, divorce, possibly, and she conveyed her plight—indirectly—to the persons she believed cared about her the most, Gay and Paul. But she found little help. Gay had to give all her attention to her own hard lot, for she, too, had married a "monster," albeit a dissolute charmer rather than a brute. Paul's reaction, however, was a severe disappointment.

Early in 1909 Katherine Anne wrote him a long letter arguing passionately for women's suffrage and women's independence, an oblique presentation of her predicament. When Paul finally wrote, he addressed her by her childhood name, "Callie." Her "vehemence" had taken him by surprise, he said, and he dealt directly with the suffrage issue. "Dear, why should you butt your head against hard facts, there is no practical reason for allowing you the ballot. I admit it would gratify their vanity, but aside from that it would be of no earthly use to women. It would not help the moral or economic conditions and would bring the millennium no nearer . . . The world's greatest need today is of good mothers which is the master profession for women requiring every art and talent to perfect, of women who live close to their children, who will bear impressions of her training all through life. The farther away a woman gets from the thought that she was made to be the helpmate of man, and the mother of his children, the farther she will be from her usefulness." Paul also carefully registered his unequivocal disapproval of divorce in case she was considering such an extreme action: "What effort you make for equality renders you unwomanly and consequently less deserving of the deference which is a woman's portion. American women enjoy more liberty than any other nation on the earth and what are the results. Divorces, soul mates and numerous other evils."

Paul's hard stance against women's rights contributed to Katherine Anne's decision to make a final effort to do whatever she could to change the tenor of her marriage. Encouraged by the Koontz family, Katherine Anne decided to join John in his Roman Catholic faith, and she began to take the required instruction. Harrison, more than ever the rationalist, who had cited the notion of the virgin birth as a particularly silly idea, was not pleased, but in the end he preferred religion to divorce. Katherine Anne subsequently was baptized in Houston's Church of the Annunciation, at the corner of Texas Avenue and Crawford Street, 5 April 1910, by the Reverend Father Thomas Hennessy. She took the baptismal names "Maria" and "Veronica."

Even before she married into the Koontz family, Katherine Anne was familiar with many aspects of Roman Catholicism. As a child she had been "proselytized" by her aunts Ione and May and by her governess Ella Mudd. She also had the limited experience of convent school, and she had been so much fascinated with beautiful nuns in Gothic literature that she had claimed the convent life as a goal when she grew up. The rich history of the church, its distance from the plainly garbed Calvinism of her grandmother, and the sonorous liturgical drama of its rituals appealed to her imagination. In a specific way, the church's hierarchy and laws imposed a comforting pattern on her life, and the paternalism of the church provided a substitute for the kind of protection she had wanted from Harrison and never received.

Within her newly acquired religious allegiance Katherine Anne found diversion and a new area of literary exploration. She also was cautiously pleased with the little house John was building for them in the Heights area of Houston. Evidence that Katherine Anne had a miscarriage or stillbirth in 1910 or 1911 suggests that her new hopefulness might have been expressed in a pregnancy.

If Katherine Anne had any illusion that the house, which they named "Inglenook," would be a place of security and happiness for her, reality reasserted itself when they moved in. John's habits of violence, drinking, and chasing women proved again fundamentally unchanged, and the beatings he gave her, provoked by his drunkenness and her flirtatiousness with other men, continued to be a serious threat to her life. But she had to contend also with the humiliation of his infidelities, which she called "a vulgar handing over . . . to public shame." He frequently visited prostitutes, and at least five times during their marriage he moved in temporarily with women to whom he had taken a fancy. According to the divorce decree, Katherine Anne knew their names and addresses.

Another cessation in their marital strife was brought about when William D. Cleveland and Sons gave John a position as traveling salesman. Thus, late in 1911 he and Katherine Anne left Inglenook and Houston and moved to Corpus Christi. After five years of an unhappy marriage, she was suspended between despair and resignation, and the initial solace she had found in her adopted faith was diminishing. She was to discover, however, in Corpus Christi and in the years 1912 and 1913 some unexpected pleasures. John's extended absences spared her his unwanted attention and afforded her increased opportunities to write fiction and poetry and to read. When she grew restless in their cramped rooms in the Tourist Hotel at 607½ Mesquite Street, she explored the busy port full of world travelers. She rode the modern streetcars around the old city and took long walks on the white-sand beach that edged a crescent of the Gulf of Mexico.

At 505 Chaparral Street, in the center of the two-block business district, was the Corpus Christi Book and Stationary Company, a newsstand and cigar store that sold textbooks and school supplies and carried a wide selection of current publications, very different from the "older" books available in public libraries. There Katherine Anne discovered Gertrude Stein's early works, Joyce's *Dubliners*, literary magazines new to her, and newspapers in a half-dozen languages. For the next year she hungrily absorbed a world of radical ideas and looked more carefully at the pioneering "new woman," with whom she was beginning to identify, in violation of most of the values of her mother and grandmother and of all that her father and brother—to say nothing of her husband—countenanced.

Shortly after Katherine Anne and John's move to Corpus Christi, she wrote a poem that she submitted to the *Gulf Coast Citrus Fruit Grower and Southern Nurseryman*, a recently established trade journal. Her "Texas: By the Gulf of Mexico" was published on the cover of the January 1912 issue. Ostensibly an appeal to northern businessmen to move to Texas, the awkwardly rhymed poem was full of self-conscious Elizabethan diction and flushed with echoes of Edgar Allan Poe and the sentimental language of her parents' Victorian love letters. Signed "Katherine Porter Koontz," it was her earliest published creative piece.

Katherine Anne at this time began to think seriously about a break from John Koontz. She knew that it would be difficult. To go far enough away to escape his wrathful chase would take money neither she nor anyone she trusted, such as Gay, had, and it was nearly impossible to finagle extra money from her husband by ruse of inflated claims of domestic expenses. John was tightfisted, especially with his vain wife, who would have liked pretty clothes, fine leather shoes, and other luxuries, especially perfumes. With a vague plan in mind that would take time to carry out, she began to squirrel away a nickel here, a dime there, secreting her little stash in an old kid glove of her mother's.

The one expense John seemed willing to assume in his wife's behalf was the cost of her travel when she decided to visit a friend or relative. Sometimes, as with the Marfa trip, it was recompense for an especially brutal attack. But in other instances, when she wished to go see Gay or Baby or in 1908 attend the funeral of Thomas Gay in Menard, he was quickly agreeable to providing train fare. A trip that proved particularly pleasurable was one she made in December of 1912 when she went to Dallas to visit Gay while Gay's husband was working in Oklahoma. Gay, in fact, needed Katherine Anne's help after the birth of her first child, a girl Gay named Mary Alice for their mother (and, coincidentally, for their younger sister). This beautiful baby with an apricot-like dimple in her chin, the first child of her generation with whom Katherine Anne shared a blood tie, was an immediate delight.

Before leaving Dallas, Katherine Anne was already thinking about a future time when little Mary Alice could visit "Tante Katherine."

Only a few months later, she made another trip, and this one, unlike the trip to Dallas, was nearly as desperate as the trip to Marfa in 1908. She had undergone an operation that required a period of recuperation at a safe distance from her husband. The surgery, which had been performed under ether to remove an ovarian cyst, carried the usual danger of infection. Baby and Gay arranged for her to spend a month at Spring Branch, in the blackland country near Houston, with the Heinrich von Hillendahl family, prosperous German immigrants with whom the Porters were acquainted.

Ten years later Katherine Anne took the surface details of that visit for a story she eventually titled "Holiday." "At that time I was too young for some of the troubles I was having, and I had not yet learned what to do with them . . . It seemed to me then there was nothing to do but run away from them, though all my tradition, background, and training had taught me unanswerably that no one except a coward ever runs away from anything. What nonsense! They should have taught me the difference between courage and foolhardiness, instead of leaving me to find it out for myself. I learned finally that if I still had the sense I was born with, I would take off like a deer at the first warning of certain dangers." After staying long enough to watch the spring come in and acknowledging that her journey, like the Marfa trip, had been a ritual of temporary escape, she returned to Corpus Christi to take up the struggle again while she gathered the money for a final break.

When Katherine Anne rejoined John in their cramped apartment, they reached an armed truce: They would stay together but would not resume sexual intimacy. He would take his pleasure elsewhere. He would provide food and shelter for her, she would continue her usual pastimes of reading and writing, and they would avoid the scandal of divorce. He might have considered the arrangement permanent, but she did not. Although she welcomed the respite from his sexual attention, she was never certain when he would turn violent. She had not changed her mind about leaving him as soon as she could.

In the spring of 1914 Katherine Anne discovered that her childhood friend Erna Schlemmer had moved to Corpus Christi with her husband, Glover Johns, who had bought the local Ford automobile agency. The reunion at the Johnses' pretty Cliffside home in the North Beach was a happy one. Katherine Anne liked Erna's husband, and she was delighted with their year-old son, little Glover Jr.

Katherine Anne spent many happy days with Erna, but she also recognized a depressing contrast between their lives. In Kyle, although
the Schlemmer family had been prosperous, their house was similar to
the Porters' house across the street, and the daily lives of both families
had been limited to what comforts the time and place afforded. After
Harrison and his children left Kyle, the economic gap between the two
families grew wider. Erna's father held a series of diplomatic posts in
Europe, where Erna had gone to boarding school, and when her father
was appointed to the prestigious position of postmaster at Austin, the
Schlemmers returned to Texas and moved into a fine home in the state
capital. Erna went to the University of Texas, and her 1910 wedding
was a social event of the Austin season. With the exception of an artistic career, Erna seemed to have everything that Katherine Anne
wanted, including a child. Believing that she, too, could still find happiness, she was more determined than ever to leave John Koontz.

Between the spring of 1913 and February of 1914 Katherine Anne
had plenty of time to think about the failure of her marriage and the
ramifications of her planned action. She knew that running off would
be considered disgraceful by nearly everybody, including Erna, who
was "straitlaced" and "conventional" and admitted no exceptions in
her belief that marriage vows were permanent. Katherine Anne began
to justify her planned bolt from "that preposterous marriage," and one
may suppose that her rationalization went something like the explanation she offered in 1927: "Marriage—that old fortress of civilization—
is thus adjusting itself to the new order. Something had to give way;
and it is better to bend before the storm than to break and go down." In
other terms she was telling herself that the "one-man-one-woman-
until-death sort of marriage," as she described it, went out at the end of
the last century with the horse and buggy. Modern women, that is,
"new" women like herself, were going to outdistance the storm.

CHAPTER SIX

The Wild Dash from Texas

February 1914–May 1918

She knew now why she had run away to marriage, and she knew
that she was going to run away from marriage, and she was not
going to stay in any place, with anyone, that threatened to forbid
her making her own discoveries, that said "No" to her.

I got out of Texas like a bat out of hell at the earliest possible moment.

Late in February of 1914 Katherine Anne counted her modest accumulation of money, gathered her personal belongings, treated herself
to a new wardrobe she boldly charged to John's account at a Corpus
Christi department store, and boarded a train. Such flights would
become a pattern in her life.

She liked to use the word "wild" to describe a leap toward liberty
and adventure. But her description of her escape in 1914 as her "wild
dash" into the "wilder world" was braver sounding than was war-
ranted by her anxious little flutter of independence as she boarded the
train in Corpus Christi to begin the thousand-mile journey northeast
to Chicago. In retrospect she liked to simplify her dash from Texas as
a desire for freedom from restrictive conventions. She told Caroline
Gordon that she had run away from the South because she had no
intention of "not thinking what I please, nor of conforming where
conformity would cramp and annoy me." She also said that she had
run away from an unenlightened society's attitude toward women
who wanted to be artists. "I had to leave Texas because I didn't want
to be regarded as a freak." Perhaps in the abstract all of that was true.
But the story or the timing would have been different had she children dependent on her, had she a family home to welcome her, or had
her marriage to John Koontz been tolerable.

In the early days of her separation from home and Texas she accepted responsibility for the paralysis of will that had kept her with Koontz for nearly eight years, but she was more inclined to look for others to blame. Most of her rage was directed at her husband, but she was also angry with Harrison for failing to provide for his children and thus making her desperate enough to marry so young and so unwisely. Because "girls whose fathers did not take care of them get a curse on them," she told Gay, "other men feel that they need not care for them either." She was unable to bring herself to single out her brother, Paul, for reproach, but he was snared in the collective blame she placed on her family. She told Gay that she was still amazed to think of the crimes John Koontz had committed against her while not one of them "lifted a hand."

After arriving in Chicago and finding a cheap room in a run-down boarding house, Katherine Anne dressed in her best outfit, a bright blue suit with matching hat, and went to the *Chicago Tribune*. She recalled the experience: "The City Editor, I've forgotten his name, consented to see me and I asked for a job. He asked me if I'd ever had any experience and he asked me how could he hire me if I didn't have any experience and I asked him how could I get any experience if nobody hired me and he said that was a good thought and hired me at 15 dollars a week and sent me to the Essanay studios to get a story about the moving pictures and what they were doing."

When she arrived at the Essanay Film Manufacturing Company, newspaper located in a wooded area outside of Chicago, she joined a quickly moving line of people going into the studios. Ahead of her she saw a man pulling a few people out of the line. When Katherine Anne reached him, he said to her, "Hello, little boy blue," and took her out of the line to join others in a makeup room. Someone blew a whistle, and the whole group was led to a courtroom set where big movie cameras were whirring. After the scene was filmed, a boy came by and put a yellow ticket in her hand. When she turned it in at the designated window, she was handed five dollars and told to be back the next morning at eight o'clock. "I was hired," she declared, "and didn't even know it." She stayed, she said, because she quickly figured out that five dollars a day was more than the fifteen dollars a week the newspaper would pay her. She appeared in two films. One was the full-length film *The Song in the Dark*, and another was probably the feature film *From Out the Dregs*, which she remembered as *From Out the Wreck*.

The melodramatic plot of *The Song in the Dark* consists of two separate episodes in the lives of Angela and Richard, who have loved one another since childhood. In the first episode Angela purchases a canary, which she discovers has been purposely blinded by the vendor to make it a better singer (and thus more marketable). Horrified, she convinces her brother George, a lawyer, to prosecute the vendor for cruelty toward innocent creatures. In the second episode Angela has an accident that leaves her blind. During her initial dark days, she wonders why her little canary can sing so cheerfully when it is never to see the light of day. She answers that question herself and, feeling her way to a piano, plays with newly discovered emotion.

Katherine Anne had a part as one of the jurors in the courtroom scene of the second episode. She became flustered when movie idol Francis X. Bushman, playing the young attorney, stepped before the jury and droning cameras to emote with deep-voiced passion. For a few weeks, she was thrilled to be part of moviemaking and was optimistic that she, too, might have a screen career. But as the weeks wore on, it became increasingly clear to her that she was likely to be permanently relegated to crowds in street scenes. In addition, the long hours and the noisy confusion on the sets left her exhausted at the end of a working day. She spent her evenings alone in her small room in the dingy boarding house, munching stale crackers and dried-out cheese, reading novels, and trying to work on a short story. Discouraged, she returned to the *Tribune*, hoping to reclaim her earlier job. She was firmly rebuffed, however, and her only newspaper publication during this period was "Brother Spoiled a Romance," her "letter" to a *Tribune* columnist, the account of her adolescent suitor's banishment by her brother. Without money or another job, she had no choice but return to Texas. The only memorable "artistic experience" she had in Chicago, as she recalled, was to see the Abbey Players in John M. Synge's *Playboy of the Western World*. *The Song in the Dark*, however, had made an impression. Blindness was to become one of her personal fears and a significant motif in her fiction.

As Katherine Anne prepared to leave Chicago she learned that both Baby and Gay needed her. Baby, who had married a man named Herbert Townsend in 1913 and had soon become pregnant, had been widowed before the child was born in 1914. With barely enough money for the long train ride back to Texas, Katherine Anne arrived in Beaumont to help take care of the infant boy, whom Baby allowed Katherine Anne to name "Breckenridge." Several weeks later Katherine Anne took a train to Gibsland, Louisiana, to look after pregnant Gay and two-year-old Mary Alice since Gay's philandering husband had left her still again. Gay's baby boy was born with a broken arm in midwinter in an unheated house with only Katherine Anne and a country doctor in attendance. When Katherine Anne found an old woman to carry on, she set out to look for a job in order to support Gay and the children.

In the rural area of Louisiana little work was to be found, especially for women. She discovered, however, that local preachers were booking entertainers in the three-state region and that she could earn twenty-five dollars for each engagement on the backwoods lyceum circuit. She made a long red flannel dress with a white train and a medieval headdress and worked up a program of songs taken from Francis Child's *English and Scottish Popular Ballads*. She long remembered the country people who came in wagons and surreys to see her perform and especially the downtrodden women in her audience, rocking their babies while they sat and listened.

Katherine Anne opened her program with a selection of mournful ballads about untimely deaths, missed chances, and betraying lovers. In addition to her childhood favorites such as "Lord Randall" and "Bonny Barbara Allen" (the first song she remembered learning), she always sang "Mary Hamilton," a ballad about a handmaiden to Mary Queen of Scots who bears and drowns a child sired by the Queen's lover and is consequently convicted of infanticide and hanged from the gallows in Edinburgh. For an encore, she changed the tone and sang a sassy rendition of "Oh, Careless Love":

> Oh, when my apron strings was low
> He followed me through wind and snow,
> But now they rise up to my chin
> He goes right by and won't look in.

"They yelled with laughter, Honey," she recalled sixty years later, as she sang for a nephew the verse she had never forgotten.

When Thomas Holloway returned to Gay and his children, Katherine Anne left Gibsland for Dallas to find work and to follow through with divorcing John Koontz. She found a cheap room in a boarding house at 1520 Ross Avenue, but she could find no better work than addressing envelopes for two and a half dollars a day. She knew that she was legally entitled to some help from Koontz, however, and she wrote to him in Corpus Christi announcing her intention to sue him for divorce. He agreed not to contest it.

On her birthday she met with Mike T. Lively, a Dallas attorney, to begin the proceedings. John Koontz signed the account of his abuses against his wife, waived his right to appear in court, and promised to send her fifty dollars a month for living expenses. The divorce was granted 21 June 1915, one day past the ninth anniversary of the wedding. In her suit, Katherine Anne also asked to have her name changed to "Katherine Porter," a legalization of her nearly complete identification with her paternal grandmother. She soon slipped into the habit of giving her name as "Katherine *Anne* Porter."

John Koontz sent Katherine Anne the promised alimony for only a few months. Taking no further legal action against him, she continued to work at poorly paying jobs in Dallas as she struggled to support herself. Frustrated and weary, she began to consider remarriage as a way out of her dilemma. She continued to embrace the notion—contrary to her independent stance on women's rights—that women should have men to take care of them. And despite the brutality of her former husband, she retained a firm belief in the possibility of finding romantic love and a perfect man. We have an idea of the paradox marriage had become in her mind in 1915 when she later defined the attraction of marriage: "It is famous for its random assortment of surprises of every kind—leaf-covered booby traps, spiders lurking in cups, and pots of gold under rainbows, triplets, poltergeists in the stair closet, and flights of cupids lolling on the breakfast table." For nine years she had contended with the booby traps and the spiders, but she was still willing to take a chance on finding the pots of gold and the flights of cupids. On 7 September 1915, before a justice of the peace in Fort Worth, she married H. Otto Taskett, a handsome Englishman.

She had met Taskett in Houston through Koontz's employment with William D. Cleveland and Sons, a firm that did business with Taskett's family, who owned a tea importing business. She told a trusted friend in the last decade of her life that the afternoon of the wedding Taskett told her to get ready to take a train for New York, where they would embark for England. When she objected, he left without her. In another version of this marriage, she declared that she refused to have sex with Taskett. She said that for a long time after her first marriage she was "frigid as a cucumber and never did really get over it altogether." In all her versions of the marriage, it was never consummated. Soon, she said, Taskett told her to get a divorce.

She was discouraged as she rented a room in another boarding house on Ross Avenue and set out again to support herself. The best job she could find was that of a clerk in the tie department of Neiman Marcus. She was unusually tired in late October when she began coughing up blood-streaked sputum and carrying a fever. She feared the worst, and, indeed, before the end of November she was diagnosed with tuberculosis.

Because she had no money for private care, doctors sent her to the County Detention Home at 5704 Lindell Street. She had no choice but to accept the imposed exile that was reminiscent of her grandmother Jones's confinement in a lunatic asylum. The charity hospital, which she called "a fearful place," took in the poorest of the poor and isolated tuberculosis patients in inadequately staffed wards. Weighing only 102 pounds, she was housed with shriveled, dying women and fed a meager diet of thin soup and dry bread. Several months later, in the early spring of 1916, her brother, Paul, who was working in the oil fields and still unmarried, had her admitted to the J. B. McKnight Hospital in Carlsbad, Texas, near San Angelo.

Katherine Anne remembered the McKnight Hospital as a "rather pleasant place, with awfully nice men and women leisurely strolling on well-manicured lawns between widely spaced buildings." In truth, however, it was a place of rigid rules and few pleasures because medical science at the time had determined that tuberculosis should be treated with enforced quiet and freedom from any possible excitement. Rooms were painted pale gray and white with no color, and the library was without books. In the early weeks Katherine Anne was forbidden to read, write letters, or receive any visitors. Her physician ordered that her upper face be covered with a dark green cloth several hours a day to make sure her "restless eyes" did not cause a sudden rise in bodily temperature.

Soon, however, Katherine Anne was among those patients who violated the rules to alleviate the gloom. A natural entertainer, for the sake of her fellow sufferers she sang ditties and composed comic doggerel verse about the medical routines at the hospital. "This is a land of hell-fire things," she wrote. She also loved to talk and tell stories, even if she had to whisper lest the enforcers put a stop to her communication. A photograph Gay took of her at the hospital in the spring of 1916 shows her in bed with flowers, smiling wanly, her hair long. In another photograph she is at the center of an admiring group of sick women.

Katherine Anne's best friend at the sanitorium was Kitty Barry Crawford, who had been a reporter for the *San Antonio Express* before marrying Garfield Crawford, a reporter for the *Fort Worth Telegraph*. Together they had founded the *Fort Worth Critic*, and before Kitty developed tuberculosis, she had given birth to their daughter. When Katherine Anne and Kitty were not discussing books or ideas, they talked about their youths and their families. Katherine Anne gave lively accounts of the Porters and other people in Kyle and retold her grandmother's stories of antebellum Kentucky and the Civil War. Kitty remembered, however, that Katherine Anne was uncomfortable with direct questions about her past.

Katherine Anne was a patient at J. B. McKnight for seven months. When she was released in the summer of 1916, she was considerably improved, but she still needed hospitalization. She had been offered, however, a position at the Woodlawn Sanitorium, three miles north of Dallas. She was to be admitted to the hospital as a patient, but she would be paid a small salary for teaching tubercular children confined there. Paul had recently married and adopted Baby's son, Breckenridge, and Katherine Anne would be able to earn enough money to relieve him of the financial burden of her care.

She established a school at the hospital that she called "Academy Oaks," where she helped twelve children keep up with their grade levels in regular schools. A natural teacher who communicated easily with children, she delighted her pupils with brightly colored pictures and little folk dances she walked them through. The *Dallas Morning News* carried an account of her school, praising the skill and thoroughness with which she taught her young charges, and as a result townspeople contributed money to buy Christmas gifts for the children.

Katherine Anne seemed to have put behind her for the moment the bad memories of her marriages, and she liked to think that her father and brother had forgiven her for her scandalous divorces. In a Christmas letter to Harrison ("Darling Old Dear") she reported that she had gained needed weight and that the hospital fed her "outrageously," refusing to let her turn her hand "except to teach the kiddies." She referred to a lover only as "Himself" and told how he pampered her. Another "nice man" was giving her a bottle of her favorite perfume, *La Boheme*. Her high spirits were reflected in the affection she sent her family: "And then, Youngun, you know all this would be dust and ashes in my mouth if it wasn't for knowing that my Darling Old Dad and Sissers and my one goat of a bruvver are all getting along so fat and fine, making money and keeping well. If it wasn't for that I would want to die."

Katherine Anne knew now that more than anything else she wanted to be a writer. Even while she was at Carlsbad, she wrote feature stories that she sent off to Dallas and Fort Worth newspapers. She decided that after her release, following Kitty's example, she would look for salaried employment as a professional journalist. She had become acquainted with the managing editor of the *Dallas Morning News*, and she believed that he might help her get a position on the newspaper when she was released from the hospital the following spring. She reported this expectation to Harrison and assured him, "So you see, I am going to come out of this all right."

In the spring of 1917, however, she did not take a job with the newspaper. She had undergone another romantic disillusionment and decided to leave Dallas. At the end of 1916 or early in 1917, Katherine Anne married again. In 1939 when she was purchasing land in Louisiana and had to identify herself legally for the court records, she swore that she had been married to, and divorced from, a man named Carl von Pless.

Carl von Pless was probably visiting Texas relatives when he met Katherine Anne. The grandson of German immigrants who had arrived in New York in the 1850s from Mannheim, Germany, he was the fourth of nine children in a prosperous German American farming family not unlike the Hillendahls. He was one of the primary models for Adam, the handsome, blonde, apple-cheeked soldier in Katherine Anne's short novel *Pale Horse, Pale Rider*, and the mythical lost love of her youth. Although she translated the failure of her third marriage into the death of her ill-starred fictional lover, in reality Carl von Pless, who remarried in April 1917, lived until 1954.

For the rest of her life, Katherine Anne refused to tell anyone outside her immediate family about her first three marriages. She usually conflated them into one, describing "it" in various and contradictory ways. In 1937 she said it was a three-year marriage that ended when she ran off to be writer. On another occasion, she said she got married to "a rich man who shut me up." In the last decade of her life she identified her first husband as John Pleskett, a conflation of *John* Koontz, Otto Tas*kett*, and Carl von *Pless*. Still another account included her "instant realization" on her wedding night that she was "totally unprepared for marriage." "I don't like to talk about it, and I never mention it," she said, "but it was twenty-six years before I married again." It was twenty-six years between her first and her fourth weddings. In Cat Porter's style she had revised the first and wiped out the second and third.

In the summer of 1917 Katherine Anne left Dallas to stay with Gay and her two children in Dubach, Louisiana. She had been there little more than a month when she received an invitation from Kitty Crawford, who had returned to Fort Worth from Carlsbad still unwell. Kitty wanted Katherine Anne to stay with her and her family and take over her columns in the *Fort Worth Critic*. Katherine Anne quickly accepted, and the 15 September 1917 issue of the paper carried her photograph and a hyperbolic introduction: "The exuberant young person above is Miss Katherine Anne Porter, late from the staff of several prominent newspapers. She has come to Fort Worth to devote her young life to the CRITIC. Miss Porter likes things which many people consider frivolous and of no consequence—Society and the many small factors which go toward making life pleasant and interesting are among her hobbies. She also originates beautiful stories for children."

Katherine Anne's introduction appeared in "Society Gossip of the Week," a mélange of a dozen or so brief stories that carried the byline of "the Town Tattler." Through the fall of 1917, after Congress had approved President Woodrow Wilson's declaration of war on Germany and millions of American men had registered for the draft, she used the "Society" column to promote the War Services Board and make *Critic* readers aware of the desperate need for help at nearby Camp Bowie's overcrowded hospital. She also became publicity chair for the Red Cross Corps. She was taxing her energy, however, and soon after the first of the year she became so weak she feared another breakdown in her health that would send her back to a sanitorium. She took a train to Beaumont, Texas, where Baby was still living, and stayed with her through the winter.

In Fort Worth, Kitty improved even more slowly than had Katherine Anne. Concerned, Garfield Crawford began to look for a place in a different climate where his wife might have a better chance for faster recuperation. When they decided she should go to Denver, she wrote to Katherine Anne, hoping that she might go there, too. Paul, believing that Colorado might be good for his sister, stepped forward again and provided enough money for her to join her friend.

In late spring of 1918 Katherine Anne boarded a train for Colorado, finally leaving Texas more or less permanently.

CHAPTER SEVEN

Apocalypse in Denver

May 1918–October 1919

In the old symbolism, the Red Horse is War, the white horse is plague.
I can't remember the other at the moment.

In the middle of May, Katherine Anne and Kitty were admitted to the Oaks, a tuberculosis sanitorium at Adams Memorial Hospital in Denver. They had been at the hospital only a week when Kitty received a welcome visitor, her old college friend Jane Anderson, who had become a successful writer with an international reputation. Fresh from adventures on the European front and exuding an air of cosmopolitan self-confidence, Jane explained that she had rented a cabin on Cheyenne Mountain in nearby Colorado Springs, and she persuaded Kitty to leave the hospital to join her.

A week later Katherine Anne received an urgent letter from Jane, who, although still legally married to the musicologist Deems Taylor, had had a succession of lovers, apparently including Joseph Conrad. She had invited her current lover, a young Gilbert Seldes, the future editor and cultural critic, to join her and Kitty, and she wanted Katherine Anne to come to the cabin, too, and alleviate the awkwardness of a threesome. "It is, perhaps, unforgivable of me to ask you to assume responsibility when you have no strength for it," Jane wrote, "But, you see, K. Barry is so defenseless when she is ill like this . . . She must be protected." Jane also told Katherine Anne that she was demanding "the right to know" her, "to be with" her. Flattered, Katherine Anne found it impossible to resist Jane's plea. The money Paul had provided for her hospitalization was more than sufficient for her share of the cabin's expenses.

After drawing Katherine Anne to the cabin, however, Jane dismissed her as provincial and uninteresting. Kitty, unable to endure the unpleasantness and the disappointment, returned to the hospital, while Katherine Anne was left to deal with Jane, who took drugs for her "war-nerves" and made frequent, impulsive trips away from the mountain with Seldes in tow. After they left for the last time near the end of the summer, Katherine Anne never saw Jane again, although she became well acquainted with one of Jane's other lovers and followed her notoriety a quarter of a century later when Jane, labeled "Hitler's Lady Haw-Haw," was tried for treason against the United States.

When a laboratory test in August showed no evidence of an active tubercle bacillus, Katherine Anne decided to stay in the dry, cool climate of Colorado. By September she had moved into a boardinghouse at 1510 York Street and found a job at the *Rocky Mountain News* as a reporter for a weekly salary of fifteen dollars. Her beat was the city and county courts. For the next month she turned out articles about murder trials, grand jury proceedings, labor and land-boundary disputes, divorces, and other lawsuits. Her very first pieces contained florid description and sly wit that were quickly squelched by the uncompromising copy editor, Frank McClelland, whom, along with the city editor, "Wild Bill" Shanklin, she would remember with gratitude. Many members of the staff were young people like her struggling to become successful journalists or artists, and she became good friends with society editor Margaret Harvey and reporters Helen Marie Black, Lucille Clayton, and Eva Chappell. They described Katherine Anne as "the epitome of Southern feminity," a "pretty girl"—some thought her "glamorous," while others described her as "the baby doll type"—who entertained them with vaudeville songs and lively stories about her family's past.

Her coworkers also recalled a mysterious air about her and the same occasional detachment her fellow inmates at Carlsbad had observed. Since her new friends were unaware of her marriages and knew only the barest details of her illness, she was easily able to make them believe she was younger than she was, a deception that helped her "erase" some of the bad years. But, in fact, her ordeals between 1906 and 1918 had matured her well beyond her twenty-eight years. The world-weariness of Miranda in *Pale Horse, Pale Rider*, her short novel set in 1918 Denver, was her own state of mind at the time.

Her standard news stories about divorce and civil litigation were given only passing attention in September of 1918. Of overriding concern to the readers of the *Rocky Mountain News* were the front-page accounts of the Allied offensive in Europe and articles about Denver's nearby army training camps. Katherine Anne, despite a real sympathy for the Allies, considered herself a pacifist. She and her friends at the *News* were reading Siegfried Sassoon and the other war poets and listening to the dissenting voices from the left wing. "Some of us," she said, "were cheering our heads off for the Russians."

She had to be careful about expressing her views, however. The Sedition Act of 1918 had instituted the levying of heavy fines or even imprisonment against any person criticizing the army or navy or obstructing the sale of U.S. war bonds by volunteer salesmen who descended on neighborhoods and workplaces. Katherine Anne, who was threatened "direly" by government officials who told her she didn't have "the right attitude toward the war," was terrified of committing sedition. She decided to apply to the Red Cross for overseas duty, an action she could take that would be patriotic without violating her pacifism. She wrote to a friend, Marcellus Foster, president of the *Houston Chronicle*, and asked him to send a letter to the Red Cross in her behalf. Before she had to make a decision about leaving her job, however, devastating influenza reached Denver, and she was among those laid low by it.

The previous spring the so-called "Spanish flu" appeared in San Sebastián, Spain. At first it seemed an ordinary influenza with typical chills and fever. Although it was highly contagious, deaths from it were rare, and by summer it seemed to have spent itself. In September, however, it returned with suddenness and force and twenty-five times its springtime strength. It spread rapidly over the world, attacking especially young adults between the ages of twenty and forty. Death could occur as quickly as two days after the onset of symptoms: first a dull headache, burning eyes, and violent chills, and then body aches, high temperature, and delirium.

By 2 October, with the city's second flu death, Denver health officials became convinced that the deadly epidemic rolling across the country (nearly forty-five thousand cases reported in army camps alone) was a threat to Denver. The city virtually shut down. All public gathering places—churches, theaters, schools, Red Cross workrooms, dance halls—were closed. In spite of precautions the disease swept through the city, and the death toll moved toward its final tally of more than sixteen hundred. The epidemic was now called a "pandemic," and many associated it with the war. Some Christians saw it as a fulfilling of the prophecy of Revelations, with the pale rider Plague foretelling the end of the world.

Katherine Anne was struck in early October. When she awoke one morning with the dreaded flu symptoms, she called Bill Shanklin at the *News* and *Denver Post* reporter A. D. Stone ("Stony"), whom she and Kitty had known in Texas. Bill immediately sent a doctor, who wrote out a prescription and ordered an ambulance to take Katherine Anne to a hospital as soon as space was available. With the help of a fellow boarder ("a young boy . . . I did not know at all," Katherine Anne recalled), Stony and one of Katherine Anne's friends from the *News*, probably Eva Chapelle, looked after her while trying futilely to find an available hospital bed. To compound their frustration, the landlady, who was threatening to put Katherine Anne out "on the sidewalk," was yelling shrilly about "the plague" and her responsibility for her other boarders. In desperation, Stony, who knew that nursing care around the clock was needed for the increasingly ill Katherine Anne, called Kitty, who was still a patient at Adams Memorial.

Kitty appealed to Dr. John Holden, director of Adams Memorial and a member of the Denver Board of Health, who telephoned the landlady and threatened to have her arrested for cruel and inhumane treatment. By the following day he had found an available bed for Katherine Anne in a makeshift area at the county hospital. Kitty then sent a cable to Gay, telling her Katherine Anne was gravely ill.

Gay hurried to Denver, where she found her sister in a hospital hallway, apparently awaiting death and the undertaker. She telegraphed Harrison, Baby, and Paul that she feared the worst, and the *Rocky Mountain News* set Katherine Anne's obituary in type. Harrison, "inexpressibly sad," as he wrote to Gay, began to plan Katherine Anne's funeral and her burial at Indian Creek near Alice's grave. But he told Gay that he was "still hopeful" and that if Katherine Anne were conscious, "Tell her Papa sends his undying love to his stricken child."

Although Katherine Anne came perilously close to death, she stabilized and slowly began to rally, claiming that she had had "what the Christians call the 'beatific vision,' and the Greeks called the 'happy day,'" a feeling of unsurpassed joy in the moments before death. Prior to the joy, however, there had been the recognition of imminent annihilation, which she described in *Pale Horse, Pale Rider*: "There it is, there it is at last, it is very simple; and soft carefully shaped words like oblivion and eternity are curtains hung before nothing at all. I shall not know when it happens, I shall not feel or remember, why can't I consent now, I am lost, there is no hope for me. Look, she told herself, there it is, that is death and there is nothing to fear. But she could not consent, still shrinking stiffly against the granite wall that was her childhood dream of safety, breathing slowly for fear of squandering breath, saying desperately, Look, don't be afraid, it is nothing, it is only eternity."

When she regained consciousness in the hospital, the first object she saw was a framed print of *The Virgin and Child Surrounded by Flowers and Fruit*, by Peter Paul Reubens and Jan Breughel. She asked for it as a memento, which she kept for the rest of her life. Like her springtime birthday and her birthstones (emeralds and pearls), as well as, in some respects, her self-selected name, it became talismanic proof of her identity and her being.

Katherine Anne finally emerged from the hospital several weeks later, having been only vaguely aware of the celebrations in the street when the Armistice was signed November 11. She was crippled from phlebitis in her left leg, her right arm had been broken in a fall, and she was bald. Bill Shanklin, who paid her weekly salary while she was ill, welcomed her back at the *News* as soon as she was strong enough to work, even though she had to type with her left hand and wore turbans and hoods to hide her baldness. Thin and frail, she was grateful for Bill's suggestion that she take time off for a long holiday recuperation. She immediately left for Louisiana to stay with Gay and her two children.

Late in January 1919 Katherine Anne returned to Denver, moved into the Park View Hotel, and resumed her work on the *Rocky Mountain News*. She wore gay bandannas over her newly grown short hair, now white instead of its original black. A fellow reporter recalled her "enthusiasm and gayety" as almost "supernatural" and praised her for "asking a corner of no one." Not long after her return she was moved from her job as reporter on the court beat to drama critic and feature writer. One of the most important periods of her apprenticeship was underway.

From February to August of 1919 the *News* published more than eighty-one pieces signed by Katherine Anne. Articulating a set of artistic standards that she would apply to her fiction writing, she discussed the lamentable American predilection for things foreign (describing an unnamed woman who was surely Jane Anderson), the difficulties of being an honest critic (who had to disregard the sensibilities of advertisers), and the scourge of sentimentality in American theater. She also railed at playwrights who could not seem to write a play "in which the heroine does not lug her past around as if it were a ball and chain."

In the late spring Katherine Anne joined Denver's little theater and began appearing in some of their productions. Among the theater performers and their Denver patrons were many men who admired her and asked her out for dinner and dancing. The man who interested her most was Park French, the Denver Players' manager, whose wife had died in the influenza epidemic and left an infant son. An architect by profession, he fell in love with Katherine Anne and before long coaxed her into agreeing to marry him. Since the engagement was to be a secret until a respectable mourning period had passed, she wore his diamond ring on a chain around her neck.

Katherine Anne had a still unsatisfied taste for luxuries, especially beautiful clothes, and French seemed to promise a life full of such material comforts. By the summer of 1919, however, she was less emotionally dependent on anticipated patronage and better able to dress herself stylishly. She was writing a column she called "Let's Shop with Suzanne," and area merchants paid her well to mention them in it. One of her friends recalled Katherine Anne's purchase of a trousseau "from the skin out" the time her "ship came in" in the form of a fat check.

She spent the early summer of 1919 in relative contentment. A minor celebrity in Denver's artistic circles, she was admired for her beauty, her acting, and her increasingly sophisticated *News* articles. But in July she received devastating news. Jules von Hillendahl, whom Baby had married, telegraphed Katherine Anne that beloved little Mary Alice Holloway had died of spinal meningitis. Katherine Anne was grief-stricken and disbelieving, full of regret for not having spent money to bring the little girl to Denver for the summer (and thus, she believed, to have saved her). Mary Alice had seemed to Katherine Anne a part of herself, the "shy soul" of her own "young years." Mary Alice's premature death was another reminder of Mary Alice Jones Porter's untimely death that had precipitated years of hardship for the children she left behind. Katherine Anne tried to push the pain of losing Mary Alice into the private receptacle that held all other memories she found impossible to face.

She was in the process of learning that her truest art came from deep pain and that she needed ten or twelve years to establish artistic distance. In her work at the *Rocky Mountain News* she also had discovered that simple language was the best language. Although in later years she objected strenuously to being called "a newspaper woman," feeling that the label diminished the idealized "artist" she wanted to be, her journalistic apprenticeship in fact had been crucial to the development of her artistic techniques.

With her success at the *News* Katherine Anne had become increasingly confident about her talent as a writer and more realistic about the limitations of her talent as an actress or performer. In one of her condolence letters to Gay she told her sister that one of the sadnesses about Mary Alice's death was that her little niece had not lived to see Tante's success or reap the rewards of that success. "I never said anything, because I have been seemingly such a failure, but I knew it was only my long preparation for fine work." She referred enigmatically to "the next stage of my development" and promised Gay, "I shall write well some day—as well as anybody in America has ever written."

"The next stage" was to go to New York, the literary center of the country. "I had to go to New York," she said. "I needed literary people whom I respected. I needed conversations." She was encouraged by Eva Chapelle, who had already moved to Greenwich Village and promised to help her find work and lodgings. It was not so hard to leave Park French, as she had known all along it would not be. He made it easier by his impatience with her protracted grief over Mary Alice's death. There was simply no place for him in the next phase of her life, which would be devoted to art. New York and the still wilder world awaited.

CHAPTER EIGHT

Greenwich Village

October 1919–October 1920

That after-war life . . . had revolt, and disillusion, and hardship, and the privilege of sinking or swimming.

Katherine Anne arrived at Grand Central Station 19 October 1919, daunted by the dense traffic and jarring noise in the streets surrounding the terminal. Planning to stay with Eva Chapelle until she could afford a place of her own, she asked a policeman for directions: "Where is Greenwich Village? And how do I get there?" In the post-Armistice Village Katherine Anne would discover an amicable group of intellectuals, pacifists, social reformers, artists, and feminists and be relieved to learn that in the endless talk within coffeehouses, bars, and salons—in serious conversations about art, sex, and politics—there would be little talk about families and pasts.

Katherine Anne quickly found a job with the Arthur Kane Agency writing publicity releases for movies. Soon she was promoted to publicity manager and transferred to the Select Studio in East Orange, New Jersey. Although she was paid well (twice what she had earned at the *Rocky Mountain News*), the work carried a heavy responsibility and required a burdensome attention to details. Moreover, she had to spend three hours a day on subways, ferries, and streetcars to arrive at the site of her "ghastly job," as she described it to Gay, consisting mostly of "sublimated reporter's work." It was, on the other hand, respectable employment, the kind of hack work she was willing to do in order to support what she called her "artist work."

Within a few weeks Katherine Anne moved into a studio apartment at 17 Grove Street. She filled it with purple furniture and brightly colored pillows and painted her floor and fireplace black. "The wilder the place looks," she exclaimed, "the dearer it is to me!" There was that word "wild" again, which near the end of 1919 not only expressed her feeling of liberation and hope for adventure but also anticipation of free-flowing creativity.

Katherine Anne was quickly taken up by Eva Chappell's left-wing circle that included established writers Gertrude Emerson and Rose Wilder Lane; radical journalists Kenneth Durant, Mike Gold, and Helen Black; Bessie Beatty, the feminist editor of *McCalls*; and Floyd Dell, socialist novelist, poet, playwright, and editor of the *Nation*. In the last months of 1919 and the first few months of 1920 she met Edmund Wilson and Edna St. Vincent Millay, the young intellectual Malcolm Cowley, and political activists and writers Ernestine Evans and Genevieve Taggard. At a Village bar she became friends with Mexican pianist Ignacio Fernández Esperón (Tata Nacho), poet and critic José Tablada, and artist and theorist Adolfo Best Maugard.

Katherine Anne began to write her family long letters describing her exciting life in the Village. On Christmas Eve she had begun a round of two-day parties with a crowd of writers and editors who had exchanged gifts at Bessie Beatty's before attending midnight mass in a Syrian church where an Oriental dancer "tinkling and rattling with brass and crockery jewelry" had read their palms ("a weird thing," she said). She had eaten "funny stuff" and drunk Turkish coffee in a Syrian restaurant and had run races in the snow with a man she knew only as "Bill." A big bear of a man named "Harold," "a young editor" (apparently *Dial* editor Harold E. Stearns), had talked about poetry, philosophy, and classical music while steadily consuming bathtub gin. As he became more and more drunk, he became less intellectual and more amorous, finally crushing her in a big hug that broke one of her ribs. After a night of unrelieved misery, she was taken by friends to St. Vincent's Hospital.

Although Katherine Anne described a free-wheeling life in the Village, she actually had retained in her personal habits and outward demeanor strong elements of the conventional and the decorous. Even as a "liberated woman" who smoked cigarettes and who dyed her bobbed hair henna-black, she was not a member of that group of plainly garbed women who read Freud in public places, passed out leaflets advocating birth control, and made speeches to radical organizations. She would not relinquish fashionable clothes and luxuries in order to make a political point. Neither was she at that time the speech-making kind of woman. Her favorite forum was a small group of persons with whom she could discuss ideas and art and whom she might entertain with a vaudeville song or a well-told story.

Katherine Anne was feeling good about her prospects in New York, "the city of opportunity, surely," she wrote her family. She signed a contract with the Asia Publishing Company for a collection of rewritten foreign fairy tales that were to appear one each month in *Everyland*, a monthly magazine of world friendship for girls and boys, after which they would be published as a book. Katherine Anne intended to dedicate the book to the memory of Mary Alice Holloway.

By Christmas, she had completed three of the tales, one from "Eskimo-Land," one from India, and one from Kashmir. She told Gay that in writing the tales she pretended she was telling the stories to Mary Alice and wrote each one thinking, "Mary Alice would love it told this way." She would not have reminded herself that she had honed her skills in telling stories to children in the tuberculosis hospitals in Dallas only a few years earlier.

She made another commitment that she hoped would lead to additional artistic successes. Adolfo Best Maugard and his friend Adolph Bolm, a choreographer whom she had met in Denver, were collaborating on *Ballet Mexicana* for Anna Pavlova, and they asked Katherine Anne to write the libretto for it. Having seen relatively little classical ballet up to this time, she became nearly obsessed with her newest artistic passion. She told Gay, "I seem to care for nothing but ballets, with the music that goes with them." Although she expected to earn little money for the libretto, she explained to Gay, "The gift will be paid back to me by the world—to have your work used by an artist is the greatest of all compensations."

When Katherine Anne felt good about herself and her creative work, she was inclined to feel nostalgic about her father, brother, and sisters. In spite of her ambivalence toward Harrison, alternating between blame and sympathy, she wanted him to be proud of her and to forgive her unconventional decisions and disreputable actions. She assured him that, approaching the age of thirty, she still looked good and was not becoming obese. Although she could not imagine herself living among them again, she reached out to them for understanding and love. "I love all of you, really and truly," she wrote, and "I wish our lives might run along a bit closer together." A few months later she pled with them: "I wish you would say you love me now and then. You never do. Not right out, like that—I love you."

Although, like Harrison, Katherine Anne leaned toward socialism when she arrived in Greenwich Village in the fall of 1919, communism was replacing socialism as the Village's preferred political theory.

By the end of 1919, she was an ally of the Communist movement, strengthened in the Village by the government's anti-radical campaign against "Reds" that had begun in December with the deportation of the anarchist writer Emma Goldman, who had fought for freedom of speech and birth control and had spent time in prison for advocating violence among the working classes and obstructing the Sedition Act. By 1920 Greenwich Village was seemingly overrun by government agents who arrested young women found smoking in the streets and raided tearooms they claimed were harboring dangerous Reds.

Like communism, Freud's theories were a special rage among intellectuals in Greenwich Village in 1919 and 1920. His ideas seemed to support the Village credo of living for the moment, appreciating the nude body's natural beauty, and practicing sexual freedom. After her divorce from John Koontz, Katherine Anne had moved easily from one romantic liaison to another. Although two such romances had led to marriage, most affairs had been careless and passing. Now Freud lifted the guilt from casual sex and nudity. Such freedom from provincial-minded prudery was pleasing to Katherine Anne, who was proud of her legs and breasts, which men told her were exquisite.

Katherine Anne had settled into a routine of hard work, doing "a dozen things at once," as she wrote Gay, "but all productive, and leading to the same end." Among the "dozen things" was her agreement to rewrite for the magazine *Asia* another fairy tale, this one for adults rather than children. Katherine Anne chose "What Happened to Hadji," which she retitled "The Adventures of Hadji: Legend of a Turkish Coffee House." In her version of the tale Hadji, a spice merchant, proves to be gullible and foolish, but his unnamed wife is a wise woman who ultimately saves him from prison by a clever ruse. Versions of both Hadji and his wife would appear in many of Katherine Anne's original stories and novels.

This story, published in the April 1920 issue of *Asia*, led to another financially attractive offer by the publishers, who had received a manuscript of a stiffly narrated autobiography by a young American woman once married to a Chinese student. They offered to pay Katherine Anne well to re-write it, and they would cover her expenses for a trip to Michigan to interview the author. The work was only ghostwriting, but the money made it worthwhile.

In addition to the freelance writing Katherine Anne was doing for *Asia*, she was still fulfilling her time-consuming and energy-draining duties for the Arthur Kane Agency. Despite her desire to finish the book of retold fairy tales for *Everyland*, by the late spring of 1920 she was nine short of the twelve specified in the contract. Neither had she completed the ballet libretto. Although in January she had given no indication to her family that she considered her move to New York temporary, she began to say that it always had been only a stopover and that she expected to go along to Europe as some of her friends were doing. She started to save money again for travel, for another "wild dash," as much away from commitments as to new experience. She wrote to Harrison for her birth record in order to apply for a passport, and she mentioned specifically going to Spain.

Her Mexican friends in the Village, however, were telling her stories about the Mexican cultural revolution. "Nothing has happened in Spain for four hundred years," they told her. "It's dead. But in Mexico something exciting is going to happen—is already happening. We're in a period of great revolutionary change in every aspect of our lives. So why go to a country that's already dead or on its way to dying?" What they said made sense to her. Moreover, Mexico did not seem foreign. It rather was her "familiar country." In childhood she often had crossed the border near San Antonio, and she had spent much of her past life in Texas towns that had as many Mexicans in the population as Anglos. She even knew a little Spanish. The commissioned work for *Asia* would make the trip affordable, and the decision to go was made still easier when friends such as Ernestine Evans, an editor at the *Christian Science Monitor*, arranged freelance work to be sent from Mexico. She also was pleased to accept an offer from a group of American bankers who wanted her to establish and edit the *Magazine of Mexico*, aimed at an audience of American businessmen.

In the late summer Katherine Anne made a trip to Ann Arbor, Michigan, to spend six weeks interviewing Mae Tiam Franking, whose life story she would retell as *My Chinese Marriage*. It is likely that she and Mae Franking became friends. They were nearly the same age, twenty-nine and thirty, and, like Katherine Anne, Mae had flouted social conventions and suffered the consequences. Mae also understood another kind of suffering Katherine Anne had endured, for her husband, Tiam Franking, had died of tuberculosis the previous year. Katherine Anne would have very little to say, however, about the trip. There is no evidence that she wrote Mae after she left Ann Arbor or that she was aware of Mae's own death from tuberculosis six years later. She apparently wanted to put the Ann Arbor project out of her mind because she considered ghostwriting degrading and far removed from the artistic writing she really wanted to do. When she returned to Ann Arbor more than thirty years later she pretended it was her first visit, as if denying the 1920 visit would deny the work.

In the middle of September Katherine Anne returned to New York to complete preparations for her trip to Mexico. When she received her passport in the early fall with a year's visa instead of the six months she had requested, she thought it was a good portent. She collected letters of introduction to American consuls in Mexico and spent the remainder of September and part of October disposing of most of her meager household possessions and packing what she intended to take with her: her typewriter, a few clothes, and her notes for Mae Franking's memoir.

CHAPTER NINE

Revolutionary Mexico

October–December 1920

I went running off on that wild escapade to Mexico, where I attended,
you might say, and assisted at, in my own modest way, a revolution.

Late in October Katherine Anne began her long journey by rail to
Mexico City, having put together a sequence of trips that included
stopovers to visit members of her family in Texas. When she reached
Houston, she went along to Spring Branch to stay a few days with Baby
and Jules. Harrison and Gay joined them on the weekend, and they all
spent an evening at the Turnverein, where they drank so much beer
they were tipsy and boisterous when they staggered home along a
woodland path. Katherine Anne saved the memory as a fleeting image
of a happy family, and she would make the Turnverein a scene in her
story "Holiday." But privately her spirits were low. She could not avoid
revisiting the dark corners of suffering that Texas represented: her
grandmother's death, her adolescent vagabondage, her disappointing
marriages, her poverty after her divorce from John Koontz, the months
confined to tuberculosis wards, and the death of Mary Alice Holloway.

After crossing the border at El Paso, Katherine Anne boarded a
Mexican train that was packed with soldiers of every age and rank,
accompanied by their wives (or mistresses) and children. Hundreds
more men, women, and children were clinging to the roofs of the rail-
cars, where women were preparing tortillas, frijoles, and chilies on
charcoal braziers. She recalled the train's rumbling "across the barren
windswept desert" and pulling into Chihuahua at evening, when she
saw on the roof of her own coach what looked like "a militarized
mobile kitchen, with bayoneted rifles silhouetted against the darkening sky, gray-white smoke oozing from the hot braziers."

She became increasingly aware of the breadth and persistence of
Mexico's long civil war as the train wound through small pueblos such

as Delicias and through larger towns such as Irapuato. By the time the train pulled into the Estacion Central de Buenavista in Mexico City on 6 November, she had seen the ruins of buildings leveled by cannon fire and haciendas burned by angry peons. On crumbling walls that bore evidence of bullet fusillade she had seen painted slogans: "Viva la Revolucion!" "Muerta a la Tirania!" and "Pan, Tierra y Libertad!"

The revolution that Katherine Anne "ran smack into," as she later told an interviewer, was the Obregón Revolution, the then most recent in the series of violent insurrections that had begun in 1910 when Francisco Indalecio Madero, a wealthy statesman and reformer, in alliance with middle-class landowners, bandit-soldiers such as Pancho Villa, and peasant leaders such as Emiliano Zapata, overthrew the despotic Porfirio Díaz, who had ruled Mexico for more than thirty years with the support of the Roman Catholic Church and an oligarchy made up of urban millionaires and a favored group of *hacendados*. For the subsequent ten years of shifting alliances and changing power, in the most ruinous civil war in Latin American history, one regime after another was overthrown. Presidents and their ministers were routinely murdered as more than ten million people died in bloody battles and devastating raids. Following the successive coups and presidencies of Madero, Victoriano Huerta, and Venustiano Carranza, in September of 1920 Alvaro Obregón was elected president of Mexico. He would formally ascend to power in December.

Mexico City was a world apart from the Mexican border towns Katherine Anne had visited in her youth. Sitting on a high plain with smoking volcanoes visible in the distance, the city seemed suspended in the arid blue sky. Grand buildings, some of them four centuries old, faced one another across wide boulevards filled with both modern automobiles and burro-pulled carts. Beyond the center of the city, neighborhoods varied from patrician affluence to abject poverty. Everywhere were pure colors, simplicity, space, splashes of grandeur, and an air of primitive mystery. When Katherine Anne later thought of her first extended trip to Mexico as her "wild escapade," she was visualizing such a panorama, which seemed to promise a release of her creative force and, at the same time, adventure.

She registered at the Hotel Regis on the Avenida Juarez and set out to look for a less expensive room and to locate persons to whom she carried letters of introduction. The radical reformer Agnes Smedley had given her the names of Thorberg and Robert Haberman, and Katherine Anne easily found Thorberg, a tall, cosmopolitan Swede, at the offices of *El Heraldo de México*, where she edited the English-language section of the paper. Thorberg immediately offered her a job writing for the newspaper and directed her to a large, affordable apartment in a *pensión* at 20 Calle Eliseo, within walking distance from the Zócalo, the historic patterned garden in the center of the Plaza de la Constitución. Katherine Anne was pleased that the landlady served *comida Mexicana* in the boarders' dining room: rice cooked with peppers and spices, coarse spinach mixed with onions, croquettes of fried beans, a pudding made with an exotic fruit pulp, and strong, hot, aromatic coffee.

Katherine Anne soon found Jorge Enciso, director of the National Museum, and Manuel Gamio, a renowned anthropologist. Gamio invited her to go with him to meet William Niven, an elderly archaeologist who was digging prehistoric sites. She later used Niven as a model for the character Givens in her story "María Concepción," and she made him the subject of her essay "The Charmed Life," a somewhat fictionalized sketch in which she calls him only "the Old Man" who impressed her with his "authenticity" and his dedication to his work.

The 9 November edition of *El Heraldo de México* carried Thorberg's introduction of Katherine Anne to the English-speaking community. "Miss Katherine Anne Porter, a young writer of much charm and promise, has just arrived in Mexico from New York. She is here to study Mexico, and to gather material for a book and a great pageant-play on the stirring history of this romantic land." The same issue included an article by Babette Deutsche about the ballet being designed by Adolfo Best Maugard with "libretto by Miss Katherine Anne Porter."

Katherine Anne shared artistic, intellectual, and political interests with the Habermans, who had been active in the Socialist Party and pacifist organizations for several years. Within the first week after her arrival she accompanied Thorberg to a meeting of Consejo Feminista de México, the Mexican feminist council, presided over by Elena Torres, a feminist organizer, whose salary was paid by the chief of police. "How civilized these Mexican radicals are," Katherine Anne noted. "They see the just thing and do it with no fuss at all." She was so inspired that she became the seventy-ninth member of the council.

Through the Habermans, Katherine Anne met important revolutionaries: Luis Morones, a large swarthy man who was head of the powerful labor union Confederación Regional de Obrera México (CROM);

Samuel Yúdico, chief of the Central Garage, a repository for federal weapons; the flamboyant Antonio Diaz Soto y Gama, who "for seven years had ridden the hillsides with his gang clutching both the Bible and Marx's Das Kapital"; the handsome and charismatic Felipe Carrillo Puerto, a member of the House of Deputies and a strong defender of Bolshevik principles; Plutarco Elías Calles, the anticlerical minister of the interior; General José Villereal, recently named minister of agriculture; and José Vasconcelos, rector at the National University and Obregón's choice for minister of public instruction. All these men were "holders of the government reins," she pointed out to her family.

Under the influence of her radical new acquaintances, Katherine Anne agreed to teach primary ballet in Vasconcelos' Institute of Social Sciences and to collaborate with the Habermans on a revolutionary textbook of English to be used in the institute. She intended to be an active member of the Mexican Feminist Council, and she offered to help Morones with the labor movement. "I expect to be connected by a small thread to the affair," she told her family.

Most of her revolutionary activity in the final two months of 1920, however, consisted of writing articles for *El Heraldo* that were infused with the political values of the revolution. Her first piece, appearing 22 November, was a review of *Mexico in Revolution,* by Vicente Blasco Ibañez, whom she attacked for dismissing president-elect Obregón as a militaristic opportunist rather than the idealist Kathcrinc Anne wanted him to be. Her next signed piece, "The Fiesta of Guadalupe," appearing 13 December, was an account of the feast of the Virgin of Guadalupe, which entwined ancient pagan rites with Catholic rituals. Her article was resolutely sympathetic to the Indians and strongly critical of the Catholic Church.

None of her acquaintances was more firmly opposed to the church than Robert Haberman, who claimed to be an atheist, placing in the social revolution whatever faith he had. He had shocked some of the other radicals when he shouted, "Long live the Devil—Death to God." In December Katherine Anne coauthored with him an article they titled "Striking the Lyric Note in Mexico," which was published in the January issue of the socialist *New York Call.* Haberman supplied the reference point of the essay, the history of Mexican labor strikes against foreign-owned factories, but the descriptive style and ironic tone were hers. She closed the essay with an idyllic picture of happy strikers marching to the thrumming of mandolins playing tuneful native melodies: "La Pajarera," "Cielito Lindo," and "Estrellita."

In mid-December, at Thorberg's request, Katherine Anne took over the editorship of the English-language section of *El Heraldo*. The supplement was canceled Christmas Day, but in the two weeks Katherine Anne edited it she raised funds for an orphanage and a free school with clinic and child-care facilities for the poor, and she started a petition drive seeking commutation of the death sentences of two Mexican citizens convicted of murder in New York City. Having argued in behalf of the Mexicans on the grounds that capital punishment was "abominable," she liked to think that she contributed to New York governor Al Smith's ordering new trials.

Just as there was an artistic wing to the revolution that would become increasingly important, there also was an intellectual and theoretical faction influenced by such men as Gamio, who employed scientific objectivity to underscore his reasoning for social change. Katherine Anne became a student to his vast knowledge of Indian culture, hoping to learn as much about the country's history as she could in order to better understand the present events. Despite appearances to the contrary, she had not completely accepted the fervor and idealism of her revolutionary friends. Emerging out of the radicalism of Greenwich Village, she had planned to write articles and perhaps a book on the state of current affairs in Mexico. Shortly after her arrival, however, she recorded in her diary, "Why not story on impossibility of writing a story at short notice on Mexico? Maybe I shall write a few, but curiously enough—It may be five years before I can really write about Mexico . . . The thing is too complex and scattered and tremendous. I want first of all to discover for myself what this country is. Everybody I meet tells me a different story. Nothing is for me but to wait, and gather my own account."

She later wrote in a fragment of a memoir, "The non-politicals [the artists and scientists] thought I had come there to study their Indian Arts and Aztec and Maya design." On the other hand, "the politicals thought," she said, that "I was there to assist at their revolution and to write good things about it and them for the devilish American Press and magazines." If the "politicals" were unaware of her reservations about the revolution, they had not read carefully enough her political writings. It was the artist as well as the skeptic discernible in Katherine Anne's 17 December report in *El Heraldo* of the funeral of General Benjamin Hill, Obregón's nephew and minister of war, who had died of "food poisoning" at a banquet in his honor. Her impressionistic account shows that she shunned the opportunity to sentimentalize and politicize what was most likely an assassination:

> Under a brilliant morning sky, clean-swept by chill winds straight from the mountains; with busy people thronging the streets, the vendors of sweets and fruits and toys nagging gently at one's elbows; with three "ships" circling so close above the trees of the Alameda one could see the faces of the pilots; with the air live with the calls of bugles and the rattle of drums, the Minister of War, General Hill, passed yesterday through the streets of the city on his final march, attended by his army.
>
> Life, full and careless and busy and full of curiosity, clamored around the slow moving metallic coffin mounted on the gun carriage. Death, for the most, takes his sure victories silently and secretly. And all the cacophony of music and drum and clatter of horses' hoofs and shouts of military orders was merely a pall of sound thrown over the immobile calm of that brown box proceeding up the life-filled streets. It sounded, somehow, like a shout of defiance in the face of our sure and inevitable end. But it was only a short dying in the air. Death, being certain of Himself, can afford to be quiet.

Later she said that she had come to Mexico full of idealistic hopes for the revolution but after about six months had become disillusioned. Her private notes and evidence within some of the pieces she published prove that her illusions vanished much more quickly. Her early frame of mind is revealed in a three-part review she published in *El Heraldo* in December. Summarizing the plot of the novel *Caliban*, by W. L. George, she said of the character Janet, "She has that deadly female accuracy of vision that cannot be deceived. That would believe if it could, and knows it cannot do so. That loves illusion and cannot endure it." As critic-biographer Thomas Walsh suggested, she was writing about herself.

During her first two months in Mexico, Katherine Anne completed the first installment of "My Chinese Marriage" for *Asia*, and she drafted articles on Mexico for Ernestine Evans at the *Christian Science Monitor*. She also had put together most of the first issue of the *Magazine of Mexico* for the "rich American oil magnates," whom she was careful not to alienate and lose the money they would pay her as managing editor, but careful also to criticize to her revolutionary friends, who were vehemently opposed to American oil interests in Mexico (as in fact, philosophically, was she). Her contributions to her art, aside from the literary elements she was injecting into some of her newspaper articles, lay primarily in notes for stories.

Although some of those notes were linked to the revolution, most had come from her association with the "non-politicals" and from some of her "adventures," such as the Cordovonga bullfight (the subject would be the difference between "adventure" and "experience"), her walking tour with the artist Winold Reiss outside Mexico City in late November (the subject was death), and the time she smoked marijuana at Cuernavaca (the subject, the difference between illusion and reality). She thought she might do a three-part story set in Gamio's Teotituacán, to be woven together with folklore, legends, and superstitions. She was fascinated with the experiences of artist Gerardo Murillo, who had changed his name to "Dr. Atl" to signal his alliance with his Aztec roots, and filmmaker Robert Turnbull, whom she met at Niven's excavation at Azcapotzalco.

"Life here is a continual marvel to the eye and to the emotions," Katherine Anne wrote her family at the end of 1920, and she tried to give them a sense of her interesting life, just as she had done almost exactly a year earlier in Greenwich Village: "There are [a] thousand delicious things to tell you—of amazing contrasts and amusing situations. How one goes to a party at Chapultepec Castle one afternoon and drinks tea and champagne with the President—a former marauding General and in no time at all attends the Lottery ticket sellers ball in company with the greatest Labor leader in Mexico—and many others—and dances until two o'clock with one eyed men, and marvelous carbon colored Indians in scarlet blankets, who dance divinely—and one staggers home in the gray of the morning with vine leaves and confetti in one's hair. And goes that afternoon to a bull fight."

It was her marvelous adventures with which she entertained them, but she also felt good about her creative work. She told them that although her own life was "a welter, as far as experiences are concerned," she had achieved "plain sight of the things I have set my heart upon." Despite all the past years of failure, she assured them, her life now was "neither inutile or desolate" but renewed "itself daily from enormous sources." The proof of her optimism about her creative energy was found, as usual, in the love and affection she sent to her family. "I love all of you, I do love all of you terribly, and you are the very background and foundation of my life, which I cannot get away from, and which I would not get away from—if I lose any part of it, I would lose too much!"

What she had lost, and very quickly, was her idealistic expectations for the revolution. In Mexico in the last months of 1920 her creative energy nevertheless had been set free. Her belief that her artistic achievements were "nearly in plain sight" was justified.

CHAPTER TEN

Adventure and Betrayal in Mexico

January–August 1921

Adventure is something you seek for pleasure, . . . for the illusion of being more alive than ordinarily. . . ; but experience is what really happens to you in the long run; the truth that finally overtakes you.

Most of her stories are about the lurking dangers of betrayal.

Katherine Anne's essay "The Mexican Trinity," an analysis of the complicated forces at work in the social revolution, was not published until the summer of 1921, and "Where Presidents Have No Friends," her longer article on the history of the Obregón Revolution and United States involvement in it, did not appear in print until 1922, but she started to take notes for both pieces almost as soon as she arrived in Mexico City and began gathering her "own account," as she had warned herself she must do.

She explained "the Mexican trinity" as an unholy alliance of Oil, Land, and the Roman Catholic Church, and she saw a source of trouble in Article Twenty-seven of the Mexican Constitution that authorized the government to break up large landholdings, divide the acreage among the Indians, and charge taxes and royalties on oil. Every square mile of Mexico would be under government control, old haciendas would be destroyed, church lands would be confiscated, and American use of Mexican oil would become much more expensive.

Among the players in this intricate political dance were President Obregón, who was trying to carry out Article Twenty-seven; Albert B. Fall, who had landholdings in New Mexico and who, as Senator Fall in 1919, had called for American intervention in Mexico; and Pablo Gonzáles, a former general, who had fled to the United States to plot in exile the overthrow of the Obregón government. He was one person among a good many others who convinced Katherine Anne that Mexico's president could really trust no one.

Her knowledge of Mexican and U.S. relations was reinforced early in 1921 by Paul Hanna, who had been sent to Mexico City to do a set of articles on Mexico for the *Nation*. With President Harding's succeeding Wilson in office and designating Albert Fall secretary of the interior, many were concerned that there soon would be war between Mexico and the United States over oil. Porter and Hanna spent many hours together in January and February discussing Mexican politics and American interests. She described him as "an enlightened human being of a rare order," who "saw Mexico perfectly straight, without hysteria, prejudice or any other objectionable attitude."

Equally responsible for Katherine Anne's continuing connection to revolutionary politics was Joseph Jerome Retinger, a Polish diplomat, friend of Luis Morones, and one of Jane Anderson's lovers. By the time Hanna arrived, she was seeing Jerome Retinger regularly and planning several enterprises with him, including a biography of Morones he wanted to write with her help. Retinger, who held the title of Docteur ès Lettres from the Sorbonne and claimed to have a connection to Polish nobility, was cosmopolitan, knowledgeable, and sophisticated. Katherine Anne credited him with educating her in international politics.

In January Katherine Anne went with the Habermans to the convention of the Pan American Federation of Labor at the San Angel Inn. Present at the meeting were all of Mexico's important labor leaders as well as Samuel Gompers, the delegate from the United States. Before coming to Mexico Katherine Anne had disliked Gompers's antisocialism and his attacks on pacifists, but in light of her association with Morones, who had ties with Gompers's American Federation of Labor, she ignored her earlier aversion and even gave Gompers a good-bye kiss at the train station. Because she was one of only five women present among nearly seventy men, she was perceived by many persons as a committed revolutionary.

In January Katherine Anne also had been visiting the archaeologist William Niven in his shop near the Zócolo, and, according to her later, partly fictionalized account, "The Charmed Life," Niven showed her some letters that raised her hair and made her blood run cold because, she said, "there was enough political dynamite in those casually written letters to have blown sky-high any number of important diplomatic and financial negotiations then pending between several powerful governments." In her reconstructed account of the scene, Niven refused to get rid of the letters because they contained "a lot about ancient Mexican culture," and she went away troubled.

Such inconclusiveness, however, was not the outcome of her discovery of the letters. With or without Niven's permission, she copied out on his stationery the letter she thought was the most damaging, and she took notes on some of the others. All the troublesome letters were sent from San Antonio and written by only one man, retired army major Harry S. Bryan, who several years earlier had lived in Mexico City, where he had manufactured raincoats. In the transcribed letter, written in late December after the death of General Benjamin Hill, Bryan rejoiced that Hill was dead and predicted the assassination of Obregón. He pointed out to Niven, "You have been told just what is going to happen." Other letters revealed that Bryan had met Pablo González in Laredo, Texas, and accompanied him to Washington to introduce him to Albert Fall and other important persons in the American government. Bryan then had gone to Mexico with messages from González to another dissident militarist, Sidronio Méndez, who sent word back that forty-five hundred troops were ready for action if the American consul in Mexico City and Obregón failed to come to terms. "Sidronio Mendez, apparently serving Obregon, is the general of these plans, confidante of Gonzalez," Katherine Anne concluded, and one of the supreme betrayers in the plot.

She sent word to Morones through Retinger, and she gave Hanna a copy of the transcribed letter. Late in February Hanna returned to the United States to write his series of articles, and Retinger undertook a clandestine trip to Washington under the auspices of Morones. Any doubts they had about Bryan's inside information would have been dispelled had they access to U.S. government records, including those of the Military Intelligence Division (MID), which documented the counter-revolutionary movement. Encouraged by oil companies to create an incident in Tampico that would justify American military intervention, González had stockpiled arms and gathered a ragtag army in preparation for an invasion in May. Randolph Robertson, U.S. consul at Nuevo Laredo, reported that Bryan and González had visited him on their way to Washington, where they would promise elimination of Article Twenty-seven along with the overthrow of Obregón. Fall apparently had guaranteed recognition by the United States if all factions unfriendly to Obregón should unite and cross the border.

Hanna's effort to disclose the plot appeared in his fifth and last article (April 27) in the *Nation*'s series on Mexico. The whole story, as Hanna and Katherine Anne saw it, was one of betrayal. She wrote in her diary that Retinger, who had been jailed in Laredo by Robertson, had been willing to sacrifice Niven for the good of the revolution ("What's the life of one old man against a world of cause?"), and she concluded that by copying the letter in the first place she had betrayed Niven, who while not altogether apolitical was nevertheless more of a dedicated scientist than a counter-revolutionary. She had been in Mexico long enough to know that hastily convened tribunals or assassins sent in the dark of night could act very quickly to execute those convicted of, or simply suspected of, plotting against the government.

In mid-April she received a disturbing letter from Hanna, who had gone to Washington to try to extricate Retinger from his predicament. Hanna had been shocked to learn from the Polish legation that Retinger had no connection with the Polish minister, Prince Lubomirsky, as he had claimed, and from Gilbert Seldes, that Retinger's acquaintances accused him of blackmail, default on personal loans, and lying. Despite her unpleasant memories of Seldes and her awareness that Seldes and Retinger were rivals for Jane Anderson's affections, Katherine Anne believed that his story about Retinger was true, "especially in the pitiable trivialities." "As for me," she wrote Hanna on 19 April, "I have given the letters and telegrams to the people they were meant to reach. And as much as they could do has been done . . . The rather ridiculous episode seems to be finished."

But it played out a little longer. In late April at Morones's request she went to Laredo to visit Retinger and to try to convince Robertson to release him. Having raised one thousand dollars bail, she learned that whatever amount of money she had was useless because Robertson was determined to deport Retinger to Poland. She found Retinger lying on his back in a dirty little cell, chain-smoking, and reading crime novels. He "entertained" her for two hours, she said, with his stories of persecution. Before she left him, she got him a new supply of cigarettes and crime novels, writing paper, soap, and socks and left him with a vial of sleeping tablets. When he wrote her afterwards complaining about his uncomfortable plight, she observed in her diary, "My friend R., who is in prison in Laredo (. . . for various political complicities, a born mischief maker and genius of intrigue) writes that his cell is very hot, the place is full of cockroaches, and the food abominable. He would be pained to know how very little I care."

Katherine Anne felt betrayed by Retinger in personal ways that had nothing to do with politics. In the early weeks of 1921 she had imagined herself in love with him, later identifying herself as his mistress. That claim was probably not true, although it is likely that they played at romance. Her relationship with Retinger, who had a reputation as a man of weak sexual drive, was more intellectual than physical, and their meetings were more public than private, generally taking place in the Mexico City cafés crowded with artists and intellectuals. This kind of ethereal and romantic love affair was especially satisfying to her, and it was no wonder she felt betrayed when events and Hanna's revelations forced her to admit that Retinger was merely "a complex and fascinating liar."

Her numerous other romantic liaisons throughout the year affirm that their relationship was not at any time the serious or committed one her "mistress" label implied. In her December 1920 letter to her family she had called "the beautiful bandit" Felipe Carrillo Puerto her "beloved," and while it is unlikely that they were mutually devoted lovers, it was common knowledge that they had an affair. She told repeatedly about a day on which they had gone rowing in a shallow lagoon in Chapultepec Park when their boat sprang a leak. She jumped ashore while he sank into the water. They changed clothes and danced that night at their favorite Salón de Mexico, where he taught her to tango. No love letters between them have survived, but she kept all her life a photograph he gave her inscribed "To my dear friend, Catarina, from Felipe."

Katherine Anne's social and sexual activities of 1920 and 1921, in fact, had been carefully documented by the special assistant to the U.S. attorney general, a young J. Edgar Hoover, and officers of MID, who had been closely watching her since her arrival in Mexico. Hoover reported that she was said to have been on "intimate terms" with Colonel Harvey Miller, the MID representative in Mexico City. Upon being questioned by his superiors, Miller reported that Katherine Anne was "personally known" by him, that she was "an attractive, clever and cultured young woman of about 35" (she would have been horrified to see four years *added* to her age), and that "to all appearances she is a lady born and bred." He further stated it was "a fair inference" that she had "been on intimate terms with a few of the Mexican officials" such as "Morones."

Whatever the nature or extent of her passing fancies, the most serious and affecting of her love affairs in 1921 was her relationship with

Salomón de la Selva, a handsome, well-educated Nicaraguan poet who had taught in universities and colleges in the United States and had been an intimate friend of Edna St. Vincent Millay. Three years younger than Katherine Anne, he had been reared in a prosperous Nicaraguan family whose ancestors included Indian chiefs, Spanish conquistadors, and an English noblewoman. Passionate about both literature and politics, he joined the British army shortly after his *Tropical Town and Other Poems* was published in the United States. A model of the sophisticated and sensitive Latin lover, in the early months of 1921 he captivated her.

From February through April, while her affair with De la Selva was evolving, Katherine Anne engaged in revolutionary activity and also amusing experiences such as acting in a commercial film produced by photographer Roberto Turnbull. The movie was a comedy about a young man who works in a cellar and falls in love with the legs and feet of a señorita passing by the cellar's high window, searching thereafter for the woman he knows only by her pretty legs. Turnbull used Katherine Anne's legs for the elusive woman, paying her with the seventeen pairs of shoes in which she had been photographed all over Mexico City. She enjoyed telling that after the movie appeared in theaters, she met a Mexican artist who gazed at her legs and feet and murmured, "Oh, I know you, I know you." Her tidy conclusion to the adventure, usually told with merry satisfaction, was no doubt another enhancing of the facts to make a better story.

Turnbull also made several posed photographs of a costumed Katherine Anne between 1920 and 1922, and he probably also made the nude photograph of her she kept all her life and copied to give to selected friends. She recalled that Turnbull, praising her "physical attributes," especially her "famous legs," once had lifted his head from the black curtain draped over his camera and said with astonishment, "My God, you've got breasts, too."

In the midst of an active social life Katherine Anne still found time to write. Early in 1921 she finished the last three installments of "My Chinese Marriage" for *Asia* and wrapped up her work on the first and second issues of the *Magazine of Mexico*, work she considered mere reporting. But she was taking notes for "real" stories and novels based on the lives of her new acquaintances or stories they told to her. She wrote a sketch of Mary Louis Doherty, a young American social worker she had met in January and become friends with, calling her "a modern secular nun" with "the look of one who expects shortly to find a simple and honest solution" to the puzzles of the revolution. She also recorded a scene she witnessed between Mary and the revolutionist Samuel Yúdico, who had come to Mary's apartment to serenade her, ultimately the beginning point of "Flowering Judas." The longest draft to survive from the first half of 1921 is "Trinidad's Story," intended to be a section of a novel-in-progress she called her "Mexican book," which was to comprise four portraits of revolutionaries: Samuel Yúdico, Robert Haberman, Angel Gomez, and Felipe Carrillo Puerto. "Trinidad's story" was included in the portrait of Carrillo Puerto.

Trinidad, a convent girl kidnapped by the captain of a bandit army who rapes her and passes her around to his men, escapes with the help of a sympathetic young soldier and arrives alone in Mexico City, where she is found by "Felipe." As he listens to her story, he falls in love with her and avenges her by finding and killing the captain. Felipe expects Trinidad to be relieved and peaceful, but she weeps terribly and has a mass said for the captain, whom she hated. One of the messages in the story is that simple men cannot understand complex women, a theme also in "Hadji."

Katherine Anne was working on "Trinidad's story" in May when she reported crying a great deal. During her affair with De la Selva, according to Mary Doherty, Katherine Anne discovered she was pregnant and decided to have an abortion. It apparently took place in the early part of May in the town of Guanajuato, several hours by train from Mexico City. Among notes that she labeled "A Diary of Uncertainties" is the enigmatic remark, "That house in Guanajuato was a rook's nest of uncertainties. Why do foreigners behave either like fiends or fools in Mexico?"

The risks associated with abortion in 1921 in Mexico were high. Illegally performed in clandestine places under unhygienic circumstances without even the few safeguards a "modern" clinic might have provided at the time, the procedure could be fatal. Katherine Anne considered the possibility that she might die, and her thoughts, as she recorded them in her diary and notes in late April and early May, were on death and the failure, again, of love. One fragment reveals her attempt to begin shaping the experience into fiction, but her fear and depression were real: " 'I am going,' she thought, opening her handbag and rummaging without plan among the folded nightgowns and handkerchiefs and perfume bottles and stockings, until she found a clean handkerchief . . . Now between one minute and another everything is changing, . . . nothing can be again as it was . . . [L]et me begin again to live in the present . . . I am counting the days, and I weep for what I have [lost], and I am afraid of the time coming when I must explain my failures and my sins to one, who is both judge and executioner, who will not listen . . . What cure is there for the wounds I have given and received, what pardon? Let me face it now." She added, "Just me along to the appointed place, with hard unfriendly hands." Another note reads only, "I have set my sails for death."

She blamed De la Selva for her suffering, and through the years her remarks about him were especially vitriolic. Most of her observations illustrate his resistance to her intelligence and knowledge. "A woman is good for only one thing," she has De la Selva saying, and one note is bitterly humorous: "If Salomon met the Virgin Mary," she declared, "he would introduce himself as the Holy Ghost."

On 15 May, her birthday and, ironically, the designated date for Golzález's invasion, Katherine Anne was warned to stay inside. Obregón declared that meddling foreigners who disregarded the Mexican Constitution would be expelled from the country, and someone from the consulate told Katherine Anne her name was on the deportation list. Frightened and anxious, she packed her bags and waited. In the meantime her money ran out and she was hungry, the realization of an old fear that had survived from childhood. She secretly entered the Habermans' nearby apartment and stole a dozen tortillas and a bowl of mole. "Starvation is very hard on the flesh," she observed, "and the idea of death is very hard on the nerves. I should like to deny that I am terrified but I am."

The deportation crisis and the hunger of May passed, but Katherine Anne continued to be despondent. With her abortion she had betrayed a standard of maternity represented by her mother and grandmother, and De la Selva had proved to be another lying lover who had betrayed her trust. Moreover, she continued to worry that she had betrayed Niven, a feeling of guilt that sharpened with a sequence of events that took place in June. Five men, including Sidronio Mendéz and his son, were executed for plotting against the Obregón government. In her diary Katherine Anne wrote, "Five conspirators, all they could lay hold of, executed within three days." She added, "How on earth can this concern me? Yet it does." She feared that by copying Bryan's letter to Niven and sending it to Morones she had brought about the deaths of several people. She must have worried that Niven could be next.

It is doubtful that Katherine Anne's revelation of Niven's letters was responsible in any way for the political executions. Betrayal and disloyalty had long been so much a part of politics in Mexico, as Katherine Anne had pointed out in "Where Presidents Have No Friends," that Obregón, who was well aware of the counter-revolutionary movement to overthrow him, had been alert to every nuance. That logic, however, escaped her complex emotions at the end of June.

Fighting her depression, Katherine Anne tried to resume her earlier activities. In June she signed a contract to teach primary ballet in several of Vasconcelos's girls' schools for four pesos a day, but she repeatedly failed to show up for class and after several weeks Vasconcelos fired her. Neither was she doing any political writing. She was trying hard to have pleasant experiences and forget the unsettling and fearsome events of May. In the early summer she climbed the volcano Popocatepetl with the artist Xavier Guerrero and afterward visited the village of Amecameca. "I shall come back some day to live in Amecameca," she promised herself in her diary. "There shall be a tiled fountain in the garden, with ducks and ferns and figs and pomegranates growing along the walks." She also said that "a silence" must hang over this home in Amecameca, "so enormous that any spoken word shall sound quite unnecessary." Since childhood and especially since her troubled marriage to John Koontz, her yearning to escape from pain and misery was inevitably expressed as a need to escape to silence. It was also a wish to escape to the solitude necessary for her creative work. Her desire to decamp again grew stronger and stronger. Through the rest of the summer she planned her bolt, which finally was possible when Kitty and Garfield Crawford sent her train fare to Fort Worth. Near the end of August Mary Doherty and Retinger, who had returned to Mexico City after finally being released in Laredo, saw her off at the Estacion Central de Buenavista, where she had arrived nearly ten months earlier.

In later years Katherine Anne was inclined to conflate her trips to Mexico and describe them as if there were no difference among them. But it was the first trip that left the deepest mark on her psyche. "Mexico," she said, "is a place that will grapple your soul to it if you don't look out and get out in time—I think I did, but I wasn't the same girl at all when I left that I was when I went in. Oh not at all!"

CHAPTER ELEVEN

Mexican Bounty:
The End of an Apprenticeship

August 1921–September 1923

*Here in Mexico there is no conscience crying through the literature of
the country. A small group of intellectuals still writes about romance
and the stars, and roses and the shadowy eyes of ladies, touching no
sorrow of the human heart other than the pain of unrequited love.*

Katherine Anne arrived in Fort Worth the first week in September of
1921 and moved in with the Crawfords in their white-frame house in
the 1600 block of College Avenue. To earn fifty dollars a month she
agreed to write articles for Garfield Crawford's *National Oil Journal*,
supplementing that salary with earnings from a shopping column for
the *Fort Worth Record*. Kitty also persuaded her to be publicity chairman for a committee promoting the establishment of a tuberculosis
sanitorium in Fort Worth.

A few weeks after her arrival, Katherine Anne went with Kitty to
see the play *Suppressed Desires*, performed by the Vagabond Players
of the newly formed Fort Worth Little Theatre. Founded by a brother
and sister, Hunter and Rosalind Gardner, the company produced its
plays in the Gardners' renovated barn behind their house on Lipscomb
Street. When Katherine Anne went backstage after the performance
to congratulate the actors, she so much impressed the Gardners with
her beauty and charm that they asked her to join their troupe. She
was praised in the local paper for her performance in November
in *Poor Old Jim*, a comedy, and in December as "Columbine" in *The
Wonder Hat*.

Katherine Anne's popularity in the amateur theater circle drew the
admiration of many men (including Hunter Gardner), who competed
for the pleasure of accompanying her home after her performances.

One of her suitors was an aviator who took her on an exhilarating ride in a rickety, open-cockpit airplane. Jane Crawford Jenkins recalled her child-eyed impression of Katherine Anne in this period: "She always wore beautiful clothes and shoes with very high heels, and . . . she always seemed to be dashing in to change and rushing out again."

To escape the busy Crawford household and make time for her fiction writing, Katherine Anne rented an attic bedroom from Mrs. Arthur Goetz, who lived nearby on Pennsylvania Avenue. For the several months she lived in Fort Worth she worked on "The Dove of Chapacalco," the Angel Gomez segment of "The Book of Mexico." The "dove" is twenty-year-old Vicenta, mistress of the archbishop since she was fourteen. For six years she developed her mind while the archbishop extorted money from the Indians. When she meets the revolutionary Gomez, he convinces her to join him in plotting to free the enslaved Indians, but she rejects his declaration of love and proposal of marriage. She wants neither marriage nor children, she tells Gomez, only freedom.

Molding Vicenta with the materials of her own experiences as a "convent girl" who had shrugged off the nuns' and priests' teaching and as a sex slave in the "prison" of her first marriage, where she educated herself by voracious reading, Katherine Anne made Vicenta a victim of all men who thought women "good for only one thing," words she had attributed in 1921 to De la Selva. Like Vicenta, she had chosen domestic liberation, but she had chosen it for art, not revolution. The timely political messages in "The Dove of Chapacalco," however, subsume the larger themes of love, marriage, and motherhood. In the fall of 1921 Katherine Anne was unable to come to terms with the conflicting aims of politics and art, and progress on the work fizzled.

She blamed her failure to finish "The Dove of Chapacalco" on her out-of-control social life that made it hard to muster the concentration demanded by creative work. "I'll never get any writing done here, and there is no use trying," she wrote Baby that fall. She had a strong desire to return to New York and find a job that would allow time for her fiction writing. Kitty and Garfield Crawford, sensitive to her frustration, gave her train fare and money to live on for a few weeks.

She arrived in Greenwich Village in early January and moved into Madame Katrina Blanchard's old boardinghouse at 61 Washington Square South. With many friends and acquaintances nearby, however, she quickly slipped back into her sociable habits. In the first three months of 1922 she finished nothing to submit for publication. Then at the end of March, when her prospects for income seemed especially bleak, she received an unexpected telegram from Retinger:

GOVERNMENT APPOINTS YOU AMERICAN ORGANIZER OF MEXI-CAN ART EXHIBITION IN WASHINGTON TO BEGIN MAY STOP TOTAL SALARY THREE THOUSAND PESOS AND EXPENSES STOP DURATION TWO MONTHS APPROXIMATELY STOP IMMEDIATE PRESENCE MEXICO INDISPENSABLE STOP IF YOU ACCEPT WIRE IMMEDIATELY AND NECESSARY MONEY FOR TRIP WILL BE CABLED INSTANTLY

Since Katherine Anne left Mexico the summer before, the so-called Mexican Renaissance had been ignited by Diego Rivera, and the ancillary popular arts movement had been flowering under Obregón's patronage. During the centenary celebrations in September the public had responded so enthusiastically to the "Exposition of Popular Art of the Centenary" that Obregón had established a department dedicated to the native arts at the national museum. He had been convinced by Retinger that a similar exposition exported for display to the United States would enhance his government's chances for U.S. recognition—and that Katherine Anne Porter was the best person to select the items for the exhibit and write a pamphlet to accompany it. She wired her acceptance and persuaded Kitty to make a longed-for trip to New York and stay in her apartment while she was away, entrusting to her care her pet, a ring-tailed monkey named J. Alfred Prufrock.

Katherine Anne arrived in Mexico City 5 April and immediately set to work. In a letter to George Sill Leonard, art editor at the *Century*, she described her daily routine: "I read in an immense hall littered with beauty and great windows opening on the patio garden. Diego Rivera comes there at times . . . Indians from the country help to assort pottery and painted boxes and serapes more beautiful than ever I imagined serapes could be, and great silver embroidered saddles and spurs that glitter like jewels." She singled out Diego Rivera, Adolpho Best Maugard, and Xavier Guerrero as the artists who helped her form her "point of view" and place her "sympathies," an acknowledgement of their contribution to her evolving aesthetic.

None of the artists was quite as important to her as Rivera, who recently had begun *Creation*, his first mural, at the Escuela

Preparatoria, a beautiful, colonial-era building in the center of the city. After Katherine Anne watched him work, she said, "I was struck with the certainty that I was in the presence of an immortal thing. And as I stood before two enormous clasped hands, on paper, pinned in place over the charcoal outline on the wall, I was touched with the same feeling I had when I was 12 years old and saw for the first time the 'Praying Hands' of Dürer. I felt like weeping with pity for the struggling, suffering, human life."

Many women came to admire the "master," and some helped with the drudge work associated with his murals, such as mixing his paint. "She is mixing my paints," in fact, was Diego's euphemism for having a sexual affair with one of his female admirers. It is not clear whether Katherine Anne had any sexual involvement with him in the spring of 1922. The artist David Siqueiros, whom she also met that spring at Diego's studio, told Hank Lopez that "little Cati," as he called her, was "very beautiful and witty and spoke Spanish much better than most foreigners." Everyone knew, he said, that she "had had affairs with that Nicaraguan poet, with Felipe Carrillo, and even Diego Rivera. She was one of those pretty señoritas, mostly gringas, who supposedly mixed paints for him." Katherine Anne confirmed to Lopez that she, indeed, had mixed Diego's paints "because that was the chic thing to do in those days," but she didn't suggest that the phrase implied anything beyond its literal meaning.

At Mexico City cafés Katherine Anne often joined Diego and his model Lupe Marín, who soon would be his wife, Best Maugard, Covarrubias, Retinger, and De la Selva. Despite the pain she had endured from two of her former lovers, one of whom had fathered the child she aborted and both of whom by 1922 she privately regarded with contempt, she continued to socialize with them. She allowed herself that kind of hypocrisy as long as she bared the truth to herself in private notes, which she always set down for possible artistic transformation later. One evening she was with De la Selva, Diego, and Lupe at Los Monotes, a popular café that served cheap and filling food, when the four of them spontaneously decided to go on an excursion to the Niño Perdido, an old convent in an old part of town, where the cobbled streets were littered with broken glass. Katherine Anne and De la Selva danced to a little orchestra playing in a nearby pulqueria, after which he made a poem, "something about the nuns in the convent who looked out on dancers of other days . . . . . and tonight their ghosts with ghostly partners, come and dance again—the nuns are dancing with small bare feet, over broken glass in a cobbled street . . . . . for me, he said."

At the end of May, Katherine Anne's pamphlet was finished, and the exhibit was ready for transport to the United States. Her final job was to arrange exhibition space in New York and Washington. Confident that the remaining tasks for the Mexican Popular Arts project would be carried out smoothly, she returned to New York in July and moved back into Madame Blanchard's rooming house, ready for some solitude and time for her own writing. Kitty had already gone back to Texas, frustrated with caring for J. Alfred Prufrock and dealing with Katherine Anne's wild Village friends, who, unaware that she was away, occasionally came by to pelt her windows with pebbles to summon her out for fun. The monkey, whom Kitty left in the care of another boarder, died.

In August those who traveled with the exhibit to Los Angeles to prepare for its opening at the Los Angeles Museum in October encountered a delaying tangle of bureaucratic obstacles and had to cancel the reservation at the museum. The exhibit finally took place in November in two stages at smaller galleries. In trying to secure gallery space in New York and Washington, Katherine Anne was even less successful. She had met a wall of disinterest in, and occasional hostility toward, Mexican art, owing largely to the strained political relationship, between Mexico and the United States, that the project, ironically, was intended to help overcome. She was "bitter as gall that politicians could have been allowed to do so much destruction, so much damage; that internal politics, and oil and finance could ruin art."

Despite Katherine Anne's disappointment with the exhibit, her two-month stay in Mexico had inspired her to resume working on her Mexican fiction. "One evening," she recalled, "I was talking to a man who said, 'Oh, I wish you would stop telling your stories and letting them go into the air. Why don't you put them down?' I told him I *was* putting them down. He said, 'I want you to finish *this* story and let me see it.'" She agreed and wrote for seventeen days and nights: "Oh, I wanted to quit writing it," she remembered, "but I finished it, finally, and called it 'María Concepcion.' The next day, I called my editor friend, the one who'd goaded me into doing it, and said, 'I've got the story' . . . Three days later, his magazine sent me a check for six hundred dollars. It was the old *Century* magazine, and the editor, of course, the literary editor, was Carl Van Doren."

The "editor friend" was George Sill Leonard, and the source of the fascinating story was a woman she had seen at Niven's dig at Azcapotzalco whose gracefulness, beauty, and inherent gentleness seemed to reflect a natural royalty. In the story the woman Katherine Anne called "María Concepción" had been married to the archaeologist's foreman, Juan, the previous year in a formal church ceremony. As soon as María Concepción was pregnant, Juan had taken up with a fifteen-year-old village girl, María Rosa, who accompanied him when he ran off to join the army. In two years they came back, María Rosa pregnant with Juan's child. Two weeks after the child was born, María Concepción, whose child had been stillborn when Juan abandoned her, went to María Rosa's house, stabbed her to death, and claimed the child for her own. The villagers protected María Concepción according to an ancient, primitive law of justice, and even Juan bitterly forsakes his profligate ways to reassume his position as head of his household.

In his diary Niven mentioned no such story about his foreman and the foreman's wife, but among photographs in his collection is one of Katherine Anne standing between them. She must have imagined traits of strength and weakness in each of them, weaving from her remembered images a many-layered story with political and feminist messages and universal themes. The character María Concepción, another strong woman who is ultimately victorious over a weak, swaggering, betraying man, was a version of Hadji's wife, Cat Porter, and the strong woman Katherine Anne wanted to be.

In "María Concepción" Katherine Anne subordinated the political theme—the absurdity of revolutionists' trying to civilize the primitive Indian—to the universal theme of primitive justice. And she integrated her personal experiences with lost children and betraying men so finely in the story that they were invisible to her family and friends. "María Concepción," which appeared in the December 1922 issue of the *Century*, was Katherine Anne's first piece of original fiction to be published. Her apprenticeship to her art had officially ended.

"María Concepción" was selected for inclusion in *The Best Short Stories of 1922*, and Katherine Anne entered 1923 with the pleasant feeling that she had been, at last, launched. Inspired to keep on writing, she was working on several different stories about Diego Rivera and a new novel called "Thieves Market" that was supplanting "The Book of Mexico." In two fragments Katherine Anne calls a character based on herself "Laura" and in other scenes calls her "Miranda," using the name "Laura" for a character based on Mary Doherty. It is the earliest evidence of her choice of names for the most outwardly autobiographical of her fictional characters.

Having moved out of Madame Blanchard's rooming house and into an apartment with the actress Liza Anderson at 15 Gay Street in the Village, Katherine Anne was part of a lively social circle. She also was not without a "beau," having embarked in the winter of 1922–23 on a love affair with Charles Sumner Williams, a socially prominent, Harvard-educated bachelor and a successful businessman rather than an artist or a revolutionary. He was her own age and wild about her. Within a few months they were engaged to be married.

Although she wasn't eager to remarry anytime soon, she was spending more time with Williams and with friends at weekend house parties or in Greenwich Village cafés than producing writing that would bring in money. Just when there seemed to be nothing immediate to which she could resort except marriage to Sumner Williams, Frank Tannenbaum, a left-wing writer with connections in Mexico, asked whether she would be interested in returning to Mexico to edit a Mexican number for the magazine *Survey Graphic*. She would, indeed. Once again, she gathered up her typewriter and manuscripts, packed her trunks, and left Greenwich Village for her third trip to Mexico in as many years.

She arrived in Mexico City in early June. Retinger was in Europe, De la Selva had returned to Nicaragua, and Thorberg Haberman was in the United States preparing to divorce Robert, but many of her artist friends were still around, hanging out especially at the café Los Monotes. Although the name "Los Monotes" translates as "big monkeys" or "big puppets," in Mexico in 1923 it referred specifically to the "big caricatures" on the walls painted by the owner's brother, José Clemente Orozco. Katherine Anne called Orozco the "wild man of Mexican art" and praised his "really gorgeous record of Mexican lowlife."

Between 1920 and 1922 Katherine Anne had been aware of the well-seasoned art of caricature in Mexico, but in 1923 she regarded it with an intense new interest, studying not only Orozco's paintings and drawings but also those of Miguel Covarrubias, who had drawn a caricature of her in honor of her 1922 birthday, after which she declared that his "impish understanding" of the personalities of his subjects belonged to "metaphysics." In "María Concepción" with simple language and pure visual imagery she had practiced an economy related to caricature, and many of her other published pieces had been tinged with the irony that underlies caricature and its nearest relative, parody. She began to consciously employ both modes in her writing.

In the summer of 1923 Katherine Anne went with the American writer Carleton Beals to see the frescoes in the National Preparatory School. In the summer of 1923 most of such frescoes were remnants of older murals that had decorated the school for nearly two centuries, but new murals were in progress, and Rivera's *Creation*, which she had seen in progress the year before, had recently been completed. The colors in the mural were magnificent, but the general public thought the figures in *Creation* were ugly and referred to them as "Diego's monkeys." There were calls in the conservative press to "whitewash" them.

Katherine Anne picked up her earlier drafts of stories about Diego, quickly finished one she called "The Martyr," and sent it off to the *Century*. She was pleased that Van Doren accepted it for the July issue. Like all her planned stories about Rivera, this one presents an aesthetic theory alongside an observation about contemporary Mexican politics. In "The Martyr" Rubén, "the most illustrious painter in Mexico," is in love with his model, Isabel, but she runs off with a rival artist who has come into money. The desolate Rubén begins his public display of grief, expressed in his escalating obsession with food and his unending talk about Isabel, whom he has exalted beyond all reason. Although his friends know that Isabel is far from the idealized woman Rubén claims her to be (they call her a "she-devil"), they participate in the charade. When Rubén suddenly dies at the café "Little Monkeys"—a witty allusion to Los Monotes and also "Diego's monkeys"—having eaten one tamale too many, they declare that he died from unrequited love.

Just as "María Concepción" illustrated the difficulty of "civilizing" the Indian, "The Martyr" illustrated two other obstacles to the success of the cultural revolution: the absence of committed artists who could touch the hearts of the Mexican people and the Mexican preference for the romantic and sentimental over reality. She feared that Rivera's self-aggrandizement and the artistic community's adoration of him would interfere with the forward direction of the artistic renaissance. In the story, Rubén idolizes Isabel, just as admirers had begun to idolize Rivera and as she herself had done only the year before.

In 1965, when Katherine Anne's collected stories were published, she said that "The Martyr" was her "little tirade against Diego Rivera and his wild woman Lupe Marin." She might also have said it was her literary caricature of them, for the story contains the laceration, wit, and economy of Orozco's paintings and Covarrubias's drawings. Her lampoon of Rivera and Lupe was satisfying, and she directed her newly exercised satiric technique to other subjects she considered more deserving of her malice. The person who topped her list in 1923 was Salomón de la Selva.

Her most detailed portrait of him appears in the unfinished story "The Lovely Legend" (another of the "stories about Diego") as the Nicaraguan Amado (the lover), a degenerate alcoholic, an immoral and sentimental romantic, and an inferior artist, who tells Rubén "endless tales of erotic personal experience in the sub-cellar stratum of romance" and recalls his lovers (many of them whores) as embodiments of colors and smells (one is "rank as a wildcat"). He composes a poem for a young convent girl who dances for him "on broken glass with her white feet bleeding," a variation on lines from the poem De la Selva composed for Katherine Anne the year before. She also has Amado complaining, "Ah my memories! Some day they will cease to rise coolly in me a perpetual fountain. I shall be as dry as the basin of the Lost Child," a simile that conjures the image of a womb prematurely emptied of a baby. She appended a note to the title: "I dedicate this story to the characters in it, and I freely acknowledge my debt to one of them for some of the more intimate details here related."

She wasn't through with De la Selva. Not only would he appear slightly disguised in several other stories, she also composed parodies of his poems and original satiric poems inspired by him. The most deeply serious, and venomous, were the several she called "witch poems." One of them, "This Transfusion," embodies emotionally laden images of blood and pain that may be associated with birth or abortion:

> *You need not be afraid, I shall not wound*
> *Your pride with my edged scorn,*
> *Nor flagellate with my despairs*
> *The surface of your heart:*
> *For this my hate*
> *Is not a lash, nor thorn*
> *But a measureless, distilled*

Vial of torment endlessly refilled.
And it shall fix upon your senses so,
Shall of your slakeless fibres be such part
As your wild blood shall mix within your veins
My hard, enduring pains,
Incorporate with your immediate being,
And if your pulse should quicken, it shall be
To the sole desire of death, the ease of hell,
From this transfusion that was the life of me.

Since 1919, when she was writing feature stories and reviews for the *Rocky Mountain News*, Katherine Anne had given serious thought to art and the artist's role. In Mexico between 1920 and 1923 she worked out the relationship between politics and art. Her *Survey Graphic* article on *corridos*, indigenous ballads celebrating the legends and folklore of Mexico, defines her final position on art versus politics. She pointed out that, although since 1910 revolution after revolution had risen, there was not a single revolutionary corrido. "Instead," she said, "the stories in the ballads are always concerned with immediate fundamental things, death, love, the appalling malignities of Fate." She called these subjects the "eternal verities," and they were at that point a fixed standard in her aesthetic.

In July Pancho Villa, the hero of a hundred corridos, was gunned down by one of his enemies many thought backed by Plutarco Elías Calles. Katherine Anne was "shaken" by his assassination, but, ironically, the death of that old antagonist helped achieve what the popular arts exhibit had failed to do, U.S. recognition of Obregón's government.

With her work for the *Survey Graphic* issue finished, Katherine Anne returned to New York in September. Her commitment to the ideal of art over propaganda was finally clear.

CHAPTER TWELVE

Friends and Lovers in New York and Connecticut

September 1923–April 1927

I have suffered a great deal from love, or rather, the impossibility of finding an adequate substitute for illusion.

As soon as Katherine Anne returned to New York in late September she wrote to Sumner Williams breaking their engagement. She much later had seemingly sincere regrets that she let Williams go, but this breakup was part of her already established pattern of rejecting stable men in favor of unpredictable cavaliers who could offer her little in the way of security, either financial or emotional. Before the end of the year she had another impracticable "beau" in Francisco Aguilera, a young Chilean graduate student and instructor at Yale whom she met on a blind date at a New Haven dance. She preserved among her papers a clipping from the campus paper, which reported that "Miss Katherine Anne Porter, author of note and a contributor to Century Magazine" would be the guest of Francisco Aguilera of the Yale faculty over the weekend and would stay at the Faculty Club during the visit. It was a society note that pleased and amused her, but its decorous air was hardly an accurate herald of the alliance.

Aguilera had the combination of charisma and intellectual interests that appealed to her. He was handsome, debonair, well-educated, fluent in several languages, sensitive to literature, and ethereally romantic. Although he bore a genteel courtliness and the fashion of an earlier generation (most of his life he would wear spats), he was, in fact, nine years younger than Katherine Anne.

Soon after the New Haven weekend he was "unconditionally" hers, he told her, and at the end of January he made his first trip to see her, during which they consummated their affair. He referred to her apartment as their "enchanted medieval castle" (he was translating Ronsard at the time) and romanced her with poetic tributes to Proust, who moved him so much he was "paralyzed," he said, and "on the verge of tears, out of sheer aesthetic emotion." He dedicated translations to her and wrote poems in her honor—"Chilena a Katherine Anne Porter" is his title for his translation into Spanish of Shelley's "With a Guitar, to Jane," which begins, "Ariel to Miranda—Take/ This slave of Music, for the sake/Of him who is the slave of thee." Katherine Anne credited Aguilera with presenting her with the name "Miranda" for her autobiographical character, but she, of course, had chosen it for a fictional alter ego the previous year, and he apparently had been inspired to call her Miranda only after she talked about planned Miranda stories.

After the weekend in which the affair was consummated, Katherine Anne heard nothing from him for four weeks. "You should come here and take the spring sun with me, mi Amado Funebre," she wrote. "We would not talk unless we chose, and the gay spring winds could blow away the restlessness of our hearts." Aguilera returned for another romantic rendezvous but followed it by another mute period. A month later she received a letter in which he conveyed by a remote tone his intention to bring their brief affair to an end. He was giving up his work toward a PhD at Yale and returning to Chile. "Write me," he concluded, "telling me of your work, of your life, of your plans. Think of me, and pray for me. Teijo, Francisco."

Her affair with Aguilera effectively over, in mid-April Katherine Anne had an amorous encounter with Aguilera's friend Alvaro Hinojosa, who wrote her praising their recent "night of happiness" together. Although he declared that he was looking forward to the hour when he would embrace her again, there is no proof that they saw one another a second time or even that she answered his letter. Before the middle of May Katherine Anne suspected that she was pregnant, and she must have considered the possibility, or likelihood, that the father was Hinojosa.

After Aguilera told her of his plan to return to Chile and before she knew she was pregnant, she considered trying to secure a foreign assignment in France. Now everything was changed, and she had to decide what to do about the pregnancy. When she was invited to join a group at the Connecticut farm of Liza Anderson and John Dallett, who recently had married, she accepted, and she sent Aguilera a cryptic note: "Señora Doña Catalina Bien-Querida de Francisco announces another change of plans. She will not go to Paris this summer. No. Instead, to the country, in Connecticut, to live in an old long deserted inn; and it is hinted that she may remain there all winter, too. Seclusion. Silence, Solitude. I love the liquid hiss of the syllables. I love the things themselves. And I shall need them."

She also wrote a letter to Genevieve Taggard that was deceptively cheerful, asking her to send a reply that would reach her on her birthday, May 15. "I love my birthday," she declared. "I was always so happy to have been born!" The insincerity of the bravado was underscored by the fact that the letter accompanied the witch poem "This Transfusion," which she was offering to the *Measure*, which Genevieve edited. "It is very personal—all my poems are," she said; "all poetry is, all life is, but I love it very much, and want you to see it . . . . . It was written out of a definite mood communicated by a tremendous experience." The mood and the tremendous experience of her 1921 pregnancy and abortion were surfacing again, and the venom she had aimed at De la Selva could now be redirected to Aguilera or Hinojosa.

Katherine Anne went to the farm when she was only a few weeks into the pregnancy. She had not firmly decided what to do, and she discussed abortion with Ignatius McGuire, a medical librarian and poet who was another visitor at the farm. She asked him whether he knew how and where she might get an abortion. Whatever advice he gave her, she soon made a decision to carry the baby to term. She convinced herself that the child would be a girl, and she intended, she said, to name her Miranda. On the bottom of Aguilera's last letter to her she wrote the name "Miranda Aguilera," crediting him with siring the child.

Aguilera, who had secured a government post in Chile in the Ministry of Education and departed before the end of the year, lived to the age of eighty-one and married three times. When acquaintances in later years asked him whether he had children, he would say, "No," but add coyly that maybe there was one. His childlessness, a peculiarity for Latin men of his generation, adds weight to the supposition that Aguilera might have been unable to father a child and that Alvaro Hinojosa was the lover who impregnated Katherine Anne in the spring of 1924.

Despite Katherine Anne's loneliness and depression, the seclusion and silence at the farm after the other guests left allowed her to return to her writing and the practical matter of earning some money.

With the help of Irita Van Doren, an editor at the *New York Herald Tribune*, she was able to secure the modestly remunerative freelance work of reviewing books, and soon she finished a story she called "Virgin Violeta." She sent it to Carl Van Doren, who accepted it for the December issue of the *Century*.

Katherine Anne said that the story was based on a disgusting story De la Selva told her in 1922 about a mean and deliberate seduction of a young girl. The story that emerged two years later focused on the anguish of the disillusioned Violeta, almost fifteen-years-old and infatuated with her cousin Carlos, who has written a poem about nuns "dancing with bare feet / On broken glass in the cobbled street." When Carlos corners Violeta in the sunroom and kisses her violently, her romantic dream about her first kiss, which she expected to be warm and gentle, is shattered. Feeling frightened and ill, Violeta rejects spiritual love, taught at her convent, and physical love, represented by the predatory Carlos. She is possessed by a painful unhappiness and can amuse herself only by drawing ugly caricatures of Carlos.

"Virgin Violeta" offers a subtle criticism of the Catholic Church for fostering an unrealistic view of human love and for its paternalism that promotes sexism in the Mexican aristocratic society. As a statement about art, the story condemns sentimentalism. On a personal level, the character Carlos is a caricature of Salomón de la Selva, whose 1922 poem about the bare-footed nuns Katherine Anne incorporated in the story. The real interest in the story lies in the psychology of Violeta, Katherine Anne's recreation of her adolescent self and an early version of Miranda. If Katherine Anne began drafting the story in the aftermath of her abortion and the end of her affair with De la Selva and completed it in the equally fitting atmosphere of another failed love affair and another pregnancy three years later, the seed of it was located in the winter of 1905–06, when she, too, was fifteen and soon to experience her first romantic disillusionment in her marriage to John Koontz. "Virgin Violeta" had been "far too long in germinating," she told Genevieve Taggard.

Katherine Anne's only constant companions at the farm were Little Dig-Dig, her cat (who was also pregnant), an unnamed "watchdog" or two, and "a 38 Colt revolver to scare away ghosts and woodchucks," as she described her life in the Windham County countryside to Genevieve. All summer long she hadn't been able to get her dead niece, Mary Alice Holloway, out of her mind. She told Gay, "I feel sometimes that when I cry for her I am crying over all the other lost

things in my life, too . . . Children are the scapegoats of our love, Gay."
She began taking notes for a story about Mary Alice she called "Vision
of Heaven of Fra Angelico," with an epigraph from the Buddha: "I will
show you sorrow and the ending of sorrow."

"Dear darlin'," Katherine Anne wrote Genevieve in the fall, "had
you heard, out of the air, maybe, that I am going to have a baby about
the middle of January? Now I've passed the danger period of losing it,
I can't keep silent any longer. Write and tell me how mad I am."
Reading hysteria between the lines of Katherine Anne's letter and
imagining an ominous note in her earlier mention of the thirty-eight
Colt revolver, Genevieve worried that Katherine Anne might be suicidal, and she made a quick trip to Windham to be sure her friend was
spiritually and mentally holding up. Genevieve's concern apparently
was well founded. Near the end of her life Katherine Anne recalled the
fall of 1924 as the one specific time she seriously considered suicide:
"I did think of killing myself . . . with a pistol. I am a very good shot.
There was a comedy strip I used to love. One of the children in the
family was always being wronged, everyone was always getting mad at
him . . . . . a bloody nuisance. One day he came striding through the
room with a pistol. 'Goodbye, I am going to commit suicide.' There
was a blast. They almost jump out of their skins. Then he comes in.
'Missed.' I was afraid I would miss."

Fertility, death, and alienation were on her mind in November, when
she completed a draft of the story "Holiday," based on the month
in 1912 she spent at Spring Branch, in Harris County, Texas, with the
Hillendahl family when her marriage to John Koontz was spiraling
downward toward its end. The unnamed female narrator of the story
reveals little about herself except that she feels fragmented and grieves
over those dead who carried into the grave some part of her living cells,
"troubles" from which she needs a "holiday." Possibly an artist, she is
the observer and chronicler of the large, fictional Müller family and
their immigrant farming community that combines Marxism and patri-
archy. In the midst of the tight-knit family, which functions according
to innate laws and forces, the narrator learns elemental truths about
herself. "Holiday" was a very private story, however, and Katherine
Anne felt dissatisfied with the conclusion. She placed it among her
unfinished stories to be forgotten for a long time.

Near Thanksgiving, as her pregnancy advanced into its final phrase,
Katherine Anne moved into a boardinghouse in the village of
Windham, where she was close to human society and medical help.

She reassured Genevieve: "Jedsie Darling—You're not to trouble about me. I am doing well enough, I have been a mad-woman, and I know it, but I can't possibly come out of my trance to establish any mood of regret. So far as the child is concerned, it is all more than well—but everything else in my personal life has been a blank failure—all, I mean that touches my love." She promised, "I will see you afterward"—meaning after the birth—"I will bring Miranda . . . , and we will talk about everything for days!"

Genevieve and her husband, Robert Wolf, had invited Katherine Anne to spend the Christmas holidays with them at their New Preston farm. In mid-December, Katherine Anne sent her regrets: "I should be happy to come up for Christmas—But I have had an illness, and I shan't be able to travel—On December second my child was born prematurely and dead, and though I have never been in danger, still it is better in every way to be quiet." She added near the end of the letter, "My baby was a boy. It was dead for half a day before it was born— There seems to be nothing to say about it."

As soon as she could travel, Katherine Anne returned to the Dalletts' apartment on Charles Street. She wanted to forget about her recent ordeal and resume her ordinary life, but the past remained alive, even if buried, and the Windham experience surfaced in her art for the rest of her life. The first expressions were two lyrical poems, "Winter Burial" and "November in Windham." "Winter Burial," which contains a metaphor for a pregnancy, was published before the end of the year in the *New York Herald Tribune.* It would be thirty years before she would publish "November in Windham" with its haunting final stanza:

> *This is a country aching at the core,*
> *Dead-tired of the year's labors, weary beyond sleep:*
> *Seeded once more in stones against the yield*
> *Of a forgotten scarecrow in a field*
> *Set there to frighten birds that come no more.*

Katherine Anne's circle of friends was widening. She had met only in passing during her earlier Village residencies Malcolm Cowley, Dorothy Day, and Josephine (Josie) Herbst, and she soon had a chance to become much better acquainted with them and with Malcolm's wife, Peggy Baird, Dorothy's sister Delafield, and Josie's lover, John Herrmann. Through them she met Allen Tate and Caroline Gordon. Katherine Anne already had a good many experiences and values in common with Cowley, whose youthful, ruddy face belied the sophistication of his critical and literary skills. In 1925 she agreed completely with him on political and aesthetic issues as both of them affirmed their preference for craftsmanship and classical humanism.

Allen Tate and Caroline Gordon were the first among her literary friends to cause her to think seriously about her Southern heritage. Allen, slight and handsome, a ladies' man, talked often about "the war" (meaning the Civil War rather than the World War), carried a cane, and sometimes wore the wide-brimmed black hat of a Kentucky colonel. He was a graduate of Vanderbilt and had been a member of the Nashville group who founded the influential literary magazine the *Fugitive* (1923–1925), dedicated to discussions of poetry (often their own) and promotion of a youthful rebellion against literary nostalgia for the antebellum. When Katherine Anne met him in 1925, he was moving in an opposite direction toward an exaltation of the agrarian values of the Old South.

Raven-haired Caroline Gordon, with alabaster skin and classic good looks, was descended from several generations of Virginia Gordons and Kentucky Meriwethers, whose family legends crisscrossed those of the Skaggses and the Boones. She was college-educated, but she shared with Katherine Anne a Calvinist upbringing, serious commitment to writing, and experience as both a teacher and journalist. She had fallen in love with Allen when he was visiting his friend Robert Penn (Red) Warren in Guthrie, Kentucky, near her parents' residence in Clarksville, Tennessee. After a year struggling with poverty in New York, where they had gone to fulfill their literary ambitions, Allen and Caroline were married in 1925 and had a daughter, Nancy.

Big-boned and awkward with startling blue eyes, Josie Herbst had grown up in Iowa in a middle-class, literate family and worked her way through the University of California, in Berkeley, before joining other young literary people in New York in 1919. Shortly after her arrival she had an intense love affair with the married playwright Maxwell Anderson; it ended when she became pregnant and had an abortion. She had been roaming around Europe mingling with expatriates from the spring of 1922 until she returned to the United States in 1925 with twenty-four-year-old John Herrmann, a Communist sympathizer and apprentice writer whom she had met in Paris the year before. She was in love with him, despite his heavy drinking and womanizing.

In 1925 Josie was thirty-three years old, but claimed to be twenty-eight. In the complicated arithmetic of her and Katherine Anne's real ages and the fictional ones they provided, Katherine Anne, who was thirty-five but admitted to being thirty-one, privately believed herself seven years older than Josie rather than the two she was. Josie, at the same time, secretly believed Katherine Anne her junior by two years. Confiding many other personal feelings and private thoughts, however, Katherine Anne and Josie shared opinions about the struggle of literary women trying to support themselves and the difficulty of finding reliable, stable men. They discussed literature, painting, and politics. They also talked about clothes and food. Malcolm Cowley called them and Caroline Gordon "the talkingest women in New York."

In the early months of 1926 Katherine Anne was living in a room at 158 Waverly Place in the Village. In the spring, she had met Ernest Stock, a twenty-five-year-old English painter and former Royal Air Force pilot who frequented the Art Students League in New York, and she considered him her current beau. Josie and John rented an old farmhouse in Merryall Valley, near New Preston, Connecticut, and Katherine Anne and Stock rented the nearby house of Genevieve Taggard and Bob Wolf, who had decided to separate.

In June Katherine Anne told Genevieve that the summer was going exactly as she had hoped and that she was delighted with Ernest. "All that fullness of green and bloom you promised have come true: I am perfectly happy . . . . . never before so simply contented with what I have." In fact, she was not so satisfied as she reported. Ernest liked to pose as a victim of past failures in love, quoting verses that bemoaned the perfidy of women, and he enjoyed showing off the shrapnel scars he earned in the war after his plane was shot down. "As he ran around in his shorts," Josie said, "we were not sure he was not trying to expose the one scar in token of the other, but he won no more than comment from a [neighboring] Polish farmwife, who scoffed, 'Look at him now, running around in underpants, showing off them bony knees.'" This foolish Ernest riled Katherine Anne, and Josie recalled that he might suddenly show up at their farmhouse "as night fell, pale as an Orestes pursued down the coast of Calabria by the Furies, to beg to spend the night." In the late summer Katherine Anne decided she couldn't stand "Deadly Ernest," as she had begun to call Stock, a minute longer. She "vanished with the mist one early morning on a milk truck," Josie remembered.

Katherine Anne returned to the Village and moved into a cheap room in the rickety house at 561 Hudson Street known as "Caligari Corners" or "Casa Caligari" by its residents, who in the fall of 1926 included Dorothy and Delafield Day and Dorothy's small daughter, Tamar. Katherine Anne, who had no lingering regrets over her failed romance with Ernest Stock, was ready to resume her book reviewing and fiction writing. As it turned out, all her writing had to be set aside for a few weeks, for if Ernest Stock had left her with neither pleasant memories nor shattered illusions, he had left her with gonorrhea.

When she consulted Dr. Mary Halton, who had taken care of her after the stillbirth of her child in 1924, Katherine Anne learned that surgical removal of her ovaries was vital. She had the operation, a bilateral oophorectomy, sometime in the fall of 1926. Because surgical infection remained a serious danger, the operation was risky and required weeks of recovery. In none of her surviving letters is there any mention of the surgery or its aftereffects, and for the rest of her life she was highly secretive about both the operation and the need for it. She told none of her friends the whole truth, hinting that it had been a single cyst, and she told her family that she had a common gynecological problem that required a hysterectomy.

The surgery was emotionally crushing to Katherine Anne, for it represented the deaths of all her future babies. She considered it a tragedy equaled only by the death of Mary Alice Holloway. "It was seven years between that loss and this one," she wrote in her diary, ignoring her additional painful losses of 1921 and 1924. As a woman who had been left with an artificial menopause, she also felt sexually unappealing to men, and, at the age of thirty-six, old. For many years she would counter these feelings by pretending to lovers and husbands, as well as to close women friends, that she still had menstrual periods, even going so far as to purchase monthly hygienic paraphernalia.

When she regained her strength, Katherine Anne found with the small publishing house J. H. Sears a short-term editing job that allowed her to retreat from book reviewing. The editors proposed that she assemble a selection of essays on marriage to be published in their Royal Collection, devoted to the presentation of "Old Wine in New Bottles." Under the pseudonym of "Hamblen Sears," Katherine Anne chose twenty-four pieces by such writers as Voltaire and St. Augustine for a collection titled *What Price Marriage?* If there was a message in her introduction or a theme in the pieces she chose, it was that the institution of marriage was changing to accommodate "modern" attitudes.

When the Tates and Ford Madox Ford moved to Casa Caligari early in 1927, Katherine Anne spent as much time as she could with them and others of their mutual circle of interesting friends. She came to know well Ford, whom Caroline called "Master" and "one of the best craftsmen of his day" (at the time Katherine Anne agreed), and Hart Crane, whose kindliness and enthusiasm for art usually compensated for his emotional outbursts. An increasing number of southerners, including Andrew Lytle and Red Warren, found their way to Allen and Caroline's quarters, filled with conversation about the South.

The Tates were drawing upon their ancestral past for their creative work, as were Warren and Lytle, and Allen had signed a contract to write a biography of Stonewall Jackson that he hoped would keep him and Caroline financially afloat. Although Katherine Anne wanted to mine her own family's history for her art, she did not yet know how to do it. Instead, taking inspiration from Allen, she concentrated on choosing a subject for a biography that she could write for the commercial market.

CHAPTER THIRTEEN

Boston and Salem: Witch-Hunts and Ancestors

April 1927–August 1928

I can't think where the years have gone . . . The world grows to be a familiar place, with no dark and terrifying corners, and no shocks.

In April of 1927 Nicola Sacco and Bartolomeo Vanzetti, both self-proclaimed anarchists, were sentenced to death after seven years of fruitless appeals of their convictions in the brutal murders of two payroll guards in South Braintree, Massachusetts. Since 1920 Katherine Anne had taken notes on the protracted event with the plan of writing an article about it. When she eventually completed the long essay fifty years later, she called the affair "one of the important turning points in the history of this country." She failed to acknowledge, or perhaps to see, that in 1927 it had led to one of the important turning points in the evolution of her artistic canon.

In her memoir she traced a connection between what she considered the unjust trials of Sacco and Vanzetti and the "witches" of Salem in 1692. It is not coincidental that the week the sentence was handed down she chose her biographical subject—Cotton Mather, the man Gay long ago told her "caused witches to be burned." After writing to Mather Abbott to ask his help with her biography of his ancestor, she sent her proposal to Boni and Liveright, who were publishing Tate's biography of Stonewall Jackson.

When the executions of Sacco and Vanzetti were stayed for two weeks to allow a final appeal, writers, artists, and intellectuals in New York and throughout the Northeast were hastily organized for a massive rally near Boston's Charlestown Prison, where the two accused men were confined, awaiting their almost certain fate. On 18 August Katherine Anne arrived in Boston with members of

New York defense groups that included the Irish-born political poet Lola Ridge, John Dos Passos, Mike Gold, Helen O'Lochlain Crowe, Edna St. Vincent Millay, and Delafield Day.

Katherine Anne's services in the six-day rally included transcribing the letters of Sacco and Vanzetti and marching in the forbidden picket line that ensured arrest and publicity. Every morning she left her hotel near the Boston Common and dropped into the picket line in front of the State House. The police closed in and made the arrests after permitting the marchers one or two circuits. The same patient Irish officer led Katherine Anne to the Joy Street jail, where a middle-aged matron put her in a cell and locked the door. Two or three hours later she would be discharged, when Edward James, nephew of Henry James, posted bail for her and the others. After her release 23 August Katherine Anne took a taxi to the Charlestown Prison. She stood smoking a cigarette and, like the other silent vigil-keepers, watching with what she remembered as "unrelieved horror and fascination" the tower of the prison where Sacco and Vanzetti were executed at midnight. Back at her hotel, she joined Mike Gold, the journalist Grace Lumpkin, and the cartoonist Willie Gropper to drink bootleg gin and discuss the outrage.

The trial of the picketers took place the following day. Having thought they might gain attention for their cause by invoking the infamous Baumes' Law, which held that anyone arrested as many as four times could be imprisoned for life, the group, who certainly wouldn't have wanted to face life imprisonment, nevertheless anticipated a sentence stiff enough to righteously and indignantly appeal with attendant publicity. They were disappointed when prosecutors decided to treat them only as ordinary nuisances and their transgression as minor. Other than Katherine Anne's being admonished for trying to smoke in the courtroom and John Dos Passos's being reprimanded for reading a newspaper, the trial was unremarkable. Katherine Anne remembered that Judge James Parmenter, "portentously, as if pronouncing another death sentence, found us guilty of loitering and obstructing traffic, fined us five dollars each, and the tragic farce took its place in history." Sympathetic local women paid the picketers' fines and gave them railroad tickets back to New York.

Shortly after her return from Boston Katherine Anne wrote "Rope," a story that had been brewing for the past year and was related to her ill-fated summer sojourn with Ernest Stock and her work on *What Price Marriage?* She sent it to Paul Rosenfeld and Alfred Kreymborg, who were gathering pieces for *The Second American Caravan*. A treatment of the twin forces of love and hate in a marriage, the story contains elements of her own marriages and love affairs, including a covert reference to children. She also embarked on a love affair with Luis Hidalgo, who was in New York receiving enthusiastic attention from an American public beginning to appreciate Mexican art. A caricaturist, Hidalgo encouraged her to draw caricatures, too. She drew one of him that captured both a scowl and his *indiginista* handsomeness. She told Gay that she was considering marrying him.

In the early fall Boni and Liveright offered Katherine Anne a contract, with an advance of three hundred dollars, for a biography of Cotton Mather to be titled "The Devil and Cotton Mather." There was considerable research to do, and she quickly left New York and Hidalgo for Salem, Massachusetts, and the Essex Institute, where the court documents from the Salem witch trials and Mather family materials were held. She took a room in Barstowe Manor, a well-kept boardinghouse at 26 Winter Street, a pleasant walk from the institute, around the curve of the lovely old common surrounded by dark, gabled, centuries-old homes.

She dated her fascination with Cotton Mather and the witchcraft delusion from her childhood and the years spent in Louisiana, "where Voodoo doctors played at witchcraft." As she delved into research for the biography, however, she conceived a story that combined her turn to the region of her early life with her interest in Mather. She suspended her research long enough to write "He," which she told Gay was her attack on "Calvinism" and the petty fundamentalists of their childhood.

"He" is the story of the dirt-poor Whipple family, who are struggling to survive on a scrap farm in central Texas. Mr. and Mrs. Whipple (no given names provided) and their children, Adna, Emly, and the simple-minded son they call only "He," battle social, economic, physical, and psychological forces beyond their understanding and control. Although Mrs. Whipple protests that she is a good Christian woman and a good mother who does the best she can with her retarded son, she takes food away from him to give to the other two children, whom she also gives warmer clothes, and she sends him to take care of the bees because he "don't really mind" if he gets stung. Mrs. Whipple finally decides they can't afford to take care of him, and she commits him to the county home. As a story about love, ignorance, isolation, exile, and motherhood, "He" is effectively universal and humanistic. But it was as a story about class struggle and the suffering and poverty of a poor, uneducated farm family that appealed to the editors of the communistic *New Masses*, who accepted it for publication in their October issue.

During a December weekend in New York Katherine Anne ended her distracting affair with Hidalgo in order to devote herself completely to the Mather biography. "Transplantation spoiled the Indian Hidalgo," she wrote in private notes, in which she summarized him as "befuddled by Broadway and 'chic'" as justification for her terminating the affair. Returning to Salem, she spent the gray, cold winter of 1927–1928 in loneliness and introspection but also industry.

Because she was reading through Mather's voluminous correspondence, letters assumed an importance to her they never had before. She had had rather negative feelings about letter writing because Harrison had held epistolary art up to her as the proper enterprise for "a lady." Rebelling against that attitude, for the past twenty years she had dashed off letters to friends, family, and lovers without giving much thought to content or style. Many of her letters, she now realized, had included indiscreet revelations of her personal life, such as the letters about her pregnancy to Genevieve in 1924. Claiming she had a particular use for her letters, she asked friends and family to return any they had saved. When she received them, she destroyed some and retyped others with names and embarrassing parts omitted. She intended to be careful from this point forward about details she put in writing, and when she *did* write something unflattering about herself or somebody else, she wouldn't hesitate to tell her recipient to "burn this when you are done with it." She now regarded letters as channels for satisfying human connectedness, literary gifts to friends and family, and a running notebook that was a repository of emotion and experience she could draw on later for her fiction. Although only the year before she had admitted being not much of a letter writer, she now became one, soon calling herself an "aggressive writer of letters."

In the spring and summer of 1927 she was writing frequently to Josie, and she began to write regularly again to Gay and Harrison. She also promised her family a visit soon. She told Gay that they would "loll around and smoke and gossip until all hours," that, in fact, her "Lazy woman's notion of Paradise" was to spend it with her in "some very sunny spot." Still wanting Harrison's approval, she told him that she had "developed into a famous cook" (not yet an accurate statement). "I love to work all day at a spread," she said, "and then come out with a bouquet, and take a bow. Prima Donna cook, that's what

I am." Promising to cook a big dinner for him when she came home, she served up a recollection of a happy childhood scene to reaffirm their bond: "the nicest memory I have is of that lovely orchard you made to take the place of the old one on the Carlton place, and don't I wish I might once more pull a ripe Indian-cling peach off one of those trees." She signed her letter with "Love and a big hug from— Kinkyhead," one of his pet names for her in childhood.

As a result of her research into the Mather family and her renewed communication with her family, at the beginning of 1928 Katherine Anne became interested in researching her own ancestral lines. She looked up "Porter," "Skaggs," and "Jones" in genealogical dictionaries and wrote to Harrison asking for whatever information he had. She told him, "I suppose my interest has some connection with my being so far away from my base, as it were, it is probably an obscure symptom of homesickness." In a way it was, if "homesickness" is an adequate metaphor for her rediscovery of her region and her family as artistic inspiration. She had conceived an idea for an autobiographical novel she intended to call "Many Redeemers," which was to have three books: "Legend and Memory," a collection of family anecdotes, especially those told by her grandmother; "Midway of This Mortal Life," focusing on her own youth and young adulthood; and "The Present Day," which was to incorporate some of her political experiences in Mexico. Before the enterprise exhausted itself, it would go on for more than thirty years, expand, change forms and titles, shed pieces of itself, and shift focus. It would become the widest stream in her fictional canon.

During the first months of renewed communication with her family, Katherine Anne was also looking inward and assessing her own life. Understanding herself had a direct bearing on the creation of the autobiographical character who would unify the three parts of her novel. She wrote several pages of autobiography and introspection that, like earlier private notes she had recorded in Mexico, were a contrast to her public words and actions. She dated the two and one-half pages "Monday 27th February, 1928":

> The bad habits of my father and the grown ups that brought me
> up have corrupted me and are about to spoil my life because
> though I was critical and rebellious, I failed to criticize with
> discrimination or rebel against the really damaging conditions.
> I was romantic and egoistic, and took naturally to the examples of

laziness, inefficiency and arrogance I saw about me . . . . . Now let me take myself in hand knowing what I do about myself and the world I live in, and do my work to the limit of my capacity, without the preoccupations of vanity and fear . . . I am corrupted also with the egotistic desire to be right always, and the fear of criticism . . . . . I have thought too much about a career ever to buckle down and make one . . . . . Root of this trouble, a false point of view in those who influenced me in my childhood, my own romantic acceptance of those views, and failure to train myself in habits of concentration and of finishing one job before I undertook another . . . . . This has destroyed my health, my nervous system, and almost destroyed my vital contacts with reality . . . . . I here and now, today, take myself in hand. I will finish this job and leave my seclusion and face the world as I did before. I found much there to frighten and discompose me, but only because my sexual impulses led me into situations that I could not control or battle with. Again I came to that struggle with fixed romantic preconceptions, and strange notions of what I could and could not do. I have allowed all sorts of persons to trespass on my human rights because I was too timid to fight for them, and too lazy and indifferent to put up the battle that I knew was necessary to hold my proper ground. I always rationalized this timidity and weakness by putting a moral construction on it, I could not use the weapons that I considered (so I said) unfair.

Yet I have done a great many things much worse, because I would not do anything until the situation called for desperate emergency measures, and then I behaved without judgement and foresight . . . . . So I have harmed a great many persons as much, if not more than they have harmed me. I have harmed some of them by allowing them to trespass on me, by my weakness encouraging them to quite predatory acts against me. I have harmed others by invading their lives and living vicariously in their emotions and problems, because it was easier than standing my own ground and fighting out my own problems.

A successful life consists of developing your own potentialities without running from your environment or denying realities, or being blind about people because knowing the facts—not the inner truth, because that is one of the mysteries I have been too much occupied with—without them, and knowing when to define yourself, when to attack, and when to stand firmly quiescent.

I have been, and am, neurotic almost to a pathological degree, and I have ruled the sympathies of friends at the same time appealing to their natural instincts to exploit their knowledge of me. I have suffered a good deal because, of what I have had to give, other persons have been able to make some use. More use than I have, at any rate. Whereas disorderliness and lack of self-discipline have made my material, got from others, almost useless to me. I have taken refuge in skepticism because my mind hated to come to grips and decide important questions for itself . . . . . Now I seem unable to believe in anything, and certainly my doubts of human beings and their motives is founded in a fear of their power over me . . . . . I believe that this is an absurd and childish state of mind for me to have let myself drift into, for it has been a long process of drifting . . . Whatever is left of my will must be assembled and put again in working order . . . . . For certainly I possessed will and vitality and tremendous interest. They cannot be entirely gone.

Now I find myself having elected to do a thing that requires merely a constant exercise of my merely surface abilities, and have got myself into an emotional state over it that keeps me from working, and I find myself drifting again to a condition of inertia and apathy, a desire to give up. I seem to lack entirely that practical pride in human achievement, that keep[s] many persons going very well. It is an inversion of ambition; yet I have selected things over-difficult to do, and have never worked at a speed beyond myself, and when I was quite young I decided to set my limitations moderately. Maybe this was my mistake. For by setting my bounds, I find they are real things and have a way of closing upon me without my (conscious) consent.

Aside from the vagueness of the reference to "sexual impulses," by which she meant her indiscriminate willingness to go to bed with her lovers in exchange for romance, the assessment was particularly accurate.

One of Katherine Anne's visitors in Salem in the late winter and early spring of 1928 was William (Bill) Doyle, an aspiring playwright she had known in New York. For an agreed upon fee, she had written the first act of his play *Carnival,* and he came to see her for further work on the script. Poor critical response when the play opened in Boston, however, discouraged Doyle, and he put off paying her what he owed her. His letter to her in early April of 1928 was full of complaints, excuses, and promises: "Will write you soon again and enclose the balance I owe you. If things happen as I want them to will send more to make it possible for you to have that gorgeous sounding place near the bluest of seas."

The place by the sea that she mentioned to Doyle represented an escape from the Mather biography, for she was much more interested in stories that were forming in her mind as part of her novel. She completed two of them in Salem and sent them to Eugene Jolas for the new experimental periodical *transition*. Jolas accepted "Magic" for the summer 1928 number and "The Jilting of Granny Weatherall" for publication early in 1929.

"Magic," which incorporates the New Orleans voodoo she tied to her interest in Cotton Mather, comprises a dialogue between a wealthy woman and her maid, who entertains her with a melodramatic tale about a prostitute who runs away from her brothel only to be reeled back through "black magic" enlisted by the madam. Thematically, the terse and ironic story is about the magic of art and the iniquity of unjust class structure and apathy's collusion with evil, the latter a subject Katherine Anne addressed in her self-analysis in February.

"The Jilting of Granny Weatherall" unfolds as lyrical stream-of-consciousness in the final hours of Ellen Weatherall and progresses by a flowing sequence of memories, each illustrating one of Granny's disillusionments, beginning with her abandonment at the altar by a fiancé named John and culminating in the final "jilting" by her religion, the absence of the "sign" she expected from God: "She could not remember any other sorrow because this grief wiped them all away. Oh, no, there's nothing more cruel than this—I'll never forgive it. She stretched herself with a deep breath and blew out the light." The writing of the story was Katherine Anne's long-delayed confrontation with the death of Cat Porter. She had transformed her own painful memory into art by displacing her grief with what she imagined to be her grandmother's shock at confronting a death for which she was not prepared. The story also incorporated Katherine Anne's feelings of betrayal by John Koontz and Roman Catholicism.

Before the end of March Katherine Anne was back in her room at Casa Caligari. She was drained from the tedious research for the biography and the expenditure of creative energy that had produced three completed stories and a plan for a new novel. With promises to return to a rigorous schedule of work on Mather, she admitted to Liveright she couldn't meet the deadline to which she had agreed. Liveright sourly accepted the delay but offered no additional advance, and Katherine Anne got in touch with Irita Van Doren at the *New York Herald Tribune* and Malcolm Cowley at the *New Republic* to say she was ready to do more book reviewing. She prepared also to leave the city for the country.

Josie and John, who had married the previous fall, had been begging her to join them at the farm they had bought in Erwinna, Pennsylvania. But she had met by then another congenial couple, Clara and John Coffey, who had a farm near the Herrmanns, and when they invited her to stay with them for the summer in their old stone house, she accepted. After Allen and Caroline dropped off her and her old black cat, Theophilus, at the Coffey farm, she settled into a corner of the barn and began to work again on the Mather biography.

She was initially optimistic that the three months in beautiful Erwinna were going to be productive. But she couldn't muster any enthusiasm for Mather, and what seemed like a new and delightful friendship with the Coffeys became contentious. Promising herself that she would never spend another summer in the country, she left in the middle of August to look for a secluded apartment in New York and the right kind of paying job that would allow her to give proper attention to her writing. Having left Theophilus behind to wander the farm at his decrepit leisure, she was appalled to learn that as soon as she left John Coffey drowned Theophilus, a horribly fitting conclusion, she thought, to her disappointing summer.

CHAPTER FOURTEEN

Escape to Bermuda

August 1928–Spring 1930

I am, let me tell you, on an island, a regular doggone Miz Robinson Crusoe.

In September *The Second American Caravan* with Katherine Anne's story "Rope" in it was published, and the volume's editors, Alfred Kreymborg, Paul Rosenfeld, and Lewis Mumford, invited her to a celebration lunch at Lüchow's, during which Kreymborg suggested that she apply for work at Macaulay and Company, the publishers of *Caravan*. She followed their suggestion and soon was hired as a copyeditor. For the first time in a good many years, she had salaried employment.

On 1 October Katherine Anne moved into an apartment at 74 Charles Street that belonged to Thorborg Haberman, who was planning to spend the next year in Bermuda with her new husband, Wasilike (Basil) Ellison. She was reasonably sure that she would never receive another dime from Bill Doyle for her work on *Carnival* and, moreover, had begun to suspect it would never see the lights of New York. This disappointment coalesced with her recent self-analysis in Salem to inspire a new story, which she titled "Theft."

In contrast to "He" and "The Jilting of Granny Weatherall," which look backward to Texas and family, "Theft" was tied to contemporary events and current acquaintances and might have been intended as a piece of "The Present Day," the third book of "Many Redeemers." Most of the story is the evolving recollection of the unnamed protagonist, a woman probably in her mid to late thirties, who has felt compelled to assess her life. The story begins with the woman's emerging from a hot bath to discover that her purse, which she laid out to dry after a soaking in a rainstorm, is gone. She angrily accuses the building's janitor, who readily admits she stole the purse to give to her pretty, young niece. "She oughta have nice things," she says, "You're a grown woman, you've had your chance." Through dialogue that explores the dilemma of a woman past her prime as well as the rights of ownership (a glance at Marxist theory), the protagonist comes to realize that she has been responsible for *all* her losses. Katherine Anne said that the story, obviously set in the Charles Street apartment, was inspired by her loss of a little gold lamé purse Delafield had given her for her birthday, but one can hardly miss the Freudian implications of the missing, empty purse, a symbolic empty womb.

The bleakness of "Theft" was a mirror of Katherine Anne's mood in the early fall of 1928, but her melancholy lifted late in October when she met twenty-nine-year-old Matthew Josephson, who had grown up in Brooklyn in a well-to-do Jewish household and had developed intellectually at Columbia University and in the bohemian speakeasies and cafés of Greenwich Village. In 1920, he had married Hannah Geffen, a reporter for the *New York American*, and the two of them had wandered around Europe for a couple of years while Josephson became immersed in Dadaism. After they returned to New York Josephson tried to be a successful writer while making a living as a stockbroker on Wall Street. When Katherine Anne met him, he was an editor at Macauley and Company, which was publishing his biography of Zola.

More than thirty years later he summoned his first impressions of Katherine Anne: "intelligence and sensitiveness with her huge dark eyes and iron grey hair held back in a simple bun . . . A small woman, she bore herself with great poise, was low-voiced, soft-spoken, and full of old-fashioned airs and graces" leavened with "much wit." Several days after their meeting he invited her out for dinner and dancing in Harlem. "I remember she deployed great charm," he said, "and quite carried me away." He gave her a copy of his *Zola and His Times*, which he inscribed "To Katherine Anne Porter *Really!*" (triple underlined).

Flattered and somewhat carried away herself, she was disappointed to discover that he was married and a father. Katherine Anne angrily asked him, "What does this mean? I will not be a homebreaker." Her wrath succumbed to Josephson's intellectual charm, however, and to the convenience of an affair with him. She occasionally joined him at the apartment he kept in the city while pregnant Hannah stayed on at their country residence about forty miles from Manhattan.

Katherine Anne commemorated the inauguration of the affair with a poem she called "First Episode." As had been true in others of her affairs, she wanted the thrill of romance combined with intellectual excitement and her lover's interest in her as an artist. Josephson could provide all that, even if he could not offer continuity and stability. He could not promise her even "candour," he told her.

By the end of 1928 the brief affair was coming to a conclusion not only because Hannah had found out and delivered an ultimatum but also because Katherine Anne had run into Hannah with her new baby and had reconsidered the wisdom of carrying on an affair with a married man. She envied Hannah, a professional woman who was also a mother, and she never admitted to Josephson that she herself was unable to bear a child. On the contrary, she told him that she was determined to live long enough to be a grandmother "for the honour of the line."

Because of her disappointment in love and her failure to make any progress on the Mather biography, Katherine Anne slipped into her familiar melancholy that translated itself into toothache and respiratory illness. Her friends John Crawford, a novelist, who worked for the *New York Times*, and his wife, Becky, an intelligent and hospitable woman, were particularly troubled about Katherine Anne's condition and insisted that she stay with them at their Brooklyn home until she recovered her equilibrium. Becky bustled her off to doctors who looked at her lungs and a dentist who worked on her teeth and wisely concluded that Katherine Anne needed to get far away from mundane editorial work, Josephson, and New York in order to focus on her writing.

Becky got in touch with friends and acquaintances who admired Katherine Anne and her writing and who had money they might be willing to contribute to a fund that would give her a free year far from New York. Within a few weeks Becky had a start but not nearly enough for the year she wanted to finance. But an unexpected development made inauguration of "the plan," as Katherine Anne called it, possible. Thorborg and Basil Ellison invited her to visit them in Bermuda and suggested that she stay on in their leased house, paying her own expenses, when they went away on an extended trip. Since the vacation was within the financial range of Becky's plan, the invitation was accepted, and passage was booked.

Still emotionally fragile, Katherine Anne sailed out of New York harbor on the *Avon* in early March. She described the voyage and her condition in her first letter to Becky from Bermuda: "All the passengers wore flowers and looked cheerful, though slightly mildewed . . . The band played, British sailors rushed around saying, 'nkyew!' and

'Eaoh!' and I staggered to my cabin where I lay in a coma until four o'clock the next after noon. It was a very rough night, so I've been told. I wasn't sea-sick, anyhow not eh wommicking kind. I just lay half-conscious, too damned tired to believe that I should ever rise again." As the ship approached Bermuda, however, her spirits began a slow ascent. Once ashore, she hailed a Victoria for the six-mile trip along coral roads lined with low whitewashed walls, palms, cedars, and oleanders to Sunnyside, the Ellison's big, white tropical house, where she was to have a comfortable two-room suite in the east wing.

For the next few weeks Katherine Anne mended in pleasing company that comprised Thorborg and Basil and Delafield Day and her husband, Franklin Spier, who had rented a house across the bay for a few weeks. She learned to ride a bicycle in this place where there were no trains, factories, automobiles, billboards, or, on her end of the island, even telephones. She swam, she went fishing in a little sailboat, and she ate ripe fruit. "I lie here and enjoy the sun like a chameleon," she wrote Josephson.

Feeling the need to get to work in order to justify Becky's efforts in her behalf, she drafted a review for the *Herald Tribune* and completed the rewriting Macauley hired her to do of *Dröll Peter*, a translation of a biography of Peter Breugel for children. And she was working again on the biography of Cotton Mather. "I feel now like a Marathon runner on the last lap," she told Becky, "a little breathless and concentrated, but almost sure of the prize." Her productivity increased when she extricated herself from her indefinite arrangement with Basil and Thorborg and moved the first of May to Hilgrove, another cheaply rented house, this one large and beautiful, too, where she expected to stay eight months at least.

She was so optimistic of finishing the Mather biography that she wrote to Liveright asking for another advance, promising to send him two chapters every week until the complete text was in his hands (she estimated 1 August). Liveright sent $250 and a severe scolding ("Once more you ask for money on a book that should have been published long ago."). Two weeks later she sent him the promised two chapters and thanks for his generosity.

In an affectionate invitation to Harrison Porter in mid-June, Katherine Anne confirmed that her work was going well: "I wish, Daddy, I have wished it many times since I came to this house: that you could come here and stop awhile. The weather isn't, I'm afraid, so awfully different from Louisiana and Texas in summer, but the houses here are of white coral, thick-walled, with high ceilings and very cool. The gardens are very spacious—mine is terraced and beautiful. The sea is nearby, bluer than anything you can imagine in water." She also told him, "I weighed 105 when I came here, and now I weigh 114. So you see, it has been good for me." She promised to send snapshots.

But perhaps because she was writing frequently to her family, depression in the form of homesickness and regret soon began to seep into her sanguinity. She interrupted work on the biography to draft two poems, "Night Blooming Cereus" and "West Indian Island," which underscored her deep longing for her family's forgiveness and her increasing emotional need to return to Texas. She yearned for a "familiar country" that would receive her as "a friend, as a member of the household," would not mock her "unshared thoughts," but would say to her quietly, "So, daughter, you are late,/But come in, and welcome!" She soon had more reason to feel dissatisfied with her island sojourn. Much of her ease had been linked to her belief that she was going to finish the Mather biography at last and get the beast off her back as well as collect expected royalties. In July, however, she received from Liveright the dummy of *The Devil and Cotton Mather*, and its brash black and orange dust jacket and numerous errors in the chapter headings infuriated her. She began to call the book "The Devil *Take* Cotton Mather." Solitude, which had been essential for her progress on the biography, assumed an unpleasant weight, and she sallied forth to meet Americans who lived on the island. She played bridge and tennis with them. She went to teas and concerts. She dropped in on her native-Bermuda neighbors, and she tried her hand at cooking under the tutelage of her Trinidadian maid.

Acknowledging that the island's inspiration was exhausted, Katherine Anne reserved ship passage for 12 August. As soon as she returned to the Crawfords' Brooklyn home, insisting on paying them $25 a month for her room, she set up a meeting with Charles Pearce and Raymond Everitt at Harcourt, Brace to discuss the possibility of publishing a collection of her stories. Encouraged by their interest, she asked Liveright to stop announcing the Mather biography, and she set about working on her fiction, the writing that truly mattered to her.

In the early days of the winter of 1929–1930, Katherine Anne completed her story "Flowering Judas," which had been intended as "Yúdico's Story" in "The Book of Mexico." She described the writing of the story in a single sitting one evening upstairs in the Crawfords' house while they were downstairs playing cards. "I was out on the corner just after midnight," she said, "dropping it in the mailbox to send it to Lincoln Kirstein, who was running the Hound and Horn. And he published it."

Katherine Anne began the writing of the story with the sketch of Mary Doherty she had recorded soon after their meeting in 1921 and the impressionistic note she had set down in her diary after approaching Mary's apartment and seeing her and the revolutionist Samuel Yúdico framed by an open window: "In that glimpse, no more than a flash, I thought I understood, or perceived, for the first time, the desperate complications of her mind and feelings, and I knew a story; perhaps not her true story, not even the real story of the whole situation, but all the same a story that seemed symbolic truth to me. If I had not seen her face at that very moment, I should never have written just this story because I should not have known it to write." By the time the story was completed at the end of November 1929, the scene had assumed plot and theme, and the characters Laura and Braggioni had evolved from portraits of Mary and Yúdico to fictional beings with lives of their own.

In "Flowering Judas" Katherine Anne added a new message to her earlier analysis of the revolution's imminent failure: Like the Mexicans, outsiders also have been unable to sustain idealistic faith in the revolution and have betrayed its principles and aims. Laura pays only lip service to the revolution that rejects religion and extols the machine (she sneaks into churches, and she buys hand-made lace). Her betrayal, however, goes beyond social politics. She also betrays herself and her femaleness. Having forsaken her essential role as woman and mother, she rejects all forms of love and instead smuggles drugs to men imprisoned in filthy jails. Eugenio, a prisoner to whom she brought drugs, dies by taking the tablets all at once, and it is her indirect responsibility for his death that leads to her shock of recognition in a dream in which the dead Eugenio calls her "murderer." Katherine Anne incorporated in the character of Laura her personal failures of love and maternity, her delivery of drugs to Retinger in Laredo, her feeling of responsibility for the deaths of five counter-revolutionaries in 1921, and her self-assessment in Salem in 1927. The central idea of the story, she said, was "self-delusion."

On 1 February Harcourt, Brace sent her a contract and an advance of $100 for a book whose title story would be "Flowering Judas." Their faith in her was reinforced a month later when they offered her another contract, for the publication of her novel "Thieves Market," with an advance of $500. She decided to return to Mexico in the spring to complete the work. In addition to Harcourt, Brace's advances, to be paid in monthly installments of $100, Liveright, with her assurance that "Cotton Mather" was resurrected, grudgingly gave her $180 and promised to send more the first of June. Becky again helped by soliciting for her friend guaranteed income that would free her up for her important writing.

CHAPTER FIFTEEN

Relinquishing Mexico

Spring 1930–August 1931

I don't feel strange or exiled anywhere, and I began something here years ago that very evidently must be finished, in the long, laborious unbreakable line of personal experience that begins God knows where and ends only when the last vestiges of your existence have been demolished.

On board the SS *Havana* bound for Vera Cruz, Katherine Anne wrote Josie Herbst, "With the band playing, and dancing going on on deck, and the soft wind blowing, and stars, and all that, here am I, in a pinkish, streamerish sort of dress, and my green shawl, feeling almost human after four days and nights of ocean travel, regular food, and hours of idling in a deck chair." But she also was carrying with her a sudden, suicidal depression. Shortly before she left, she had told Gay, "It is not death that troubles me, but the boresome process of disintegration, and I don't mean to go through with it past a certain point."

After stepping ashore at Vera Cruz, she went on to Mexico City by train and from there to Xochimilco to stay for a few weeks with Dorothy Day, who was living there with her daughter, Tamar, in a small thatched hut. Dorothy, a radical feminist writer when Katherine Anne knew her earlier in Greenwich Village, was now a devout Catholic activist working among the poor in Mexico. In 1921 and 1922 Katherine Anne had idealized the flower-laden village of Xochimilco and the Indians who lived there. With its floating gardens and canals it had been a favorite excursion for her and her friends and the setting of a romantic episode with Joseph Retinger. In 1930, however, she found the reality far different from a pleasurable day trip and her earlier fantasies. Dorothy's hut was too small for the three of them, and the single glassless window had to be barricaded at night, as Dorothy explained, "to keep out drunken Indians." Nearly as vexing to

Katherine Anne as the thought of violent marauders were Dorothy's placing statues of Mary and Joseph beside her bed, praying for protection, and attempting to reunite her with her discarded Roman Catholic faith.

Katherine Anne passed her fortieth birthday, 15 May, in Xochimilco with Dorothy and Tamar. None of her letters in May and June, however, mentioned her birthday at all. The number forty, that conventional symbol of the dividing line between youth and middle-age, depressed her, along with everything else. She later gave her thoughts to the *Ship of Fools* character Mary Treadwell, who is also celebrating a "forties" birthday: "She was feeling her age . . . as a downright affront to her aesthetic sense. All the forties were dull-sounding numbers, . . . hopelessly middle-aged, so much too late to die young, so much too early to think of death at all." Katherine Anne's depression was intensified by memories of the country "where so much had happened" to her, as she told Delafield a few weeks after her arrival, revealing a fear that her return to Mexico "might have been a mistake."

Everything that dismayed her in Mexico in 1930 was not personal. Dramatic changes and losses since 1923 were obvious in the new cast of characters on the political stage. Not only had her one-time lover Felipe Carrillo Puerto been lined up against a wall and shot by counter-revolutionaries, but Samuel Yúdico, the primary model for Braggioni in "Flowering Judas," had died mysteriously in 1928, the same year Obregón, having been elected president of Mexico a second time, was assassinated before he could take office. Plutarco Calles, who had succeeded Obregón as president in 1924, Katherine Anne now regarded as a dangerous thug, and she considered Luis Morones, for whom she once did courier work, equally corrupt. Vasconcelos, the political idealist she had most admired in Obregón's first cabinet, had retreated from the capital powerless after a failed run for the presidency. Communists and socialists, potent philosophical forces in Obregón's rise to power and in the artistic renaissance, were weakened as an influential faction and hardly tolerated in the quarters that had control in 1930. The artistic revolution itself had moved from an idealizing of Mexico's pre-Columbian past to bold political propaganda and had shifted still again when Diego Rivera accepted a twelve thousand dollar commission from the U.S. ambassador to Mexico, Dwight W. Morrow, to decorate, as a gift to the people of the state of Morelos from the people of the United States, a gallery in the Palace of Cortés in Cuernavaca. Katherine Anne thought Rivera's capitulation consistent with the rampant commercialization of Mexican art and regarded him in 1930 as the symbol of one more strand of Mexico's corruption.

At the end of May she rented an old-fashioned townhouse at Calle Ernesto Pugibet 78, near the Alameda Park in Mexico City. On the second floor, off a leafy, covered balcony along a little courtyard, she had two bedrooms, a workroom, a kitchen, and a bathroom. "It is just precisely the right thing for me," she wrote Gay. She also hired a maid, a cheerful Aztec woman named Eufemia, who arrived each morning with a bunch of flowers. All that was missing from such a domestic scene was a man, and by the end of June she had found one.

He was twenty-six-year-old Eugene Dove Pressly, a native of Pennsylvania, and more recently a resident of Denver. He had never been married, and since 1928 he had been an employee of the Institute of Current World Affairs in Mexico City. He was short and sturdy without being fat (5 feet, 4 inches, 150 pounds), blue-eyed and brown-haired. Photographs Katherine Anne took of him reveal unsophisticated good looks and an apparent enjoyment of posing in the nude. He adored Katherine Anne from the moment he met her.

Despite having a man in love with her, her depression lingered, and she tried to counter it with frenzied socializing. She took day trips with Gene to Indian villages and spa towns; she went to parties at the apartment of Frances (Paca) Toor, editor of the English-language magazine *Mexican Folkways*; she dropped in at Fred Davis's Sonora News Company above Sanborns House of Tiles restaurant; she linked up with Mary Doherty and other friends at Mexico City cafés; she made trips to Taxco, a beautiful old mountain town halfway between Mexico City and Acapulco, to visit William Spratling, an American from New Orleans who had invigorated Taxco's silver industry, and Moisés Sáenz, an Obregón ally who now was secretary of public welfare; she went to Cuernavaca to see Diego's murals; she even showed up at afternoon teas and parties in the Anglo-American community. She entertained a spate of visitors—Liza Dallett, Malcolm and Peggy Cowley, Achilles Holt, Lola Ridge—and was often in the company of painters Juan O'Gorman and Pablo O'Higgins (who gave her six weeks of piano lessons), the poet Blanca Luz, and the photographer Manuel Alvarez Bravo, who took a portrait of her that disclosed her deep sadness. As a result of her intense social life Katherine Anne was soon laid up with exhaustion and a throat infection.

In her sickbed she seemed hardly aware of the 4 September publication of *Flowering Judas*. Despite its slender size and its limited edition of only six hundred copies, *Flowering Judas* and its enthusiastic reviews propelled her onto the American literary scene and permanently fixed her critical position in modern literature. Margaret Cheney Dawson's review in the *New York Herald Tribune* was typical of the acclaim: "It is a dramatic moment in the life of a patient reader," Dawson wrote, "when, after all efforts to be judicial, all carefully balanced yeas and nays, a book presents itself that compels a loud, hearty, unqualified *yes. Flowering Judas* is such a book."

Although Katherine Anne acknowledged the "lovely reviews" of her book, the praise did not lessen her depression and anxiety. She concluded, "This is all very well, but I must do better than this." She was concerned about the swift approach of the December deadline for "Thieves Market" without the manuscript anywhere near completion.

In her frustration and misery, with the exception of Mary and Gene, hardly anyone escaped her wrath and criticism. She lumped her friend Carleton Beals with "all the other God-awful mediocrities who swarm over the place eating the heart out of it like white ants," and at a party she kicked him in the shins, something she said she had been longing to do for eight years. She castigated Best Maugard for being "one of the main springs of the Tourists Board," and she criticized Frank Tannenbaum, with whom she had worked on the Mexico number of *Survey Graphic*, for his "wooden style" of writing. Paca Toor she despised, she said, and she took to task Pablo O'Higgins, who had decided "that all art was mere childishness in the face of the great oncoming wave of world change." She railed to Caroline Gordon about Catholic converts such as Dorothy Day but also lapsed Catholics, whom she called "pathological cases" who "cut away from their mother and then fester at the navel." She complained about Jews, such as Matthew Josephson, who "run from life as if Life were the Devil with horns and cloven hoofs." She attacked Moisés Sáenz for bringing "limp-haired boys" to his Taxco villa and Bill Spratling for "sleeping with his mozo."

The praise and affection she heaped upon her family during her moments of optimism and self-satisfaction had dissolved into the scorn and reproach of her wretchedness. In a mid-October letter to Gay, she bitterly recalled their childhood as "horrible," "hopeless," indecent, and uncivilized, and she also dredged up long-suppressed memories of John Koontz. "Doesn't J. H. live around there somewhere?" she asked Gay. "Or is the little bastard dead?" Declaring that he should have been killed for the crimes he committed against her, she raged, "I think if I saw him I should be tempted to do it even now. But far from having rotted away, as he should have, I suppose he is fat as a pig in his wallow." She blamed her family for many of her difficulties. "I don't really think any of you are completely indifferent," she wrote, "but I know well . . . if I had depended on the love of any of you I should have been good and dead by now."

As an escape from her depression she fantasized about a cabin she might build for herself on Caroline and Allen's property in Tennessee. She wove images in her mind that evoked all the ideal places she remembered or imagined, Indian Creek, her grandmother's Hays County farm, and Amecameca (Xochimilco was no longer in the mix), and she instructed Caroline how to prepare the landscape where the cabin would sit: "Plant a cape jessamine on the sunny side. Crape myrtle and cypress and pomegranate, red cabbage roses and arbor vitae, cedar and dogwood and I think I am leaving the yard and running wild in the woods, for I never saw dogwood in a garden—wild roses on the fence, and climbing roses all over the roof—heavens, what a place." By the end of January she had composed a song about her dream cabin:

> *There's a cabin on the river*
> *In Tennesseeeeeeeee*
> *Waiting for Meeeee!*

Because she was painfully aware that she was forty years old and had neglected her work for a long time, such gaiety was quickly displaced with even deeper despondency: "I have a new idea of Hell," she told Caroline in the same breath. "Suppose for eternity you were permitted to see your life unrolled like a scroll, and at every turning point you could then see clearly precisely where your mistakes were made, and at the same time know the thing—some very simple, absolutely simple, thing you should have done, and the mistake need not have been made, and you realize that the whole mess was quite unnecessary. I'm tied up in knots and can't write a line."

Then, in the middle of February, for reasons inexplicable, as Katherine Anne told Malcolm Cowley, she suddenly saw the leading thread of her novel, and her mood lifted. She changed the title from "Thieves Market" to "Historical Present" and envisioned it as "twelve or so interconnected stories in the style of 'Flowering Judas.'" Newly inspired to get to work and escape the temptations of Mexico City café society, she moved with Mary and Gene to a country villa in Mixcoac that had large common rooms and galleries, private bedrooms and studios for each of them, and rooms for servants.

In March she received word that she had been awarded a Guggenheim Fellowship with a year's stipend of two thousand dollars. Convincing herself that she would write better in Europe, she suspended work on the novel and resumed the madcap social whirl with dinners and parties at Mixcoac and a stream of visitors. She later wished, however, that one of her visitors in the spring of 1931 had never crossed her doorstep. Hart Crane arrived in Mexico on 11 April with a Guggenheim, having told friends that he intended to stay for a week "with my old and wonderful friend, Katherine Anne Porter." The visit that began as a friendly reunion grew intolerable to Katherine Anne as it lengthened beyond two weeks. She resented his nightly drunkenness and bringing strangers into the house at all hours of the night. At the end of April, at her suggestion, he moved into a house around the corner from hers. Katherine Anne thought the arrangement had been agreed to amiably and that they might still salvage the friendship. It was irrevocably destroyed a few weeks later when she and Gene were delayed in reaching his house for dinner and Hart, frustrated, went into the city to drink through the evening. Retuning home in a taxi, he passed Katherine Anne's gate and shouted, "Katherine Anne, you're a whore." The next morning he sent a note of apology blaming his behavior on the tequila. "I have borne to the limit of my patience with brutal behavior," she wrote in reply. "You must either learn to stand on your own feet as a responsible adult, or expect to be treated as a fool . . . To me [your tantrums] do not add the least value to your poetry, and take away my last shadow of a wish to ever see you again." Hart left Mexico City the first week in July when his father died in the United States. By the time he returned, Katherine Anne was gone, and a year later he committed suicide by jumping from a ship returning to New York from Mexico. He came to represent to her the tragedy of a gift lost to debauchery.

In the middle of the summer, the Russian film director Sergei Eisenstein invited Katherine Anne to visit the Hacienda Tetlapayac, a pulque plantation owned by the Saldívar family, where the Russian crew was filming scenes for *Que Viva Mexico!* During her three-day visit she took notes for an article about the Russian director and the complicated production of his Mexican film exploring the changing of orders in Mexico. She never anticipated, however, an extraordinary event that coincided with her visit. Felix Balderas, one of the young Indian actors, killed his sister and was hunted down in the maguey fields by another young actor. Katherine Anne was fascinated and horrified by the various reactions to the perhaps-not-accidental killing: She was not insensible to the irony that the real event was a replication of a fictional scene being filmed. She would make the killing the focal point in the article ("Hacienda") and short novel (*Hacienda*) that eventually resulted from the visit, both pieces reflecting her view of Mexico in 1931 as a land of death and corruption and vanished promise.

After she returned from the hacienda Katherine Anne had little more than a month to complete her "house wrecking," as she called it, and get to Vera Cruz in time to board the North German Lloyd ship the *Werra*, bound for Bremen. She was not departing with much cheer, however. She told Harrison, "I leave a troubled land and go to one more troubled."

CHAPTER SIXTEEN

The German Interval

August 1931–January 1932

Being on that ship was a godsent experience.

I felt the very earth of Europe shake under my feet when I stepped ashore . . . I already knew about Mussolini, and a little but not enough about Hitler.

Katherine Anne had chosen a daylight trip to Vera Cruz in order for her and Gene to have a last look at the magnificent mountains along the railway route that wound through lush ravines and skirted rocky cliffs. But fog obscured their view of the valleys, and a violent, nerve-shattering electrical storm marked their departure-eve night in Vera Cruz. The disagreeable weather, symbolic, she thought, of her past sixteen months in Mexico, abated only when she and Gene at last embarked with the other passengers on 22 August and the *Werra* slid out of the harbor and headed to the open sea.

Six days into the voyage Katherine Anne began a letter to Caroline Gordon that was an informal travel diary. Written to amuse Caroline and Allen, it also was to be, Katherine Anne said, something "to remember my first Atlantic crossing by," and she asked Caroline to save it for her. Among her fellow second-class passengers who caught her attention were a young, conservative oculist from Texas who talked about "dirty Bolsheviks"; an overweight Swiss girl, whose father had worked for thirty years as a mining engineer in Torreón; a Spanish Zarzuela company (a musical comedy troupe), whose hopes for success in Cuba and Mexico had been dashed; a blissful, newly married couple; a dying man who sat curled among pillows in a chair; a young mother with her newborn son; a little hunchback man with downy, dry hair and a shriveled face who wore gaily-colored neckties; medical students going to Gijon to finish their education; and a beautiful fifty-year-old

Cuban woman who was insane. At Havana 876 third-class (steerage) passengers embarked, all of them Spaniards from the Canaries and ports of Spain who were being expelled from Cuba because there was no work for them.

All of the crew and most of the first-class passengers were Germans. "Herr Doktors and Herr Professors and Herr Engineers and all that," she wrote, "with such typically German Frauen—vast, bulky, inert, with handsome heads and elephant legs, who drink beer all day long, swallowing a steinful in two drinks, smacking their lips and saying 'Ja, Ja!'" She took note especially of the ship's physician, Dr. Sacher, an old Heidelberg student with kind eyes and two saber scars across his cheek and forehead. Katherine Anne had gone to him for a heat rash, and after giving her a lotion he told her cheerful little anecdotes about his wife and confided that he himself had a bad heart.

All the persons Katherine Anne described in the letter would appear in some form in her novel *Ship of Fools*. She was also setting down ideas that would become themes and subjects in the novel. All around her she saw the cruelties and irrationality of chauvinism and the baleful aftereffects of the World War and the 1918 Armistice. She commented on the passengers' alienation from one another ("half of us do not salute the other half . . . not from rancor but from indifference"), homelessness ("A feeling that I was rather far from home came over me . . . and hope I might cry with joy to see some one place again."), and the indefiniteness of life's destination ("life on this ship is very uncertain, full of rumors, alarms, and excursions"). She saw the ship as a microcosm ("We have everything on board . . . this prelude is preparing me for life in an inn"), but at the time she had no inkling that she was making notes for a long novel. She told Caroline that she might have "a very short short-story" based on "this long bee-line across the water."

Katherine Anne and Gene had chosen the German ship because it was cheap, not because they expected to stay on it all the way to Germany. But when they were unable to get a French visa along the way, they had no choice but remain on board the *Werra* until it reached its termination point at Bremen on 19 September. Some junior officers recommended a cheap hotel nearby and took them to the fifteenth-century Am Markt Ratskeller to drink Rhine wine and eat pig's knuckles and sauerkraut.

The next day Katherine Anne and Gene went by train to Berlin and registered at the Thüringer Hof, a small hotel on Hedemanstrasse.

For the equivalent of six dollars a week they were to have two rooms with breakfast and maid service. And they had steam heat. "Praise God," she said, for the nights were already chilly. In the succeeding days, choosing among the city's many cafés, they dined cheaply on great mounds of meat, potatoes, and vegetable goulash. "I foresee gout to the death," she told Caroline, "but I don't know yet what to do about it."

Katherine Anne and Gene spent the remaining days of September and all of October anticipating a parting. Their money, including her most recent Guggenheim installment, was rapidly depleting, despite the low prices. Gene, after looking futilely around Berlin for work, concluded that his best chance for employment lay in Madrid, where he would be fluent in the language. Katherine Anne promised to join him in Spain when he was set up with a secure job and an adequate apartment. In the meantime, they looked for a cheaper pension where she might comfortably live alone. In one boardinghouse they were inspecting, Gene touched a cheap souvenir that crumbled under his touch. Katherine Anne was embarrassed and cried out, "Why must you touch things? Why must you always touch and destroy things?" The incident was indicative of the strain in their relationship and her increasing restlessness and boredom with him.

Analyzing what she had come to see as the liaison's failure, she drafted a lyrical poem she titled "Bouquet for October," the subject of which was an "out of season" love affair between spring-born lovers (Gene's birthday was also in May) who, with the taste of sunny Mexico still in their teeth, find themselves in unfamiliar and autumn-cold Berlin. In reality, the discord was the result of differences in their temperament and her dislike of forced domestic responsibility rather than their being dumped in an alien northern European city on the cusp of winter. Whatever the cause, she felt sad about the failure—again—of love, and she captured her deep disappointment in sharp images of approaching winter:

> We will walk in the Tiergarten: invisible
> To the little eyes buttoned up against the frail sunlight:
> Observe the dubious riches of decay, pity
> The bereaved branches, the exhausted leaves dropping
> Like tears which nobody notices.

It would appear in *Pagany* early in 1932.

The third week in October Katherine Anne and Gene found a boardinghouse for her into which she could move after he left. Owned by Rosa Reichl, a Viennese widow, the substantial, well-kept, three-story gray stone house, which had a courtyard and a small back garden, sat at 39 Bambergerstrasse, a spacious street in a neighborhood shaded by tall trees. For two rooms and morning coffee Katherine Anne would pay Frau Reichl thirty-three deutsche marks a month. The only disadvantage seemed to be the landlady's intrusive interest in her boarders, an interest that Katherine Anne feared would break into her solitude during working hours.

Katherine Anne's letter to Gene a few days after his departure revealed the stresses between them. She asked him to forget her bad behavior in recent days and blamed it on not being "altogether sane," assuring him it was not her "heart or spirit." After his train pulled out, she had gone to Zundt's for coffee, all the while, she told him, "bawling like a calf, because everything came out so badly for us."

The sadness she described to Gene was exaggerated and short-lived. With his absence came opportunities for socializing, and two days after he left, she had gone on a shopping spree, describing to him "a set of pinkish wool unnerware, a boosting-halter that would do your eyes good, two pairs of silk stockings, a black purse which I decorated with my big silver pin, a lumly pair of shoes, black with snakeskin, just what I wanted, four beautiful linen handkerchiefs, a pair of oh, God, how swell black gloves with white streaks on the cuffs, in short went quite mad, forgot to eat all day long." Gene must have been shocked and dismayed with her extravagance. Although he had quickly found work in Madrid as a translator at the American embassy for 850 peseta a month (about two hundred dollars), the job was to last only three months.

Through contacts provided by Malcolm Cowley, Josie Herbst, and other friends, Katherine Anne soon met Johannes Becher, the Communist poet and social critic, and Herbert Kline, a young Communist sympathizer and reporter for the *Chicago Tribune*, who had been accompanied to Berlin by his mother, Hermene Kline, to await the arrival of his fiancée for an early 1932 wedding. Full of youthful intellectual energy that Katherine Anne found entertaining, he was at the threshold of an award-winning career, combining interests in leftist politics, journalism, filmmaking, and the other arts.

On a mid-November evening Katherine Anne and the Klines went to a cabaret owned by some friends of theirs. "You will be pleased to learn," she told Gene, "that I was urged and urged to give my version of the rumba, and I refrained." But "all this bores me utterly to death," she declared, "I don't care if I never go to another cabaret."

She told Peggy Cowley, however, a version that rang more true: "Went out with some comrades to a pleasant den where solemn young men roamed around playing piano accordions, young actors rose and chanted mean songs agin the government, and towards the knee of the evening I rose and did my version of the Rumba, which is all the rage here, to the strains of the Peanut Vender . . . . . A very attractive young man with a nervous face tied up in interesting bowknots attached himself to me at once, and insisted on taking me home." She saw the same young man several nights later at yet another party. Drinking throughout that evening, he attached himself to her until she saw "that the notion had again got hold of him." She left early, she said, and with "a safe, sound and sober escort" (unnamed).

Through Herbert Kline, Katherine Anne met Sigrid Schultz, chief correspondent of the *Chicago Tribune* for Germany and eastern Europe. Sigrid's fashionable West Berlin apartment had become the scene of important luncheons, dinner parties, and receptions attended by a broad range of diplomats, members of European nobility, and high-ranking politicians, including the Nazi leaders. Shortly after Gene left, Sigrid invited Hermann Göring, Adolf Hitler, Joseph Göbbels, and Katherine Anne to the same dinner. Katherine Anne recalled being "morbidly anxious" to see the Nazis and was dismayed to observe when she arrived that they were not there. Hitler and Goebbels did not appear, but Göring showed up, accompanied by his adjutant, Erhard Milch.

Göring was a rising star in the Nazi Party and a trusted advisor to Hitler, later establishing the Gestapo and concentration camps for the "corrective treatment" of difficult opponents. He eventually fell out of favor with the other Nazi leaders, and in the final days of the war Hitler was forced to dislodge him from power. He committed suicide rather than face the execution ordered by the International Military Tribunal at Nürnberg. At the time of Katherine Anne's introduction to him, he was a recent widower, an art collector, a man of formidable intellectual gifts and self-indulgence, and a drug addict. But with charisma and flamboyance, he also was the most popular of the Nazi leaders with both the German people and foreign diplomats.

After dinner Sigrid's guests moved into her large parlor for schnapps, and Katherine Anne found herself sitting beside Göring on a couch near the fireplace. Speaking fluent English, he told her she was too beautiful and sensitive to be wandering around the world alone, and he reminded her that she must not forget to be a woman while she was being a writer. She replied that her whole trouble was being "too much a woman." He liked her response so much, she reported to Josie, that he kissed her heartily, "smack, smack."

She directed the conversation to politics, and he explained to her how the Nazis were going to remove from power every Jew in Germany. "We've got to restore that good clean German blood," he said, foretelling, she later thought, the exterminations that would be carried out. She argued with him, pointing out that nobody had pure blood by that time. They also disagreed about women's role in society after he remarked that "the only kind of woman who's important is a *geheiratete Frau*, a married woman." Refusing to fall into the "trap of feminine hysteria," she bore his harangue about Jews, women, and Americans, whom he considered too softly sentimental. She thought him in general to be "in the kind of candid relaxed mood which comes on when a man is tired and having a few drinks after a good meal." She believed he considered her, as a woman, no threat and "was probably playing it straight" with her.

When she finally announced that she must go, he quickly offered to drive her home, and she accepted the courtesy. Shortly after she got into the long, chauffeured limousine with him and Milch, he put his arm around her shoulder and asked her to stop by his favorite *Biergarten* for a little drink. She recalled that while she ordinarily would not claim to be *naturally* discreet, prudence having been so thrashed into her as a child that her instinct was to stay away from this strange and possibly dangerous man, an inner voice was saying, *"Why, hell yes—why not?—it might be interesting."* Ten minutes later they were seated at a cloth-covered table near a dime-sized dance floor and a four-piece band in Otto's Hofbräuhaus. When he took her home, he tried (futilely, she said) to kiss her, and he made an effort to see her again. Among Katherine Anne's papers is a phone message that her fellow boarder Herr Bussen had taken and tried to translate into English:

> Mr. Von Gehring had belled you now. He would against bell you, this afternoon between three and four a clock.
>
> Bussen

Prudence apparently asserted itself, and Katherine Anne avoided Göring for the rest of her stay in Berlin.

Throughout November and December Katherine Anne worked productively despite her flourishing social life and Rosa's hovering. She finished her article "Hacienda" and her story "The Cracked Looking-Glass," which she had begun the fall of 1926 while she was recovering from the surgical removal of her ovaries. "Hacienda" was accepted by the *Virginia Quarterly Review,* and "The Cracked Looking-Glass" was accepted by Alfred Dashiell for the spring issue of *Scribner's Magazine.*

"The Cracked Looking-Glass" emerged from a snippet of gossip Katherine Anne had heard in Connecticut about an Irish woman who scandalized her rural neighbors by keeping young boys as boarders. In Katherine Anne's hands it became a complex and many-layered story centering on Rosaleen, a romantic and superstitious woman married to a much older, practical man. With absolute faith in her dreams about lost youth, lost loves, and lost children, she also finds consolation in the wild and improbable tales she tells and the young men she befriends, each of whom, as both quasi-lover and surrogate-child, momentarily replaces in her fantasies her aged, ill husband and her nonexistent, absent, or dead children. Rosaleen's suffering and the ways she deals with it are Katherine Anne's own, and the May–December marriage in the story is a mirror reflection of Katherine Anne's chain of liaisons with much younger men, Gene Pressly being only the most recent and thus far the youngest.

The first week of December Paul O'Higgins called on her on his way to Moscow, where he had a year's fellowship from the Soviet government. He arrived dead broke, pale, and thin after a terrible trip in steerage on a French liner. To finance the rest of his trip, he brought with him paintings by Diego Rivera and photographs by Tina Modotti that he hoped to sell. Katherine Anne introduced him to Kline, and the three of them buzzed around Berlin "like drunken bumble bees" trying to dispose of "one hundred marks worth of Diego and Tina." They had no luck, but German Communist Party members raised enough in loans to cover O'Higgins's train fare to Russia, with the guarantee that Katherine Anne and Kline would sell the art after his departure and pay them back.

They were not able to sell anything at all because everybody else seemed to be hard pressed in the worldwide economic depression. Katherine Anne had not managed her expenses well, and because Gene's temporary job at the embassy would end in January, they were increasingly concerned about money. Letters going back and forth between them during November and December included discussions of alternative sources of income. They considered his translating a Spanish novel that she would then rewrite for style. They even talked of trying to set up a press of their own, like Leonard and Virginia Woolf's Hogarth, arguing prematurely over what they should call it. (He suggested "The Salamandra," and she countered with "Freehold" and "Amparo," a name she ultimately would give only to a dancer-prostitute in *Ship of Fools*.) These were fantasies, however, and she knew that the most realistic way to generate income would be to complete "Historical Present" and "The Devil and Cotton Mather." For a brief period she declared that she was going to force herself to stay in Berlin until she finished those two books at least.

Her optimism that resulted from finishing two stories and meeting interesting people started dwindling. After fighting off a sore throat for a few days, she felt a violent physical chill and realized it was the onset of her recurring bronchial ailment. A doctor who called on her at Rosa's diagnosed a lung infection and prescribed a regimen of rest and cream to help her further resist the devastating effects of the frigid and damp Berlin winter.

Between poor health and financial concerns, she had reason enough to feel despondent, but in Europe in 1931 there were additional causes for anxiety and depression. She encountered a company of soldiers on Unter der Linden "marching, almost walking, slowly and evenly under the morning sunlight. But striding easily as one man, matched in height, elegant in their long field gray well fitted coats, their formal, handsome steel helmets, the faces grim and bored and stiff with the prolonged endurance of their terrible discipline: color bad, eyes withdrawn and moveless; the pale small eyes that make all these faces seem alike."

She was frightened by Nazism, but she had no faith in any political system, including Communism, to solve the world's problems. She had freely expressed her political views to O'Higgins, with whom she had sat in a Berlin café drinking beer and contrasting her plan of action in the present circumstances with his. "I'm going to get up on a soap box and tell everybody how sick it is and what tommyrot it is until they get so irritated they lock me up. Then I'm going to write pieces about [it]," she said. O'Higgins responded, "I'm going to fight for Russia." Both of them had lamented the international hatreds, but while she saw no real solution, he was convinced that Russian Communism (she called it "the famous Russian fanaticism") could save the world. Her sentiments were already on private record in the satiric title she had chosen for the most personal of her novels-in-progress—"Many Redeemers."

In December she became gradually more depressed by the dreary, cold days and freezing nights, her lingering illnesses, the continual worries about money, and more and more evidence of eventual world war. Joining Gene suddenly made more sense to her than remaining in Germany through the winter. She planned to stop over in Paris only a few days to see old friends before going on to Madrid. She thought she might marry Gene Pressly and thus find stability. When she was approached in the city by a beautiful gypsy fortune-teller who suggested that her life was taking a positive turn, she felt as though her decision to go to Spain had been mysteriously validated.

The last week she was in Berlin, however, she received an unexpected visitor. The expatriate American writer Robert McAlmon, who had been roaming around southern France and Germany since leaving Paris in the spring, showed up at Rosa Reichl's after Kay Boyle sent him Katherine Anne's address. Somewhere along the way, he had been joined by William Harlan Hale, a twenty-one-year-old Yale graduate who was researching a book on Hitler's rise to power. Hale was young, handsome, intellectual, and literate, just the kind of man Katherine Anne could not resist. He was equally attracted to her, and for a few days in Berlin they had long conversations over dinner and wine, each apparently heady with the excitement of new romance. But the encounter wasn't altogether delightful for her. She was thrown back into uncertainty about her future with Gene, and her last letters from Berlin show a renewed anxiety and depression. She ranted to Gay about their terrible childhood and their father's failure of responsibility. She also had a disturbing dream that she described to Gene in her last letter to him before she left Germany:

> Confused as the devil. But some kind of enormous silent crowd of people, gathered for some reunion, probably religious in character. I thought some man was either killed by another, or put to death legally; I don't know which: but the crowd were gathered around him, and I stood a great distance looking on but not seeing what was really happening. Then later I went to the place where he was, and there was a little lake, dark and sinister looking; at the bottom lay several bodies: two of them women clasping newly born babies. One of them was in a kind of current, and her arm waved back and forth in the water. The newly dead man

lay nearby with a heavy cross of flowers weighing him down. There were others, too, but I don't remember them. Then my sister Alice [*sic*] came up with another baby on her arm, and a very grave, censorious look on her face, such as I remember her to have, when she is really displeased with something . . . . . I don't know what she was angry about, but it seemed to be against me, and the baby she carried was mine. She put him down on the grass and we sat without talking. And I was happy about the baby. Nothing ever came to explain the meaning of the bodies lying in the lake, nor the living baby, nor my sister's presence, nor indeed, anything . . . . . It was all very sinister, mysterious and portentous, as dreams can be, and yet without meaning even as I dreamed it . . . . . You'll think I've turned a very Rosaleen on you, always telling my dreams. But usually I can't remember them, haven't for years, and when I do they interest me very much, because they're so damned queer.

She told him to keep her letters in which she recited her dreams, "because I want them for later use, maybe . . . . . and may no psychoanalyst ever see them!" While all the symbolism in the death-filled dream is not clear, some of the meaning is apparent, and perhaps was to her even as she was telling it. Her troubled relationship with her judgmental sister, Baby, is there, as is her regret for her dead children, a measure of the depths of the new phase of her depression and her yearning to be a young, fecund woman again.

She never expected to be leaving Berlin with such a mixture of regret and anticipation. Bill Hale and Bob McAlmon saw her off from Berlin's Bahnhof Zoologischer Garten with promises to meet again in Paris.

CHAPTER SEVENTEEN

Paris, Madrid, Basel

February–December 1932

I have a feeling of continuity, of things beautifully done for their own sakes, a strong live source of belief in life, that goes on and will allow me to go with it.

"If I went to Paris I am afraid I might be tempted to live there, just to stay there for good and all," Katherine Anne had written Gene from Berlin. It happened almost exactly that way, for even in cold, gray February Paris burst upon her psyche like fireworks. She exaggerated her illness and pled the necessity of resting in Paris longer than she had planned.

After registering at the Hotel Malherbe, 11 rue de Vaugirard, on the Left Bank, she announced her arrival to Eugene Jolas and his wife, Maria, and to Ford Madox Ford, who was living in an apartment a few buildings away with his newest and last love, the young painter Janice Biala. Those four showed Katherine Anne famous Paris attractions—the Cluny, Sainte Chapelle, Notre Dame, a Bal Musette—and presented her to English-speaking literary society in Paris. They called upon Sylvia Beach in her rue de l'Odeon bookshop and lending-library, Shakespeare and Company, which had been the center of expatriate life since its celebrated years in the 1920s, and they repeatedly made the rounds of favorite expatriate cafés and bars—the Dôme, the Select, Le Coupole, Jimmy's.

Paris, however, was still a stopover on her way to an appointment with Gene, and she regretfully left Paris and went on to Madrid. She had made up her mind to go through with the marriage, and she wrote Gay and the rest of the family the news of the betrothal: "For me, this is such a good thing, because I am tired of my peculiar situation of loneliness, with hundreds of acquaintances and dozens of men who are friendly and attentive but after all, nothing to me.

I want to get rid of the crowds and noise and uncertainty and fix my life in one place with one person that I love and who loves me . . . . . And here he is! Or rather, there he is, and I'm on my way to that man, lemme tell you!"

On 14 February, the day before her departure for Spain, she also wrote a long letter to Bill Hale announcing the imminence of the marriage, and this letter revealed her ambivalence. "Why are you not in Paris, or I in Berlin, or both of us in London . . . ?" she asked Hale. She compared the step she was about to take to putting on "the old familiar hair shirt" and sacrificing "Joy." She declared, however, that she meant "to stand by it" once it was done. She signed the letter wryly, "With my love."

Given her uncertainty and regret, there was little chance that the journey would be successful. To pass the time on the long train trip she took along the poems of John Skelton that included his lyrical laments at being banished from Paris. After a twelve-hour stop in the sparkling coastal resort Biarritz and a tumultuous ride through the rolling Basque country, she pulled into Madrid in a cold wind. She went with Gene to see the apartment he had rented, and then she took to bed in her hotel room, where she lay weeping for hours, she told Caroline and Allen, "and drying up my tears for the rest of my life. Why? because I had seen Paris and could not endure the thought of being anywhere else." After only two days in Madrid, she set out again for Paris accompanied by Gene, who made arrangements to do some State Department scrap work in France for two weeks. "Well, Miss Caroline," she wrote shortly after her return, "I am in Paris. Yes mam, I made it back."

To break the news to her family that she had cancelled the wedding in Spain, she chose to write to her brother, Paul. It was a long-delayed effort ("after all these centuries," she said) to re-establish a loving connection with him, but she was careful not to flaunt her independence and impropriety. She described plucking up her courage to tell her "young man" what she thought, and he, being "the nicest person" she has "ever known," accepted her decision and escorted her back to Paris. "I know now I'll never marry him nor anybody else unless I go suddenly mad," she said, "and I'll never live in Madrid so long as there is Paris."

Gene returned to Madrid the first week of March with the plan of trying to work out a transfer to the Paris Embassy so they could be together in the city she seemed unwilling to leave. She moved into the Hotel Savoy, at 30 rue de Vaugirard, next door to Ford and Janice at Number 32. For 1,250 francs a month she had partial board, maid service, and a top-floor room with steam heat, a fireplace, and a view. She found a virginal, a small piano, that she had someone drag up the stairs, and with her typewriter in place and all her papers strewn about, she resolved to dig in and do some writing.

Working each day on "Many Redeemers," she also had a paying project Ford brokered that pleased her. Aware of her passion for late medieval and Renaissance music and poetry, he had suggested she translate some old French songs that Harrison of Paris would probably publish. She made an agreement with the owners of the small press, Monroe Wheeler and Barbara Harrison, a shy heiress who was the daughter of the former governor of the Philippines in Woodrow Wilson's administration, to translate fifteen French popular songs of her own choosing and put them in verses to match their original melodies. She would be paid 3,000 francs upon delivery of the manuscript.

In April Gene was transferred to the Paris Embassy, and Katherine Anne sublet Ford and Janice's apartment while they went to the south of France. He arrived in a spring barely warming up after a very cold winter. "One day it showers and shines by turns every quarter of an hour," Katherine Anne wrote Janice, "then comes a long day of celestial blue and cool winds, and then, by God, a hail storm, and today high winds that shriek in the chimneys and drive rain and hail through the window cracks." The change of weather had a bad effect on her weak constitution, and soon she was battling bronchitis and a fear that tuberculosis had returned. She entered the American Hospital at Neuilly the last day of April. At nearly the same time, Gene accepted a position in the American Embassy in Basel, Switzerland, at an increase in salary. He left Paris the second week of May, and she was to follow him as soon as she was able to travel. Doctors at the American Hospital found no evidence of active tuberculosis and encouraged her move to the cool mountain air.

After her release from the hospital Katherine Anne settled up her Paris life. She went to teas and parties with Monroe Wheeler, who introduced her to the American writer Glenway Wescott, with whom she quickly became friends, and she spent several days at the estate of Barbara Harrison. She made last minute visits to her favorite art galleries. She also had a wild evening with Bill Hale that ended in the wee hours of the morning at her hotel with both of them, flushed with wine, singing the French songs she was collecting. She had no more hopes, imaginary or other, pinned on Hale, although she enjoyed play-ing a lovers' game with him. "Let's continue to be as gorgeously vague as we have been," she told him; "its more in character and therefore more entertaining." She expected to keep up a correspondence with him and looked forward to reading his soon-to-be-published book on Hitler and Goethe.

The first week of June Katherine Anne arrived in Basel laden with trunks full of clothes, manuscripts, and books. Gene had taken rooms for them in the Hotel Krafft, a small pension on the Klein-Basel bank of the Rhine River. Because Gene's daytime hours during the week were spent at his job, she had time to write and to explore the hilly old section of the city where narrow cobbled streets, crowded with small French-German tea shops, delicatessens, green grocers, boutiques, cafés, bookshops, and art galleries, wound to the fifteenth-century uni-versity. Most weekends they left the town to take excursions into nearby Germany. Their most satisfying jaunt was the two-hour train ride to the Black Forest and a walk into the deep woods. She described to Josie her and Gene's creeping into bushes to make love and drinking a lovely bottle of white wine afterward, a scene that probably was a romantic fiction but also captured her good mood in Switzerland.

Much of her lovely feeling emerged from satisfaction with her writ-ing and the energetic activity of her imagination. She wasn't at all inspired to return to either "Historical Present" or "Cotton Mather"—almost ready to give up the Mexican material entirely and bored out of her mind with Mather—but she was increasingly excited about "Many Redeemers," which was coming into focus and unrolling, especially the first book, "Legend and Memory." She added a scene about a Swedish hired man, a bounty hunter, and a Hays County murder that occurred when she was a very young child, the raw materials for *Noon Wine*. She also outlined a story about her near-death from influenza in Denver during the Great War, a beginning point of *Pale Horse, Pale Rider*, intended for "Book Two, Midway of This Mortal Life," an allu-sion to Dante's *The Divine Comedy*. In this distant European city she was looking more intently than she ever had into her own past, her family history, and her native region. The process had begun in Salem. It had matured, however, in Basel.

No places were more inspiring to her than the city's art museum and the library at the university, the primary center of sixteenth-century humanism when Erasmus lived in Basel. Through Erasmus, whose *In Praise of Folly* she had loved since adolescence, she was led to Ulrich von Hutten and his *Letters from Obscure Men* and to Sebastian Brant and his *Stultifera Navis,* which she read slowly in German as *Das Narrenschiff.* At the Kunstmuseum she rediscovered Holbein and Dürer and added Urs Graf to her list of favorite painters. She dated a letter she wrote in early November, "1932—or is it 1400? Who cares?" In this atmosphere she finished the French songbook and sent the manuscript to Wheeler and Harrison. The seventeen songs she selected—carols, ballads, complaints, legends, and brunettes— represented the twelfth through eighteenth centuries. Her preface and informative headnotes were flavored with style and wit.

Her mind was wandering in the fifteenth century until she received from Bill Hale a copy of his book, *Challenge to Defeat: Modern Man in Goethe's World and Spengler's Century,* that jolted her back to the twentieth century and the problems in it. Katherine Anne praised the first part of the book for its well-founded "bill of particulars against our present times," but she took issue with the thrust of his indictment of modern artists as too effetely out of touch with their societies: "I do not believe in the artist as prophet. The prophetic gift is an accident. Goethe possessed it. Dante did not. What rule can you make out of that? It is . . . the artist's business . . . to be as good and as serious an artist as his capacities will allow, and leave judgments to the future. He might as well. He can do nothing else. Dante's austere and passionate theology is farther from the spirit of this day than are the 'personal' and 'romantic' poetry of Catullus . . . . . but Dante's poetry is greater than the poetry of Catullus, is still as living, and full of meaning as the sculptures on the portals of Sainte Chapelle, and for the same reasons." She objected to Hale's failure to set forth a plan of action against the impending world disaster. "We must fight the battle as it comes with all the strategy we have," she told him. Her critique underscored the wide gap between their ages and experiences. It was the last letter she ever would write him.

When Gene was sent to Geneva in November for some secretarial work at the International Peace Conference, she chose to stay behind in Basel to work on his rough translation of José Joaquín Fernández de Lizardi's *El Periquillo Sarniento* (The Itching Parrot), an early nineteenth-century work rich in the traditions of Laurence Sterne and political satire. But she couldn't get excited about this pot-boiler Ford had suggested, and she wished they did not have ongoing money worries. "Go burn a candle that you shall make six thousand a year and I shall write a prize novel," she told Gene.

She began to complain about Switzerland, the "muggy piety" of a monastery she visited, the encroachment of early winter. She yearned for what she didn't have (warmth, peace of mind, the company of Gene), fantasized about ideal places, and daydreamed about happy circumstances. Gene, who appreciated women's fashion, mentioned a smoke-colored chiffon dress a woman wore at an embassy event. "Oh, how I love smoke color," Katherine Anne wrote him, "and how purty it is on me. I should like a smoke colored chiffon dress, very simple and long and all line, no gewgaws, with thin silver pins in my hair and a darker smoke colored wrap collared with deep taupe-colored fur. With this I should wear satin slippers and stockings to match, but the slippers would have silver heels. So there now. And a string of emeralds around my neck while we're about it. And long smoke colored gloves in whatever material they're wearing em in now." She consoled herself with a substitute: alone in her room she wore with her yellow nightgown a warm but beautiful shawl Gene had bought for her in Paris, and she sprayed herself generously with the Molinard perfume he had given her.

At the end of November Gene accepted a post, as clerk to an under-secretary in the Paris Embassy, that alleviated money worries. Katherine Anne's spirits took wing. She wrote to Madame at the Hotel Malherbe to reserve rooms, got together all her "personal scraps" (more books and papers than clothes, she pointed out to Gene), and packed a large piece of luggage she bought cheaply at a second-hand shop near the cathedral. She tried to work on the middle section of "Many Redeemers," which she was calling "that book of Amy" (pointing to the segment's ultimate resolution as *Old Mortality*), but she no longer felt the pressure to work on the unexciting Lizardi translation. "You may gather I'm not working on Lizardi," she wrote Gene. "I'm not, honey. I'm just too excited and flurried and nitwitted for any use . . . . . Think of it, day after tomorrow is the last day of this hellish, this unpardonable month! Expect me to work? You're nerts, Mr. Pressly. A kiss on your sweet nose and eyes. I love you, you angel. Good night."

By 2 December she was in Paris, again.

CHAPTER EIGHTEEN

Paris

December 1932–January 1936

*I never saw such rainbows as I saw over the city of Paris . . . If every
soul left it one day and grass grew in the pavements, it would still
be Paris to me, I'd want to live there. I'd love to have Paris all to
myself for even one day.*

In the early months of 1933, at the lowest point of the Great Depression, the dollar, which had been so strong against the franc through the 1920s, was steadily falling. The worsening economy ultimately was the biggest reason Katherine Anne changed her mind again about marrying Gene Pressly. She called it the "well-known economic determinism," concluding that a rationally decided marriage, an "arrangement," she said, was the best kind.

Katherine Anne and Gene were married in Paris on 11 March in a civil ceremony conducted by the mayor and attended by Ford, Janice, and Ford's young daughter, Julie, who presented to Katherine Anne a ribbon-tied bouquet of heather for luck. After the wedding, the party retired to the Deux Magots to drink champagne. Sylvia Beach and her companion, Adrienne Monnier, joined them and added their signatures to the certificate. That evening Ford and Janice held a reception for about twenty-five people at their apartment; the guests danced in the courtyard until three in the morning.

Katherine Anne explained to Robert McAlmon what she wanted and expected from this marriage: "I'm very settled and happy about the marriage, dear Bob, it really gives some kind of solidity and form to my daily living that I seem badly to need . . . I like having a sense of responsibility towards some one else, it keeps me from the danger of coiling in upon my own vitals like a snail . . . Chronology has something to do with it, too: I am at that time of life when most conscious people make a final decision, a choice of some sort. If ever one is to settle a way of life, one does at my age. I shall be thirty nine [*sic*] years old next May."

The first of April Katherine Anne and Gene moved from the Hotel Malherbe to a seventh-floor flat at 166 Boulevard Montparnasse, across from the Closerie des Lilas, near the Luxembourg Gardens in one direction and the cafés Dome, Select, and Rotonde in the other. Although the apartment, which they rented for five hundred francs a month, was tiny, it allowed her to sink contentedly into the domestic routine that had appealed to her for a long time. Setting her mind to actually becoming the "famous cook" she had told Harrison in 1927 that she was, she shopped the markets daily for fish and fowl, inexpensive but good cuts of meat, and fresh fruit and vegetables. She baked her own bread rather than buy it at a *patisserie*. Although she sometimes brought home good *vin ordinaire* from a nearby Nicholas wine shop, she was learning about excellent wine from Monroe Wheeler, Barbara Harrison, and Glenway Wescott. Her newest culinary confidant was Janice Biala, a talented cook, and their correspondence throughout the Paris years was full of food talk. From Toulon, Janice sent her sausages, cherry preserves, lemon leaves for tea, and anchovies (two of them "made their debut on Russian eggs," Katherine Anne wrote in thanks). Her cooking had a dash of Southern style to it, and her touch was as light as Cat Porter's.

She wanted still more expertise, however, and she turned to Le Cordon Bleu cooking school. For three francs she could buy the school's monthly magazine, *Le Cordon Bleu Revue Illustrée de Cuisine Pratique*, which included recipes and articles on food and also a detailed schedule of the weekday classes offered at the school's two sites, one at 129 Faubourg Saint-Honoré and one at 8 rue Léon Delhomme. She could telephone ahead to reserve one of the open places in the kitchen-classroom and for a fee of a few francs, in addition to the cost of the ingredients, attend and participate in the day's cooking lesson designated either haute or bourgeoise.

Katherine Anne described a class in which she made a hearty ragout that she carefully carried home on the metro to share with Gene, and another in which she learned to roast a pig. The aroma of the ragout had so tantalized her companions on the subway that she was obliged to constantly lift the lid and let them sniff the well-seasoned steam. She remembered arriving at another class and being greeted by a big-nosed man named Jacques wearing a high toque and striped pants. Towering over her, he asked, in French, "Does Madame wish to learn to cook pastries?" She replied, "No, Madame wishes to learn to cook wild game." She subsequently went to the market and bought a huge fresh ham that still had hair and protruding leg attached. She said that was her "graduation piece." She wrote down recipes (which she referred to interchangeably as French *recettes* or her grandmother's old-fashioned *receipts*). She also kept a record of successful menus, often incorporating them in letters to family and friends. Her social life now included presiding at dinners for her Paris friends: Sylvia and Adrienne, Barbara, Monroe, Glenway, and the talented young photographer George Platt Lynes.

Katherine Anne's hostessing and domestic duties naturally took time away from her writing. By the end of June she was complaining to Janice, "Just keeping the house clean and the food cooked and the laundry done and the socks darned and shopping has been enough for me . . . My publisher is beginning to roar and so are several magazine editors, and I sit simply swamped under a two-room flat. Its too stupid, but I can not combine the two kinds of work, when both are so heavy for me." Money worries required valuable attention, too, especially after Gene's monthly income of 3,200 francs dropped to 2,400. In the middle of the summer she was further depressed by the departure from Paris of Glenway and Monroe, who sailed to New York with George Lynes, and Barbara, who left for a sanitorium in Davos, Switzerland, after a small spot of tuberculosis was discovered on her left lung. Katherine Anne spent the rest of the summer muddling along, juggling cooking and writing, and occasionally escaping from both kinds of chores.

On a cold rainy evening in the fall of 1933 Katherine Anne was visiting Sylvia at the bookshop when the door flew open and in burst Ernest Hemingway. After throwing her arms around Hemingway, Sylvia said, "Katherine Anne Porter . . . this is Ernest Hemingway . . . Ernest, this is Katherine Anne, and I want the two best modern American writers to know each other!" Sylvia dashed into the back room to answer the telephone, and Hemingway and Katherine Anne simply looked silently at one another for ten seconds until he hurled himself through the door and back into the rain, appalled, Katherine Anne assumed, to have his famous name pronounced as a writer in the same breath with someone of whom he had never heard. Sylvia, returning, seemed mystified that Hemingway had vanished. Katherine Anne didn't think it strange at all. It reminded her that she was forty-three years old and had yet to establish a big reputation, and she had been wasting her time on pot-boiling writing that didn't always produce income. She had forced herself to finish "The Itching Parrot" and had sent it to Harcourt-Brace editor Raymond Everitt with high expectations, but Everitt had recently reported to her that in his opinion "The Itching Parrot" was "too dull to be saleable."

She received a welcome jolt of encouragement in the middle of November with the arrival in Paris of Donald Brace, who told her first that with some assurance from her that "The Devil and Cotton Mather" would be completed, he would buy the contract from Boni and Liveright. She readily promised. But he had even more attractive offers: Harcourt, Brace would publish a new, unlimited edition of *Flowering Judas* enhanced with several additional stories. And he gave her another advance on "the novel," finally understanding that it was "Many Redeemers" instead of "Historical Present." Thoroughly pleased, she reported to Janice that over tea and toasted brioche she and Brace had "fraternized like a house afire" and "got everything straightened out." Adding to her sanguinity was the appearance of her beautifully produced *French Song-Book*, which was receiving praise in Paris, New York, and Chicago.

While working in the early months of 1934 on the fictional version of "Hacienda," which she wanted to include in "Flowering Judas and Other Stores" as well as give to Monroe and Barbara to publish as a separate book, Katherine Anne wrote another story that rose unexpectedly in her mind. With her attention already focused on Mexico, she was inspired to write "That Tree," a story about the conflict between a bourgeois work ethic and art. The setting was revolution-jaded Mexico, and the central characters were based on Carleton and Lillian Beals. By the end of March she also had finished some important pieces of "Many Redeemers," six stories amounting to about sixty pages, which she titled "The Grave," "The Circus," "The Grandmother" (eventually to be called "The Source"), "The Witness," "The Old Order" (later titled "The Journey"), and "The Last Leaf." In early April she sent them to Brace. Then she collapsed.

The Paris winter and the intense creative work had taken a toll. She became ill with bronchitis, and she was mentally exhausted. Everything around her seemed dark. The economy was not improving (taxes were rising), and omens of war were growing more pronounced. In Germany, Hitler was appointed chancellor, and Hermann Göring became prime minister of Prussia. Germany had begun to rearm, and Katherine Anne saw an increasing number of German expatriates, many of them Jews and artists, in Paris cafés. In the French government there were political murders and scandals in the Cabinet. She described the Place de la Concorde and the Place de la Republique as "battle fields" she stayed away from "to avoid getting shot."

Old and new grievances obsessed her, and the relationship between her and Gene became shaky. No matter that she had told her family at the end of March that she and Gene were happily settled in Paris life (she invited them all to visit), the whole month had actually been a low point in the marriage. It had never been so rock solid as a few friends such as Ford, Janice, Sylvia, and Adrienne assumed. They all liked Gene, and Katherine Anne always mentioned him to them with that awareness in mind, telling Janice the previous June, "What a feller! I wouldn't swap him for a bushel of emeralds." It was a contentious relationship almost always, bickering brought on by Katherine Anne's high-strung nervousness, her resentment of too much togetherness and domestic demands, and his crankiness and excessive drinking.

Monroe, Glenway, and Barbara were aware of the difficulties in the marriage. After Monroe went to Davos by way of Paris early in 1934 he told Barbara that he had seen Katherine Anne and that Gene was "gloomily drinking by himself" while Katherine Anne was in "very poor health and unable to write." Barbara quickly wrote to Katherine Anne urging her to join them in Davos for several weeks of rest and recuperation at the clinic. She sent her money for train fare and insisted on paying all expenses at the clinic.

Katherine Anne left Paris for Switzerland within a few days of receiving the letter. Monroe met her en route and escorted her to the Parksanatorium Davos, where a pleasant room had been reserved for her. Beautiful Davos, sitting in a high valley in the eastern area of Switzerland, was instantly soothing to her ragged nerves. A resort community laced with numerous walkways, it had long been famous for winter and summer sports and medical research. It lay against the backdrop of soaring, forest-thatched mountains.

Katherine Anne's letters to Gene from Davos confirmed the troubles in the marriage. She spoke of all their "rudeness and hatred and quarrelling" and accused him of saying and doing "shockingly cruel things" to her when she was truly ill. "It terrifies me," she wrote, "that when I really need help and sympathy I must leave you, to find it somewhere else." Separation or divorce during those difficult economic times was not an option, and Katherine Anne saw no choice but try, for the moment, to make the best of a marriage that was less than satisfactory. She extended her stay in Davos by three more weeks, telling Gene she needed more time to regain strength. She decided to return to Paris in time for her birthday, however, after he took responsibility for the "rough edges" in their marriage and told her he would love her even if she "weighed a ton."

Shortly after her return she heard from Donald Brace that he had placed "That Tree" at the *Virginia Quarterly Review*. With this encouragement, she soon finished the long, fictional version of "Hacienda." Although she adhered to the general facts of her 1931 visit to the Hacienda Tetlapayac, she added characters, some based on real persons and some invented, adjusted or expanded the original portrayals, and structured the story with conscious literary craft, exploiting the ready symbolism in filmmaking and pulque, the milky-white, reality-distorting liquor produced on the hacienda. She also developed the Mexican themes to make them more universal than political by tracing the ironic distance between ideals and their fallen representatives: The old patriarchal family of the orderly feudal system has been replaced by a chaotic web of incest, murder, decadence, dishonor, and a repudiation of traditional and natural roles.

That summer Paris was oppressively hot and undergoing change. Many American expatriates, fearing war in Europe and experiencing a renewed appreciation for their native land, had returned to the United States, where Prohibition had finally been lifted. Sylvia was worried that she would not have enough patrons to keep her bookshop open. American literature and criticism were also sharply shifting to the direction anticipated by *Scribner's* awarding John Herrmann's political story half of its 1933 prize instead of Katherine Anne's "The Cracked Looking-Glass," which had also been an entrant. Many of Katherine Anne's literary friends were among those who had developed social consciences that took precedence over their earlier devotion to art. Malcolm Cowley, Edmund Wilson, and Matthew Josephson, among many others, were now upholding social change as the proper aim of art. Katherine Anne could not have disagreed with them more. Josie Herbst had always leaned in that direction, an issue between her and Katherine Anne since the 1920s. In the summer of 1934, however, Katherine Anne had a new bone to pick with her.

Josie's story "Man of Steel" had been published in H. L. Mencken's *American Mercury* in January, but Katherine Anne did not see it until she happened upon it at Sylvia's shop in late July. The story is built around hardly disguised character studies of Katherine Anne and

Ernest Stock, who are called "Miranda" and "Ernest" in the story, and unfolds as an account of their miserable sojourn the summer of 1926 in Merryall Valley. Katherine Anne was appalled not only that Josie would appropriate the name she had chosen for her own autobiographical character and had once intended for her child who died, but also that Josie had insensitively given "Miranda" a past that included three husbands, numerous lovers that resembled men in Katherine Anne's life (one of them named "Salvador"), and a dead child buried on one of the nearby hills. Josie had even imagined "Miranda's" feelings about the loss of the child: "He had had arms and legs, a perfect thatch of hair, everything for living except life. Why hadn't he lived? Why had everything she loved withered and died to her touch?" Although she had not told Josie everything about her painful past, she had divulged more of it to her than she had to any other person. In 1931 she even had told her her real age.

Feeling horribly betrayed, Katherine Anne sat down and wrote Josie immediately: "Myself, I never used anybody I ever knew or any story about any one, complete. My device is to begin more or less with an episode from life, or with a certain character; but immediately the episode changes and the original character disappears. I cannot help it. I find it utterly impossible to make a report, as such. I like taking a certain kind of person, and inventing for him or her a set of experiences which I feel to be characteristic, which might well have happened to that person. But they never did happen, except in the story. Or if I take one episode as a starting point, it always leads to consequences which did not occur really. I believe that this is what fiction-writing means." She backed up her lecture with a discussion of her own rewriting of "Hacienda." "My struggles there," she told Josie, "taught me a great deal. For one thing, that I must not use *actual characters combined with their actual experience* [her italics]." "One must either write fiction, or report facts," she said, and "remembered events and actual personalities" should be "merely the jumping off place for the imagination" and "where your story should begin, not end."

As the fall days shortened and early winter approached, Katherine Anne was depressed not only by Josie's disloyalty but also by her own inability to write. "I am overcome by that acedia and melancholy which the wise Catholic church fathers have listed among the cardinal sins," she wrote Bob McAlmon; "they come of constant planning and constant frustration and postponement of plans, which in turn come of acedia and melancholy through which I have got myself into a place where I cannot manage my own affairs or make my own plans come through." In order to work, she told McAlmon, taking a page from Virginia Woolf, she needed a room in Paris of her own where she could keep her papers, take her hours she needed without interruption, play the piano, see the few friends who mattered to her, drink when she felt like it, and collect a few books.

A month later she had found a three-story house that met nearly all her requirements. On 15 December Katherine Anne and Gene moved to 70 bis rue Notre-Dame-des-Champs, a large, rear cottage, a pavilion, once occupied by Ezra Pound. They had six rooms, two baths and kitchen, and numerous closets. In their little walled garden full of ivy and lilac was a big atelier with a fireplace and two upper rooms. In the cottage Katherine Anne took for herself a bedroom, study, and bath on the top floor, and Gene had the same arrangement the next floor down. Although the cost of ten thousand francs a year was high for them, the house provided a combination of separateness and togetherness that was appealing. To celebrate this fresh beginning, Gene bought her a new typewriter, a silent one that muttered along, "blupblupblup instead of clatterclatter," she happily told Caroline a few days after the move. She also acquired a tortoise-shell cat she named Skipper, and she found an inexpensive little piano she had moved into the atelier.

Through Donald Brace's negotiations, the *Virginia Quarterly Review* accepted "The Witness," a sketch of Squire Bunton (called Uncle Jimbilly), and "The Last Leaf," a sketch of Masella Daney (called Aunt Nannie), to be published under the title "Two Plantation Portraits" in the January 1935 issue, and "The Grave" in April. Red Warren had asked Katherine Anne for a story he and Cleanth Brooks could publish in the first issue of the *Southern Review*, a literary journal they were establishing at Louisiana State University, where they both were teaching, and she asked Brace to send them pieces of "Legend and Memory." "The Circus" would appear in their inaugural issue in July, and "The Old Order" would appear in the winter 1936 issue.

"The Circus" is the first story in the sequence to focus specifically on Katherine Anne's autobiographical character Miranda and her emerging awareness. Grandmother Sophia Jane is persuaded to attend a circus with other family members, including some visiting relatives from Kentucky, and to allow the very young Miranda to go, too. In the surreal and horrifying experience of the circus, Miranda intimates death, cruelty, and lust.

"The Grave," which is the artistic rendering of Katherine Anne and Paul's killing of the mother rabbit in that mid-1890s summer, concludes with the last event in Miranda's rite of passage, beyond even the events in the later short novels featuring Miranda, *Old Mortality* and *Pale Horse, Pale Rider*. Although, in real life, Katherine Anne tattled about killing the pregnant rabbit and caused Paul to be whipped by their father, in the story Miranda suppresses the trauma and never tells. When the experience surfaces in her mind twenty years later, it is softened by the attached memory of her brother standing in the sunshine turning over and over in his hand a beautiful silver dove, a coffin screw, he had found in an empty grave the same day as the killing. In stories about dead mothers and dead babies, *art* subsumes the anguish.

By summer Katherine Anne had the stories together that Harcourt, Brace would publish in October as *Flowering Judas and Other Stories*. She anticipated a little money from this publication, and she was working well on "Midway of This Mortal Life," the second part of "Many Redeemers," hopeful even that she might finish her long autobiographical novel before many months passed. Artistically, she was thriving, but her marriage had not improved; and, assuming that solitude would enable her to attend seriously to her writing, she convinced Gene to make a two-month trip to the United States without her.

The week before Gene left, Josie arrived for an unexpected visit. John Hermann had run off with another woman, and a devastated Josie was escaping to Europe with a newspaper assignment that would put some time and distance between her and what Katherine Anne saw as "a smash-up . . . like an earthquake or a volcanic eruption." Katherine Anne set aside her anger over Josie's story "Man of Steel" in order to sympathize with her bereft friend, whom she hadn't seen for more than five years. After Gene left, Josie stayed four more days before going along to her assignment in Germany. Katherine Anne told Caroline how splendid a house guest Josie was, but her letters to Gene shortly after Josie's departure revealed a different story.

There was more to Josie's and John's breakup than his heavy drinking and seeking out other women. The complicated and protracted disintegration of the relationship involved his increasingly time-consuming involvement in Communist activities and also Josie's lesbian affair with a young woman, Marion Greenwood, an affair that Josie's biographer, Elinor Langer, has called "the secret" at the center of the breakup. While Josie might not have told Katherine Anne "exactly" all that had happened, as Langer put it, Katherine Anne drew conclusions that upset her. In a conversation about sexual intimacy, Josie had warned Katherine Anne that two months of celibacy while Gene was away might not be good for her, and she let Katherine Anne know that she herself would not mind a little "physical comfort." Shocked, Katherine Anne described the disturbing visit in a letter to Gene as soon as Josie left for Germany. "You might try tieing [sic] her hands," Gene replied, "and then, if she keeps up such talk in odd moments, you had better slap her hard . . . . . she may be making advances, and you had better ask her to leave the premises, or leave them yourself if you're on her ground."

Katherine Anne arranged for Josie to stay at a friend's vacant apartment on her way back through Paris from Germany rather than with her, as had been planned. But she never revealed to Josie any of her anxieties or revulsions. She left that for Mrs. Treadwell in *Ship of Fools*, who muses about such matters on the occasion of her forty-sixth birthday, the very one toward which Katherine Anne in the summer of 1935 was looking: "Women . . . so often lose their modesty, their grace. They become shrill, or run to fat, or turn to beanpoles, take to secret drinking or nagging their husbands; they get tangled up in disreputable love affairs; they marry men too young for them and get just what they deserve; if they have a little money, they attract every species of parasite, and Lesbians lurk in the offing, waiting for loneliness and fear to do their work; oh, it is all enough to scare anybody."

Katherine Anne's strategy was to keep up the pretense of contentment and happiness in her marriage to Gene in order to avoid an unpleasant confrontation. "God knows I shall be glad to see him," she wrote Josie shortly before Gene's return in September, calling him "my friend and my defender, my ally and my share of love in this world." Her relationship with Josie would never be the same, however, and the evidence of its effective dissolution is apparent in the correspondence that was sustained for another dozen years. From the time they began corresponding in the mid-1920s, humor was their common tone. They addressed one another as "Miz Plushbottom" and "Miz Montparnasse," signed themselves in similar ways, and "spoke" in a country dialect reminiscent of rural people in the Connecticut countryside. That tone changed. Everything was serious after the summer of 1935. No longer would Katherine Anne begin her letters to Josie "Josie, Old Tortuga" and sign herself "Your'n til death." She might use a perfunctory "Darling Josie" or "Dearest Josie," as she began most of her letters to her friends, but soon it would as often as not be

"Dear Josie" or only "Josie." She even pointed out the change: "You will notice," she told Josie later, "I address your letter differently . . . If its all the same to you, I'll call you by your own name from this out."

Although the abstract idea of lesbianism and homosexuality did not conform to her rigid ideals of womanhood and femininity, Katherine Anne had close friendships with lesbians such as Sylvia and Adrienne and homosexuals such as Monroe and Glenway. Since her tirades against homosexuals in Mexico in 1930 and '31, she had come to see the attraction in friendships with homosexual men who were handsome, charming, and cultivated. Monroe's relationship with Barbara Harrison, who had married Glenway's younger brother, Lloyd Wescott, the previous May, seemed to Katherine Anne a perfect example of "pure love" unencumbered with sex.

It was Sylvia who was responsible for Katherine Anne's appearance before the American Women's Club in Paris on 29 November. Although Katherine Anne originally planned to talk about Mexico and the background of her stories set there, what was most on her mind was the process of creating art out of the materials of autobiography and history. "To give a true testimony," she told her audience, "it is necessary to know and remember what I was, what I felt, and what I knew then, and not confuse it with what I know or think I know now. So, I shall try to tell the truth, but the result will be fiction. I shall not be at all surprised at this result: it is what I mean to do; it is, to my way of thinking, the way fiction is made." She included in her forty-five-minute speech the definition of the so-called American writer (she argued for individuality rather than conformity to standard subjects and styles); the necessity for the presentation of reality, whether agreeable or not, "with a truth beyond the artist's own prejudices, loves, hates" (or political positions); the importance of craft ("a little like making shoes"); and, because she was still appalled by Josie's "Man of Steel," the necessity to transmute living originals into fictional characters the originals would not recognize. Although she thought her delivery could be improved, she was generally pleased with her talk and the reaction to it. She dimly saw a possible source of income in lecturing and teaching.

In the late fall and early winter of 1935 *Flowering Judas and Other Stories* was receiving wide attention, and in both England and the United States Katherine Anne was praised as a writer superior to Hemingway, Faulkner, and O'Hara. Five pieces from "Legend and Memory" either had appeared or soon would, and Sylvia had engaged

Marcelle Sibon to translate Katherine Anne's stories for publication in *Mesures*. There were more parts of her novel already in draft or in her head, and she wanted to keep writing. But the Notre Dame des Champs house was not conducive to work, and she looked for a change of scene and new companions. She was trying to ignore the economy, the darkening clouds of war (Germany had absorbed the Saar and instituted compulsory military service, and Italy had invaded Ethiopia), the increasingly damp, cold weather in Paris, and her perennial bronchitis. Her anxiety and troubles seemed symbolized by a persistent toothache and the attempted theft of her cat, Skipper, probably destined that season, Sylvia thought, for Parisian "rabbit stew."

The winter of 1935–36 seemed to be only for enduring. She had been yearning to see her family and Texas for more than ten years. In the spring she intended to finally go home.

CHAPTER NINETEEN

Going Home

January 1936–April 1938

So my time in Mexico and Europe . . . gave me back my past and my
own house and my own people—the native land of my heart.

In January 1936 Harcourt, Brace gave Katherine Anne another advance
on "Cotton Mather" that enabled her to leave for the United States
earlier than she had planned. She departed Le Havre on 6 February on
the SS *President Roosevelt* and five days later was established in a
boardinghouse at 72 Pemberton Square in Boston. She hoped to renew
her enthusiasm for the Mather biography by living for a few weeks close
to his historical locality and his Boston grave, but all she could think
about was going to Texas. She soon left Boston, and after a long bus ride
arrived at Baby and Jules's house at 903 Olive Street in Houston, startled (and pleased) to see that beautiful and earthy Baby, who was enthusiastically raising Boston bulldogs, had gained an extraordinary amount
of weight. Mindful of their father's preference for slender women,
Katherine Anne gleefully called Baby "Jumbo" behind her back.

In mid-April Katherine Anne set out with Baby and Gay to visit
Harrison for several days at his little farm in Mission, Texas, 365
miles away. When they drove up, she saw her father looking handsome and hearty dressed all in white and talking to a field hand. When
he saw Katherine Anne he said, "Well, what are you doing here?" She
replied, "Why, I came to see you." They hugged each other and sat
talking for a long time.

Baby's twenty-two-year-old son, Breckenridge, brought his grandfather to Houston a week later, and Baby and Katherine Anne took
Harrison to visit ancestral homes, birthplaces, and graves throughout
central Texas. They veered through Menard County, where Harrison's
sister Anna was buried, and they made the 340-mile pilgrimage to
Indian Creek. None of them had been there in more than forty years.

They set forth, bearing pots of flowers, to find Alice's grave in the Lamar Churchyard. Entering the cemetery, Harrison pointed to a tall, narrow, bluish stone and told them, "It is there." Katherine Anne walked straight to it and sat down beside the neglected grave to dig a shallow hole for planting the flowers. She spontaneously wrote a poem on a scrap of paper that she buried under the soil of her mother's grass-strewn grave:

> *This time of year, this year of all years, brought*
> *The homeless one, home again,*
> *To the fallen house and the drowsing dust*
> *There to sit at the door—*
> *Welcomed, homeless no more.*
> *Her dust remembers its dust and calls again*
> *Back to the fallen house this restless dust,*
> *This shape of her pain.*

She took from the tombstone the photograph encased in glass that Harrison had placed there in 1892.

From the cemetery she went with Harrison and Baby to find the house in which she and Baby had been born and Alice had died. They talked with the two sisters who lived in the run-down house, and they walked over the old farm, gathering pebbles from the creek and taking photographs. But it was overwhelmingly sad for Harrison, who wanted to leave immediately. In contrast to her father's reaction, Katherine Anne told Gene that she felt an extraordinary lightness of heart all the way back to Houston.

There was an odd omission, however, in the journey to Indian Creek. Katherine Anne never mentioned the graves of her grandfather John Newton Jones and her uncle T. A. Jones, both near Alice's, or the fact that her mother's only surviving brother, George Melton Jones, lived a few miles from Indian Creek at Ebony. Alice's adored "baby brother" and Katherine Anne's only living uncle on her mother's side, he could have told her a great deal about her mother's early life. His adult children, a daughter he had named for Alice and a son, Hugh, the only surviving child of Harrison's sister Louellah, also lived in the area. Katherine Anne seemed peculiarly uncurious about her mother's family, preferring her idealized images to any reality she might discover.

After the trip Katherine Anne stayed with Gay at her house on Rutland Street, and their days burst with family life and Texas culture. She thought that all her nieces and nephews were good-looking and talented. She felt tender toward Breckenridge, whom she had named in 1914, and she imagined that Paul's pretty daughter Patsy might have a career as an actress. The whole family engaged in a constant round of activities from school programs to "full tilt" Houston centennial events. They played the races by day and poker by night, kept the radio going with jazz and "Texascowboy" songs, and "talked themselves quite hoarse." She told Gene, "I couldn't live here, but I'm glad I came. And in many ways that I could not describe without thinking it out, I am one of them and awfully like them, in character and in temperament."

After the long ship voyage back to France at the end of June, Katherine Anne again confronted the unmitigated troubles in her marriage. Change, however, was in process. At the end of the summer Gene learned that the State Department was sending him to Washington for an interlude until he could be assigned to another post. They spent September cleaning out their Notre-Dame-des-Champs house and sending possessions by cargo ship for storage in New York. They sailed 8 October, and by the time they reached New York and moved temporarily into a hotel, it was understood that Katherine Anne would not go to Washington with him.

Katherine Anne, eager to get on with her writing, which she had neglected for several months, met with Donald Brace, who gave her a new contract for five short novels of twenty thousand words each: "Noon Wine—Old Mortality—The Man in the Tree—Pale Horse, Pale Rider—Promised Land." It was the first evidence of her recognition that she was not working on a long novel called "Many Redeemers" but rather on a series of related short novels. Harcourt, Brace expected to publish them as a collection in the fall, and Brace gave her an advance that would support her for several months.

When Gene left for Washington at the end of October, Katherine Anne moved along to the Water Wheel Tavern, an old Revolutionary-era inn, at Doylestown, Pennsylvania. After only one week she reported to Josie that she had finished *Noon Wine*—"it turned into a mud-lark and took the bit in its teeth and galloped easily past the twenty one thousandth word."

Noon Wine, set in the area between Kyle and Austin at the site of the Thompson dairy farm, where Katherine Anne, Gay, and Baby briefly stayed in 1902, opens from the viewpoint of two faired-haired little boys who watch a stranger approaching their family's run-down farm. The foreign-looking man asks their father, Royal Earle Thompson, for work, and Mr. Thompson, pretentious but shiftless, is delighted to hire him to restore the dairy farm he has let go, much to the dismay of his sickly, pious wife. For nine years, while the little boys grow into strapping big sons, the farm flourishes, and the Thompsons know that the hired man, Olaf Helton, is responsible for its success. It is for that reason that they do not question his strangeness or press him about his past, and it is their dependence on him for their economic survival that causes Mr. Thompson to protect him from Homer T. Hatch, the fat, wicked bounty hunter who under the guise of "law and order" tracks him down as a fugitive from an insane asylum. Imagining that Hatch intends to kill Helton, Thompson impulsively kills Hatch first: He "felt his arms go up over his head and bring the ax down on Mr. Hatch's head as if he were stunning a beef." Although at the trial Thompson is let off the murder charge, no one truly believes him innocent, including his wife and two sons. Unable to face their judgment, he maneuvers twin barrels of a shotgun to a position under his chin, and, with his great toe, prepares to pull the trigger. *Noon Wine* is like "The Jilting of Granny Weatherall" in its anatomy of the human mind facing death.

Katherine Anne continued to work at breakneck speed, and in the middle of December she finished *Old Mortality* and sent it to Donald Brace, who would act, as usual, as her agent. The first section of the three-part short novel recounts the romantic family legend about the beautiful, dead Amy through the viewpoint of her nieces, Maria and Miranda, ages twelve and eight. The second section takes place two years later, when Maria and Miranda are students at the Convent of the Child Jesus in New Orleans and finally meet Uncle Gabriel, Amy's long-suffering lover and short-time husband, who is very different from the romantic Gabriel of the family legend. The third part takes place eight years later, when eighteen-year-old Miranda, married now, returns to Texas for the funeral of Gabriel and meets Cousin Eva, a spinster, scientist, and suffragette, who tries to destroy the romantic legend. Miranda rejects both versions, and she also renounces her own hastily made marriage. She asks herself, "What is the truth?" and resolves (naively) to know the answer.

The title "Old Mortality" comes from a poem Gabriel wrote for Amy's tombstone:

> *She lives again who suffered life,*
> *Then suffered death, and now set free*
> *A singing angel, she forgets*
> *The griefs of old mortality.*

Katherine Anne said she made it up to be simply representative of tombstone poetry in Texas, and such verse was, indeed, vivid in her mind in the fall of 1936 after her visits to Texas graveyards the previous spring. In addition to Harrison's poem on Alice's tombstone, she had seen the awkward poem that Thomas Gay had inscribed on the Menard County cemetery tombstone of Anna Porter Gay, the model for Amy, and she had seen the verse on her grandfather John Jones's tombstone that was assuredly composed by her mother:

> *Servant of God well done*
> *Rest from thy loved employ*
> *The battle fought*
> *The victory won*
> *Enter thy master's joy*

Despite just having written a short novel about the falseness of romantic legends, Katherine Anne would never admit that her father and mother wrote tombstone doggerel. In fact, she told Monroe that when she visited "an old cemetery last spring" she noticed that "all the mottoes and quoted verses were secular, and classical . . . . . Interesting, I think. Not religious, and not sentimental poetry, except now and then, but fine tall quotations from Shakespeare and Dante and Milton."

When Erna Schlemmer read *Old Morality* in 1939, she told Katherine Anne that she had immediately identified "little Miranda" as Katherine Anne, as "Callie, that dearest friend of my childhood." But Erna would have been aware of other aspects of the story that were not faithful to autobiography. Baby is not represented, just as she would be left out of all Katherine Anne's stories based on her own childhood. Although the exclusion can be justified on artistic grounds, at the same time, using a revisionist technique she learned from her grandmother, Katherine Anne created a world in which her baby sister, who was their father's favorite and whose birth, she believed, precipitated the death of their mother, does not exist.

Katherine Anne's two months at the Water Wheel Tavern constituted one of the most productive periods of her life, but as cold weather approached, her winter bronchial ailments predictably appeared, her creativity dried up, and her spirits deflated. Her mood was darkened by a letter from Harrison the middle of the month. He reported that he finally received the copies she sent of *Hacienda* and

Mary Alice Jones Porter, Katherine Anne's mother, at the time of her marriage to Harrison Boone Porter, Katherine Anne's father, in 1883. Reprinted with permission of the University of Maryland Libraries.

Callie Jo Russell, youngest daughter of William and Marinda Russell, neighbors of Harrison and Alice Porter at Indian Creek. Callie was twelve years old at the time Alice and Harrison honored the Russell family by giving their fourth child the name Callie Russell Porter, later changed to Katherine Anne Porter. Photograph courtesy of R. J. Koch, Callie Russell's son, from the collection of the author.

Katherine Anne Porter, on left, still known as Callie, with her younger sister, Mary Alice (Baby), and their grandmother, Catharine Ann Skaggs Porter, in 1893. Reprinted with permission of the University of Maryland Libraries.

The Porter house in Kyle in which Katherine Anne spent her third through tenth year. Photograph by the author.

Katherine Anne when she was a student at the Thomas School. She inscribed the photograph: "Aged 14 years, San Antonio, TX. Photographer, Hegemann, asked my father to allow him to photograph me for a national photography show. He won first prize in the 'Young Girl Division.' He pinned up my hair and draped me in a black lace mantilla and set me in a fashionable pose and turned me to looking about 18. However it seems to be the only likeness that survived that year—1904." Reprinted with permission of the University of Maryland Libraries.

Harrison Paul Porter, Sr. (christened Harry Ray Porter), Katherine Anne's brother in, 1905, when he wrote his first surviving letter to her. He described life aboard ship and exotic ports into which he sailed, and he encouraged her to keep writing her "fine" stories, providing the first external evidence of her early attempts to write fiction. Four years later, three years into her troubled marriage to John Henry Koontz, he wrote her a sternly worded letter arguing against divorce and women's suffrage. Photograph courtesy of Harrison Paul Porter, Jr., from the collection of the author.

Katherine Anne in Corpus Christi in 1912, two years before she ran away from John Koontz to Chicago, where she worked briefly as an extra in the movies. Reprinted with permission of the University of Maryland Libraries.

Katherine Anne's first passport photograph, 1920, shortly before she left on her first extended trip to Mexico. She had dyed her hair henna black after it turned white during her near-death from influenza in Denver in 1918. Reprinted with permission of the University of Maryland Libraries.

Katherine Anne, at left end of the third row, among members of the Pan American Federation of Labor convening in Mexico City in January of 1921. Within the group are Plutarco Elías Calles, Felipe Carrillo Puerto, Samuel Gompers, Thorberg and Robert Haberman, and Mary Doherty. Photograph in the Thomas Walsh Papers at the University of Maryland. Reprinted with permission of the University of Maryland Libraries.

Salomón de la Selva, Nicaraguan poet with whom Katherine Anne had a romantic liaison in Mexico in 1921. The affair ended when she became pregnant and had an abortion. He was the object of her mordant satire in several stories and poems. Reprinted with permission of the University of Maryland Libraries.

Katherine Anne (right) with unidentified man and woman during the Sacco-Vanzetti demonstration in the summer of 1927. Her analysis of the case and her participation in the protest resulted fifty years later in her memoir *The Never-Ending Wrong*. Reprinted with permission of the University of Maryland Libraries.

Katherine Anne in Mexico in 1930. The photograph, by Manuel Bravo, discloses her deep depression. Reprinted with permission of the University of Maryland Libraries.

Hart Crane in Katherine Anne's
garden in Mixcoac in May 1931.
Reprinted with permission of the
University of Maryland Libraries.

Eugene Dove Pressly in Mexico in
1931 when he was living with
Katherine Anne in Mixcoac, outside
Mexico City. He traveled with her
that summer from Vera Cruz to
Bremen, Germany, a voyage that
provided the surface material for
Ship of Fools. They were married in
Paris in 1933 and divorced in 1938.
Reprinted with permission of the
University of Maryland Libraries.

Katherine Anne at Berlin train station in November 1931, shortly after Pressly left for a job in Madrid and shortly before she met Hermann Göring. She inscribed the photograph "Abandoned in Berlin." Reprinted with permission of the University of Maryland Libraries.

Katherine Anne in Paris in 1933 at the time of her and Pressly's wedding. Photograph by George Platt Lynes. Reprinted with permission of George Platt Lynes II.

Barbara Harrison Wescott and Monroe Wheeler, Katherine Anne's friends and patrons, who as Harrison of Paris published her *French Song-Book* and *Hacienda*. Katherine Anne dedicated *Ship of Fools* to Barbara. Reprinted with permission of the University of Maryland Libraries.

Katherine Anne and her father, Harrison Boone Porter, during her 1936 visit in Texas. Reprinted with permission of the University of Maryland Libraries.

Albert Russel Erskine, Katherine Anne's fifth husband, in Baton Rouge, Louisiana. At the time of their marriage in 1938 she was one month short of forty-eight, and he was twenty-seven. Photograph by George Platt Lynes. Reprinted with permission of George Platt Lynes II.

Katherine Anne as photographed in New York on her 1939 birthday by the fashion photographer George Platt Lynes. *Pale Horse, Pale Rider: Three Short Novels* had just been published to glowing reviews. Reprinted with permission of George Platt Lynes II.

South Hill, Katherine Anne's house near Saratoga Springs, New York, at the time she bought it in 1941. She renovated it extensively before she sold it in 1945. It was the only house she ever owned. Reprinted with permission of the University of Maryland Libraries.

For Katherine Anne
with love and gratitude
from Eudora — as of
1941 "A Curtain of Green" (below)
Introduction by KAP
and 1973 now
and all years in between
and to come

Eudora Welty, Katherine Anne's protégé and then friend for forty years. Eudora inscribed the photograph: "For Katherine Anne with love and gratitude from Eudora—as of 1941 'A Curtain of Green' (below) intro by KAP and 1973 now and all years in between and to come." Reprinted with permission of the University of Maryland Libraries.

Charles Shannon in Marcella Winslow's Georgetown garden in 1944 during his affair with Katherine Anne. He was probably the love of her life. Reprinted with permission of the University of Maryland Libraries.

Katherine Anne, in the third row, at the Congress for Cultural Freedom in Paris in 1952. Among the American representatives were Allen Tate, Robert Lowell, Glenway Wescott, and, in the first row, William Faulkner. Reprinted with permission of the University of Maryland Libraries.

Katherine Anne in 1954 at the University of Michigan, Ann Arbor, where she was highly successful with her students. Reprinted with permission of the University of Maryland Libraries.

Katherine Anne, Seymour Lawrence, and two unidentified men at the publication party for *Ship of Fools* in 1962. Reprinted with permission of the University of Maryland Libraries.

Harrison Paul Porter, Jr., Katherine Anne's nephew, who was the closest family member to her from the 1940s through the end of her life. Having identified in him a kindred artistic spirit, she dedicated *A Leaning Tower and Other Stories* to him. He was appointed her guardian in 1977. Reprinted with permission of the University of Maryland Libraries.

Katherine Anne at a 1968 ceremony at the University of Maryland, to which she had donated her papers and personal possessions. Her friend and attorney, E. Barrett Prettyman, Jr., stands to her left. Reprinted with permission of the University of Maryland Libraries.

Katherine Anne on her eighty-fifth birthday. Photograph by her nephew Paul Porter. Reprinted with permission of the University of Maryland Libraries.

Katherine Anne Porter's grave at Indian Creek, Texas, adjacent to that of her mother, Alice Jones Porter. Photograph by the author.

Flowering Judas and Other Stories, which he called "the assemblage of your stories," but he did not comment on them at all.

At the end of December Katherine Anne left Doylestown and joined Gene in an apartment at 67 Perry Street in Greenwich Village. He was awaiting word from Washington about a diplomatic post, and she was trying to recover from the flu. In the misery of the circumstances, the unhappiness in the marriage expressed itself in the usual arguing and recriminations. She countered the wretchedness with as much self-indulgence, socializing, and occasional escapes as she could manage. She visited Barbara and Lloyd Wescott in New Jersey, where with their encouragement she turned a weekend stay into two weeks, pleading new illness to Gene and claiming she was physically unable to return to the city.

Katherine Anne was especially worried about earning enough money to support herself while continuing her writing when she received an unexpected telegram announcing that the Book-of-the-Month Club had awarded her a twenty-five hundred dollar prize in acknowledgement of the high quality of her writing. She was elated. "Now let me get to that next book," she wrote to Baby and Jules, "Huzzah. Three cheers and a couple of tigers. EEP EEP Hoohaw, as a Frenchman says when he is trying to say, Hip, hip, Hurrah . . . . . EEP EEP, I repeat, in a little voice . . . . . I got the prize, I got the prize." Recalling the speed with which she had wrapped up *Noon Wine* and *Old Mortality*, she imagined she could meet the 1 April deadline for the entire collection of short novels.

In February Gene accepted a non-government job with an oil company in Venezuela, and Katherine Anne convinced him to go to Denver to visit his mother until his departure for South America at the end of March. They agreed that the separation would be the first step in the dissolution of their marriage. After he left on 31 March, they would never see one another again as husband and wife.

Despite Katherine Anne's enthusiastic acceptance of the Book-of-the-Month-Club award and the financial cushion it created, she did not get much work done that spring on the remaining short novels. She missed the April deadline, but Donald Brace again agreed to an unspecified extension. She was doing some writing, however. In March she published two book reviews, and she also wrote a new story that had not existed in notes or apparently even her thoughts before the first week of April. "A Day's Work" formed from a conversation she overheard through the walls of the Perry Street apartment.

An analysis of the unbreachable differences in a loveless marriage between an Irish-American deluded dreamer and his weary, sour, realist wife, the Joycean story was invested with the troubles of the Presslys' disintegrating marriage.

Monroe Wheeler, the Wescotts, and George Platt Lynes were responsible for most of Katherine Anne's social diversions. They took her to plays and museums and introduced her to George's brother Russell, who was an editor at *Harper's Magazine*. She in turn entertained them at Perry Street. In his diary Glenway recorded a festive evening: "Dinner last night with George and Monroe at Katherine Anne's apartment . . . Her table handsomely set; raffia cloth and turkey-red napkins, wooden plates, and four silver goblets, and her new Russian forks of nugget silver, the handles enameled with dark flowers by some Muscovite William Morris." After dinner they went to Coney Island, arriving near closing time, going up and down the street of "games and freaks," behaving like children.

All of Katherine Anne's activities that spring of 1937 were not light-hearted. Genevieve Taggard, who had married Kenneth Durant, convinced Katherine Anne to march in the May Day parade, join the leftist League of American Writers, and contribute a favorable comment to a *New Masses* Readers' Forum on the anti-Nazi Mexican movie *The Wave*. Mingling again with some of her old radical crowd from the 1920s, she translated a Loyalist ballad for a volume titled . . . *and Spain Sings: Fifty Loyalist Ballads Adapted by American Poets*. She soon was distancing herself from Genevieve and Kenneth, however, complaining to Monroe that her Communist friends were giving her the same old arguments that she had heard from 1924 to 1927 and that now were dominating literary criticism. She felt that in none of her fictional works had she ever confused politics with art. Her views were more consistent with those of her southern friends, Red Warren, Andrew Lytle, Allen Tate, and Caroline Gordon.

By the end of April she was thinking southward again. Gene wrote to tell her he was disenchanted with the job in Venezuela and would be back in New York in July, awaiting an assignment with the government. Katherine Anne intended to be absent from Perry Street when he arrived, and she had a perfect excuse. Harrison would be celebrating his eightieth birthday on 28 June, and the family was planning a party to coincide with the Old Settlers' Reunion in San Marcos.

Katherine Anne arrived in Texas in late June, sinking into family life for the second time in a year. At the Old Settlers' Reunion on

6 July she was asked to speak, and an old gentleman announced her as "the littlest Porter girl, the curly haired one." The whole event was "pleasant as could be," Katherine Anne told Josie, "but I had no regrets and no wrenchings of the heart for any part of the past."

Having learned that Red Warren and his wife, Cinina, would be in California and the Tates would be in Michigan at the Olivet Writers' Conference, Katherine Anne had been disappointed that she would not be seeing her southern friends on this trip. But Caroline and Allen had convinced Joseph Brewer, president of Olivet College, to invite Katherine Anne to join them there for the last week of the conference. She enthusiastically accepted the offer, boarded a train, and thirty-six hours later arrived in Michigan. At the conclusion of the conference 31 July, Caroline and Allen insisted that she return with them for an extended stay at their Tennessee estate, "Benfolly." They made the car trip southward a sightseeing jaunt into the past as they visited battlefields Antietam and Appomattox, Washington's home at Mount Vernon, and "Kenmore," a famous grand house that once belonged to ancestors of Allen who were kin of the Washingtons.

Benfolly sat on a lush green slope high over the Cumberland River. The lawn spilled around the peeling, pillared house, in whose formal parlor over the fireplace hung an engraving of Stonewall Jackson and a loaded twenty-two rifle under a Confederate flag. In August life at Benfolly was intensely artistic, intellectual, and sociable. Allen was writing his novel *The Fathers,* and Caroline was trying to finish *The Garden of Adonis.* Katherine Anne wanted to work on "The Man in the Tree," a story about white southerners' guilt over slavery, while she was absorbing again the Tates' southernness. But for her the atmosphere was too convivial for the solitude she required for writing. Instead, she played with the resident cats, preserved peaches, made elderberry wine, and enthusiastically participated in lively social evenings when any of the numerous friends of the Tates dropped by.

She became friends with Brainard (Lon) Cheney, a novelist and reporter for the *Nashville Banner* and a college chum of Red Warren's at Vanderbilt, his wife, Frances (Fanny), and Cleanth and Edith Amy (Tinkum) Brooks, who in a mid-August visit were accompanied by a handsome young man introduced to Katherine Anne as Albert Russel Erskine Jr. Twenty-six-year-old Erskine was a graduate student at Louisiana State University, a member of the staff of the LSU Press, and the business manager of the *Southern Review.* Cleanth, who with Red had founded the literary quarterly, suspected that Albert was half enamored with Katherine Anne before he ever met her, for she was the "darling" of the whole editorial staff of the *Southern Review*, where three of her stories had appeared. In that summer he fell completely in love with her.

Albert Erskine was a native southerner who had been reared in prosperous, conventional Memphis society and had received his baccalaureate degree from Southwestern, the local college, where he had been Red's student. When Red accepted a position at LSU, he went along, too, enrolling in the English program. Katherine Anne observed his good looks, wit, courtly manners, and intellectual liveliness. She thought he seemed unusually mature for his age.

Like almost everyone else, Albert believed that Katherine Anne was in her early, rather than her late, forties. But the difference in age, whatever it was, seemed not to matter to him, and she ignored it. He was at Benfolly with her one week, and they were nearly inseparable, sitting on the grassy bank high above the river and talking throughout the hot, moonlit summer nights. By the time he returned to Baton Rouge and Katherine Anne prepared to leave Benfolly, the attraction between them was strong, and he was one of the reasons she decided to look for an affordable apartment in New Orleans, where she could occasionally enjoy the company of the charming Albert, less than two hours away by train. To finance her move, she appealed to Monroe for a loan, and he quickly complied with four hundred dollars.

For thirty dollars a month she rented an attic room forty feet long with bath and little kitchen on the top floor of the Lower Pontalba, a historic old building at 543 St. Ann Street, overlooking Jackson Square near the St. Louis Cathedral, whose convent school she had briefly attended in 1903 or 1904. Nearby were the Cabildo Museum, the French Market, and the wharves. She expected to seclude herself and write, but New Orleans was full of social possibilities, and she wasn't long in finding society, or it her. A reporter for the local paper wrote her up, and the article, accompanied by a photograph, released a "deluge" of social invitations, as she reported to Josie a month later.

Katherine Anne occasionally saw the Warrens, who kept an apartment on Royal Street in New Orleans in addition to their home in Baton Rouge, and her new friends, the Brookses. Whenever either couple made the seventy-five-mile trip to New Orleans, Albert was with them. But throughout September and the first half of October, she and Albert were never truly alone, and whenever she saw him he was "exhausted and cross," she told Caroline, seemingly "his favorite mood." Despite this frustration (or perhaps because of it), the excitement of the romance was growing.

Since meeting at Benfolly they had been corresponding with increasing intimacy and warmth. Finally, the weekend of 24 October Albert made the trip to New Orleans alone, and the affair that had been evolving for two months was consummated. The letters that followed were unrestrained love letters. "My Darling," she wrote him in mid-November, "I wish I could tell you how much I love you . . . , but I think it takes more words than I have."

Because Albert had time-consuming responsibilities as a graduate student and as managing editor of the *Southern Review* as well as an editor for the LSU Press, he could make the trip to New Orleans only every two weeks. This arrangement was satisfactory to her, for she was at last writing again. She had completed several book reviews, and she was working on the five short novels. In early December she finished *Pale Horse, Pale Rider.*

In writing *Pale Horse, Pale Rider*, Katherine Anne had transmuted into art and mythologized her experiences of near-death during the 1918 flu epidemic and her pacifism in conflict with anti-German hysteria and wartime patriotism. She created from her imagination a doomed love affair in which Miranda's soldier-lover, Adam, who takes care of her during her illness, contracts the flu and, ironically, dies while she lives. If the failed love affair bears most resemblance to Katherine Anne's fleeting marriage to Carl von Pless, Adam's appearance—"olive and tan and tawny, hay colored and sand colored from hair to boots"— is very like that of young Albert Erskine. "Last time I saw your eyes," she wrote him three years later, "they were a light tawny tan with quite definite green spokes around the pupil, and little occasional flecks, mustard color, the whole effect being of a very pleasant and of course I thought perfectly beautiful hazel. And your hair at times was a kind of polished tan or leather color, edging toward straw at the temples and neck, and in the light it was just a mixed, bright straw blond. And your complexion was a fine sunburnt olive."

Since November Albert had been pressing Katherine Anne to marry him, and he was urging her for an answer. His persistence led her to find an escape. She decided to go to Houston for Christmas, but before she left on 22 December, she responded encouragingly to his proposal. He went home to Memphis to break the news to his father and mother that he hoped to marry a woman who was his mother's age. Katherine Anne had barely arrived in Houston when she wrote to

Albert accepting his proposal of marriage, to be delayed only as long as completing a divorce from Gene required.

Katherine Anne postponed her return to Louisiana with the excuse that she simply was too ill to return to New Orleans. She would make the best of this separation, she told Albert, and place herself under a doctor's care and use the time to work on "The Man in the Tree" and "Promised Land." In the meantime, she made a down payment on a piece of land outside Baton Rouge near property owned by the Warrens. She also would use the time to imagine a house they would build there and name "The Cares," a symbolic foundation for their marriage. She envisioned herself in this fantasy house surrounded with books and music and industriously writing in a place of sunlight and flowers and trees. Albert, the attentive and admiring lover, was to be hovering in the background, careful not to intrude on her "artist-time."

During the four-month engagement Katherine Anne and Albert spent only one weekend together, when she took a train to Baton Rouge on 28 January. For the rest of the time they wrote one another daily and spoke by telephone regularly. Her letters to him, although love letters, were full of talk about their planned house. She discussed costs ("perhaps we'll have a $6000 house at $45 a month"), the porch ("a ten foot porch running around three sides"), the foundation ("concrete . . . I feel positively Russian about it"), surveying the land and moving the trees ("the whole thing is so fascinating and exciting, I often wonder just what I did for excitement and romantic interest before"). She told him, "My entire mind is a fire works of shooting stars, and it is so providential to have something undeniably real to work on, like a house-plan."

Her letters also included a vague account of the state of her health. Although she said that her condition was "something like the flu," she made it sound more serious—and described a recovery from "it" crucial to her future happiness with Albert. Near the end of March, when the puzzled Albert had become increasingly impatient, she explained, again, that it wasn't fair or sensible to stop in the middle of a treatment the doctor had said would probably take six months. Privately cheered by news that she had been awarded a second Guggenheim, she looked even farther ahead and reminded him that she made an unchangeable commitment to go to Olivet again in the summer. He did not know that she was also considering applying for a residency at Yaddo.

It was understandable that Albert would have been skeptical. Having moved out of the guest room in Baby and Jules's house and into a duplex apartment at 218 West Fifteenth Street the first week in January, she told him that she was working hard in her isolated and bare studio. Her letters, however, revealed anything but the solitary life she usually required for serious writing. Having advertised writing classes in the local newspaper, she met three nights a week with students, and she joined Baby and Jules in a merry round of visiting friends and relatives ("it is astonishing how much sheer motion there is in life from minute to minute"). Her good spirits were reflected in her whimsical description of their returning to town at "high twilight" with "the huge moon" staring "at us through the tangled black branches of big important trees not budding out yet."

Among her most pleasant moments was time spent with her nephew Paul, her brother's son, and her niece Anna Gay, Gay's daughter. She had barely become acquainted the year before with these delightful sixteen-year-olds, and now she had time to get to know them. She had been following Anna Gay's dancing lessons for a good while, but she was not totally prepared for the handsome young Paul. Sensitive to art and hungry for learning, he was a reflection of her own young self. He, on the other hand, saw her as an aperture to the outside world of art and ideas. The year before, when he met her at a family gathering, he had been too shy to approach her with questions. But he never forgot his first impression of her:

> . . . a small, silver-haired woman, very animated, smoking a great deal, with a fascinating voice and a mysterious accent. She wore a sleeveless white piqué evening gown made from a design by Schiaparelli. No jewelry, but . . . her earlobes were rouged! Astonished, her sisters and the other ladies made indulgent little jokes about it among themselves. Of course they had rouge on their cheeks, Aunt Baby quite a lot of it, but they thought rouged earlobes were outlandish, unseemly, just the kind of thing you would expect of someone who went off to live in Paris and exposed herself to the well-known wicked habits of the French. If Aunt Katherine was aware of what they were saying, she ignored it.

In the early months of 1938 Paul, "totally enchanted," often dropped by her apartment. Everything about her "seemed different, meaningful, glamorous" to him. He longed to peruse her "magical piles of books and manuscripts . . . redolent of marvelous soaps and powders and perfumes." He also discovered her sense of humor: "One day she played a little trick on me. She pretended that she had lost a coin under a tall wardrobe and asked me if I would retrieve it for her. Down on my hands and knees, I found my face only a few inches from the glaring eyes and gaping jaws of a very alive-looking stuffed alligator. She burst into laughter when I fell over backwards, then kissed me when she saw that I was embarrassed, and said that she was sorry. At once it was all right, and we laughed about it together."

Katherine Anne's stories about her family amused Albert ("What was an alligator doing under your bookcase, darling?" he asked her), but some things she told him didn't amuse him at all. He angrily questioned her announced intention to go to Olivet the next summer: "If you feel you must do that, then there is no question about it. Only I entirely fail to see the *must*." He continued to be frustrated, as well, by the protracted divorce proceedings and her inability to set a date for their wedding.

After consulting a lawyer in Houston, she had filed suit for divorce 11 January. Writing to Gene the same day to inform him, she revealed nothing about Albert Erskine or her plan to remarry. She said she would welcome the little money he had offered earlier, and she explained that to complete the proceedings he would receive a waiver to sign in the presence of the American Consul in Moscow. "Bless you for your goodness, my dear," she wrote, "and please think of me as well as I think of you. But you know we shall never live together again, and I think you will find it better to be free, really, to make a life of your own. This way, it is nothing for either of us." By the end of the month she had received from him one hundred dollars and the signed waiver, and the divorce was set for April.

Since the middle of January, she had been trying to reassure Albert, whose fragile patience had been strained. To convince him that she truly loved him and wanted to marry him, she intensified her enthusiasm for their house, and the plans became more elaborate. "Let's talk about The Cares and what will grow there for us," she had suggested near the end of February, in the tone of a patient mother diverting an unhappy child. "Its very pleasant to think we may have violets for lawn, and we can plant jonquil and narcissus all over, just scatter them carelessly (you, know, putting them down very carefully careless) and a great many other kinds of small grassy flowers that will grow among the grass and make a Miltonic enameled meadow."

When the divorce became final on 9 April, she set the wedding date for 19 April (one day past Albert's twenty-seventh birthday), and she wrote to tell her friends: "In the good Catholic formula for this no doubt justice of the peace wedding, I shall say, 'Pray for Albert and me at ten o'clock Tuesday morning, April 19th.'" She began to gather her belongings and to say goodbye to her family before Albert arrived in his new Willys coupé to fetch her on 17 April. Young Paul was the most difficult to leave, for she sensed his need for her. He recalled her departure as "traumatic" for him.

Katherine Anne and Albert drove to Baton Rouge for the marriage license and then to New Orleans for the wedding. Red and Cinina Warren, who were to be witnesses, went with them first to the St. Charles Bar for planter's punch, and then the four of them made their way to the Palace of Justice on Royal Street. A judge shooed them into a small office where he conducted the brief ceremony. Albert kissed her and said, "Now you are safely back home again."

CHAPTER TWENTY

Transition from Marriage to Independence

April 1938–December 1941

This is not the end of the world, it is only the end of my world. The furies really have arrived, and the terrible thing about it is that they did not come uninvited.

After the wedding Katherine Anne joined Albert in his two-room bachelor flat in Kean's Apartments on Chimes Street in Baton Rouge. Albert tried to ensure time for her writing by staying away for lunch and hiring a woman to do cooking and daily housekeeping, but Katherine Anne didn't get much writing done. She had her mind on Olivet, for she planned all along to go despite Albert's disapproval.

She arrived at Olivet in the middle of July and jumped into round-table discussions with students and other writers, met Robert Frost ("old bull-headed bore" but "a great poet and a good man"), had tea with Ford, who opened the conference, shared rum with the poet Leonie Adams, read *Hacienda* for her first evening stint (July 19), and a week later prepared an hour's talk on the short novel (relying "heavily on Henry James, good old St. Henry St. James who left us such a testament to help us out at writers' conferences"). Joe Brewer, the president of Olivet, invited her back for the next year. She reported to Albert that she told Joe, "No, I am sorry." Parodying the song lyric "Gret God, I'm feelin' bad, I aint got the man I thought I had," she "sang" in her returning-home letter to Albert, "Gret God, I'm feelin fine, I got a good man and he's all mine."

The two weeks in Michigan were stimulating and satisfying (she virtually promised to return next year), but when she reached Baton Rouge in the oppressive heat of August, she had little inclination to write. She was more interested in socializing, primarily with Red and

Cinina Warren, Cleanth and Tinkum Brooks, and several other members of the *Southern Review* staff and LSU faculty. Out-of-town visitors such as Andrew Lytle or John Crowe Ransom sometimes dropped by, and she continued to meet and make friends with new people, even showing up at campus hangouts to chat with students. When Albert's lease on his flat ran out in September, they moved to a larger apartment across the hall from the Brookses at 901 America Street.

Her spirits did not lift until April when *Pale Horse, Pale Rider: Three Short Novels* was published by Harcourt, Brace to glowing reviews. She was compared with Hawthorne, Flaubert, and Henry James and praised for flawless prose and the transformation of the novel genre into poetry. The London *Times Literary Supplement* recommended the book as "first choice" of the novels of the week. The one response she desperately wanted was one she never was to get. She had dedicated *Pale Horse, Pale Rider: Three Short Novels* to Harrison Boone Porter, her father, and although she sent him a copy of the book, hoping once more for a word of praise, he never commented on it or acknowledged the dedication.

The publication of *Three Short Novels* was important in a number of ways. Not only was the enthusiastic critical reception wider, she was now officially a novelist rather than a writer of only short and long stories. With her position in the literary world higher and firmer, she had accepted requests to speak at Vassar, Bennington, Bryn Mawr, and Shipley. When Monroe and Lincoln Kirstein invited her to stop by New York City for the lavish 10 May opening of the new home of the Museum of Modern Art, she discovered, as she reported to Albert, that the good reviews of her book had made her "a drawing card in the most New Yorkish sense of the word." She described a staggering number of luncheons, meetings, cocktail parties, art shows, and public readings, and a happy reunion with her cousin Lily Cahill, who had become a successful Broadway actress. For her birthday, 15 May, she met George Platt Lynes at his studio for a photography session before they attended a party Glenway gave for her. There was no outward evidence that she was concerned to be passing her forty-ninth birthday and looking toward her fiftieth, unless it was her frenetic dashing about and eager absorption of praise.

While she was in New York, Katherine Anne's letters to Albert revealed that their marriage was weakening further. "Where shall I go next? What shall I do?" she asked him. Then: "I must come back—darling, tell me how you feel about it. Oh do tell me really, as exactly as you can." She, in fact, had nowhere to go where she could support herself permanently. But after receiving a conciliatory telegram and two special delivery letters from him, she was prepared to give the marriage another chance. She asked Albert to forgive her "once more" and assured him she loved him. "I say it again, from the heart."

She knew that a lack of money had limited her choices. The Guggenheim had expired, and while she earned a little from her lecture tour ($100 each appearance, plus expenses), she would not receive any royalties from *Three Short Novels* until fall at the earliest. While she was in New York, however, she conceived a plan that might bring in a little money: she would pay off "The Cares" with her earnings from the trip and sell the land at a profit to a man who had expressed an interest in it. The clerk of court's office in Baton Rouge recorded that on 1 July she had bought the two parcels of land, a 1.76-acre tract from Cyrus J. Brown for $500 (cash) and an adjoining 2.5-acre tract from Mr. Brown's daughter, Shirley Claire Brown Winston, for the same amount. Two days later, Katherine Anne sold the same two tracts of land to Albert Sidney Williamson for the sum of $1,150, to be paid under mortgage with an unspecified rate of interest. It was more than a stopgap scheme to get needed money. Symbolically, the selling of "The Cares" was the annihilation of a dream.

Within the legal documents of the transaction was Katherine Anne's sworn statement of self-identification required by Louisiana law: "Mrs. Albert Erskine, Jr., nee Katherine Ann [sic] Porter, a resident of Lawful age of the Parish of East Baton Rouge, who has been married three (3) times. First, to Carl Von Pless, from whom she was divorced, Second, to Eugene Pressly, from whom she is divorced and presently to Albert Erskine with whom she is now living, the said Albert Erskine Jr. herein appearing to aid and authorize his said wife." In the style of her grandmother, by refusing to enter them in her sworn statement, she tried to wipe from existence and memory her two earliest marriages, one of which lasted nine years.

Albert was not one of the very few persons she entrusted with the truth about the number of her previous marriages. Neither did she tell him that her ovaries had been removed thirteen years earlier. She made a point of "confiding" to Tinkum that she was showing no signs of menopause and suspected that she would be fertile for a long time to come. She no doubt told Albert the same story and used a pretense of monthly menstrual periods to convince him, just as she had Gene Pressly.

The problems in the marriage were not alleviated by the half-hearted reconciliation in her 15 May letter, for she brought to this marriage not only secrets, but also the difficulties she contributed to every marriage or relationship: resentment at interference with her work, a nervous disposition, and a tendency toward depression that manifested itself in verbal attacks and weeping that morphed into hysteria. Albert later would tell one friend, "She was just plain mean." Albert, despite his good manners, would never accommodate her with passivity, and he took as uncompromising an attitude toward her moods and capriciousness as he took toward manuscripts he edited. For the better part of the next year the two of them would struggle along, arguing privately, escaping from one another whenever possible, receiving visitors as buffers, and, essentially, putting up a front. In the early summer she convinced Albert to move with her into a house, at 1050 Government Street, that provided a separate bedroom for each of them.

Among the visitors that summer was the young Mississippi writer Eudora Welty, who came to Baton Rouge with the editor Herschel Brickell and his wife. Katherine Anne would remember receiving that "quiet, tranquil-looking, modest girl" in the Erskines' house that warm summer day. Eudora, who described herself as "tongue-tied all the way through lunch," recalled stimulating conversation (with Katherine Anne at the center of it), convivial drinks, and Albert's lovely manners and attentiveness to his wife. She went away with "an abstract memory of happiness" in the household.

Other visitors that summer who were deceived about the state of the Erskines' marriage were W. H. Auden and his companion Chester Kollman. During the several days' visit Katherine Anne and Albert played Mozart recordings for them, served them mint juleps, drove them to St. Francisville to show them "decayed Southern grandeur," and talked and talked about literature. Katherine Anne gave the two men her room, pretending it was a guest room, while she slept on a cot in Albert's room. In his letter of thanks Auden praised their hospitality and declared that he expected to be Katherine Anne and Albert's "friends for life."

In late July Katherine Anne returned to Olivet. With the success of *Three Short Novels* and her additional experience speaking at colleges, she was more comfortable with students. She had reunions with John Peale Bishop ("man of the world") and George Davis, editor of *Harper's Bazaar*. Sherwood Anderson, whom she had not met before but with whom she had corresponded a little, supplied "the rough-diamond note." Edmund Wilson was there, and he wrote to Allen Tate that John Bishop, Padraic Column, and Katherine Anne Porter put on "wonderful shows." Gossip circulated that Katherine Anne Porter, who didn't care a lot about sex (it made her nervous), had been delighted to escape the demands of her lusty young husband. She promised Joe Brewer that she would come back to Olivet the next summer.

When she returned to Baton Rouge, Albert, who had successfully completed an important segment of his graduate work, left for a trip to Memphis to visit his parents. In her solitude, she finally was working well. Soon she wrote a story that was tangential to the long novel. "The Downward Path to Wisdom" focuses on a child named Stephen, who is caught among quarrelling parents, a grandmother, an uncle, and a servant, all of whom not only fail to understand his child's innocence and needs but withhold from him the love that would have redeemed him. Loveless, he learns to hate all of them. The story was accepted by George Davis for *Harper's Bazaar.*

The late summer and early fall, however, brought letdowns and anxieties. She was badly disappointed to learn that she had been snubbed by the Texas Institute of Letters, which had awarded its annual prize to J. Frank Dobie's *Apache Gold, Yaqui Silver* rather than her *Three Short Novels.* On 1 September Germany invaded Poland, and two days later France and Britain declared war on Germany. World War II had begun. Katherine Anne had premonitions of disaster, and Albert was concerned about the draft that would accompany U.S. entry in the war.

On 31 December 1939, Katherine Anne and Albert entertained Delmore Schwartz and his wife for a New Year's weekend that featured a roast suckling pig with lavish side dishes. What Schwartz remembered as odd about the visit was Katherine Anne's feigned struggle to stay up late with him and Albert and her declaration that it was her age that made a difference in her stamina. She was "talking all the time of being 20 years older than either of us," he recalled. Although the causes of the disintegration of the Erskines' marriage were surely more complicated than age difference, she had directed attention to what everyone else would consider the fissure in the union.

The New Year's Day dinner was Katherine Anne and Albert's last domestic scene anyone would remember. As 1940 began, she let it be known that she would be available for lectures at colleges and writing workshops such as Bread Loaf, and she wrote to Elizabeth Ames, director of Yaddo, asking for a residency whenever possible, the sooner the better. Almost immediately Mrs. Ames confirmed an opening from 3 June through 31 July. In the meantime Albert moved into the LSU Faculty Club.

Shortly before the separation she finished "Notes on a Criticism of Thomas Hardy," which marked her foray into literary criticism. Taking as her starting point T. S. Eliot's disparaging estimation of Hardy, she defended Hardy and criticized Eliot for pious orthodoxy, which she thought had no place in either art or criticism. The essay, which was published in the summer issue of the *Southern Review,* was as much a statement of her current religious belief ("There is at the heart of the universe a riddle no man can solve, and in the end, God may be the answer") as an analysis of Hardy's art.

Criticism was a two-edged sword, however. Before she left Baton Rouge for Yaddo she took time to compose a careful letter to Lodwick Hartley, a professor at North Carolina State College of Agriculture and Engineering, who had written a critical article on her work that appeared in the spring issue of the *Sewanee Review.* It was the first published scholarly analysis of her fiction. She read it with interest and, for the most part, satisfaction, but she took issue with Hartley's suggestion that some of her stories contained sentimentality: "Myself I think half the evils of human relationship are rooted in sentimentality, which Joyce defined as . . . the feelings of one who wanted the pleasures of a situation or relationship without having to pay the price." She also reiterated her position on "the feminine point of view": "At the risk of being called a feminist, (slimy word) I wish to say that I do not believe that my faults are specially womanly, or my virtues specially masculine . . . I write as I do . . . as an artist, with an almost complete lack of self-consciousness as to sex."

Katherine Anne arrived at the Saratoga Springs train depot 3 June and was met by the Yaddo chauffeur, who drove her to the four-hundred-acre estate on which sat a stately Victorian mansion surrounded by a vast lawn, formal gardens, and dense woods. The great house had been built by banker and philanthropist Spencer Trask and his wife, Katrina, an amateur novelist and poet, who named it "Yaddo" after their four-year-old daughter's attempt to pronounce "shadow." After the deaths of all their children the Trasks converted the estate into a place of inspiration and hospitality for artists. Elizabeth Ames, tall, beautiful, stern, and talented, had been director since 1926.

In the grand central hall Katherine Anne was met by Mrs. Ames, who took her to the high tower and her quarters, a long, narrow bedroom and study with leaded, paned sash windows and a gray marbled bathroom with a huge, deep tub. Enchanted, she thought, "Maybe I could live here." She had expected to stay at Yaddo only until the middle of July, when she would leave for Olivet, but Elizabeth Ames arranged for her to return to Yaddo after the Michigan stint and to stay until the first of October.

In August Katherine Anne left Yaddo long enough to give a lecture at the Bread Loaf Writing School at Middlebury College, where she met Carson McCullers, whose first novel, *The Heart Is a Lonely Hunter*, she and Albert had read together in Baton Rouge. Katherine Anne had thought then that Carson might be another young southern woman like Eudora Welty whom she could sponsor and befriend, but the eccentric, heavy drinking, overtly bisexual Carson proved to be far different from the shy and decorous Eudora. At the end of the conference Carson approached Katherine Anne saying she admired her stories immensely and hoped Katherine Anne hadn't minded her when she was drunk. Katherine Anne's response had been noncommittal, but she summarized her to Albert as "tiresome to what a degree." "So I think I shall give her up as a hopeful youngster," she said. "She's rotten to the bone already."

Katherine Anne's interest in having a house of her own had revived with her delight in the Saratoga area. Without any substantial income, however, she knew that purchasing a house would be impossible, and she passed the word that she would be available for bookings on the college lecture and workshop circuit. Soon she accepted offers to speak at Cornell, Wells, Briarcliffe, and Skidmore. She also agreed to return to Olivet as an artist in residence for three weeks in January. Elizabeth Ames solved the problem of where Katherine Anne would live between her college stops by offering her rare wintertime room and board at Yaddo and extending her stay until June 1941.

In recent months Katherine Anne had met editors who talked to her about leaving Harcourt, Brace, and she was seriously interested in doing so. Bennett Cerf wanted her to move to Random House, and representatives of Simon and Schuster, Doubleday, Viking, and Little, Brown had also let her know they would welcome her and pay off her contractual debts if Harcourt, Brace would agree to such a transition. Her interest in leaving her original publishing house was tied more to her embarrassment and frustration at failing to fulfill contracts than it was to disagreements or displeasure with her editors there. She thought that with a new publisher she could have a fresh start.

After the literary agent Maxim Lieber approached Harcourt, Brace in her behalf, however, Donald Brace and Lambert Davis called upon her to tell her firmly that they had no intention of releasing her. "I just sat and kept my own counsel," she told Caroline Gordon, "and felt like a problem child being renovated by the family." The outcome was that she made more promises and signed four new or revised contracts, and they gave her more advances. She was obligated to finish the Cotton Mather biography and the remaining two short novels, "Promised Land"—now retitled "No Safe Harbor"—and "The Man in the Tree," as well as a third short novel she was calling "The Leaning Tower." The three short novels and several new stories would be combined in some yet unspecified way to constitute the second and third books. The fourth contract called for an unnamed book of fiction, either a novel or another collection of short stories. She planned to produce a book a year for the next four years. "Prospects, which often glow," she told Caroline, "are positively blazing at the moment."

"No Safe Harbor" however, had become troubling to her, for she had begun to think it wasn't a short novel at all but might instead be rather long. For the moment she would set aside the writing of it while the whole work unfolded in her mind. Directly related to it was "The Leaning Tower," which was inspired by the little plaster Tower of Pisa that Gene Pressly had broken at a Berlin pension in 1931. Her diary notes and letters to Gene about her fellow inhabitants at Rosa Reichl's boardinghouse and the recollected atmosphere and experiences of Berlin formed the background of the tale about illusion, cruelty, suffering, decadence, and the potential fall of civilization. Her autobiographical representative in the fictional work is Charles Upton, who shares with Miranda a romantic sensibility (including crying jags), naiveté, and a desire to know the truth. Like Laura in "Flowering Judas" and Miranda in *Pale Horse, Pale Rider*, he intuits an awful truth in a dream that concludes his story. She finished the short novel before the end of the year and sent it to Red and Cleanth for the *Southern Review*.

In addition to income from Harcourt, Brace, she had received a good fee for her appearance 2 December on the radio program *Invitation to Learning*. But she was never an efficient manager, and she rarely could resist extravagant purchases of clothes and perfume. For the holidays she bought three expensive dresses, a stunning feathered hat, and a turquoise evening gown complemented with a black velvet coat and dark red snakeskin shoes. Her money had been further depleted by shipping costs for her filing cabinets and trunks sent from Baton Rouge, a dental bill for cosmetic crowns, and payments to Gay toward the nursing care of Harrison, who recently had suffered a paralytic stroke and now was an invalid in Gay's house.

Swamped with expenses, she nevertheless continued to think about buying a house. She told Albert that if she did not have a house of her own and "somehow enough to live on," she feared she might end in "a home for aged paupers." "You may laugh," she told him, "it *does* sound funny, and it could happen." She was now certain that she wanted a house near Yaddo.

Albert, who had arrived in Connecticut to take up a job with New Directions in Greenwich, came over to Yaddo to spend a few days with her. Christmas Day they lolled around her quarters at North Farm listening to records he had brought her that included Corelli's *Christmas Concerto* and Bach's *Wedding Cantata.* After highballs they went into Saratoga Springs for a roast beef dinner at the Worden Hotel. As she described their reunion after a six-month separation, it sounded romantic and nearly perfect. Although her and Albert's lives, she told Elizabeth Ames, were "probably not going to be lived in the most conventional sort of way," the bond between them was "mysterious and deep," providing "confidence and joy." "It is really love," she said.

But despite her idealized portrait of the Erskines' marriage, there would be no reconciliation. In the first letter Katherine Anne wrote to Albert in the new year, she told him, "Oh how glad I am we are separated. Now we can be at ease with each other." The marriage would play itself out for another year and a half while she rechanneled the energy she had spent in maintaining the fantasy of it.

CHAPTER TWENTY-ONE

"Ah, the House . . . the House"

January 1941–August 1942

The truth is, I want to have a house of my own, where I can put my books and papers and little dear worthless belongings and I want to sleep and wake in that house, and work in it, and fuss with it a little, for the rest of my days.

When that Dope Goering remarked en passant that America would be an inside job, well, I could only hope it wasn't so. But now I lie awake nights fearing it may be true . . . God knows the air is full of signs and portents. Did you happen to see that perfectly wonderful profile of Harry Bridges in a New Yorker . . . in which he described the methods of the FBI? It was frightfully amusing, and I mean frightfully. I laughed with my hair on end.

Katherine Anne initiated 1941 with a Twelfth Night party in her quarters at Yaddo's North Farm. Moving among holiday wreathes and two dozen tall, lighted green candles, she played records for her six guests and served Kentucky eggnog and liver pâté she made herself. She had a happy feeling about the year ahead and a growing desire to make a permanent home in the area. "I do so like this old oaken, iron-bound character of the upstate New Yorkers," she wrote Albert. "I get along like a house afire here, and feel wonderfully settled in my mind and heart."

In the middle of January Elizabeth drove Katherine Anne to Ballston Spa, about ten miles from Yaddo, to look at a house she had heard about. When they reached the summit of the Albany Post Road that overlooked the valley, Katherine Anne saw her dream house, a two-story, seven-room house sitting on a knoll behind tall maples surrounded by rolling woods and meadows and facing a forest preserve of eight thousand acres of pine and spruce trees. The elderly woman who was selling it told her two hundred dollars would hold it until 1 May, when the remaining eighteen hundred dollars of the asking price was due. "I have looked at old houses in Pennsylvania and Connecticut, Massachusetts, even a few days in Vermont," she wrote to Glenway. "I have seen literally hundreds. I know at a glance what is there, and this is my house. That is settled. I am going to have it."

Katherine Anne mentally renamed the estate "South Hill" and made plans for remodeling the house: tearing off porches, taking partitions out, adding plumbing and heating and a new lighting system, turning the cellar into a basement. She expected to move in 15 May, her fifty-first birthday. "And here I am," she wrote Albert at the end of January, "happy in some way that I never was before . . . ; if only I can have my place to stay and be able to work to keep it pleasant and to care for it properly, I want nothing more . . . And everything I lost before in this world will come back to me there. Just think, when I plant a tree now I can stay to see it grow, when I work and spend what I have on the house, I do not have to leave it just when it is becoming pleasant to live in. Just think, never again do I have to depend upon any one else for anything, and I can make what plans I like, then carry them out in my own time and way, and the house and the whole landscape around it will look as I would like them too, little by little, year after year." To earn money for the house she made commitments to speak at several colleges and to participate in two *Invitation to Learning* programs. Between engagements she had the security of Yaddo, for Elizabeth promised to support her while she talked her way into a remodeled and beautifully furnished South Hill.

Because Elizabeth's support extended to protecting Katherine Anne from as many distractions as possible, she turned down Josie's request for a place at Yaddo for the winter on the grounds that an additional guest might disturb those already in residence. Since Katherine Anne was one of the few persons remaining through the winter, Josie reckoned that Katherine Anne was responsible for the denial. She wrote Elizabeth an angry letter and sent a copy to Katherine Anne. Katherine Anne's letter to Josie in February was mildly apologetic ("regrets for not having been more serviceable in the Yaddo business"), but she declined Josie's request to read her recent *Satan's Sergeants* and write an overview of her canon. There would be no further correspondence between the two of them for the next year and a half.

Despite all the speaking engagements, by 1 May Katherine Anne was short of the eighteen hundred dollars to pay for South Hill. She was nevertheless able to assume ownership of the house by taking out a short-term loan. Renovations that she considered necessary before she actually moved in would have to be delayed until she had enough money to proceed.

In June the arriving summer fellows at Yaddo enlarged the colony's society and changed its winter makeup. Katherine Anne was delighted to see Eudora Welty among the newcomers, but she was not at all glad to see Carson McCullers, who seemed to be obsessed with her, following her about and seizing every opportunity to be in her presence or speak to her. One evening she went to Katherine Anne's room, pounded on the door, and begged, "Please, Katherine Anne, let me come in and talk with you—I do love you so very much." After ordering her to go away, Katherine Anne was relieved to hear (she thought) Carson retreating down the hall. She was shocked, however, when she opened her door to discover Carson lying prostrate across the threshold. "But I had had enough," Katherine Anne told Virginia Spencer Carr, McCullers's biographer. "I merely stepped over her and continued on my way to dinner. And that was the last time she ever bothered me."

Except for the two weeks at Olivet, Katherine Anne spent the rest of the summer working on her house and writing. She was enjoying the company of Eudora, whose career was moving ahead splendidly, much to the pleasure of Katherine Anne, who thought of Eudora as her protégé. In the summer of 1941 Eudora was reading the proofs of *A Curtain of Green and Other Stories* and waiting, along with her editor at Doubleday, Doran, for Katherine Anne to write the introduction to it that she had promised.

Eudora was assigned to the farmhouse with Katherine Anne, and their bedrooms were across the hall from one another. Eudora could hear Katherine Anne's little typewriter stuttering along, wondering whether she was working on the introduction. What Katherine Anne was working on so single-mindedly, however, was "No Safe Harbor." One day she tapped on Eudora's door and held out a sheaf of typed pale-blue pages. "You may read this," she told Eudora, "if you like." It was the first sixty pages of the novel. Eudora was flattered, sensing that Katherine Anne's offer constituted a "gift of . . . confidence."

As the summer deepened, so did the friendship. They talked about their common favorite authors (Rilke, Joyce, Forster, Homer) and played stacks of French records on Katherine Anne's wind-up gramophone ("from Piaf back to Gluck, back to madrigals, the opera *Orphée*"). Eudora was also drawn into Katherine Anne's flourishing domesticity that included compiling recipes and laying in a cache of bottles of choice wine for the soon-to-exist, temperature-controlled, wine cellar in her house.

Knowing she needed transportation to get to and from her house, Katherine Anne bought with her meager funds a brand new, shiny black Studebaker car that she named "the Champ." She had not quite learned to drive, but Eudora was a good driver and willing to take the wheel as they made frequent trips from Yaddo to South Hill to see how work was progressing or just to lounge in the presence of the house, stretching out on the shady, grassy lawn, puffing on cigarettes, and talking about *Ulysses.* Sometimes Katherine Anne would pluck on a little ukulele and sing old ballads. They also drove into Albany and bought French antique dining-room chairs and a roll of ruby-red carpeting for the stairs. The purchases were put in storage alongside Katherine Anne's other possessions to wait until the house was ready.

In July Katherine Anne received a long letter from her nephew Paul a week before his twentieth birthday. She had not been feeling very kindly toward her family. Anna Gay had disappointed her badly by hauling off and getting married the previous August instead of dedicating herself to a career in dance. Baby's and Gay's letters in the past six months had been full of complaints about Harrison, who since his stroke had been an irritable trial to his caretakers. She also had received a few strange letters from Harrison himself, who ranted with paranoid obsession against Baby and Gay. Paul's letter, on the other hand, was a happy surprise. His interest in music, literature, and painting had increased and matured since she saw him last in the spring of 1938, and she recognized in him a kindred spirit.

"When I was your age and younger," she wrote in reply, "it seemed to me I was on a desert island quite literally. No one to talk to about the things that interested me, and not only indifference, but an active hostility to the way my mind was growing, and the direction my life had to take." She encouraged him to find his "own place" and his "own people" and to send her anything on earth he wanted to write (in "confidence"). Because he expressed an interest in Thomas Mann, she recommended a reading list: *Death in Venice, Disorder and Early Sorrow, Mario the Magician,* and *Buddenbrooks.* She urged him to read E. M. Forster, Yeats, and Virginia Woolf. The correspondence continued with rapid fire.

After the first deadline for the introduction to Eudora's *Curtain of Green* had come and gone and Eudora had returned to Mississippi, her editor, John Woodburn, drove over to Saratoga Springs to discuss the delayed introduction with Katherine Anne. Surprised, he came away with it in hand. Eudora, grateful for Katherine Anne's work in her behalf, said, "All her generosity, her penetration, serenely informs it, doing everything in her power for the book and for its author, as she'd intended to do all the time." Her introduction to *A Curtain of Green* and an essay called "Now at Last a House of My Own" were the only new pieces of writing Katherine Anne finished in 1941.

Buying "the Champ" and furnishings for South Hill had absorbed her skimpy earnings, and her financial plight worsened through the year. Desperate, she made agreements to write still more books. In June she signed two contracts with Doubleday, Doran for a biography of Erasmus ("Erasmus of Basel") and an account of a fifteenth-century murder trial indirectly related to Joan of Arc ("The Trial of Berthe de Fauquemberge"). Doubleday, Doran paid her an advance of $1,000 with an additional $1,000 payable upon receipt of the completed manuscripts. She also signed a contract in November with Viking to assemble an anthology of stories that might sell as a college textbook. Viking gave her an advance of $1,250 and guaranteed her another $1,250 when she delivered the manuscript. The anthology was due April 1, 1942; "Berthe" was due July 1, 1942; and "Erasmus" was due July 1, 1943. The $2,250 was gone almost before it reached her hands.

On 23 January 1942, Harrison Porter died. Katherine Anne wired talisman roses to the mortuary and mailed letters of consolation to her family with a promise to send, later, her share of the funeral expenses. In her letter to Baby, who had been the child closest to their father, she encouraged her to get on with her life, but in her letter to Gay and Paul she revealed her own sadness and regret:

> After all the rage and hatred and anger, and the last weakness and fear, it is ended; and tonight I looked at the cold stars and the half-moon in the deep sky, and could think only of our little, old sad father lying alone for the first night in his grave; and he seems to me like my own child, as if I had grown very old and he was newly born again . . . . . And this morning I saw the first sun he would not see, and though we had waited for this day, still all day my mind has been suspended, blank, and my heart full, as if I were still waiting, as if something else could happen. But it will not, and now I hope we can go our ways in peace and forget some of the evils we have known, and that the old grudges will die . . .

> Death is not an unhappy ending, it is simply the end. It is only
> unhappy for the living who remember what went before . . . . .
> I can think of nothing but the little tired man folded away to
> sleep and to go to dust forever . . . . . it makes me very lonely and
> tired, too.

Her grief was deepened by the cold, dark Saratoga winter and Albert's pressing her for a speedy divorce since he had fallen in love with a young New York woman he wanted to marry. After considering various options, Katherine Anne decided to go to Reno, Nevada, in the spring, live there for six weeks, and get a divorce without any fuss. Only thoughts of South Hill brought her happiness in the early months of 1942. "I visited my house yesterday," she wrote John Peale Bishop, "and it is lovely, lovely. A dear good sweet place, full of light and air and modest space. I shall live there some day when this time of my life will be only a bad, half remembered dream."

Another part of the bad dream was the war and the paranoia and controversy that surrounded it. These days she was especially critical of the tactics of the Federal Bureau of Investigation (FBI) and the Office of Strategic Services (OSS), which, she was convinced, abused loyal American citizens. The poet and editor Donald Elder, for example, who in a spirit of liberal patriotism had been trying futilely to get a job in defense work, became convinced that the FBI was obstructing his efforts because of his liberal politics. Katherine Anne told Elder to not "let the gestapo discourage" him, and she declared that she herself was in "such a cold and grim fighting mood" she would "enjoy a good fight with the FBI or almost anybody on the other side." Her own resolve would soon be tested.

By 9 May Katherine Anne was a resident of Reno, living in an inexpensive, small studio apartment at 303 Hill Street, a discreet distance from the gaudy gambling district that looked like an Old West movie set. She also had found a lawyer she could afford. He was George A. Bartlett, a former judge who had served in the U.S. Congress and written a satiric novel on divorce. Since his retirement from the bench, he had steadily performed weddings and taken divorce cases that interested him, adjusting his fee according to his client's ability to pay. When Katherine Anne met with him, he set his fee at one hundred dollars, and they became instant friends. She was routinely invited to his home, gladly received by his wife and daughters, and placed on their guest list for parties and dinners.

It seemed as if the six weeks in Reno were not going to be so bad after all. Katherine Anne had a ready-made, small social circle, and she planned to spend many satisfying hours of each day working on the books under contract to Doubleday, Doran and Viking. She observed with only detached interest Reno's "gambling hells," fancy-dress cowboys, "seriously loose ladies," and "prosperous, frustrated women" there like her to get a divorce. She cooked her daily steak and asparagus in her own little apartment, worked at her writing during the day, and socialized a little in the evening.

On Katherine Anne's birthday a young FBI agent called upon her to ask questions about her friends and probably about herself as well. She must have been asked about Josie, who after being denied residency at Yaddo had presented herself to the government for wartime service and had been placed in the independent intelligence and propaganda agency known as the OCI, the Office of the Coordinator of Information, "to determine what is left of the German will to live." Accused of being both a Communist and Fascist and charged with taking secret documents out of the OCI, she was being investigated by the wartime House Un-American Activities Committee (HUAC).

Contained in Josie's FBI report filed in the Salt Lake City office are routine biographical facts that many of Josie's acquaintances could have supplied and also information of a more personal nature: Herbst "has a violent temper, a revolutionist attitude and has caused trouble wherever the opportunity presented itself. She is described as having the utmost contempt for the American form of Government and for the so-called American 'liberal.' She is said to be a great follower of STALIN and a personal admirer of this man. She is not known to have been an admirer of TROTSKY nor to have been actively affiliated with the TROTSKY Communists." According to an unattributed "amplification" in the field investigation report, Herbst had made statements to the effect that Earl Browder was too "timid"; she had attempted to use the American Ambassador to France to get German Communists into America; and she had published a magazine story in which she said she had voted the Communist ticket.

Josie's biographer, Elinor Langer, concluded that Katherine Anne was the report's "Informant I," who had asked for confidentiality after making "derogatory" remarks about Josie. It certainly is reasonable to assume that Katherine Anne provided some of the information contained in the FBI report since we know, as she reported to Donald Elder, that she had been interviewed by the FBI in Reno in the middle of May, and the Salt Lake City report on Josie was dated 16 May. And Katherine Anne might have commented about Josie's temper and Josie's distaste for liberals and the American form of government. But there are peculiar and dubious statements in the report, too, and without a tape or a transcript of the interview or interviews, it is impossible to distinguish between what Katherine Anne might have said and the agent's interpretation of it, or, for that matter, between what Katherine Anne might have said and what others said, since the background investigation of Josie was, according to Langer, "a full-scale mobilization involving offices and agents all over the country eliciting an undifferentiated hodgepodge of opinion."

Some facts about Katherine Anne's FBI interview, however, can be confirmed. According to FBI report 77-841, filed at Albany, New York, 12 May, "[name excised] Yaddo Artists' Colony advised that KATHERINE ANNE PORTER was not presently residing at the Colony, but could be reached before the 15th of June at 303 Hill Street, Reno, Nevada." As Katherine Anne described the interview to Donald Elder, she had been "tracked . . . down" to answer questions about "friends." It is likely that she was asked about more persons than Josie. Gene Pressly had offered his services to the U.S. Army and the OSS, and despite his earlier service with the State Department could have been the subject of background verification during wartime. Malcolm Cowley, working in the Office of Facts and Figures (OFF), was also being investigated, as was Elder. In fact, in her June letter to Elder, Katherine Anne seemed to be sending him an oblique message of assurance: "I was really happy to be able to tell [the FBI] that so far as I knew [the friends] had no political consciousness whatever . . . . . They ask the strangest questions, don't they?"

Several scenes can be imagined. She described her "FBI man" as "young, good looking, very tall, the typical FBI sleuth," and if he created the right mood with dinner and wine, on her birthday, no less, she might have talked freely and intemperately. She also might have been intimidated. Her own FBI file at the time included the following entry: "A confidential informant who has furnished reliable information in the past advised that one Katherine Anne Porter was a sponsor of the Second Congress of American Writers held in New York City on June 4, 5, 6, 1937, under the auspices of the League of American Writers." Whatever Katherine Anne told her young FBI man, the meeting must have been severely unsettling to her and, more than her pending divorce, might have accounted for the "very dark place" to which she told Tinkum she had descended in the last part of May. Her neat summary to Elder of the interview's conclusion ignored the wounding emotion that had to surround it, whether that of fear or guilt or both.

Katherine Anne and Albert's divorce was final on 19 June. She thanked Judge Bartlett for his charming management of the "unwedding ceremony at the court house," and she celebrated the event with him at a "noisy party" that evening at his home. A week later she described to him her "very real and happy serenity of spirit," but she revealed somber thoughts to Tinkum as she translated Jean Auel's lines that had inspired an earlier title of her novel-in-progress:

> Which of us but has had
> His promised land, his day
> Of ecstasy, and his end in exile!

The summer of 1942 ended Katherine Anne's effort to succeed at marriage. She had concluded that husbands were the enemy of art, and, with some exceptions, her attitude toward husbands of her friends changed. While she might be charmed by a handsome fiancé of a young friend, when he became a husband her references to him darkened. Husbands could even drive an artist crazy. She claimed that Virginia Woolf's "madness" began in 1913, the year of her marriage to Leonard Woolf. "I want to know," Katherine Anne wrote in a marginal note in Woolf's *Diary*, "why she killed herself when all the evidence is that she enjoyed life even at its worst, and wanted 'ten years more.'?" The answer was clear. In publishing his wife's diaries, Leonard Woolf also had betrayed her, just what Katherine Anne expected of husbands.

Katherine Anne also saw the divorce from her fifth husband as her freedom from sexual "duty." Recalling Socrates' comment that it was like having a tiger off his back, she said she actually felt that way at age thirty. What she probably meant was that had she really been past sex in 1920 she would have avoided the whole bad experience with Salomón de la Selva in 1921, Francisco Aguilera in 1924, and Ernest Stock in 1926. "I'll tell you what I've always thought about sex," she told her nephew Paul in 1972, "and I still think it after quite a varied experience. It is a crashing bore unless you are so dead in love with a person that you can't live without him." She said there were only two men she had felt that way about, but she never named them.

On 20 June Katherine Anne flew to Bloomington for a five-day writing conference at Indiana University. She threw herself into a busy schedule of lunches, poker evenings ("which I love"), and lecturing ("Can you imagine people who will *pay* me to talk, when you

know so well I talk cheerfully for nothing!" she wrote Judge Bartlett.)
She was happy to see old friends, especially John Crowe Ransom,
who was "pretty marvelous." She was also pleased to meet
Dr. Alfred Kinsey, who since 1939 had begun conducting interviews for
the thousands of sexual histories that would form the statistical base
for his revolutionary *Sexual History in the Human Male* (1948) and
Sexual History in the Human Female (1953). Kinsey was particularly
interested in artists, and he interviewed her. She made a good story
out of it: Kinsey neutrally asked her, "Have you ever made love to a
dog?" "Why, no, Dr. Kinsey!" she reported exclaiming. "Have you?"
She must also have told him that she was "cold as a cucumber" in
matters of sex because he asked whether she had read the works of
Richard von Krafft-Ebing, whose *Frigidity in the Human Female* at
the turn of the century had been groundbreaking.

After Kinsey went through the rest of the questions on his list,
they had a pleasant conversation about food, music, art, and literature. She wrote him after the interview, "I was only half joking when
I remarked to you that I might have something to say to you on the
subject of sex; but I suppose nothing much is new to you by now.
Still, a half-joke can be quite serious, and I did mean it, and shall be
delighted to be interviewed on the subject of the erotic element in
the arts, including as you say, literature." On Valentine's Day 1952
Kinsey wrote to her ("Dear Katherine Anne") to thank her for her
"very considerable contribution" to his research and "to our thinking on various important matters."

On 27 June she took a train from Bloomington to Boulder for the
five-week Rocky Mountain Writers' Conference. Her future after
Boulder was undecided. Although she had accepted an offer from Sarah
Lawrence College for a temporary replacement position, she impulsively broke the contract when she received a proposal from LSU to fill
in for Red Warren for a year. Near the end of July, however, Elizabeth,
responding to her news that she intended to spend the next academic
year in Baton Rouge, wrote her a long letter that touched her heart.
Describing how she had spent scarce wartime gas driving to South Hill
to sit on the doorstep for a couple of hours, Elizabeth told Katherine
Anne, "God speed the next year quickly and your return to that lovely
place which seems to ask and ask when its mistress will be there."

The way suddenly seemed clear. She cancelled her agreement
with LSU and from Boulder went straight to Yaddo, where she was to
stay until she could get her house into livable shape.

CHAPTER TWENTY-TWO

South Hill and Washington, D.C.

August 1942–January 1945

I make plans and decisions in my firm, sensible rational states of mind, and then in my irrational states I find myself to my horror trapped in my own decisions.

In the summer Katherine Anne put together "The South Hill Book," a combination guest book, diary, and photograph album that was to contain a complete account of her house. On 28 August Elizabeth Ames wrote in the book, "Glory be to God that K. A. has moved in!" "This is my own house," Katherine Anne wrote on 12 September, "my very first, and how miraculous it seems that I need never move these books and such and myself, again." But the diary entries simultaneously disclosed an undercurrent of depression initiated by flu, a painful strain in her right eye, and money worries. The plumber was threatening to put a lien on the house unless she paid the remainder of what she owed him, and she had not settled her account with the building contractor. She suddenly recalled Ford's favorite superstition—"To see the new moon through any obstruction is very bad luck"—and noted that she was looking at the new moon through reading glasses, a window pane, a metal screen, and tree branches.

In the "murderous cold" winter of 1942–1943 pipes throughout the house froze, and a bone-chill seeped through crevices in the old walls. Katherine Anne's car, "The Champ," had to be towed away, frozen. "Well, of course its very flattering," she remarked to Caroline Gordon, "to have all Hell and all Nature combine to turn in and help me celebrate my first winter on my own farm, and as people keep telling me, 'Well, at least nothing more can happen, this is about all this climate can do,' I don't really believe them." Disillusioned, she made a secret pact with herself that she would not spend another winter at South Hill.

Harcourt, Brace had grown tired of waiting for "No Safe Harbor" and made plans to bring out *The Leaning Tower and Other Stories.* She dedicated the collection to her nephew Paul, who had been drafted into the army about the time she moved to South Hill. But income from that book was months away. Barbara, Lloyd, Glenway, and Monroe concluded that the best solution for her financial problems was for her to finish her books under contract, and they insisted she accept their gift of several months stay at a nearby rural inn. Escaping South Hill before cold weather arrived, she made her departure sound casual: "just throwing a suitcase full of clo' and a few books and a manuscript in the Champ and rolling right down the Hudson river road to a place which promises me food, fire, a roof and no housework."

The place was the Harbor Hill Inn at Cold Spring, New York, across from West Point. She arrived in early October, expecting to stay until January. But sitting in an inn with nothing to do but write did not work this time, and she was able to tap neither her creative well nor the motivation that activated her writing at Doylestown. She spent her time writing letters and battling the onset of flu.

In late November she was surprised to receive a letter from Josie, who seemed sad over the break in the friendship. "People ask me how you are but I have nothing to tell them. I wish I had." She signed the letter "With love, Jo." After a month Katherine Anne matched Josie's effort and wrote a long, friendly letter with no mention of the hiatus in the friendship.

Early in 1944 Katherine Anne learned that John Peale Bishop, who held an appointment as Fellow of Regional American Literature at the Library of Congress, had had a serious heart attack and would be unable to continue in the position. She wrote to Allen Tate, who also was at the Library of Congress, having assumed its first Chair of Poetry, to ask whether it would occur to "anyone in power there to offer such a fellowship to a literary femme sole,—to me, if I must speak right up." With the support of Librarian of Congress Archibald MacLeish, such an offer was quickly forthcoming, and she unhesitatingly accepted it. Allen and Caroline, who were renting a house in the Anacostia section of Washington with Lon and Fanny Cheney, invited her to live with the four of them. She arrived in Washington on 19 January, looking forward to new experiences and a new scene. On 20 January she signed the oath of office and was officially appointed to the Society of Fellows of the Library of Congress.

A pervasive air of seriousness and edginess hung over wartime Washington. The streets were thronged with soldiers, military bureaucrats, refugees, and royalty from neutral countries. International conferences took place in carefully guarded mansions. It all seemed like an anachronistic backdrop to the work Katherine Anne was to do in the library, researching source writings of pioneers and transient visitors in early America, focusing on her ancestral relative Daniel Boone and the period from 1769 to 1820 in Kentucky.

Her reunion with the Tates and Cheneys was initially delightful. At the Anacostia house, dubbed "the Bird Cage" in honor of a so-named whorehouse in one of Lon's novels, she joined lively conversations and enjoyed the frequent dinner parties. At one she met Marcella Comés Winslow, a young portrait painter and friend of the Tates. When Marcella's husband, Colonel Randolph Winslow, of the U.S. Army Corps of Engineers, was sent to England, she decided to wait out the war with Mary and Johnny, her two young children, in a pleasing old house on P Street in Georgetown. Marcella's letters to her mother-in-law, the writer Anne Goodwin Winslow, included epistolary snapshots of Katherine Anne from the time the two met until their friendship ended more than twenty years later. "KAP has pure white hair, short, curly," Marcella wrote in February, after Katherine Anne had agreed to sit for a portrait. "She is short, about your height [5 feet, 2 inches], thin, and has lovely gray-blue eyes, a youthful unlined face, high forehead, pointed chin. She is animated in a very ladylike way and fascinating to talk with. No airs or mannerisms, a good sense of humor and the ability to say devastating things in a charming way."

After only a month Katherine Anne discovered that the Bird Cage had become too small for comfort. The high-strung Caroline had turned on Katherine Anne with a vengeance, perhaps, her biographer Veronica Makowsky suggested, out of resentment that Katherine Anne's critical reputation, resting on a much smaller body of work, had surpassed hers in the twenty years since their days as struggling writers in Greenwich Village. Caroline and Allen's daughter, Nancy, recalled her mother and Katherine Anne quarreling over a jingle about a turkey, Caroline insisting not only that Katherine Anne's rendition was wrong but also that Katherine Anne was stupid not to know the correct one. Finally, when Caroline provoked a hysterical argument with Katherine Anne over a broken bottle of perfume, Allen asked Marcella whether Katherine Anne could move in with her. Marcella was delighted. Not only did she admire Katherine Anne, but she needed the extra sixty dollars a month Katherine Anne would pay for room and board.

Katherine Anne and Marcella took in as many social events and gallery openings as they could. At Caresse Crosby's art gallery they met Eleanor Clark, a young writer, and Corporal Charles Shannon, a handsome young southern painter. At another gallery they encountered, of all people, Francisco Aguilera, who had returned to the United States and assumed a position in the Hispanic Foundation at the Library of Congress. Katherine Anne told Marcella that she was "madly in love with [him] once and, literally almost murdered [him]." They also ran into Mary Doherty, who recently had moved to Washington with her sister Peggy to take a government job.

Katherine Anne became an integral part of the Winslows' lives. She was fascinated with the history of the Winslow family, delighted to learn that the seventeenth-century dissenter Anne Hutchinson was a distant ancestor and declaring she hoped to write a biography of that brave "heretic" after she finished "Cotton Mather." She developed a warm friendship with Marcella's mother, Honora Comès, who often stayed at the P Street house to help with Mary and Johnny, who adored Katherine Anne, calling her "Miss Poter" in exaggerated southern accepts. Her compulsion to please or to entertain as strong as ever, Katherine Anne announced that living again in the midst of a Roman Catholic family had restored her own lost faith.

Katherine Anne was teaching Marcella to cook, and together they hosted small dinner parties in the snug, formal dining room and cocktail parties in the lush little garden. Their most lavish event of the spring was the party they had on Katherine Anne's fifty-fourth birthday. The menu included Smithfield ham (which Marcella contributed), liver pâte (Katherine Anne's specialty), beaten biscuits (like Cat Porter's), and a cake from the Washington restaurant Avignone Frères. Spending fifty dollars on the party, she hired a man to do it all ("Thank goodness," Marcella said). Some of the guests were Russell Lynes; Ann Holloway Hemmerly, who was living in New York while her husband, Walter, was in the service; Eleanor Clark; Mary and Peggy Doherty; Lincoln Kirstein, the patriotic millionaire aesthete who was now a private at Fort Belvoir; several South American diplomats; Herbert Schaumann, a young German poet who had forsaken the Nazis and joined the American army; and Charles Shannon. The Tates were included as well. Katherine Anne and Caroline were on friendly terms again since they weren't living under one another's noses.

At the beginning of the summer Marcella left Washington with her children to spend a couple of summer months at a seaside resort. For the time they were away Katherine Anne rented the P Street house with Mary and Peggy Doherty. The three women hired a maid for routine housework, and they often welcomed friends and acquaintances into the house for drinks or dinners. Eleanor Clark and Charles Shannon were frequent visitors, and Shannon took Katherine Anne out to dinner alone once a week. On the evening of 8 July, after dinner out, he asked whether he might stay over. She put him in a spare third-floor bedroom adjacent to hers. Although the romance was still chaste at this point, the interest was building. The next morning they breakfasted late in the garden, which was abloom with roses, before going to the National Gallery to see a tribute to Antoni Gaudí. They returned to P Street for dinner, and when he left at midnight, they embraced for the first time. Five days later he arrived about six-thirty in the evening. After they dined and sat in the garden until late, they spent their first night together.

There were not many days in the remainder of July that they were not together. He brought her shells he had collected in the South Pacific and gave her gardenias; they dined at the Aldo Café or at P Street. On the few days they were apart, they wrote letters to one another. Katherine Anne's letter to Barbara Wescott in late July acknowledged the affair with Shannon but put a particular slant on it: "I have a charming and gifted young man very much in love with me, and you know that is a kind of illumination. He is too young for me, of course, they always are, always will be, no doubt: but you will be glad to hear that, after a long time and far overdue, I have arrived at years of discretion in this matter, so never fear I shall do anything foolish. I am running the show this time, and it is plain that everybody will have a better time that way."

It is not surprising that Katherine Anne was drawn to Charles Shannon, who was a courtly and witty young man from Montgomery, Alabama. Not only was he handsome and articulate, he also was liberal-minded and passionate about art. At age twenty-nine he already had an impressive record. After graduating from the Cleveland School of Art, he returned to Alabama and built a studio in the woods near Montgomery. His award-winning paintings, which focused on African American people in the South, helped him establish and finance New South, a venture promoting the arts, including supporting an eighty-five-year-old former slave who painted Montgomery street scenes.

The romantic tryst had a miserable core to it, however, for Charles confessed to her at the end of July that he was married. Marcella, who returned to Washington a day or so later to take Mary to the dentist, dropped into P Street to see Katherine Anne and found her in "bad shape," distraught over Charles's deception. Katherine Anne nevertheless chose to keep the affair alive. She had several engagements in New York City the last weeks of August, and Charles got passes to see her, always arriving with bouquets of white roses. Sometimes they stayed in hotels, and sometimes they stayed at an apartment Lincoln Kirstein made available to them.

Katherine Anne's seven-month appointment at the Library of Congress ended in August, and she set about disengaging herself from Washington. She had a little money that would have gone a long way toward getting South Hill into livable shape, but she had no intention of returning to her house. She had decided to go back to the free room and board and the warmth and security of Yaddo.

The Leaning Tower and Other Stories was published 16 September. The first printing of ten thousand sold out in eight days, and the second printing sold briskly. The reviews were almost all "wonderful," Katherine Anne reported to Gay. She was praised for her fastidious technical skill, her subtlety and genius of character analysis, her translucent prose. She was called over and over again an "artist." Many reviewers found the title story, "The Leaning Tower," horrifying in its depiction of prewar Germany.

In early October Charles Shannon traveled to Saratoga Springs to see her. After a night together at the Pine Tree Studio at Yaddo, they had a bitter quarrel about his marriage. She thought then that she would never see him again, but a month later, blaming her strung out nerves for the row in October, she arranged to meet him in New York when she went to participate in a radio broadcast. Monroe Wheeler lent her his Park Avenue apartment, and for several nights she and Charles dined in and made love between dashes off to social engagements. As soon as she returned to Yaddo, she fell ill with pneumonia and was sent to a Saratoga Hospital. Charles immediately wired white roses, and two days later he arrived, sitting by her side for hours and eating hospital meals with her. When he left, they both wept.

Released from the hospital 23 November, she felt well enough to travel a week later to New York City, where Charles had reserved a room in her name at the Commodore Hotel. For three days he gave her gifts: Friday it was violets; Saturday it was a pink camellia; Sunday it was a red ostrich leather cigarette case. She gave him a recording of Alice Raveau singing Orpheus in Glück's opera *Orpheus and Euridice.* They ate out every night at intimate little restaurants, dancing or listening to music afterwards. She had accepted the fact of his marriage and the end of the affair, for she knew that his wife was due to arrive in New York from Alabama the next day. A month later she wrote him a long letter in which she tried to destroy "so far as I was able everything that had been between us."

Writing regularly again to Josie, Katherine Anne atypically mentioned nothing of Charles Shannon or their romantic affair. Instead she described her own political activities that had been given energy by her strong feelings about the war and her worries about Paul, whose outfit had been shipped to the European front. She had never even voted in an election before, but now she was working industriously for Roosevelt and Wallace. She was named vice-chairman of the National Women's Committee and made speeches in Saratoga, that hotbed of "Deweyites and Nazis," she told Josie, who was still so disillusioned with the American government that Katherine Anne feared she would fail to vote. "I imagine I can see everything wrong with the administration that you can," she wrote, "Congress, the State Department, name your own list: but I also think the alternative is considerably worse, and I am at the point where I will take a chance with the lesser evil . . . . . I'm all out for saving the pieces now and trying to change things by working from within."

She was becoming ever more deeply involved in the lives of Paul and Ann, playing artist-mother to both of them. When she was in New York she went to watch Ann work at Celli's studio, delighted to see, she reported to Gay, that Ann had become "a good, sound, professional dancer, with a nice, precise technique." She decided to spend a little of her own diminishing money to have Ann's teeth fixed, an investment in Ann's art as much as a generous gift from an increasingly doting aunt. For Christmas she sent Paul an inscribed copy of *The Leaning Tower and Other Stories* ("our book," she called it since it was dedicated to him). His letters, coming now from France, were beautifully written, and she mentally made plans for sending him money to finish his education at the Sorbonne in Paris when the war ended. When she acknowledged the possibility that he might not survive the war ("I know about this war, in my bones," she wrote Josie), she went to the local blood bank and gave a pint of blood, saying to herself, "This one is for Paul."

In December Katherine Anne received a letter from Jules Goldstone, a Hollywood agent, asking whether she would be interested in coming to California to work for a major studio as writer and advisor. She was, yes, very much interested in the offer. Goldstone was able to negotiate a contract with Metro-Goldwyn-Mayer (MGM) for fifteen hundred dollars a week for thirteen weeks, after which if both she and the studio exercised options for her to continue, she would be paid two thousand dollars a week on the understanding that she would stay six months longer. She saw the job as a chance to "get a little nest egg against old age" and give a little to her family (meaning especially Paul and Ann). "Well, Old Taurus is the money sign in the Zodiac, as you know," she told Gay, "but I have wondered when and if he was going to get to work for me . . . . . Looks as if he meant business this time . . . You can spread the news, angel." She also had been handed an opportunity for another wild dash—away from Yaddo, winter, the burdens of owning South Hill, the unfinished novel, editors and publishers who were hounding her, and reminders of her newest failure in love.

CHAPTER TWENTY-THREE

California

January 1945–September 1949

I remember songs about California:
California, here I come
Right back where I started from . . .

Or

O, my dear, do you remembah
California in Septembah?

Or

The Miners came in 49
The whores in 61
They got together right away
Hence the Native Son.

"I have a prejudice against California," Katherine Anne had remarked to her father in 1936, "I can't think why except all the people I ever met from there were astrologers, or New Thought Maniacs, or Coúe disciples, or just full of the newest Hindu philosophy; and you can imagine how my rationalist mind would spew all that up." Although the aim of her statement was to remind her father of their common rationalism, it was true that she had never imagined the Pacific West as her intellectual or creative home. At the beginning of 1945, however, she was willing to accept Hollywood money to climb out of debt and ready to take advantage of the southern California climate to break her pattern of wintertime bronchitis.

By the end of January she was busily involved in her studio assignment and feeling well, reporting she was "full of energy." She quickly saw, however, that working on "falsified and romanticized" Hollywood scripts was not a natural outlet for her creative imagination. The only satisfying part of the whole experience was the money she was earning. In addition to paying off debts, she wanted to save money for "the children," as she called Paul and Ann.

In early February Ann arrived in California at the invitation of Katherine Anne, who thought that while Ann's husband, Walter Hemmerly, was in the service, Ann could see California for the first time and also find a job. Katherine Anne found a roomy house to lease at 333 Twenty-fifth Street in Santa Monica, where she unpacked the possessions she had brought along (including the virginal and a thousand records). In mid-March she bought a car, which she and Ann christened "Ole Honey" (Ann drove it—Katherine Anne was still an incompetent driver), and hired a man to clean the house and a woman to do the laundry. She purchased California clothes: black tailored slacks and blouse, white platform shoes, a wide white belt, white china beads. Despite her prejudices expressed to Harrison a decade ago, she talked approvingly about astrology, offering to have charts done for selected friends.

Her energy and contentment and assimilation in Hollywood solidified after her thirteen weeks at MGM ended. Midway in the contract, she went to Sidney Franklin to ask him to be "amiable" and release her when the contract expired. When he told her he would like for her to stay, she called his behavior that of a husband who, "like a wounded stag," calls her "an unreasonable woman" and asks "What have I done, what have I done?" and "Who ever said I didn't love you?" Like her contracts with publishers, it was another version of *marriage*, in which she habitually felt trapped and "jailed." Franklin, however, let her go without rancor.

Shortly before Ann left in June, Robert Lewis, a director at MGM, offered Katherine Anne his house to live in while he spent two summer months in New York. Glad to escape the expense of rent since the money she saved from her MGM salary was steadily decreasing, she moved into his house at 201 South Bentley Avenue in Los Angeles, and when he returned at the end of August, she took a small, four-room, upstairs apartment at 843 Sixth Street in Santa Monica that rented for a pleasingly modest sixty-five dollars a month.

Soon afterward, Lewis invited her to a large dinner party where she met Judy Garland, the conductor Richard Hagemann, the singer Richard Hale, and Luise Rainer Odets, the Austrian actress and wife of the leftist playwright Clifford Odets. Katherine Anne was invited to dinner at the Odetses' home the next week, and from there her social life multiplied as she became a popular guest within Hollywood circles. In the group at the Odetses were Theodore and Helen Dreiser and Charlie Chaplin and Oona O'Neill. Mrs. Odets showed the guests her four-month-old baby, and many of the other women were pregnant. "Not a woman opened her mouth all evening except me," Katherine Anne wrote Caroline Gordon, content to distinguish herself as the artist among the mothers.

In the fall of 1945 she reviewed two books, George Willison's *Saints and Strangers*, an account of the Pilgrims who had settled Plymouth Plantation (including the Mathers), and Glenway Wescott's *Apartment in Athens*. She found it easy to praise the book by Willison, whose wife, Toni, she had met and become friends with in Paris, but Glenway's novel, which he said he had written as his "war work" to "show how bad the Germans are," presented her with a dilemma. She badly wanted to praise his novel, but it violated her aesthetic standard of the separation of art and politics. The way she escaped the trap was to argue that Glenway had done something more valuable than his claim, for he had shown the *universality* of "Germanism." It was that streak in all of us, she declared, "that made possible the Germany we know today."

Payment for the reviews was small, and her savings had dwindled to almost nothing. It was anxiety about money combined with her acknowledgment that she was not in the right mood to work on any of her books that made her receptive to Goldstone's renewed urging to take on another job with another Hollywood studio. In the middle of October she signed a contract with Paramount Pictures for fourteen weeks at two thousand dollars a week. She was to work with Charles Brackett (who produced *Lost Weekend*) and the dramatist Jacques Thery on an adaptation of Victorien Sardou's *Madame Sans Gêne* for Betty Hutton. She and Thery were constantly at odds, however, and she stayed away from the studio for days at a time in pique and frustration. By the end of her first fourteen weeks she was as bitter about Paramount as she had been about MGM. Paramount, however, acted on their option and extended her contract indefinitely in order for her to finish the script.

When her Hollywood friends asked her whether she was having an affair with anyone or who her current lover was, she pretended she was being faithful to a man she left behind in the East. Privately, she

was manufacturing the materials of romance in the intense correspondence she had begun with Herbert Schaumann in 1944 even
while her affair with Charles Shannon was flourishing. In 1945 he
was calling her his "best-loved being." She was calling him "darling"
and asking him to visit California.

Schaumann was homosexual, and although she suspected it, she
wasn't sure. At one point in the correspondence she explained to him
the various kinds of love. "I was reading again in W. B. Yeats' memoirs," she said, "and came upon a paragraph I marked for you: Yeats,
quoting his father: 'There is not more desire, he said, in lust than in
true love, but in true love desire awakens pity, hope, affection, admiration, and, given appropriate circumstances, every emotion possible to
man.'" "This is a lovely kind of truth," she told him, "and we should
know it best by now."

Love was an ambiguity Schaumann failed to clarify at the time, and
she engrossed herself in a fiction featuring a handsome young man
who admired her as an artist, a cosmopolitan intellectual with whom
she could discuss ideas and art, and a man young enough to be a
replacement for the children she lost. When he sent her a photograph
of himself as a child, she analyzed it: "Your little childhood picture is
touching as children are; it is their confidence in their world, and its
brief bloom, that pretty fairly breaks the heart. Such a sweetly dressed
cherished looking baby, and I like best the one where you lean warmly
over your mother's shoulder, blissful, limp, hands lying asleep on her
breast and shoulder, still part of her." She projected her own history
onto Schaumann's mother: "She has such handsome hair and a fine
figure, but already her face is that of a woman ravaged by her temperament, incurably disturbed . . . . . It is a deep look, and there is a great
deal more to the face than that . . . . . Maybe it is the little face next to
hers shining with love and confidence that makes the tragic contrast."
Katherine Anne understood the psychology of this kind of displacement more than a decade ago when she explored it in the character of
Rosaleen in "The Cracked Looking-Glass." Applying it to herself was
another matter.

In the early months of 1946 Toni Willison, who wrote to ask
whether Katherine Anne realized that the George Willison whose
book she reviewed was her husband, mentioned in passing that they
were looking for a house in upstate New York. Katherine Anne
told them about South Hill, and they went to Saratoga Springs to
see it. They soon made her an offer that she accepted. Never a good

businesswoman, however, Katherine Anne carried the no-interest mortgage herself and despite her need for money told them they could delay the first payment for several months.

In March Paul arrived in Santa Monica after his tour of duty finally ended, drained from combat, mind-weary and directionless. He remembered the long-awaited reunion with his aunt as "incoherent babble, kisses, hugs." She had invited him to come "to rest, eat good things, read in her library, and recover." Knowing that Ann had lived with her six months the year before, he assumed she meant for him to stay with her. When he saw the tiny one-bedroom apartment and a cot for him in her small living room, he knew the visit must be temporary and he would have to find a place of his own. She told friends about the "heavenly reunion" with "blessed Paul" and rejoiced in his handsomeness and his family resemblance to her ("We look like mother and child," she told Monroe.). But he was sleeping in her work space, and she thought that she could get to work on her writing if *only* he were not there.

While he combed advertisements for an apartment to rent, she bolted to the Lucerne Valley in the high Mojave Desert of San Bernardino County, having heard at the studio about a dude ranch that offered silence and remoteness, isolation that should allow her to finish at least the Sans Gêne play. By the time she returned three weeks later, Paul had found an apartment on the beach nearby. He had learned firsthand about her tightly strung nerves that were the underside of her kindness, wit, and charm.

Part of her temperamental personality was an impulsiveness that defied reason. When she was in the Lucerne Valley, she had gone out driving with people she had met at the ranch; the group happened upon eighty acres of mountain property for sale. Without any deliberation she immediately looked up the owner to tell him she wanted to buy it. She had no checkbook and only $9.50 with her, but by borrowing 50¢ from one of her companions, she was able to give the owner $10 as a good faith promise, which he acknowledged with a receipt written inside a match cover. She met him the next day at the bank to formalize the transaction, which included a down payment and a mortgage he would carry on the remainder of the $10,000 price.

She had yet to realize any money from the sale of South Hill, and apparently forgetting the several frustrating years and outlay of money spent getting her Saratoga Springs farmhouse to the point of near-comfort, she ignored the enormous task of replacing the new property's rustic little house with one suitable for her and ignored as well the fact that the climate in the high desert was neither mild nor predictable. The second day she was at the ranch, a violent snowstorm blew a window out in her room in front of her worktable, and she was hit in the head with a piece of sash that caused a minor fracture and several weeks of headaches.

To hear her talk about it, however, her house on the mountain in the desert would be the perfect place. "I am already putting myself to sleep nights planning my house," she wrote to Albert Erskine. "It is beautiful, spacious, full of light and mountain air, the machinery all works, it glows and glitters with cleanliness and order without anybody turning a hand, the colors are all perfect though I can't quite see what they are, and no unpleasant person has ever yet knocked at that door . . . . . You never saw such a house, and neither did I, and perhaps nobody ever will. And yet it exists and I am living in it . . . . . and I mean to make a good try at putting it where others can see it, too." Even while she was weaving the dream, some part of her recognized the illusion.

Katherine Anne and Paul spent several evenings a week together "talking about everything on earth." He had an especially interesting story to tell her about his visit with Sylvia Beach in Paris after he completed an army-sponsored course in French language and culture in Dijon the previous August. At Shakespeare and Company he had found tiny, white-haired Sylvia, thrilled to meet the nephew of one of her dearest friends. Sylvia, who took her hostess duty seriously, decided he should meet Gertrude Stein, and she escorted him to Stein's place (then in the rue Christine), told him goodbye, and assured him Stein would be glad to see him if he sent in a note saying he was Katherine Anne Porter's nephew. Paul nervously followed her advice and was badly embarrassed when he heard Stein thunder, "Who in the hell is Katherine Anne Porter!?" Christopher Blake, another young American GI, who was present, tried to explain who Katherine Anne Porter was. Stein became friendly and insisted Paul come in to visit. When he left an hour later, she gave him an eight-by-ten-inch glossy photograph of herself on which she wrote, "To Paul come again soon Paul" and signed her name. Blake related the curious event to friends, one of whom laughed and said, "The bitch. She knows perfectly well who Katherine Anne Porter is." Blake, who was fond of Stein, wondered why she would go out of her way to be cruel. Some suspected it was retaliation for Katherine Anne's parody review of Stein's *Useful Knowledge* in 1928.

Paul was present when Herbert Schaumann came to California to visit Katherine Anne in August of 1946. Unable to sustain her fantasy love affair in the face of Schaumann's homosexuality, she collapsed in tears and physical illness. Schaumann was shocked that Katherine Anne had misunderstood his feelings for her. Accusing him of deception, she was once again disappointed in love. In September she wrote him, "Love me as you did, if you can, . . . and I will love you. There will be nothing 'useful' in this love, no ordinary human satisfactions, we can't build any continuing city on it here." The illusion of love was the thread that connected this fictional affair to "No Safe Harbor," her long novel-in-progress, where she was developing a Plato-like symposium on love and to whose third part she affixed the epigraph, "And here have we no continuing city." The quotation from Saint Paul, whose name she considered synonymous with asexual love, was an allusion to the failure of hope.

In the last months of 1946 numerous crates and trunks full of papers and possessions began to arrive in Hollywood from Saratoga Springs after the Willisons moved into South Hill. Perusing reams of notes, she was inspired to piece together a memoir of the last Christmas she spent with her niece Mary Alice Holloway ("A Christmas Story"), which she sent to *Mademoiselle*, where it would be published near the December anniversary of Mary Alice's birth. She worked some on "No Safe Harbor," mostly to revise and sharpen scenes she had already written. She read a lot. She devoted attention to her current resident cat, Jupiter. She wrote many letters, as usual, but there was no longer any mention in them of her mountain or the house she had planned to build. In the fall she placed her property with a realtor, hoping at least to recover her original investment. She made a will—Gay, Paul, and Ann were the primary beneficiaries. She named Glenway Wescott her literary executor.

In the fall of 1947, with her mountain unsold and with increasingly importunate letters from the owner, who still held her original mortgage on it, little or no money to expect from royalties, and no progress on the unfinished books, Katherine Anne became worried enough about future income to accept a job with yet another Hollywood studio. She agreed to write for Columbia and the producer Robert Rossen a loose adaptation of Chekhov's story "La Cigale." She had worked only a week or so on it when Robert Rossen was called to Washington to answer questions before the House Un-American Activities Committee, which had just finished its business with the Hollywood Ten, the group of producers and screenwriters who were imprisoned for refusing to name colleagues who had been sympathetic to, or members of, the Communist Party. "My God, it chills my blood," she wrote Russell Lynes, "it is just the thing that was happening in Germany in 1932 and on, and in France from 1934 and on, and is happening everywhere now as if that war had never been fought." The practical consequence of Rossen's summons was that she was obliged to give up the project, return the advance of three hundred dollars Columbia already had paid her, and forget about the fifteen hundred dollars a week she had been promised.

In early November the owners of her Santa Monica apartment gave her notice that they needed the place for themselves and she would have to move within thirty days. Her financial condition was worse than it had been since she arrived in Hollywood. In addition to the bad business decisions, she had spent freely on Paul and Ann as well as herself. She also had paid off every debt she owed to friends. She had to sell her car, Ole Honey, and resort once again to asking for personal loans to tide her over. With embarrassment she also wrote to George and Toni Willison, explaining her plight and hinting she might have to turn over the mortgage to a bank. For the short term she accepted the invitation of her friend George Lynes, who had arrived in Hollywood with an extended assignment from *Vogue,* to move into the guest wing of the big house he had rented.

To earn money quickly, Katherine Anne turned to unfinished essays and soon wrapped up one on Gertrude Stein that she had begun ten years earlier. Her admiration for Stein in 1912 had changed to disdain, visible in her 1928 parody of Stein ("Second Wind") and a letter to Lincoln Kirstein in 1933 in which she said, "I doubt the veracity of *all* Gertrude Stein's portraits, judgments, and conclusions about *everything.*" The new essay was a literary caricature of Stein as appallingly possessive and prideful.

Because the essay was essentially an analysis of Stein's *Everybody Autobiography,* Russell Lynes published it in *Harper's Magazine* as "Gertrude Stein: A Self Portrait." Those who had tired of Stein's verbal gymnastics and the Stein legends appreciated it, but because the story of Stein's dismissive remark to Paul in 1945 had circulated in Parisian and American artistic circles, other persons assumed that Katherine Anne's piece was retaliation for Stein's rebuff. Some also thought the piece particularly harsh in view of Stein's death the previous year. Charles Shannon wrote Katherine Anne a letter of affectionate disagreement, and Josie Herbst took exception only a little stronger. "Much as I like almost everything I ever saw of yours, I have to dissent on your Stein piece," she wrote in January 1948. "It reads so persuasively but it isn't Stein. She was all that your piece divulges but that isn't the whole story. Not by a long shot . . . but . . . I shall welcome to the skies anything I see you write, even when I disagree with it." Josie signed the letter, "Best wishes, good luck, good health and my affections that will survive everything but the atom bomb."

Katherine Anne began to draft a long letter to Josie in which she further explained her view of Stein, but she never mailed it. In the meantime, Josie put together her rebuttal to Katherine Anne's essay; and, given her mildly expressed "dissent" in her January letter, Katherine Anne had to be shocked by Josie's "Miss Porter and Miss Stein" in the May 1948 issue of the *Partisan Review*. Josie accused Katherine Anne of a broad attack on modern art, which, she pointed out, had also been denounced by Hitler. ("Is there any relevance in the fact that Hitler condemned modern art and burned the books?" she asked.) She also linked Katherine Anne's attack on Stein to the censure of Russia's three leading composers by the Central Committee of the Communist Party. Aware of Katherine Anne's public opposition to Nazism and Communism, she had delivered a particularly brutal and unjust blow. She also took the liberty of quoting not only Katherine Anne's essay on Stein but an earlier, personal letter from Katherine Anne, who had mentioned the horrid fascination Stein held for her. The friendship that had survived more than twenty years, staggering along the last dozen of them, was finally over in May. The two women who once had been affectionate, confiding friends never wrote to, or saw, one another again.

The Stein dispute was not the only issue in the collapse of the friendship. Equally devastating was Katherine Anne's passive refusal at the end of 1947 to review Josie's novel *Somewhere the Tempest Fell*, which contains a scene with shallow characters blatantly modeled on Glenway, Monroe, and George Platt Lynes, who gather in the Paris garden of a woman clearly modeled on Katherine Anne. Besides being offended at an attack on some of her dearest friends, Katherine Anne would have been reminded of Josie's betrayal in "Man of Steel." Josie's letter that contained her mild complaint about Katherine Anne's essay on Stein was really more about what she considered Katherine Anne's failure in the matter of her book. "I would have appreciated even harsh criticism to silence," Josie wrote bitterly.

Also contributing to the death of the friendship was Josie's lack of self-confidence at a low point in her life when she decided both to stop writing fiction and to avoid intimate relationships. She suddenly saw Katherine Anne as the undeserving victor in what apparently was a power contest. Katherine Anne was gathering a following while Josie was losing the small reading audience she had when literature and politics were appreciated as bedfellows. Katherine Anne seemed, too, to be growing more maturely beautiful and animated, while Josie was descending into what her biographer described as a "grandmotherly quality." In an earlier letter Josie had commented on a photograph of Katherine Anne accompanying an article about her in a Hollywood newspaper: "I thought your picture in the paper was enchanting, but then, what is the use, you will always have the kind of face that holds its own. Mine holds its own too, in its way, but not so flattering as yours does. And my pictures are foul and always depress me no end."

Katherine Anne had done nothing to neutralize Josie's envy but rather encouraged it, exaggerating her success in Hollywood, chatting about several producers' interest in making movies out of her short novels, and recounting with lively detail an interview with a *Time* reporter. She implied that California, the lush land of flowers, was for her nearly perfect. In the last letter she ever wrote to Josie, who had remained an avid gardener, she described the morning crop of roses she had cut and a new camellia bush she had planted. She talked as if she were in high gear, buzzing around the summit of a blooming world, working well, looking forward to finishing her novel. Wrapped in her own misery, Josie was unable to see that under Katherine Anne's fanciful description of contentment and industry there was a painful melancholy.

For the better part of the past year Katherine Anne had been George Lynes's guest, posing in expensive clothes and jewelry for his fashion photographs and relishing the social life at the big house. While there she met Christopher Isherwood (and impulsively pulled his hair when he mocked her southern accent and called her the Joan of Arc of Texas) and saw again Truman Capote, who also was on assignment from *Vogue.* Although she had been friendly with him at Yaddo, in Hollywood she saw him in a new light when he came to dinner wearing a flashy silk scarf and a yachting cap and talking about all the celebrities he had met. She decided then that she didn't much like Truman after all, and he became an object of ridicule in entertaining stories she told for years.

Katherine Anne feared she would overstay her welcome at Lynes's and was anxious to be on her own again. Her plight was resolved at the end of December when George and Toni Willison began to send her monthly house payments in order to avoid a bank mortgage and she received a little money from the owners of the Eighth Street apartment for all the lemon and camellia trees she had planted in an extravagant arbor. She also accepted a tour of colleges and universities that would begin in April and end in July.

In early February 1948, at the request of Wallace Stegner, director of the Creative Writing Program at Stanford, Katherine Anne made an appearance at Palo Alto. She had met Stegner at Bread Loaf, and in the 1930s she had corresponded with Yvor Winters, who also was on the creative writing faculty. She also discovered several Texans on the English Department faculty, including the chairman, R. F. Jones. At her formal talk and the party in her honor afterward, she was dazzling, and Jones and other senior professors immediately thought it would be wonderful to have her at Stanford for a whole year. When she left for engagements at Midwestern universities, Stegner and Jones were trying to work out details of an offer.

At the two-week writers' workshop at the University of Kansas in the summer, Katherine Anne met Isabel Bayley, a well-educated, pretty, thirty-seven-year-old woman who had been a lieutenant in the U.S. Air Force W.A.C. and had worked for the FBI during the war. W. Hewitt (Hew) Bayley, her husband of nine years, was a handsome, engaging man who shared her experiences and her interest in literature and ideas. Katherine Anne formed a friendship with them that would last her lifetime.

The wear and tear of traveling caught up with her after the Kansas stop. She cancelled her last scheduled engagement on the tour, a lecture at the University of Washington, in Seattle, and traveled seven hundred miles by train and boat to a small hotel George Davis had recommended in Ludington, Michigan, to rest for a few weeks, work on her writing, and make a decision about where to go next and what to do. While she was there she received an offer of an appointment as half-time lecturer at Stanford for twenty-five hundred dollars. The advantage was that the salary would start on 1 September, but her duties wouldn't start until January 1949, when she would teach one noncredit course in each of two succeeding quarters.

She was offended, however, that her courses would be noncredit. "It makes me feel rather marginal," she wrote to Stegner. "It puts literature and the artist in their place, all right, something not to be taken too seriously in academic life." Her complaint was understandable, but it also reflected her insecurity in the academic world. Remarking on all the forms she had filled out for the Stanford personnel office, she wrote, "At one point I had to break down and confess that I was just merely a professional writer and nothing else much . . . . . I hope they knew this all along and weren't expecting a long row of Ph.D's, M.A's, D.D's, and so on. Hell, I'm not even a D. Litt." With some misgivings she nevertheless decided to accept the appointment, while she continued eastward, taking advantage of the delay of her duties at Stanford to go to New York to visit Ann, who was in the process of divorcing Walter Hemmerly.

Katherine Anne arrived in Palo Alto in early November with her virginal and eleven suitcases full of clothes, books, manuscripts, crystal clocks, and Paris perfumes. She was temporarily put up in a campus guesthouse while she chose a place to live. First, she rented a rural cabin in La Honda, about sixteen miles from Palo Alto, assuming that remoteness would protect her from her own gregariousness, but the unheated cabin was cold and the trip to Stanford required four hours on connecting buses. She finally moved into a dark, cave-like two-room basement apartment under the garage of a professor's house within walking distance of the campus.

Although Katherine Anne could have limited her class to as few students as she wanted and could have evaluated students' work before admitting them, she did neither and allowed everybody to enroll who asked. Reading and marking dozens of manuscripts and seeing students during scheduled office hours, she soon began to complain about having no time to do her own work. She compounded the drain on her time by her inability to refuse any invitation to lunch, dinner, cocktail party, or musical performance. Wives of the English Department faculty took her up, and in addition to cementing her friendship with Yvor Winters's wife, Janet Lewis, she became especially friendly with the wife of R. F. Jones. She also became friends with Anne and Richard Scowcroft; Richard was the newest member of the English Department. Often a guest at the Scowcroft home, she exhibited her compulsion to entertain by telling fascinating stories about her experiences in Mexico and Europe and her family in Texas, weaving vague impressions of impoverished gentility and freed slaves hanging about. She also occasionally broke out in a song or dance or performed a particularly witty and "ungracious" imitation of Truman Capote.

In the late spring, after recovering from a bout with pneumonia, she vanished from Palo Alto for a month or so without telling anyone at Stanford she was leaving. In March she had received a letter from the chancellor of the Woman's College of the University of North Carolina conveying a wish to grant her an honorary doctoral degree at the university's May commencement. After she agreed to be present, she learned that the university did not underwrite the cost of her travel or the four hundred dollars for the academic hood. Money that Donald Brace sent her allowed her to go, but the experience at Greensboro was not altogether pleasing because she shared the honor with a North Carolina woman who had political connections in the state and wrote amateurish local history novels. Katherine Anne was appalled that no distinction was made between herself and the "Teep," she told Monroe, and that "with identical grave ceremony and high-flown citations for services to literature, we received our identical hoods and got identical applause."

Nevertheless she had her first Litt.D. and an academic robe and hood to prove it, and she looked forward to wearing her new "costume" at the Stanford commencement, where she felt looked down upon by most of the English Department faculty. Jones was startled to see her in full academic regalia in front of him in the graduation procession. She still wouldn't speak to him, however, although she remained friendly with his wife.

In the summer Katherine Anne was embroiled in an event more unpleasant than the tension between her and the Stanford English Department. As a member of the Society of Fellows of the Library of Congress, she had participated in the awarding of the 1949 Bollingen Prize to Ezra Pound for *The Pisan Cantos* as the best book of poetry by an American author published in 1948. Although some persons and newspapers such as the *New York Herald Tribune* lauded the award for the sharp line it drew between politics and art, the selection caused fury in many circles. The *New York Times* ran the headline "Pound, in Mental Clinic, Wins Prize for Poetry Penned in Treason Cell." Robert Frost called it "an unendurable outrage." Robert Hillyer, a Pulitzer-prize-winning poet and president of the Poetry Society of America, stirred the controversy with two long articles, 11 and 18 June, in the *Saturday Review of Literature*, charging that *The Pisan Cantos* were part of a conspiracy against American ways of life and literature and warned that the FBI had been alerted. The Hillyer articles were introduced into the record of the House of Representatives, and the question of whether Fascism had infiltrated the Library of Congress came before the Congressional Joint Committee on the Library of Congress. The result was that the government barred the library from thenceforth awarding the Bollingen Prize, which in 1950 would be resumed by the Yale University Library.

Katherine Anne was incensed at Hillyer's accusations of conspiracy and "ruthless mockery of our Christian war dead." In a five-page, single-spaced letter to the editor of the *Saturday Review*, she defended the selection of Pound for the Bollingen award while she explained again her position on the separation of art and politics: "I am glad that he [Pound] is being cared for, I pity his madness; the evil he has done is hateful to me, I reject it without reservation; but I remember the light that used to shine from his pages when he wrote about something he knew with his heart—poetry—and the beautiful translations, or paraphrases, from the Chinese and the Provençal, and how well he knew that art was not a marginal thing, but lived at the center of being by its own reality; that it was no decoration, but the foundation stone itself; no matter, he cannot commit treason against that, it is beyond the reach of his mortal part." When the *Saturday Review* refused to publish her letter, she circulated copies among her friends.

While the Bollingen brouhaha was going on, Katherine Anne was teaching her last class at Stanford, a "Problems in Fiction" class in the summer term. Among those who signed up was Herbert Steiner, a handsome twenty-seven-year-old GI from Seattle who admired her greatly and had felt badly let down the year before when she cancelled her appearance at the University of Washington. Steiner provided an especially detailed portrait of Katherine Anne in a classroom, describing her method of teaching as a combination of lecture, performance, and inspiration. She was organized, but she spoke without notes. On the first day of class she handed out a large bibliography of recommended reading that ranged from the eighteenth century to the present. She read favorite passages from Henry James, Kafka, Mann, Gide, Smollett, and Colette, with whose "sadness and longing" she identified. She also read passages from "No Safe Harbor," telling the students, "No one is ever going to a safe harbor." Always strikingly dressed (usually with a flower on her shoulder), she constantly adjusted her glasses, moved her hands, and smoked while she read. She talked often about "loss." Her voice was "lovely to hear, throaty, sexy," he remembered. "I never saw such silence in a class."

Despite her obvious success in the classroom, Katherine Anne considered the Stanford year a miserable experience, and she told Steiner she was firmly resolved to do no more university teaching. When the summer term was over, she packed up some of her belongings, put others in storage, and, with relief, left California for the Northeast.

CHAPTER TWENTY-FOUR

New York City and France: The End of Something

September 1949–September 1952

I know well that if I were not a writer, if I did not have that pro-found solid ground of life-long love and interest to stand on, I would not take the trouble to live another day. But that gives meaning and hope to everything, it is quite literally why *I have lived and what I live* for.

When Katherine Anne wearily left Palo Alto in mid-September, despite her earlier vow to give up university teaching, she actually saw no possibility for steady income other than "trouping," as she called it, which would drain the energy she needed for her writing. It was a vicious circle. She wrote a long letter to Donald Brace in which she outlined the "ghastly" situation at Stanford, where she was regarded as "public property" like "something in a zoo" and beset at all hours of the day and night by eager and curious students. She asked for fifteen hundred dollars immediately to get settled and then four hundred dollars a month for six months. "By that time you will have the novel and it might b[e] published by then . . . I could finish if I were not bedeviled for a little while."

Brace was mildly sympathetic, but change was underway at Harcourt, Brace, and he did not have the free hand he once had. He was also distracted by his own declining health. Her request consequently was only partially and grudgingly granted (basic living expenses), with the accompanying exhortations to finish the novel more pointed than usual. To save money, she moved in with Ann in her little apartment at 304 East Forty-ninth Street.

Ann was preparing to remarry, and Katherine Anne was outspoken in her disappointment. Hoping Ann would profit from her aunt's mistakes, she had advised Ann to "look well and long at any man who proposes to marry you. Don't load him down with all the virtues and qualities you would *wish* him to have, and then be disappointed when it turns out that he hasn't them at all." When Ann firmly let her know that the decision to marry Walter Heintze, a Swedish designer, was unchangeable, Katherine Anne conceded defeat and began to plan Ann's wedding for the following spring to "Walter II."

Living with Ann, whose schedule for rehearsing and performing was irregular, did not provide Katherine Anne with an atmosphere congenial to serious creative work. Neither was the money Harcourt, Brace provided enough for her to live on comfortably. Surrendering to the circumstances, she resumed the very activities she had wanted to avoid, accepting numerous speaking engagements at colleges and universities and the Poetry Center of the Young Men's–Young Women's Hebrew Association, which her friend John Malcolm Brinnin was heading, and making commitments for book reviews and articles for commercial magazines. With an increased influx of money she was able to rent two floors of a six-story house at 108 East Sixty-fifth Street. Forsaking all pretense of seeking solitude, she invited Ann to move in with her until her spring wedding.

In February, while elaborate wedding plans were underway, an event occurred that would be talked about for years. Dylan Thomas arrived in New York at Brinnin's invitation, and Harvey and Ann Breit invited Katherine Anne to a large party in Thomas's honor at their home on the lower Eastside. After barely managing through the evening to stave off the clumsy overtures of Thomas, who had been drinking heavily since his arrival in New York, Katherine Anne decided to leave the party early. In hat, coat, and gloves, she was intercepted by a guilefully polite Thomas, who told her how glad he was to have met her. Before she could respond, he grabbed her, lifted her toward the ceiling, and, in front of the startled guests, held her there "as if she [had] no more weight than a doll," according to Brinnin. Despite his hands under her skirt and his announcement that he intended to sleep with her, she kept her aplomb. Brinnin told Thomas firmly that the party was over and managed to take him away. Brinnin gave an account of the event in his *Dylan Thomas in America*; Sidney Michaels reconstructed it as a scene in his play *Dylan*; and Karl Shapiro made a poem about it.

For Ann's wedding Katherine Anne tried to re-create the lavish and legendary nineteenth-century Kentucky wedding of Cat Porter.

She had dogwood and smilax sent up from the South at considerable expense, and she hired Monroe's butler. She made sure there were sumptuous quantities of food and champagne, and she flooded the flower-laden and candle-lit apartment with recorded music. About a hundred of Ann's friends from the ballet showed up, and Gay came from Texas.

After the wedding Katherine Anne, finally alone, was able to return to her writing. In the last five months of 1950 she published three excerpts from the existing manuscript of "No Safe Harbor," three essays, and four book reviews. Those days she selected with particular care the books she reviewed, making sure that she could praise them. In her review of *The House of Breath*, however, the first published novel of William Goyen, a fellow Texan, with whom she had been corresponding for the past three years, she took seriously her role as mentor and felt obliged to instruct him in the art of fiction. While she praised his full, rich writing, she issued a strong warning to her young friend: "Mr. Goyen has not availed himself of any of the precautions against self-revelation that is so useful in the objective method. Here are the most extravagant feelings, the most absurd recklessness of revealment, at times there is real danger of the fatal drop into over-pathos."

Goyen, who told her his novel had been written with her and her "great work" as his "guiding principle," called on her to deliver his thanks in person, and during the whirlwind visit he told her he loved her. Flattered, she was nevertheless holding back. The fact that he was thirty-five and she was sixty had little to do with her restraint. She felt sure that he was homosexual, and she had no energy for another pointless love affair.

She saw Goyen again in January on his way to Yaddo. Since their last meeting he had sent her several love letters and wired flowers for Christmas. He urged her to come to Yaddo to see him as soon as she could, and against her better judgment she made the trip the second week in February. As soon as she arrived, Goyen sent her a secret note asking, "Please don't be mean to me." While she was there he convinced her that he was at least bisexual, and they became lovers.

The British poet and editor Stephen Spender characterized Katherine Anne as Goyen's "lover or near-lover" with whom he seemed "to be playing an elaborate game" in which "the excess of his expressed affection" concealed "a considerable evasiveness in a game they both play and in which she is perhaps as elusive as he." Goyen and Katherine Anne knew the rules for the game: She made a shrine of the bed they slept in at her apartment and pressed the flowers he sent her. They wrote paeans to one another's photographs and lamented being apart, justified by both of them as the price of their "art."

Katherine Anne was fully aware of the fabrication even while she was constructing it, her double vision evident in two pieces she wrote on 14 July. One was a letter to him in which she called him "my darling" and "my love" and told him he was always on her mind and in her heart. "I hope you like being there." The other was a private note she dashed off to herself: "About Bill Goyen, . . . He is so totally self absorbed, I am beginning to think he never saw another human being in his life . . . He is a peeper and a pryer and a natural intruder on other's lives, and calls it a search for 'truth' . . . He damages everything he touches, with a heavy-handed kind of insensibility . . . I understand now why he talks about love so much, longs for it, . . . he hasn't got it in himself . . . He said to me once during our early friendship, when I thought very well indeed of him—he is all-too-plausible—'Oh, I am afraid you will find me out, and if you do, you *can't* love me!' Poor man, that is true." The habit she had established by the 1920s of setting down truthful private notes that were the beginning points for artistic rendering—but contradictions of her public words and behavior—was still thriving. She continued the collaboration with Goyen for another year.

Her relationship with another young Texas writer was entirely different. She had become acquainted with William (Bill) Humphrey, an instructor at Bard College, in Annandale-on-Hudson, New York, and later the author of *Home from the Hill* (1958), after he invited her to speak at the college in 1950. Although in those days she generally received $250 plus expenses for college appearances, she was so appreciative of Humphrey's and his wife's, Dorothy's, admiration of her that she agreed to come for $50. She was aware of Humphrey's works even before she heard from him, having recognized her influence on him in two of his stories published in *Accent*. Humphrey told her that she was his one teacher and that for models he kept favorite paragraphs from *Noon Wine*, *Old Mortality*, *The Old Order*, and "The Cracked Looking-Glass" near his typewriter and always assigned his students her essay on Gertrude Stein.

Since 1940 Katherine Anne's protégés had been growing in number, and she gave time and support to them, writing letters of recommendation for fellowships, awards, and grants and reviewing their work both privately and publicly. She continued to offer advice and encouragement to James Powers, Isabel Bayley, Eudora, Peter Taylor, and many others. She was always pleased when her sponsorships bore fruit, such as Eleanor Clark's Guggenheim fellowship. She was honest with them, however. She was critical of Humphrey's *Home from the Hill*, and at a certain point she told Isabel Bayley, in effect, that she was wasting her time, that her intelligence was not the creative kind, and that she should turn to something other than fiction writing.

Katherine Anne learned again that the college circuit was especially wearing, and despite her need for money, she gave up such speaking engagements for the last half of 1951 and tried to make a living writing reviews and articles. In October she published "Marriage Is Belonging," a rumination inspired by her artificial affair with Bill Goyen, memories of her five disastrous marriages, the recent divorce of Red and Cinina Warren, and the separation of Albert and Peggy Erskine. In November she published reviews of E. M. Forster's *Two Cheers for Democracy* and *The Short Novels of Colette*. The three pieces were all she had to show for the year.

Before the end of 1951 she began to discuss with Eugene Reynal at Harcourt, Brace the possibility of gathering a substantial body of her nonfiction to be published as a book. He agreed to the project but said that he, Robert Giroux, and Catherine Carver would be editors of the book rather than Donald Brace, who was more and more unwell. The title piece was to be "The Days Before," her 1943 essay on Henry James. Rather than giving her another advance, Reynal, at her suggestion, hired her as a literary adviser who was to show up in their offices one day a week.

Reviewing and trouping were still her logical contingencies for earning money quickly. She asked editor friends for specific books to review, and she scheduled a college tour in the South, where she could enjoy reunions with Southern friends. She was in Jackson, Mississippi, 7 March to make an address at Millsaps College, and she stayed with Eudora and her mother, Chestina, in the Welty home on Pinehurst Street. Mrs. Welty was aghast that Katherine Anne had nothing at all prepared for her talk at the college. "What are you going to talk about?" she asked. "Well, I don't know yet," Katherine Anne told her. "Whatever comes into my head when I see the audience." Despite this casualness, Katherine Anne was brilliant that evening as she talked about the role of the artist in the modern world. From Jackson she went to Greensboro, North Carolina, and from there to Columbus, Mississippi, to give a talk at the Mississippi State College for Women.

She managed also a stopover in New Orleans, where she saw Peter Taylor and Andrew Lytle, who came up from Florida for the reunion. She swung back to Jackson for an automobile jaunt along the Mississippi coast with Eudora. Katherine Anne remembered the whole tour as "fine" and "joyful" and a "shimmer of greenery and warmth."

Soon after her return from the South, Katherine Anne received an invitation to join the American delegation traveling to Paris for the five-week-long International Congress for Cultural Freedom. Making the trip from the United States were Allen Tate, Glenway Wescott, Robert Lowell, Virgil Thomson, James Farrell, Janet Flanner, William Faulkner, and W. H. Auden, among others. Distinguished companies from Boston, Vienna, Berlin, Rome, London, and Geneva were to perform symphonies, operas, and ballets. The Paris Museum of Modern Art had made its main exposition rooms available for two hundred masterpieces selected especially for the event from museums in the United States and Europe. On 5 May Katherine Anne boarded the *Queen Elizabeth* with a merry company of friends and relatives seeing her off. She arrived in Paris six days later.

Like the other participants, she knew less than she thought she did about the Congress for Cultural Freedom (CCF), which had been established in 1950 to bring together Western intellectuals and artists opposed to Communism and to generate support for anti-Communist enterprises that carried the message of intellectual and artistic autonomy. The CCF, however, was secretly founded, controlled, and financed by the CIA, which was fighting the cold war by attempting to contain the left, win over the European intelligentsia to U.S. capitalism, and expose the failures of progressive social movements. By hiding behind bogus foundations, such as the Farfield, and channeling money through legitimate foundations run by sympathetic capitalists such as Rockefeller, Ford, and Carnegie, the CIA was able to carry out covert political activities, which included setting editorial policy at selected magazines, subsidizing certain authors and their publishers (T. S. Eliot's "Four Quartets" was translated at CIA expense and airdropped into the Soviet Union), and pressing Hollywood studios to produce films that illustrated the intellectual and artistic benefits of capitalist independence.

In 1952 Katherine Anne was among a large number of distinguished artists and intellectuals who were happy to accept the CCF's first-class accommodations in a month-long testimonial to artistic freedom. And being in Paris was as wonderful as she knew it would be: "God knows,

I was never so happy to get back to any place in this world," she wrote Paul. "The light there, even the lighting of the streets at night: the endearing French habit of not turning on street lights at this time of year until nearly nine o'clock, leaving that long twilight which is so strange and beautiful in a city: in the crowded centers of course, the cafés light up, but that is all. And the lively, moving skies over Paris: did you ever have time to sit and watch the cloud shapes on a sunny day? I love the way you can see in half a dozen directions at every *place*: and the green vistas of trees with the sunlight filtered through as if the underside of the leaves were lighted. Oh well, its Paris, and the city for me."

She went to lunch and dinner at favorite restaurants. She revisited the Louvre and the Cluny. She had a bittersweet experience in discovering that a Mexican art show was the remnant of the collection she had organized in 1922. She went with Robert Lowell to light a candle in St. Germain-des-Pres for the sake of old times; she became friends with his new wife, Elizabeth Hardwick, a native Kentuckian; she had lunch with Janet Flanner; she lingered over tea with Glenway and the young, charming Luis Flores; and she took comfortable pleasure in a reunion with her French translator, Marcelle Sibon. She had long conversations with Cyril Connelly, Stephen Spender, and Louis MacNiece. "Over and over again," she said, "I would be walking along the street and some one would suddenly be at my elbow whom I had not seen for years, and there was always time to sit for an hour at a little table on a side walk and talk awhile."

The CCF festival began 28 April. The formal addresses took place 16 May, and Katherine Anne was selected to speak in behalf of the American delegation. Her talk, however, was not so good as others she had given, and some persons who were aware of her brilliant success as a speaker were disappointed. Her notes for it, published in 1970 as "Opening Speech at Paris Conference (International Exposition of the Arts, 1952)," reveal an incoherence and inconclusiveness that resulted from trying to cram everything she wanted to say into her allotted fifteen minutes. Her summarizing statement, however, was naïve: "This delegation of Americans was not chosen to come here on the basis of our political beliefs and that is a good thing. We came strictly as artists."

Nobel-prize-winner William Faulkner spoke as a member of a panel at the closing meeting. At the end of the session, after Faulkner received a standing ovation for his brief remarks, Katherine Anne,

Glenway, and Lowell approached the podium to pay their respects to their countryman. Apparently not recognizing them, he strode between them without speaking. Katherine Anne felt snubbed (Glenway reported that she was "furious"). Although she judged Faulkner still "a wonderful author," she concluded that it was "much too late to know him personally," and she made a literary caricature of him: "He looked a sober, trim, beaknosed little bantam fighting cock . . . He is tiresome in his anti-intellectual, anti-literature posture, insisting he is only a farmer: if one mentions another writer, he says, with an exaggerated Mississippi accent, 'Why, he's one of these literary fellers, isn't he?' which can be funny for awhile, but it doesn't last well. Mind you, when I said he looked sober, I know damned well he drinks like a southern author: and he does quite a lot of cavorting among the ladies."

By the time the festival ended 1 June, Katherine Anne had made arrangements to go to a remote inn where she could rest and write. She intended to return to Paris later in the summer, and, after a trip to New York to settle up her affairs, she thought she would come back to live in Paris for good. On 2 June she boarded a train that eight hours later reached the northwest coast of France. She could hardly have chosen a more out-of-the-way place than Le Moulin de Rosmadec, at Pont-Aven on the coast of Brittany. In the little town, where hardly anyone knew a word of English, and in the fifteenth-century inn (once a mill), where she was the only registered guest, she felt pleasingly isolated. "Already I am smoothed out and re-newed and easy in my mind," she wrote Bill Goyen, describing a "roaring to write" attitude.

But despite the congenial fifteenth-century atmosphere of the idyllic Moulin de Rosmadec, she found it impossible to write even the fifteen-hundred-word preface for "The Days Before." Instead, she wandered into simple churches; she watched local Breton artisans; she visited the nearby River Goyen and scooped up a little vial of its water to take to Goyen. Contributing to her creative stasis was the fatigue she brought with her to Brittany. Her hectic, month-long socializing in Paris had been interspersed with spells of sickness that ranged from digestive upsets to a fainting spell.

After she was at Pont-Aven about a week, she learned that she immediately had to vacate her New York apartment, which was being sold. She had to rely on her maid Guinelda Archibald ("The Priceless"), friends (Bill Goyen and Cyrilly Abels), her Harcourt, Brace editors Carver, Giroux, and Reynal, and Ann—"a perfect regiment of angels"—to find another apartment for her and oversee the moving and storage of her staggering quantity of belongings. With her consent they rented an apartment for her at 117 East Seventeenth Street.

Katherine Anne blamed the move for her inability to write the preface for the collection of essays, but she also had little heart for the task after she received the edited manuscript. She strongly regretted that she hadn't been able to revise the old pieces and write new ones (an article on art and neurosis and biographical essays on Rimbaud, Erasmus, Jane Austen, Emily Brontë, Eleanor Roosevelt, and Gide). The collection depressed her in other ways, too. To make the book publishable she had allowed Carver to cut, paste, select, and edit the nonfiction, something she would never have allowed anyone to do to her fiction, and some of the essays hardly seemed her own. In reading over the pieces she also was reminded of their span of difficult years. "All this whole collection," she wrote Carver, "represents such a struggle for survival, for expression, such difficulties trying to make something whole out of fragments of time and energy, such loss and waste, as makes me even now deathly tired to remember."

She left Pont-Aven on 5 July and returned to Paris. After she registered at the Hotel d'Islay on the rue Jacob and found the page proofs waiting for her, she tried unsuccessfully to write a preface. As a substitute, she mailed a two-paragraph "foreword," in which she defended the nonfiction she had been forced to write in order to afford a little time to write the fiction that mattered. She nevertheless anticipated the book's earning enough money to ease her "problems of existence," as she told Reynal, and she liked the dust jacket (Paul Cadmus's lovely drawing of her against a white background), having averted the publisher's use of an unflattering photograph of her taken the day she sailed. "I pulled myself together and forced myself to look at it, as one might stare down a Gorgon," she wrote Carver. "Please don't show it to anybody, and above all, don't ever let it slip out and get published." At age sixty-two she disclosed her insecurities about her fading beauty.

During the course of putting together *The Days Before* she had become increasingly dissatisfied with her relationship with Harcourt, Brace and aware of the bad decisions she had made early on in shunning the service of agents. In May before she sailed to Europe she enlisted the help of agent James Oliver Brown to try to get her three books reprinted in paperback and to persuade someone in Hollywood that *Noon Wine; Pale Horse, Pale Rider;* "The Cracked Looking-Glass"; or *Old Mortality* would make good movies. Victor Weybright at New American Library (NAL) told Brown flatly that Katherine Anne was "too special to be read" by the persons who bought NAL's books. She had to face the fact again that she was branded an effete writer out of the reach of the average reader who bought cheap paperbacks that made authors wealthy and publishers content. She released some of her bitter frustration to Brown: "I am still the 'meticulous stylist' writing her 'filagree prose.' Jesus, I am sick of it. But I can't be stampeded at this date, no more than I was then."

Brown was the first person to spell out to Katherine Anne exactly how much of her Harcourt, Brace owned and the restrictions on any agent she would hire. "I did not know that my publishers controlled all or nearly all of my subsidiary rights," she wrote to Brown in shock. "Of course, God help me, I still hardly even know what they are, nor what I might expect from them, properly handled . . . I hardly know how to reconcile this state of affairs with a simple truth—that I am on most friendly terms with them and they do a great deal for me, but always in advances of money and so on, which just plunges me more and more deeply into debt."

The same day she wrote Brown, Katherine Anne also poured out her frustration to Catherine Carver: "My mind is peculiarly set in just one state, deep down, under all the surfaces which do somehow help to keep me going from one day to the next: just horror. Just exactly that." Alarmed, Carver encouraged her to go on a little trip and forget the unpleasantness across the ocean. A week later Katherine Anne apologized for the "tone" of her letters that worried Carver, nevertheless dramatically comparing herself to "those captives of American Indians staked out on an ant-bed."

Katherine Anne realized how much she missed Donald Brace, and at the end of July, after stiff letters from Carver, Reynal, and Giroux, she wrote to him in despair. "It had begun to look as if you were really freed forever from my small but annoying affairs—no, no such luck for you! . . . I am back with a whole row of frustrations, bafflements, discrepancies between this and that, and apparently no hope of any kind of change." She said, "I am writing this as my very last hope, and if nothing is done, why then, I am done, too. I can at any time take a job as lecturer in a college or University, I can go on trouping the country lecturing, I can write articles until kingdom come for any number of magazines, but you see, I've been doing that all these years to support myself while trying to write, and I am exhausted. I am exhausted and I am sick of the utter endlessness of the prospect. I know every one says, 'finish the novel and your financial troubles will be over.' I am going to finish it, in between other jobs, of teaching, lecturing, writing. But if what I have already published had been handled properly by some one who really knew how to use all the possibilities, I shouldn't have had to go on to this point of despair."

It was nearly two weeks before she received a reply from Brace, who had taken time to review her contracts and discuss the situation with Reynal and Giroux. He explained in detail the binding legal agreements that had been made with the French and English publishers for the previous books and pointed out that different arrangements could be made only for future books. Without the encouragement from him she had hoped for, Katherine Anne stood by what she had told him at the end of July. She was relinquishing the attempt to finish her writing under contract. She also had given up trying to return to France to live and was resigning herself to lecturing and teaching at colleges and universities. She put her name on the waiting list at American Express for passage as soon as possible to New York and to an apartment she had never seen.

She sailed on the *Niewe Amsterdam* from Le Havre on 13 September.

CHAPTER TWENTY-FIVE

Michigan and Belgium

September 1952–February 1955

My what a fuss I do make about taking a little lecturing job in a uni-
versity, but of course, no one thing is ever just that, it is connected
with everything else, and I have turned up so many stones and planks,
every sort of thing from radio and moving pictures to buying a house
to love and marriage, and the same crawly organisms come romping
out, and don't think I don't know they are in my blood, too. I am a part
of this filth, something in me against my will and my spirit, consents
to it: or I wouldn't be in this world . . . it is very hard sometimes not to
despair altogether, and of myself first, because I know myself best!

Katherine Anne had barely settled into her little three-room apartment
on East Seventeenth Street when *The Days Before* was published.
It was reviewed more widely than any one of her previous books,
and most of the assessments were enthusiastic and congratulatory. In
the *New York Times Book Review*, Carlos Baker wrote, "Reading
these essays is as easy, as pleasant, and as rewarding as reading a fine
novel." Impulsively, Katherine Anne sent an inscribed copy of the
book to Ezra Pound at St. Elizabeth's Hospital in Washington:

> *For Ezra Pound, Poet*
> *With the gratitude and*
> *Recollection of more than*
> *Half my lifetime*
> > *Katherine Anne Porter*
> > *26 September 1952*
> > *New York*

Pound's response was not what she expected. In her book he read for
the first time her review of his *Letters*, and he wrote to her to say he

saw in it an unfriendly influence of Mark Van Doren. She hastened to answer Pound's letter, to assure him of her admiration, and to defend herself against having been "led" by Van Doren or anyone else. She promised to stop by St. Elizabeth's and discuss those points with which he took issue.

For the remainder of the year, she enjoyed the success of *The Days Before* and the December wedding of Red Warren and Eleanor Clark, at which she was matron of honor and Albert Erskine was best man. Although she and Albert had not seen each other for more than a decade, they had kept up a cordial correspondence in which the intimacy of husband and wife had been replaced with the professional relationship of editorial advisor and author. Seeing him at the wedding, however, reminded her of the failure of her hopes in 1938 when Red had been best man in their wedding. Later, when she read Simone de Beauvoir's *The Second Sex*, in a marginal note near a passage on marriage ceremonies she referred to Eleanor and Red's wedding and to "the monster, the best man," calling up her inclusive label for men who failed in any degree to live up to her romantic ideal.

Her nephew Paul continued to please her, however, and she was delighted that he moved to New York, where they could attend musical performances, ballets, and museum exhibits together. She had reluctantly accepted the fact that he was not going to pursue a career as a writer, just as she had bowed to Ann's decision to pull back from professional dancing in order to be a full-time wife and mother. She stopped trying to be her nephew's and niece's artistic "mother."

In the late winter of 1953 she still felt she had unfinished business with Ezra Pound. After speaking at Washington and Lee University and Sweetbriar College at the beginning of March, she passed through Washington on her way back to New York and spent two days with the now-widowed Marcella Winslow at the P Street house. Marcella thought Katherine Anne seemed less well, noting signs of exhaustion in the spasms of coughing that left her gasping for breath. Despite fatigue, however, Katherine Anne asked Marcella, who had painted Ezra Pound in 1948 and continued to call upon him at St. Elizabeth's Hospital, to take her to see him.

To visit Pound one had to get permission from the Pounds and the superintendent of St. Elizabeth's, a grim, dilapidated insane asylum that dated from the nineteenth century. Marcella secured the permissions and escorted Katherine Anne to the hospital on 4 March. Once cleared by officials, they were admitted to the visiting room in

Howard Hall, a barred prison ward Pound called "the hell-hole." Katherine Anne thought Pound in fine spirits. "Where he was," she said, "the air was not hospital air, or the air of madness; he is profoundly eccentric, he is really a Fascist by a kind of emotional *bent*, and I cannot, cannot understand one word of his economic theories: so I tried without I hope being too obvious, to keep the talk on poetry and personal history . . . He *is* in prison, you know; and it seems strange to me now how free he was—all the walls disappeared."

Katherine Anne returned to Washington to speak at the Corcoran in April, and Mary McGrory, a columnist at the time for the *Washington Star*, described the event: "Although of an age to be a grandmother, Miss Porter somehow still commands the aura of the Southern belle. Her snow-white hair frames her delicate features and a gray elegant dress brought out her beautiful deep-set gray eyes. Her throaty drawling conversation is sprinkled still with the 'La, me's' of her Texas and Louisiana girlhood. Miss Porter charmed the audience right out of their seats."

Katherine Anne's talk had not been only charm and lightness, however. Mindful of her distinguished political audience that included Justice William O. Douglas, she had also commented on the congressional inquiries into Communism on campuses. She called the investigators who "maul" and "paw over" the fine arts—"the only things that outlive everything else"—"not only perfectly ignorant but perfectly malignant" and warned, "We will pay a big price for this kind of foolishness." She told the audience that students were frightened and angry and felt "contempt" for the senators conducting the investigations.

She was torn between a long-term university appointment and radio work supplemented by very brief appearances on campuses and at the Poetry Center. The performer in her would have liked to become a radio personality, and it looked like a real possibility when she accepted an offer from NBC to read poetry on Sunday mornings. A notice in *Variety* called it a "permanent feature." "Look who's landed in show biz!" she wrote her cousin, the actress Lily Cahill, in early May. She told Lily that everybody, from radio people to her "serious writing friends, poets, novelists, critics," was saying, in the same gay voice, "You're IN!" But even while she was telling Lily all this, exaggerating their common ground in "theater," the intellectual and practical part of her was ready to accept a year-long appointment the University of Michigan had offered. Her decision crystallized when NBC failed to continue her readings at the end of the thirteenth week. She notified officials at the university in Ann Arbor that she was coming.

Isabel and Hew Bayley sublet her apartment for the year, enabling her to leave her belongings in place and providing her the peaceful thought of having a "home" to which to return. After Stanford, she also tried to be smart in her negotiations with administrators who were setting up her year. She was satisfied with the proposed schedule of two courses each semester, and she demanded that her courses be offered for credit. In the fall term one course was to be a workshop in creative writing and the other was to be a survey of contemporary poetry.

After she arrived in Ann Arbor by train 14 September, she was given lodgings in the Michigan League, a university inn for campus visitors, provided an office suite in Angell Hall, and assigned a full-time secretary, Mary Cooley, who had long experience dealing with temperamental writers. From all accounts, Katherine Anne's undependability in meeting appointments (and sometimes classes) and her unchanged habit of accepting invitations for more social events than she could possibly attend were a challenge to Mary. But Mary later said that Katherine Anne completely won her over, that she saw behind her charm a great intelligence and generosity and was happy to devote her time and energy to making her year at Michigan successful.

Perhaps not so charmed were the hostess who prepared an elaborate dinner party in her honor only to receive a telegram from her an hour beforehand saying she was unwell and unable to come; or the dean, whose saucer she appropriated for serving cream to the stray kitten she adopted; or regular faculty members who resented her taking over the kitchenette in the faculty lounge to cook midday meals for herself, the aroma of steak and onions wafting down the halls into classrooms. Mary herself must have wondered whether charm had its limits when Katherine Anne asked her to teach her to drive the little four-speed, column-shift Hillman-Minx that Isabel and Hew had lent her. After one panicky lesson, Katherine Anne refused to drive again and Mary had to keep it in her own backyard. Surprised that Katherine Anne had no money when she arrived, Mary also worried constantly about her mismanagement of her finances. When Katherine Anne made trips away from Ann Arbor for television appearances in New York or Washington, she always returned without anything saved from her fees, but with accessories she couldn't afford: a black fox stole, a beautiful purse, an expensive string of cultured pearls.

As at Stanford, she was glad to take her writing students' manuscripts to read and comment on outside of class, but she spent class time reading from favorite writers and some of her own works. She held some of the writing classes in students' apartments and dormitory common areas. Most students were so enchanted with her that another faculty member resentfully labeled them her "fervents." One young man told her ten years later that he had shaped his whole life according to the opinions she had expressed that year.

A young journalist in Ann Arbor in 1953 recalled the special attention Katherine Anne gave her. On a cold rainy day Jeanne Rockwell entered a dingy campus coffee shop to buy a Coke. She asked a small white-haired woman in a purple velveteen cloak sitting at the counter having lunch whether it was all right to take the nearby stool. The woman gestured permission, and it suddenly occurred to Rockwell that the woman eating a sandwich in small bites and sipping tea with lemon might possibly be Katherine Anne Porter, who, she had heard, was in town. After observing the delicately drawn jaw, aristocratic nose, and noble line of brow and exchanging pleasantries with her, Rockwell had to ask: "You're not Katherine Anne Porter, by any chance?" Rockwell recalled "flashing eyes" raking her appraisingly before the nod. Embarrassed later to remember that she had blurted out, "I write too," Rockwell recalled Katherine Anne's instantly expressed interest, "the voice low, the words beautifully articulated." Rockwell thought, "In her dark beautiful cloak she seemed a mythical figure, the Hera of another world, surrounded by flights of birds, able to divine the nature of auguries. Somewhere inside, I wept invisible tears wishing she'd tell me what to do." When Rockwell invited Katherine Anne to dinner at her house with her husband and little son, she came. Rockwell called Katherine Anne "a lively patron saint of literature . . . to generations of women all over."

Late in the fall semester, Katherine Anne began to feel worn out and ill. The poetry class met for three hours a week, the writing workshop two, and each of nine advanced students had an hour-long private conference with her every week. Marking papers required an extraordinary amount of time, and other duties and social engagements consumed still more. The long train trips to New York, Baltimore, Philadelphia, and Washington for readings also soaked up energy. Back in Michigan in the increasingly cold weather of late fall, concerned that she might come down again with bronchitis, she checked herself into St. Joseph Mercy Hospital for seclusion and rest.

Her self-diagnosis was "nervous exhaustion," and an accommodating physician agreed.

At her request hospital nurses placed a No Visitors sign on the door of her private room. After she had been there about a week, David Locher, a library science graduate student who worked on the hospital switchboard, heard that the writer Katherine Anne Porter was in the hospital and asked the hospital chaplain to arrange for him to meet her. He found her sitting in bed in a kimono, surrounded by books and magazines. Although he intended to stay only a few minutes, he stayed an hour while she talked and talked. Locher, a gentle, religious young man who wrote poetry and made rosaries, was awed to be "in her presence." He asked whether she would give him written permission to enroll in her Recent American Fiction class the next semester, and she readily consented. She inscribed the book he had brought, "December 3, 1953, a dark day in hospital but not an unhappy one." David Locher would become her lifelong friend.

Shortly after she arrived in Ann Arbor, Katherine Anne had applied for a Fulbright Grant to teach abroad, requesting France, preferably Paris, in order to do research for "The Trial of Berthe de Fauquemberg," her medieval murder mystery. The competition for France was heavy, however, and early in 1954 she was offered instead a place in Belgium at the University of Liège for the academic year 1954–55. She accepted it with little hesitation. She would have to sublet her apartment for another year, and she would have to "pack up, pull up, and get the hell out," she told Cleanth and Tinkum. But "I might just as well be working in Liège as Ann Arbor," she said. "I aint never going to get no chance to do nothing nohow in the literary way . . . . . There is only so much of me, and I have only so much energy, and so I resign. But I'll never get over the notion that I could have been a good writer under a luckier star, or perhaps on some other planet."

Before the spring semester was very far underway, Katherine Anne began to show new signs of fatigue. As at Stanford, the weariness revealed itself in her complaints about student demands infringing on her personal time (ignoring, as usual, the fact that she encouraged it) and in her increasingly frequent failure to show up for class. David Locher recalled guiltily cutting class one day only to run into Katherine Anne, discovering that she was cutting class, too. Her excuse was that she was too bone-weary to face energy-draining classroom talk. Then in late March she collapsed in the classroom. She was talking along easily about Henry James, she told Monroe, when a pain "about the size of the palm of my hand started just under the lower ribs slightly to the left and spread and expanded and grew agonizingly all over my midriff and up to the shoulder and into the jawbone and down the left arm." She broke into a sweat, put down the book she was discussing, laid her head on the table, and told her students, "Oh, I'm so sorry, so very sorry."

She was taken by ambulance to the university hospital, where her attack was determined to be angina pectoris rather than a full-blown heart attack. The word was sent out erroneously by the student newspaper, however, that Katherine Anne Porter had suffered the latter, and when the Associated Press picked it up and newspapers all over the country began reporting it, friends, relatives, and even total strangers who admired her writing reacted with alarm. Calls, letters, and telegrams poured in from all over the world, and she spent much of her time in the hospital answering them.

She told everyone that it had been a very slight attack and nothing to worry about. But she, in fact, had had two similar attacks in 1952, one in April, shortly before she left for the Congress for Cultural Freedom, and a second in May, when she had collapsed in Ciro's in Paris. At that time a Paris doctor had recommended nitroglycerin as a safeguard, but whether she ever filled the prescription is not known. She said that doctors at the University of Michigan hospital simply told her to "SLOW DOWN!" She intended to do that, she told Monroe: "In fact, it might be fun." One of her reasons for diminishing the attack was to make sure the Fulbright committee did not hear about "the scandal," as she called it, and conclude that she was not up to the year abroad.

Regardless of the jolly face she assumed to others, the attack sobered her, and she resolved to take care of herself during her remaining months in Ann Arbor. The attack also reminded her of the passing time ("I am really old now," she remarked to Glenway) and of her unfinished books with their unpaid advances from Harcourt, Brace. She now wanted seriously to get back to her writing.

Instead of working on the books under contract, however, she wrote "A Defense of Circe," a clever retelling of the Circe episode in *The Odyssey*. Circe is a mythological "new woman" who, "smilingly with her natural grace," transforms Odysseus and his men into "groaning, grunting, weeping, bewildered creatures" to be penned in a sty. Even wise Odysseus, born from the seed of Zeus, is no match for Circe; but Katherine Anne understood Odysseus's longing for "home," and she probably equated his "long black ship . . . breasting the wild sea" for ten years with her protracted writing of the ship voyage that constituted "No Safe Harbor." She sent the essay to Cyrilly Abels at *Mademoiselle*, where it was published in the June issue.

The remainder of her time at Ann Arbor was pleasant enough. She judged stories for a literary prize, finished up her classes successfully, and accepted a Litt.D. at commencement. She threw a couple of big parties for her students, one in the home of a faculty member and the other in a park outside of town. (David Locher noticed that the park seemed familiar to her, and although she claimed never to have seen it, he later suspected she had been there in 1920 when she visited Mae Franking.) The summer session, in which she taught another seminar on creative writing, passed quickly, and in August she left Ann Arbor for New York.

She sailed out of Hoboken for Europe on 17 September on the SS *Ryndam* and arrived in Rotterdam eight days later. From there she went to Brussels, expecting to stay only a few days before traveling on to Liège. She no sooner arrived in Brussels, however, than she collapsed with bronchitis and took to her bed in the hotel for two weeks. When she reached Liège on 11 October, she saw and felt signs of approaching cold weather, and she was disappointed in the nondescript apartment at 25 Avenue des Platanes that her Belgian host, Dorothy Deflandre, had chosen for her. Under different circumstances she might have been pleased with her schedule, one lecture a week at the University of Liège and later talks in other Belgian and European cities. But her health was poor, and she was depressed. "I am melancholy to a point I have not known since Germany, Berlin in 1931," she told Glenway. She reported to several persons that she was having bad dreams.

She accepted an invitation to read her story "The Circus" in London over the BBC in December, and she decided to extend the escape from Belgium with trips to Paris and Rome. She enjoyed the luxury of the Hotel Connaught in London's Carlos Square (pure linen and a silk comforter on the bed, roast beef and Yorkshire pudding served on silver and porcelain). But she did not linger. She went along to Paris to buy clothes before flying to Rome, which she reached Christmas Eve. She went to midnight mass at Ara Coeli and Christmas Day attended a children's fair in the Piazza Navona. Ecstatic, she toured the city as fast as she could. "I'm glad I never saw Rome until now," she wrote on a postcard to Glenway, "for how could I dream anything so new and fresh and gay could happen just by finding another city?"

The change of weather and the hectic schedule had been too much for her frail constitution, however, and she was ill when she returned to Brussels. Dorothy Deflandre placed her in a comfortable hotel in lieu of sending her to a hospital and arranged to move her into an apartment in Brussels, from which she could commute once a week to Liège. Rest in a hotel room was not sufficient, however, because the influenza with which she was diagnosed was severe. She was sent to the Edith Cavell Hospital for three weeks.

Through the rest of January she gradually improved and doctors thought she could finish her Fulbright assignment, which included scheduled lectures in Spain, France, Sweden, Luxembourg, and Denmark. But when she left the hospital in early February she realized she was not up to the rigor of the schedule, and the Fulbright committee released her from the commitment. By the end of the month she was at the Gallia Palace Hotel in Cannes, waiting for the *Andrea Doria* to take her home.

CHAPTER TWENTY-SIX

Ship of Fools: *The End of a Long Voyage*

February 1955–September 1961

It is customary to say, one is born and dies alone. Not true about birth, at least, which mother and child most certainly share, and not just in the body. Death is a solitary thing.

Before Katherine Anne left Belgium, she bought a winding sheet of fine linen in which she expected eventually to be buried. The death wrap was emblematic of her bone-weariness, depression about her unfinished novel, and concern about her health. A few months after she arrived in New York, however, it was not her own death but the deaths of persons close to her that she had to face. In July her cousin Lily Cahill died of a stroke following complications from the chronic bronchial infections she had battled all her life. On 19 September Katherine Anne's brother, Paul, died, and the next day Donald Brace died. She did not know until later that in June Adrienne Monnier also had died, having taken a fatal dose of sleeping pills. When Katherine Anne heard about her death, it seemed only fitting that it occurred in the summer of 1955.

Reliving their childhood and adolescent hardships, Katherine Anne saw her brother's death as momentous: "We four were the family, and look, until yesterday we were all living." She identified with Lily as an artist, and she envied her professional success despite struggles with illness and poverty. Donald Brace's death was more than the loss of a man Katherine Anne once considered a dear friend. It further loosened her bond with Harcourt, Brace and constituted the real beginning of her break with the firm.

The deaths reminded Katherine Anne again of the urgency to complete her unfinished business. In the summer she found a house in

Southbury, Connecticut to which she could withdraw, "determined," she said, "to be a writer." By August she was fairly well settled in the two-story, six-room house, which sat on a grassy knoll above a main road. On the second floor she created a workspace in the glassed-in sundeck. "Now my days are tremendously long and slow and there is no sense of loneliness or isolation," she told Glenway.

Having waited a respectful time after Donald Brace's death to extricate herself from Harcourt, Brace, in mid-October she wrote to William (Bill) Jovanovich, president of the firm for the past year. "I am now, and have been for a great while, almost utterly discouraged about my relations with Harcourt, Brace and Company," she wrote, citing what she regarded as the mismanagement of her affairs. "The truth is," she told him, "all my beautiful beginnings and long serious work have just run into what looks like a blind alley." She asked for specifics about her total debt to Harcourt, Brace and which of her rights the publisher was willing to sell.

Bill Jovanovich, a reserved scholar and hard businessman, had none of the courtly patience of Donald Brace, but he was unwilling to let her go without making some effort to keep her. He offered her four hundred dollars a month for the next year and reported that he was dispatching to Southbury one of his secretaries to help her sort the manuscript pages of the long novel and sending John McCallum, newly promoted to vice president of the firm, to convince her of the high esteem in which she was held by Harcourt, Brace. She succeeded in intercepting the secretary—the thought that a stranger would be pawing through her papers horrified her—but she graciously welcomed McCallum to her house on 27 October.

Jovanovich and McCallum thought their appeal had worked, but two days after McCallum's visit she wrote anything but acquiescent letters to each of them. She explained her immediate need for a substantial sum of money to pay off an accumulation of debts and expenses and described the monthly four hundred dollars as about half of what she had hoped for. She asked, again, for a specific report on her debt to Harcourt, Brace and a list of titles, with proposed contents, of books she had signed contracts to write.

What she did not express to either Jovanovich or McCallum was her rage at their implication that she was owned by Harcourt, Brace. Both Jovanovich and McCallum had spoken of having inherited her and her great debt, and when she told them that another publisher had offered her three times as much as their four hundred dollars a month, they complained about the lack of ethics of a publisher who would try to take away another publisher's *"property."* Jovanovich had told her that such a publisher was only after her *"name!"* She replied, "Well, if my name is the only thing I have to peddle, maybe I had better peddle it to the highest bidder while it is still hot!"

Even before McCallum's visit, Katherine Anne was seriously discussing a move to Atlantic–Little, Brown with the young director of the Atlantic Monthly Press, Seymour Lawrence. She had known Lawrence since 1954, when, as the energetic special assistant to the editor of the *Atlantic Monthly*, he wrote to ask whether she had a new story or an independent portion of her novel-in-progress that the *Atlantic Monthly* could publish. Although she told him she would be delighted to send him a section of the novel, because she soon left for Liège nothing more of the mutually expressed interest developed until the following April, after Lawrence, who had become associate editor at the Atlantic Monthly Press, went to New York to her East Seventeenth Street apartment to discuss the publication.

Katherine Anne liked and respected the twenty-nine-year-old, Harvard-educated Lawrence, who had a talent for recognizing geniuses and publishing their work. Not especially handsome, he was warm and witty, as well as very smart, and he greatly admired Katherine Anne and her art. Their relationship proceeded formally, and from June of 1954 to the end of November 1955 they addressed one another as "Mr. Lawrence" and "Miss Porter."

In the fall of 1955 she invited him to Southbury for lunch to discuss the section of "No Safe Harbor" she finally was offering to the *Atlantic Monthly*. Present also was Cyrilly Abels, her good friend on whom she more and more relied for advice. Lawrence recalled a wonderful lunch of broiled lamb chops, fresh garden vegetables, brown bread Katherine Anne had baked that morning, and a vintage wine. They were standing in her driveway as he was preparing to leave for Boston when she suddenly said to him, "Mr. Lawrence, my dear friend and publisher Donald Brace died this year and there is no one else at Harcourt, Brace I know or trust. Can you recommend a good publisher?" He didn't hesitate a moment before replying, "Miss Porter, I wear two hats: I'm an editor at the *Atlantic* but I've also been recently appointed Director of the Atlantic Monthly Press. Our books are published under the joint imprint of Atlantic–Little, Brown and we would be honored to be your publisher." Katherine Anne replied, "Why, Mr. Lawrence, I believe that's a proposal and I accept."

After Lawrence returned to Boston, he wrote a friendly letter to her in which he offered to send her a fountain pen in exchange for her bread recipe. She answered immediately, delighted to send the recipe and an explanation of the psychological benefits of bread baking. Even though their association was still very formal at this point, the exchange was symbolic of the differences between her potential relationship with Lawrence and the one she had had with Donald Brace, who would never have stepped into this domestic territory. It was also a mark of Lawrence's shrewd understanding of the kind of editor and publisher Katherine Anne wanted and needed. The next year he asked her to be godmother to his first child, Macy, another act far different from anything ventured or imagined by Donald Brace, who in his letters to Katherine Anne never referred to his wife or daughters by their given names.

The day after she sent her bread recipe to Lawrence she wrote another letter to him, feeling him out about the willingness of Atlantic–Little, Brown to meet her demands. On 9 November he wrote back to say that the board of directors had approved all her requests: The firm would pay off Harcourt, Brace, and she would be given twenty-five hundred dollars immediately with a promise of four hundred dollars a month for the next year; she was to receive 15 percent royalty on each copy of the novel sold, and only 10 percent would go to the publisher for the sale of moving-picture rights. She was also promised that no book Atlantic–Little, Brown published by her would go out of print during her lifetime. Pleased with Lawrence's response, she wrote to William Jovanovich on 20 November to tell him of her resolve to move to Atlantic–Little, Brown, a decision she called "final." Her association with Harcourt, Brace was not over, however, for the firm refused to hand over the rights to her five books they already had published. She was not at all surprised, but it hardly mattered at this point. Her dismay at remaining partially tethered to Harcourt, Brace was considerably less than her satisfaction with Seymour Lawrence and her new contract with Atlantic–Little, Brown.

Lawrence wrote to her at the end of November to say he wanted to address her as "Katherine Anne" but hesitated since he was "the junior member." Her next two letters to him ignored his indirect request, but finally in mid-December she wrote a "Dear Seymour" letter in which she described in some detail the novel on which he had gambled. From here on he would be "Seymour" to her, not "Sam" as his other authors and friends called him. For both of them it was the beginning of a remarkable professional relationship.

Through the late winter and spring of 1956 she had worked well on the novel, now titled "Ship of Fools," forcing herself to send Lawrence at regular intervals batches of the manuscript she was revising, expanding, and retyping. But she began to feel depressed about it for a number of reasons beyond her growing acknowledgment that there was yet more to do than she had anticipated. She was again frustrated about money. The up-front payment disappeared in a month or so, and the four-hundred-dollar monthly stipend really did not go far. She also had been upset by some letters she received after the publication of the first *Atlantic* excerpt. Several readers had pointed out a technical error in her description of the Jew Julius Lowenthal's preparation for prayer, and another reader, who identified himself as an American foreign correspondent, had been so shocked and offended by a racial slur one of the characters directs to Lowenthal that he called Katherine Anne a "thoroughly vile" woman for even writing the words. In the first case, she was appalled at her error and acknowledged that there were some matters in the novel that would require research. In the second instance, she was dismayed that the angry reader had missed her point. She justified the scene to Lawrence: "It *is* offensive, spoken by an offensive character, and I meant it to be so."

She was also put out with Lawrence, who had written the copy for the catalog announcing publication of the novel. She rebuked him for his praise of her as "the most distinguished woman writer" of the present day:

> At the risk of being called a horrid name like Feminist, I object, always have, to being called a *woman* writer; men say this I am sure without really knowing they are making a faintly derogatory discrimination: they do after all set the standards, nobody can deny that, and to say I am considered the most distinguished *woman* writer is to say I am not judged by the great standard. If I am distinguished, please allow me my level of distinction in the first-rank company. I am not ashamed to be in the company of Emily Brontë, George Eliot, Virginia Woolf, but they certainly belong in the company of Flaubert and Turgenev and Henry James and—make your own favorite list. I consider *Wuthering Heights* the purest act of genius in the world of the novel; nobody male or female has ever beat Emily Brontë at that!

So it is not contempt of my kind, nor of their level of gifts, but just simply that I must be judged as an artist, and not a woman artist. How does it sound to say, T. S. Eliot is one of the most distinguished men poets, etc? If you really believe I belong in the first rank, then don't please put me by implication at the head of the second.

Early in 1956 the agent Jeff Hunter had set up a fall tour for her through the National Concert and Artists Corporation (NCAC) with the support of Atlantic–Little, Brown, which had looked at the expedition as part of the promotion of her novel to be published in November. By the end of July she was calling the novel genre "an Instrument of Torture," and it was clear that the circuit was not going to be a victory campaign coinciding with the appearance of *Ship of Fools.* Obliged to go through with it, she moved into the Jefferson Hotel in Washington to avoid housekeeping and to rest up. Within little more than a month, between 31 October and 25 November, she made fifteen appearances, for which she received a total of six thousand dollars. After paying NCAC and Hunter their fees and subtracting the cost of travel and advertising, she had far less to show for the jaunt than she had hoped.

Lawrence and the officers and board members of Atlantic–Little, Brown were disappointed that she had not completed the novel, but Lawrence did not scold or deliver recriminations. He advised her to keep focused, to exercise self-discipline, and to avoid the distractions of too many friends and too much socializing, but he did so in a completely sympathetic way, tempering his advice with praise and encouragement. He revealed an exceptional understanding of her fragile personality and her equally fragile creative force.

In the spring of 1958 she received two significant offers that would take care of her financial needs from September of 1958 through May of 1959. For the fall semester she was offered the position of writer-in-residence at the University of Virginia, in Charlottesville, and for the following spring semester she was offered the first Glasgow visiting professorship at Washington and Lee University, in Lexington, Virginia. She accepted both and prepared to vacate her Southbury house. She intended to finish the novel, however, before she went to Charlottesville. She asked Lawrence to find her a remote inn in which she could seclude herself for several weeks.

Lawrence booked Katherine Anne for a month into the Outpost Inn in Ridgefield, Connecticut. She led him to believe that as she retyped the manuscript in triplicate she would easily revise as she went. Then the whole novel would be finished. She even discussed with him a photograph for the dust jacket. But after only three weeks she confessed to him, "I am going more slowly than I like . . . I am tired enough to die, and am just starting on a long winter of hard work in a new place, and this haunts my sleep!" She talked about suicide and told Lawrence that she envied Colette, who had married "a protector." Lawrence wisely backed off, hoping she would find the creative energy to finish the novel.

Katherine Anne arrived in Charlottesville in mid-September cheerfully ready to perform her light duties as writer-in-residence. She was asked only to visit literature and writing classes occasionally, to be available for weekly conferences with a few individual students, and to give four public talks or readings. In return, she was given a stipend of five hundred dollars for each of the five months and provided comfortable living quarters in town as well as offices in the library and on the fifth floor of Cabell Hall, which housed the English Department. Her flexible schedule also gave her the freedom to leave Charlottesville for extended periods.

The estate of Emily Clark Balch underwrote the writer-in-residence program that had been inaugurated with William Faulkner's residency the year before. Katherine Anne was satisfied with the honor the invitation carried, and she was enchanted with the University of Virginia. The lovely rolling campus with its pillared Greek revival buildings sitting at the edge of the Blue Ridge Mountains evoked the colonial eras of her ancestors. She was sure that her mother's "collateral relatives" must still live "in bunches over in Roanoke." "It is almost strange how at home I feel," she declared. Soon she was referring to "Yankees" as out of touch with the reality of the South.

Instead of working on the novel, Katherine Anne took advantage of her light schedule to undertake a cross-country speaking tour in October and November that included stops at a half-dozen universities. The highlight was an engagement at the University of Texas on 22 October. The lecture hall overflowed that night, and two additional rooms had to be opened up with piped-in sound. Elegant in a formal blue gown, Katherine Anne walked onto the stage and bowed to her audience. "I look upon this as a kind of beautiful family gathering," she said. She reminisced about growing up in Kyle with her grandmother. "People ask me what I write from, and I say, I write from experience, but I say experience is anything that happens to me . . . a flash of memory, a nightmare, a daydream . . . You can't start a work of art anywhere except where life starts."

At the party afterward in her honor someone broached the idea of her donating her literary papers to the University of Texas. She happily embraced the suggestion. A week after she returned to Charlottesville she received a letter from Harry Ransom, vice president of the University of Texas. "I know Texas," he wrote. "I think that you know it too. Therefore I believe you will understand the sincerity and conviction with which the Administration has voted to establish in the new Library Center the Katherine Anne Porter Library." She responded quickly and ecstatically: "Your decision to establish in the Library Center a library in my name is the kind of honor I never imagined for myself, not being much concerned with honors, but now it is bestowed, I am enraptured with it, it seems now to be just what I should have chosen for a moment in my life—if I had been choosing! It is a gentle, lasting kind of glory, as if one had managed to merit well of the Fatherland without quite knowing how." She was confused, however. She thought that the library center was a complex of buildings and that the library to be named for her was an individual building. In fact, the center was a single building and the library to be named for her was a room in it. At the time, no one at Texas seemed to recognize the misunderstanding anymore than she did.

At Washington and Lee in the spring semester, her schedule was even lighter than it had been at the University of Virginia. Although Charlottesville had charmed her with its Jeffersonian echoes and its horse-country gentility, Lexington was even more parochially southern and rigidly historical. She was pleased to be the first woman to teach at the all-male school, and everyone she met seemed to be a descendant of some famous historical figure. "I love this place," she wrote Edward Schwartz, "a small town of world-travelers and polylinguists and good families and beautiful old houses and furniture and portraits and silver and manners."

Students, faculty, administrators, and townspeople sought out her company for social events and enthusiastically came to hear her speak. A particular delight was her reunion with Erna Johns's son, Glover Johns Jr., a professor of military science and commandant of cadets at Virginia Military Institute, also in Lexington. A warm and intelligent man, he was enchanted with Katherine Anne, whom he called "Miss Callie." His wife, Rita, another poised beauty, often invited Katherine Anne to luncheons and tea parties.

In January Katherine Anne had a nostalgic encounter with Charles Shannon in Montgomery, Alabama, when she made an appearance at the Air Force Library. She recalled his "golden glory" when they had been lovers, and she believed that he had been one of the few men in her life who truly loved her. Shortly after seeing Shannon, she ran into Jordan Pecile, a young naval officer she had met seven years earlier when she gave a talk at Cornell and he had been the student assigned to escort her around campus. He was articulate and sophisticated, and when he suggested further meetings and hinted at romance, she was receptive. Unlike most of her lovers and quasi-lovers since her breakup with Shannon, Pecile was heterosexual.

She joined Pecile in Williamsburg on Valentine's Day for lunch at Chowning's Tavern. He was twenty-seven, two years younger than Charles Shannon was when she met him, but instead of the fifty-four she was in 1944, she now was nearly sixty-nine. Even though the imminent love affair was another May-December one, she was willing to ignore the age difference if he was. She called him "Giordano" and began writing him love letters, occasionally meeting him at inns outside of Lexington for romantic rendezvous.

By the end of April she concluded that he was too young for her and not romantic and gentle enough, but she didn't want to give him up completely. "I don't want us to lose each other altogether," she wrote. "Why should we?" For the rest of the year she created him in an image she chose, and Pecile was apparently willing to sustain the relationship on her terms for a little while.

Soon after the affair with Pecile began, Katherine Anne received word that she was among eleven American novelists to be awarded major grants-in-aid by the Ford Foundation. Cleanth had nominated her, and she had struggled to get the required financial forms completed by the imposed deadline. Doubtful that she had provided all the necessary information, she was surprised as well as pleased at the news. The promise of thirteen thousand dollars for the next two years would give her time to finish the novel. She wrote to tell Lawrence the good news.

In the early summer of 1959 Katherine Anne got in touch with John Prince, a young friend of the Tates, who was a caterer and a broker with a local real-estate firm in Washington, D.C., and asked him to find her a house to lease in Georgetown. He soon located a pleasing red-brick colonial at 3112 Q Street NW, around the corner from Marcella's house on P Street and only a few blocks from the house on Twenty-ninth Street he shared with his wife, Catherine. The only inconvenience

Katherine Anne saw was that the basement of the house was already rented to a young man named Rhea Johnson. The price and the location were right, however, and she signed a two-year lease.

From the time she settled in her house until the end of December 1959, her life was hectic, with social activities dominating her days and evenings. She had become friendly with Barbara Thompson, a young reporter who interviewed her in 1956 and was calling on her now for a long interview that eventually would be published in the *Paris Review.* Katherine Anne also added to her social list her eye doctor, with whom she began a decorous affair. John and Catherine Prince were now friends with whom she took in ballets, symphonies, and art shows and exchanged lunches and dinners. Although Katherine Anne had attended and observed classes at the Cordon Bleu, John actually had completed a course there. He wasn't sure he believed Katherine Anne's "wild boar" story, but he considered her a connoisseur of wine and a wonderful cook. He recalled especially her "Devil Sauce," bread, and roast goose, which he said was the best he ever ate.

The other renter, Rhea Johnson, was an agreeable young man who worked in a government office and did more or less whatever she asked him to do. If she wanted him at a dinner, he would be there. He also offered to help her sort through her papers, and he was one of the few persons she allowed to do it. While he was rummaging through the trunks, baskets, and filing cabinets, he came across several unpublished stories she had forgotten. She submitted "The Fig Tree" to *Harper's* and, after adding only a concluding paragraph, sent "Holiday" to Lawrence for the *Atlantic Monthly.*

Katherine Anne had accepted an October speaking engagement at UCLA, and the day before her departure, to her horror, Lawrence showed up unexpectedly. Panic-stricken, she locked herself in her bedroom and refused to see him. In frustration Lawrence appealed to John Prince, who had a key to her house and was willing to risk her displeasure by letting himself in to try to reason with her. It was to no avail; she was in hysterics, claiming that with the trip ahead of her she was too nervous to see anybody. Whatever thoughts Lawrence went away with she never knew. The next morning, when John and Catherine picked her up to take her to the airport, she was smiling and cheerful, the previous day's crisis apparently forgotten.

When she returned from UCLA she was very tired, and the usual depression accompanied the fatigue. She declined social invitations, telling friends that she really must get some rest and finish the "retyping" of her novel. Before December ended, she was ill with pneumonia. In a few weeks she had a fall that laid her up with a mildly sprained back.

As the holidays passed she gradually emerged from her sickbed and re-entered the social stream, throwing parties, giving lectures, and appearing on the television show *Camera Three*. In the spring the U.S. Department of State asked her to go to Mexico for a month-long residence at the University of Mexico, the purpose of which she saw as spreading "the gospel that North America is *not* just a shambles of Barbarians who eat ketchup and drink coco cola with their meals." She accepted the State Department invitation, and she asked Ann, who had been diagnosed with breast cancer and had undergone a mastectomy and chemotherapy, to accompany her. She wrote to Mary Doherty, who had returned to Mexico, to say she was coming, and she broke the unwelcome news to Lawrence.

Katherine Anne arrived in Mexico with Ann on 25 May and stayed through most of June. She and Ann lived well in the Hotel Imperial, and she was honored and interviewed seemingly continuously. Although showing Ann the sights and taking her around to meet her old friends such as Dr. Atl and Xavier Guerrero was pleasant, much about her return to Mexico, "where so much had happened" (a phrase she continued to associate with the country), was unsettling.

When she returned from Mexico she resumed feverish socializing, her desire to be pleasing and to entertain stronger than ever. In August her former Michigan student David Locher called on her when he traveled to the area with a friend. She insisted that he spend the night in her guest room and that she prepare a special meal for him. She introduced him to daiquiris, showed him her treasured pieces of furniture and her garden in the backyard with a Judas tree, and pointed out two large filing cabinets full of unfinished work and two large baskets full of articles *by* her and articles *about* her. She autographed books that she then gave him; she played favorite old records for him; she gave him manuscript pages by which to remember her. But mostly she talked and talked: She told him of the novel she had to finish before time ran out and of her admiration for Joan of Arc. She sang songs for him that she remembered from her days on the Lyceum circuit, and she demonstrated a ballet turn or two. She also told him sadly that she had lost children in all the ways one could.

When David arose the next morning about 7:30, he was shocked to see Katherine Anne with a cut on her temple and a bruise on her cheek. Their daiquiris had not mixed well with the sleeping pill she had taken, and she had fallen in the bathroom during the night. When he left at 9:00 that morning, Katherine Anne took a taxi to the Georgetown University Medical Center. The inch-long cut required stitches, and she was warned to stay away from alcohol as long as she was on medication such as the tranquilizer she had taken sporadically since 1954.

In October she went to Macon, Georgia, to participate in a panel discussion at Wesleyan College with Caroline Gordon, Madison Jones, and Flannery O'Connor. The subject was "recent southern literature," and the panel was moderated by Louis Rubin Jr. The most pleasant part of the event for Katherine Anne was seeing again Flannery O'Connor, whom she liked personally as much as she admired her writing. Flannery was startled when Katherine Anne asked about a particular chicken she had seen at Flannery's house two years earlier. "I call that really having a talent for winning friends and influencing people," Flannery remarked.

For the remainder of 1960 Katherine Anne balanced an active social life with progress on the novel. Unaware that she was actually working well again, Lawrence wrote her at the end of November to express his disappointment that he had yet to receive the final chapters of *Ship of Fools*. He said he had hoped they could "shout the good news from the rooftops." He asked her, "When *may* we shout?" He softened his implied complaint with snapshots of the children, including her godchild, Macy, and friendly talk about his family. He sent roses at Christmas. On 28 December she wrote him a long letter in which she answered his crucial question of 30 November: "Seymour darling," she said, "the god-damned book will be ready soon. Oh yes, I can see my way through the thing now . . . this should be Our Year, and it shall be. Bless you for everything."

In the middle of January, Lawrence wrote to Katherine Anne to tell her of Atlantic–Little, Brown's "eagerness" to have the remaining chapters of *Ship of Fools*, which he referred to as "one of the most magnificent and enduring works of fiction of our time." "Eagerness" was understated, for what he had been instructed to do was to go to Washington and work with her until he had the rest of the novel in his hands. In her reply four days later she seemed agreeable to the visit he proposed. He had to be startled when he received a telegram from her on 4 February in which she apologized for an "inertia" and told him that that to escape the misery of the "unbearable pressure" she had

accepted an invitation to give readings and lectures at several universities in California. She also had agreed to an appearance afterward at
Oberlin College in Ohio. She expected, moreover, to be in New York
in May for another guest shot on *Camera Three* and for the spring
meeting of the National Institute of Arts and Letters. What he didn't
know was that she also had halfway promised Cleanth and Tinkum
that she would accompany them on a trip to Greece later in the year.
But she told Lawrence in the telegram that while she was in California
she would try to finish the novel. "Don't call or write," she said.

Despite her vow to isolate herself, she was drawn into a constant
round of social events that she made no effort to resist. But rather than
wearing her out, as Lawrence feared, the trip to California seemed to
restore her health and good spirits and reversed her earlier, bad feelings
about California. Her letters from the University of California at
Riverside, where she delivered the Regents Lecture, and from La Jolla,
where she read "A Defense of Circe" to a group of oceanographers,
were brimming with praise for the students and the lovely southern
California weather. When she returned after a month, she seemed
truly ready to face the novel.

During her absence Lawrence had concluded that if she were ever to
finish *Ship of Fools*, she had to be removed from social opportunities.
He suggested, and she accepted the idea, that he find a remote inn on
the New England coast where she could retire and do nothing much
but write. The inn that seemed to be just the place was the Yankee
Clipper Inn at Pigeon Cove, on Cape Ann, in Rockport, Massachusetts.

Katherine Anne wrote Cyrilly Abels at the end of May, "Nobody
knows where I am except for Jesus and my editor. I have the happiness
and the ease of mind and spirit I always have when there will be no
telephone, no mail, no telegrams, no radio, no television, no visitors,
with breakfast in my room and the whole wonderful but too short day
in which to work." She wasn't altogether avoiding company, however.
Lawrence in his wisdom knew that she might rebel against total isolation and made arrangements with her friend John Malcolm Brinnin,
who lived in nearby Gloucester with his companion, Bill Read, to keep
an eye out for her. The three of them dined together nightly, with
Katherine Anne presiding over jolly conversation and pouring good
wine, which Lawrence provided.

Lawrence was sanguine enough about Katherine Anne's intention
to persevere to the finish that he left on a vacation with his family.
He was ecstatic when he received a telegram from his secretary on

30 June: "The Ship is in port. Congratulations. KAP back in Washington." The word spread quickly, and colleagues and friends reached Lawrence to celebrate the good news. In a letter to one friend, he basked in the editorial success many thought he would never achieve: "The midwife gratefully accepts and appreciates all congratulations . . . It was a marvelous challenge and worth every effort. When you have an author as fine as she is and a book of such major dimensions as *Ship of Fools*, then nothing should be spared."

The manuscript was essentially complete, but it had to be proofread one more time, and minor refinements needed to be made. Although Katherine Anne was truly exhausted mentally, she agreed to return to the Yankee Clipper Inn the month of August for one more push. She wrote to Lawrence in mid-August that she felt "mangled" from the past weeks. She also had regrets that she had let the novel become the beast that it had been for at least twenty years. "The horrible thing is that it was all so damned unnecessary," she wrote, "but its done and can't be undone." She dated the completed manuscript thus:

Yaddo, August 1941
Pigeon Cove, August 1961

CHAPTER TWENTY-SEVEN

Success and Failure
in the Aftermath of a Novel

September 1961– December 1966

Seymour, darling, nothing fails quite like success.

In July Katherine Anne had told Cleanth Brooks: "All I want now, my dear, more than frankly, *ferociously*, is just plain green folding money in wads and hunks; and what do I want it for? To spend, darling, to buy a house with a garden and a canoe and a catboat and a little car— I'm tired of taxicabs—and a huge emerald, my birthstone, and I can't live or die without one much longer; and really what I want too is the kind of freedom from daily bedevilments that a certain amount of money *can* buy. I'm not in the least afraid of being vulgar on this subject; I think money used in certain ways could be fun and nice for everybody around . . . . . I would love to be able to give pretty parties."

Despite a profound weariness that had set in after she finally completed the novel, restlessness as well as a desire for immediate money compelled her to again take up speaking and lecturing the last months of 1961. The first week in October she was at Marshall University in Huntington, West Virginia, to appear at a convocation and talk to literature classes. When she walked into one classroom packed with students lining the walls and sitting on the floor, she clapped her hands with delight and said, "Oh, I wish I had a book. I might read a story." Her host, Dr. Mervyn Tyson, chairman of the English Department, quickly found a copy of *The Norton Anthology* and handed it to her. Chuckling, she scanned the biographical headnote. "To see what they are saying about me," she said. And then she read "María Concepción." "She talked and talked!" Tyson remembered. "And everyone loved her."

Tyson, his wife, and young daughter took her to dinner in Ashland, Kentucky, about twenty miles away. On the return trip, they passed one of the many industrial plants in the Appalachian conjunction of eastern Kentucky, southern Ohio, and southwestern West Virginia. With gaseous light ablaze against the dark hills, the plant might have appeared oppressively industrial and polluting to some persons. Katherine Anne, however, was enchanted. She said it looked like "fairyland." Back in Huntington, they passed by a house in which a brutal murder recently had been committed. Katherine Anne was gripped by the details: a wife, whose husband kept a bloodhound that had helped solve the case, had been killed by the gardener. Tyson thought she might be planning to write a story about it. At no time had she given a hint of her fatigue. The performer had simply risen to the occasion and given a good show.

She spent the remainder of 1961 and January and February of 1962 anticipating the publication of her novel and fighting a growing exhaustion. In March, Lawrence brought her up to Boston to receive congratulations all around from the staffs of Little, Brown and the *Atlantic* and to see the first copies of the book fresh from the bindery. She inscribed a copy for him:

> For Seymour, the real hero of the campaign with my friendliest love and reconnaissance, now and always!
>   Katherine Anne
>   Friday 2nd March 1962
>   In your office at Atlantic Monthly Press
>   Bless you!

Lawrence could hardly contain his exuberance. Having convinced the Book-of-the-Month Club to make the novel its April 1962 selection, he expected it to earn a huge amount of money. He cautioned Katherine Anne to prepare to invest and protect her earnings so that she would be financially set for the rest of her life. She gave very little attention to what he said. At the St. Regis Hotel in New York in early March for an interview, Katherine Anne remarked, "Believe me, I wish I could have all this. I love wealth and luxury . . . I love to be pampered, to be a woman, to stay in a hotel like this one."

Ship of Fools was published to elaborate fanfare 1 April. Lawrence and Atlantic–Little, Brown hosted a party in her honor 2 April at the "21" Club in New York City. Present were a substantial number of critics, editors, reviewers, publishers, booksellers, and many of her friends and family members, including Barbara Harrison Wescott, to whom *Ship of Fools* was dedicated. Katherine Anne should have been in her element, enjoying the success of the day, but she seemed instead dazed by it all, and weary. William Maxwell, editor of the *New Yorker*, had gone to the party expecting "the beau monde," he said, but instead found a lot of drunken publishers and publicity people. "KA was exhausted from the massive hullabaloo, had been vomiting all day, and was in a state of impermeable excitement. It was like shouting at somebody through the thick plate glass of a restaurant window. I couldn't see that anything had been done for her pleasure, only her apotheosis, which she was bravely enduring." For the remainder of the week she was a guest on television shows, had lunch with newspaper and magazine reporters, recorded interviews for radio programs, autographed copies of *Ship of Fools* at the Gotham Book Mart, and sat for publicity photographs. All these events took place while the first reviews of *Ship of Fools* were appearing.

Mark Schorer's "We're All on the Passenger List," the lead review in the *New York Times Book Review* on 1 April, was important and influential: "This novel has been famous for years," he wrote. "It has been awaited through an entire literary generation. Publishers and foundations, like many once hopeful readers, long ago gave it up. Now it is suddenly, superbly here. It would have been worth waiting for for another thirty years if one had had any hope of having [it]. It is our good fortune that it comes at last still in our time. It will endure, one hardly risks anything in saying, far beyond it, for many literary generations." Words and phrases such as "brilliance," "magnificent," "heartbreaking," "comic," "great ironic style," and "unique imaginative achievement" sparkled in the review and would be repeated in many others. Schorer compared *Ship of Fools* with George Eliot's *Middlemarch* and Joyce's *Ulysses*. In the numerous other reviews in the spring very few negative words were uttered against it.

Lawrence reported to Katherine Anne on 23 April that *Ship of Fools* was number one on the best-seller lists in the Sunday editions of both the *New York Times* and the *New York Herald Tribune*. The following day he was able to tell her that the film rights to the novel had been sold and that her name was to be featured on theater marquees. Secker and Warburg were preparing to release the novel in England, and translations into many other languages were underway.

The money rolled in. Book club members paid $5.95 a copy for it; others bought it for $6.50. Stanley Kramer paid $400,000 for the film rights. Katherine Anne, however, was not to get all at once the "wads and hunks" of green folding money she was anticipating because her contract with Atlantic–Little, Brown specified an annual limit of $30,000 to her earnings on the novel. The approximately $27,000 Katherine Anne received at the publication of *Ship of Fools* was nevertheless more money than she ever had at one time. And she did what she always said she would do first when she had the money: she bought that big emerald ring. She made a down payment of $2,000 on a twenty-one-caret emerald surrounded by two carets' worth of twenty-four diamonds and signed a sales agreement to pay installments of $500 a month until the full price of $13,000 was paid. "These material pretties," she wrote Barbara Wescott, "will be a kind of dessert, something nice—I don't care for desserts, let's say brandy and coffee, at the end of what has been, after all, a long, strenuous but exciting party!"

She also went on a shopping binge for designer clothes and accessories, particularly hats. She carefully chose expensive ensembles that she would enjoy wearing repeatedly, and she particularly liked the styles of designers Pauline Trigère, Geoffrey Beene, and Christian Dior. Lawrence, who had joined in the hunt for the "perfect" emerald, also went on at least one shopping expedition with her. "See how publishers spend their time?" he said gleefully. "Ladies hats and emeralds. What a life."

Because the limitation-on-earnings clause did not allow her to buy the kind of house she wanted, before she left on a month-long vacation in Europe with Ann she rashly wrote to Bill Jovanovich to ask whether he would reconsider selling Little, Brown the rights to the titles Harcourt, Brace owned, imagining that her new publisher might reprint in remunerative paperback editions her earlier three fiction collections. An irate Jovanovich, seeing the phenomenal commercial success of *Ship of Fools* and recalling the many years Harcourt, Brace had expected to publish the novel, spoke of betrayal and told her flatly that he had no intention of relinquishing the titles Harcourt, Brace owned. Katherine Anne concluded that she simply *had* to finish another book that would have a contract separate from that of *Ship of Fools* and thus not bind her to the $30,000 limit. She thought she could complete most quickly an anthology of short stories that could sell as a college textbook. Lawrence told her that Atlantic–Little, Brown would be pleased to publish it.

Katherine Anne's relationship with Lawrence was not so good as it had been. She became convinced that his dire warning that the tax man would claim more than 90 percent of her earnings that exceeded $30,000 was an oversimplification of the tax laws, and she suspected that she had once again been unwise in allowing her publisher to act as her agent. While she acknowledged Lawrence's role in bringing *Ship of Fools* to completion, she was no longer certain that he would place her interests above his own or those of his employers. When she learned that Cyrilly Abels had left her position as fiction editor at *Mademoiselle* and was striking out on her own as a literary agent, Katherine Anne turned her business affairs over to one of her closest friends.

Reviews of *Ship of Fools* continued to appear through the summer and fall. A passionately enthusiastic review was written by Dorothy Parker, who exclaimed, "My God, here is a book," and two British reviewers called it "outstanding" and "a great universal novel." Negative assessments and those that damned with faint praise, however, also appeared by fall and included reviews in German newspapers and magazines. Herbert von Borch's review in *Die Welt* carried the headline "Die Deutschen sind allzumal grausam, böse und fanatisch" (The Germans are Still Cruel, Evil, and Fanatic) and a subhead that called *Ship of Fools* "Dokument des Hasses" (a document of hatred). Ultimately, the most devastating review appeared in October in the American magazine *Commentary*. Written by Theodore Solotaroff, the long review titled "'Ship of Fools' and the Critics" was unmatched by any other English-language review in its wrath and personal attack. Assailing Schorer and all other reviewers who had praised *Ship of Fools*, Solotaroff accused Katherine Anne of snideness, failure to understand history, and a lack of "consciousness." The novel, he said, revealed "little more than misanthropy and clever technique." He objected to the "clammy connection between sex and evil" (the result, he said, of the author's "contemptuous and morbid attitude toward human sexuality") and, specifically, to her characterization of Julius Löwenthal, the only Jew aboard the ship. In creating Löwenthal, Solotaroff said, Katherine Anne had re-created "the stage Jew of modern literary tradition" and in the process proved herself "morally vicious."

Josie Herbst concurred wholeheartedly with Solotaroff. Shortly after the novel's publication she herself wrote a five-thousand-word review for *Commentary*, but according to her biographer, her review was abandoned in favor of the one to be written by Solotaroff, who was associate editor of *Commentary*. In letters Josie wrote within a few weeks of the novel's publication, she made some of the same points Solotaroff would make later. "There is not only no lovemaking [in *Ship of Fools*] but no fornication worthy of the name," she wrote Katherine Anne's old nemesis Alfred Kazin, and "there is only one Jew aboard to play pariah." To Daniel Curley she questioned all of Katherine Anne's "moral attitudes."

Katherine Anne was not only angry and dismayed at the negative reviews, she was also shocked. She concluded that no one who reviewed *Ship of Fools* had really understood what she was doing or saying. "Even those who praised it," she told Red Warren, "didn't put their finger on the point." "I wrote the damned book on purpose," she told Caroline Gordon; "I don't take back one line, I wish I had made it tougher—I nearly sprained my soul pulling my punches at certain places—and not one reviewer even the best has yet guessed the real theme and point of that book."

Set in 1931, the novel opens in August in Veracruz, Mexico, from which the *Vera*, a mixed freight and passenger ship, is preparing to sail. It concludes twenty-six days later, when the passengers disembark in Bremerhaven. Seventeen of the twenty-five major characters are Germans returning to their native land after a stay in Mexico. The other eight are Swiss, American, and Swedish. There are about twenty-five other important characters of various nationalities as well as several hundred German crewmembers and 876 Spanish deportees from Cuba.

Divided into three parts, "Embarkation," "The High Seas," and "The Harbors," with epigraphs from Baudelaire, Brahms, and St. Paul, respectively, the episodic narrative unrolls from an ironic-voiced omniscient narrator who limits the viewpoint to first one character then another after the opening frame in Veracruz that establishes controlling themes. Major scenes, enacted on deck, in steerage, in cabins, and in passageways, involve the divorcée Mary Treadwell and her encounters with various men on board; William Freytag, who is denied a place at the captain's table when passengers learn his wife in Germany is Jewish; the Zarzuela company of "dancers" who profit at the expense of the other passengers; Ric and Rac, unloved and warped twins of two of the dancers; the American artists Jenny Brown and David Scott, who alternate between loving and hating; the love affair between Dr. Schumann, the ship's physician, and the insane noblewoman La Condesa, who is a drug addict; and the Basque woodcarver Etchegaray, who loses his life saving the bulldog Bébé, who is thrown overboard by Ric and Rac. In their sexually charged pursuit of one another Siegfried Rieber and Lizzi Spöckenkieker provide comic relief.

Other characters, such as Julius Löwenthal, the Jewish manufacturer and salesman of Catholic church furnishings; Captain Thiele, the Nazi-minded ship's captain; the religious zealot Wilibald Graf and his callow nephew, Johann; William Denny, a sex-crazed, bigoted engineer from Texas; the complaining hunchback Karl Glocken; Frau Rittersdorf, who spies on her fellow passengers; a political agitator; two priests; a mild-mannered little widow whose husband's corpse is in the hold of the ship; an alcoholic lawyer and his family; an educator and his wife, who own the bulldog; an idealistic bride and groom; a new mother traveling with her Indian nursemaid; and a Swiss hotel keeper with his wife and eighteen-year-old daughter, serve to illustrate the themes of alienation, intolerance, chauvinism, self-delusion, the complexities of love, and apathy's collusion with evil.

Ship of Fools, a variation on *The Odyssey* and a classic satire in the spirit of Erasmus, Swift, and Laurence Sterne, is full of lacerating wit and pronouncements on human folly. Of the many ironies, the strongest lies in the voyage itself: all the passengers think they are journeying to a better place than the one they left, and a significant number believe they are going *home*, that haven of comfort and love. What they all are going to, of course, is the near-collapse of modern civilization.

Katherine Anne remarked in her prefatory statement that she was "a passenger on that ship," and most persons assumed she meant that the ship's society was a microcosm of humanity, which naturally included her. She said elsewhere that she was part of each character on that ship, suggesting that she understood the motivations and feelings of her characters. But there is a more literal meaning to her statement. At least three of the female characters are heavily autobiographical, and many of the others represent people in her past life. Some of the events on board the *Vera* correspond to her most painful personal experiences.

Jenny Brown and David Scott represent Katherine Anne and Gene Pressly largely as they were in 1931 when they made the voyage from Mexico to Germany. The lonely, childless Mrs. Treadwell remembers her "sixteen-year-old heart" and looks back over her failures at love and motherhood much as Katherine Anne had done periodically from the late 1920s. Motherless Frau Rittersdorf, who once considered "marrying into the Spanish race" and keeps a notebook in which she records sharp comments and observations about her fellow passengers, is Katherine Anne's caricature of herself. Katherine Anne even brought her sister Baby onto the ship in the form of the bulldog Bébé, a "joke" based on Baby's having bred bulldogs for many years. The loutish William Denny represents John Koontz, and her second and third husbands, Otto Taskett and Carl von Pless, are represented in the Karls and Ottos in the narrative. It is Otto Schmidt's widow who sails on the ship, and Otto and Kathë Hutten are the owners of the bulldog. Frau Rittersdorf sends herself flowers from former husbands Karl and Johann. Katherine Anne gave the arrogant, authoritarian, anti-Semitic captain of the ship the name "Thiele," after a family that owned a butcher store in Kyle before the turn of the century and to whom her third husband was related.

In more ways than one *Ship of Fools* encompasses Katherine Anne's life and art. It has echoes of the "older" literature she first loved in childhood and reread in the 1930s, and it reverberates with the 1920s and 1930s modernist aesthetic that emphasized using old literature in a new way and focused on a protagonist who is searching for truth and self-identity but does not find them within the boundaries of the fictional work. Because of the protracted writing of *Ship of Fools*, it reflects the themes and techniques of the other fictional works Katherine Anne wrote concurrently, and it folds in her external experiences and her internal life over the course of sixty years. When she finally finished it, her creative vein was exhausted.

Having decided to escape to Europe for a year, Katherine Anne arrived in Rome in mid-November to spend six months in the Hotel Eden on Via Ludovisi. Cards and letters through April chart a heavy schedule of shopping, sightseeing, soaking up celebrity, and visiting with friends and acquaintances who stopped by, such as Barbara Thompson, who had married a Pakistani diplomat, Barbara and Lloyd Wescott, and the young writer Walter Clemons. At the end of June she decided to spend the rest of her year in Paris in a little apartment in the Villa Adrienne, at 19 Avenue du Géneral Leclerc. Despite a void she felt in the city because of Sylvia Beach's death the year before, she set about continuing her love affair with Paris. By the time she left Paris for the United States at the end of October 1963, she reported being in "very good health and spirits."

Her good mood was instantly tempered. "I arrived home to an assassination," she said, shaken like the rest of the country, when President John F. Kennedy was shot and killed in Dallas on 22 November. She adored the Kennedys, had been invited to their White House several times, had corresponded with the president about the arts, and was mindful of their appreciation of her. She was among the thousands who went to see his body lying in state in the Capitol. Within a few months she wrote a tribute to Jacqueline Kennedy ("Her Legend Will Live") for the *Ladies Home Journal*.

She returned from Europe with the resolve to find a house to buy. Before Christmas, John Prince showed her a house at 1515 Twenty-ninth Street, across the street from his and Catherine's. Owned by Minna Curtiss, Lincoln Kirstein's sister, the restored eighteenth-century brick house was lovely, with a private garden and large, ornate rooms big enough for all Katherine Anne's possessions, including chandeliers and cupboards, tables, swaths of fabric, and paintings she had bought in Europe—these were arriving almost weekly by ship. Prince thought she could get the house for ninety thousand dollars, and Katherine Anne's enthusiasm was high. She told him, "Honey, you know my weakness," and "Don't try to save me from myself."

Katherine Anne wrote to Lawrence to ask about an advance for the anthology of short stories that would allow her to make a down payment on the house, and he persuaded Little, Brown CEO Arthur Thornhill to offer a fifteen-thousand-dollar advance *if* Katherine Anne sent along the preface first. John Prince subsequently made Mrs. Curtiss an offer for ninety thousand dollars, which she accepted on the condition that she receive the full amount within thirty days. John arranged with his employer to hold a good-faith deposit check from Katherine Anne that could initiate the mortgage application process, and he wrote up a binding contract that she signed. The traditional Twelfth Night Party at the Princes' home a few days later was an unusually lively affair. Katherine Anne prepared the customary goose, and she insisted that everybody traipse across the street to see *her* house.

On 10 January John received a special-delivery letter from Katherine Anne, announcing that she was giving up the house "and all hopes of it, finally, for good." "The pressure is simply too great," she wrote; "my resources are not adequate, and I cannot afford the terrible impasses that my search for a house always brings me to." Mrs. Curtiss, however, refused to cancel the contract. A desperate Katherine Anne hired lawyers to help extricate her from the messy dispute, and a disgruntled Thornhill came through with the requested advance in order to pay the legal retainers. Katherine Anne was scared and emotionally exhausted as she checked into a hospital in New Jersey to be near the supportive friendship of the Wescotts and Monroe Wheeler. Several weeks later, the lawyers negotiated a settlement, and John Prince relinquished his commission on the aborted sale. Her friendship with the Princes was over, and Katherine Anne felt cruelly let down by her publisher. Blaming Thornhill for initially holding back the money that would have made purchasing the house easy, she told Lawrence that it was "dreadful the way an agent or an editor or publisher tries at once to lay hands on everything you ever did and tie you up forever."

In March Lawrence told her he was leaving Atlantic–Little, Brown to join Alfred A. Knopf as editorial vice president, and he asked her to go with him. She at first declined, but when he pointed out that it was he who had had faith in her and her novel and not the "skeptics" at Little, Brown, she lost little time altering her decision. "Dear Seymour! Hello, I'm back!"

After she informed Arthur Thornhill that she wished to leave Little, Brown, Thornhill reminded her that she still owed the firm three more books. "I am sorry to be so mercenary," he wrote, "but the latter factor is significant in that as an officer of a corporation, my actions are accountable to the stockholders who probably would take a dim view of my releasing valuable assets." It was, of course, the wrong approach to her, and Lawrence took advantage of Thornhill's blunder. "This talk of 'assets,'" Lawrence said, "may very well be true but an author is a human being and no self-respecting publisher would make a legal attempt to force an author to stay."

Katherine Anne felt good about the decision to go with Lawrence to Knopf, where Cyrilly was able to work out an attractive contract, but what contributed most to her good feeling in the summer was that she once again had found a house she loved. Although buying it was out of the question, she had been able to lease it for an indefinite period, or "for life," as she reported to Caroline Gordon. It was a two-story, eleven-room red brick Tudor at 3601 Forty-ninth Street NW in Spring Valley in northwest Washington. She moved in 1 June and soon began to receive houseguests and throw the "pretty parties" that had been her dream for years.

By this time in her life she had collected what she described as an "unreasonable" amount of furniture and books and other treasures, and she finally had a house big enough for all of it. In her thirties, after an adolescence and young womanhood in which she had few possessions (a wooden Buddha figure her brother gave her in 1904, photographs, a few prints of favorite paintings, her mother's old kid glove), she began to hoard more and more things, putting them in storage in whatever city she was leaving and retrieving them whenever possible, even temporarily. Admitting that she was the magpie of her family, by the time she was in her fifties, she had a staggering mass of belongings, some items that she bought in Europe quite valuable and all them ornate. She had recently acquired a Cupid and Dolphin fountain from Pompeii, an Orpheus-Euridice-Hermes bas-relief from Naples, and a golden-glass chandelier from Venice. She already had marble tables and sideboards, a seventeenth-century gold-leaf headboard, a four-hundred-year-old Spanish chair from Avila, and yards and yards of oyster white silk she was saving for curtains and a bedspread. "My taste, once so Puritan as a reaction from the Family Gewgaws," she explained, "is getting more and more Baroque, most lavishly gold-leafed, more extravagantly brocaded." She had left her Puritan taste behind in the style of her fiction.

In early November, President and Mrs. Johnson invited Katherine Anne to the White House for a dinner in honor of twenty-five American intellectuals and artists that included Leonard Bernstein, Lionel and Diana Trilling, Richard Rodgers, James Baldwin, and Agnes De Mille, among others. She was a special success that evening. Soon afterward Baldwin nominated her for the Prix Formentor award in Majorca (she didn't win), and she was asked by the State Department to return to Mexico the last part of November for two weeks of lectures and public readings for the Instituto Cultural Norteamericano. Although her last visit in Mexico had not been particularly satisfying, she readily accepted the offer.

In Mexico City she was more of a celebrity than ever before. At a coffee or rum reception after one of her lectures, she met Enrique (Hank) Lopez, an attorney and coeditor of *Diálogos*, a Mexican literary journal, who asked to interview her for a special issue of the magazine on American writers. "I'll do anything for Mexico," she said. "I've always considered this my second home." Despite her professed fondness for Mexico, the country held more painful memories than happy ones, and the first subject she brought up to Lopez was Salomón de la Selva. "He was one of the most evil men I've ever known," she said. "An absolute scoundrel, who thought nothing of seducing the teenage daughter of his best friend and then bragging about it." She admitted to Lopez, however, that there had been "something strangely compelling" about De la Selva, "a certain sinister magnetism that made him hard to resist." She talked about revolution and political intrigue in 1920s Mexico, a marijuana party she attended, Diego Rivera, and the "horrible nightmare of Hart Crane."

The painful recollections that Mexico generated and the intense schedule took a toll, and she collapsed with overwrought nerves and bronchitis, confined to the Hotel del Prado under a physician's care while the final lectures were cancelled. At one point, she thought she was dying and asked for last rites. A week's rest barely restored her energy sufficiently for her to make the return trip to Washington on 4 December.

After the first of the year, Lawrence, who had not been satisfied with his move to Knopf, announced that he had signed a contract with Delacorte Press to recruit authors and edit their works, which Delacorte would underwrite and produce. When Katherine Anne agreed to go with him, he offered her a two-book contract with an eighty-five-thousand-dollar advance. Knowing he was unlikely to get what he asked for, he nevertheless specified an October delivery of a collection of her essays, poems, and occasional writings and delivery of the Cotton Mather biography exactly a year later.

At nearly the same time she made the pact with Lawrence, Harcourt, Brace decided to capitalize on her expanded celebrity and bring out her stories and short novels in a single volume. Although she had considerable ill will toward Bill Jovanovich, the project pleased her, and she agreed to participate in the arrangement of the pieces and to write a brief preface. The collection was to comprise all the short stories and short novels in *Flowering Judas and Other Stories*; *Pale Horse, Pale Rider: Three Short Novels*; and *The Leaning Tower and Other Stories*; and it was to include as well the two early stories "The Martyr" and "Virgin Violeta" and the two stories published in 1960, "Holiday" and "The Fig Tree." She had an opportunity to put in proper sequence the seven pieces she now titled *The Old Order*, constituting another short novel. She concluded the brief preface with an eloquent send-off: "To part is to die a little, it is said (in every language I can read), but my farewell to these stories is a happy one, a renewal of their life, a prolonging of their time under the sun, which is what any artist most longs for—to be read, and remembered. Go little book . . . . ." *The Collected Stories of Katherine Anne Porter* appeared in September 1965 to enthusiastic reviews in the United States and Great Britain that underscored Katherine Anne's value as a writer of short stories and short novels. She was still loved, despite the controversy of *Ship of Fools*.

Katherine Anne had become an important enough writer to get the serious attention of academic critics, and since Lodwick Hartley's article in 1940, that attention had expanded. A good many master's theses and doctoral dissertations already had been written on her work, and in 1957 the first monograph had appeared, *The Fiction and Criticism of Katherine Anne Porter*, by Harry J. Mooney Jr. Sometimes graduate students initiated correspondence with her while writing theses or dissertations, and she had a chance to correct the record or try to steer them in the right (or at least a different) direction. By 1964 there had been additional books, one by George Hendrick, who included a biographical chapter, and one by William Leslie Nance, who attributed a "principle of rejection" to her that angered her.

She was reminded that whether she liked it or not, she was going to be the subject of not only critical studies but biographical studies as well. She decided to take matters in her own hands and choose her biographer. Hank Lopez had come to New York on legal business and made a trip to Washington to call on her. She asked him, in much the same way she had approached Lawrence about being her publisher, whether he would be interested in writing her biography. Pleased with the tone and respect in the interview of her he had published in *Dialogós* and *Harper's Magazine*, she thought she could count on the same distance and discretion in a whole book. He quickly accepted the offer and immediately set up a schedule of interviews to be taped. For the better part of a month he was her guest while also functioning as her would-be biographer.

In the fall, *Ship of Fools*, directed by Stanley Kramer with screenplay by Abby Mann, opened in movie theaters, and her Q Street housemate, Rhea Johnson, escorted her to a Washington theater to view it incognito. Although publicly she said that she was pleased with the adaptation of her novel, she actually was displeased with some changes. She did not object to advancing the ship journey to 1933 in order to emphasize the progress of Nazism, and she found no fault with the casting or the excellent performances of George Segal (David Scott), Lee Marvin (William Denny), José Ferrer (Herr Rieber), Simone Signoret (La Condesa), Elizabeth Ashley (Jenny), Vivian Leigh (Mary Treadwell), Michael Dunn (Karl Glocken), or Oskar Werner (Dr. Schumann), or with the cinematography of Ernest Laszlo and the set direction of Joseph Kish (the latter two won Academy Awards for *Ship of Fools*). But the film bore the marks of Hollywood sentimentality. Mann and Kramer made the hunchback into a dwarf who acted like a Greek chorus; they made Julius Löwenthal into a merry and wise Jew who regarded all people with understanding and patience; they added a hint of homoerotic tension to the friendship between Captain Thiele and Dr. Schumann; and near the end of the voyage they killed off Dr. Schumann, teetering on the edge of soap opera. Kramer's direction nevertheless was brilliant, and he revealed a keen understanding of the original work. All the characters, he said, were "aspects of Katherine Anne Porter herself and of what she feels and responds to." Beyond Katherine Anne's original conception, it was his shrewd directing of his excellent cast, his timing of the numerous scenes, and his playing off pairs of characters against each other that accounted for much of the success of the film.

Believing herself to be permanently out of favor with some literary critics, Katherine Anne was surprised and pleased in March when she won the National Book Award for her *Collected Stories*. At the awards ceremony in Philadelphia Hall on 15 March, she was described as "a dedicated and uncompromising literary artist, successful almost in spite of herself." Asked by a reporter what it meant to her to be called "a dedicated artist," she replied, "It's simply the form of your life." Two months later she learned that she also had won the Pulitzer prize for fiction.

The accolades and recognition continued. In June the University of Maryland, which had inducted her into their chapter of Phi Beta Kappa in 1963, awarded her a Doctor of Humane Letters degree, and in December she was instated in the American Academy of Arts and Letters, having been nominated by Glenway and Red, who, mindful of Katherine Anne's resistance to "memberships," thought the honor could nevertheless benefit her psychologically. Cleanth Brooks, at the invitation of the Nobel Committee of the Swedish Academy, nominated her for the Nobel prize in literature. He had nominated her once before, after the publication of *Ship of Fools*, and in nominating her again three years later, he addressed the issue of the popular success of *Ship of Fools* and, by implication, the small critical controversy that had surrounded it: "I should like to put in nomination once more," he wrote, "the name of Miss Katherine Anne Porter, surely one of our most distinguished writers of fiction, and probably our most brilliant stylist." He said, "I can think of no writer in English in the last generation whose stories would match hers in subtlety and power," and he said he hoped that the committee would not allow the great popular success of *Ship of Fools* to "put her work at a discount." She had not won the Nobel prize in 1963, and she did not win it in 1966. Neither would she win it when Cleanth nominated her a third time.

Before the end of 1966 she dealt with her other disappointment, her realization that the University of Texas was not naming a library building after her and had never intended to do so. That honor, she had said in 1959, was more important to her than "the Nobel Prize and a Congressional Medal rolled into one." But like the Nobel prize, her very own library in Texas would elude her. There had been no correspondence between Katherine Anne and anyone at the University of Texas about the library since 1959, and whether she understood that the Academic Center and Undergraduate Library, which opened in 1963, was "her" library—or whether she even knew that such a library was completed—is not known. Shortly before *Ship of Fools* appeared, an article about her in the *Christian Science Monitor* mentioned that the University of Texas was building a two-million-dollar library for contemporary literature to be called the Katherine Anne Porter Library. There is no evidence that Harry Ransom, or anyone else at Texas, corrected the story. By 1966, however, the truth had dawned on her.

She was deeply disappointed and terribly embarrassed. With no further delay, she decided to donate her papers, which she had placed temporarily at the Library of Congress, to the University of Maryland, where she knew she was held in high esteem. The College Park campus was also reasonably close to her Spring Valley home, and she would be able to work in her papers at her leisure. She made a phone call 11 October to University of Maryland president Wilson H. Elkins, and in mid-December she publicly announced that the University of Maryland would be the repository of her papers.

She wanted to end the year with crucial measures that would organize her life. With her papers on their way to their new home and her biographer selected, she asked her attorney to draw up a will that would reflect her bequest to the University of Maryland. She made a party out of the will-signing. Then she suffered a gallbladder attack complicated with exhaustion and emphysema. She spent the holidays in the university hospital, in Baltimore.

CHAPTER TWENTY-EIGHT

Spring Valley and College Park

January 1967–December 1971

Bobby Kennedy has called one of those fool things that goes over falls a "ship of fools." Is nobody ever going to mention my name?

Katherine Anne's attorney, E. Barrett Prettyman Jr., presided over her will-signing party at the end of 1966. She had known Prettyman since 1962, when shortly after the publication of *Ship of Fools* he had looked her up in the Washington telephone directory and phoned to tell her how much he liked the novel. Charmed, she invited him to call on her at Q Street. She thought little more about him until she attended a dinner party in 1966 and was seated next to Justice John Harlan, for whom Prettyman had clerked at the Supreme Court. During the course of dinner-party chat Katherine Anne confided to Harlan some of her legal problems, and he recommended Prettyman as someone she might consult. She wrote to him on 28 May to ask him to help her write a will, and since then he had represented all her legal interests.

Barrett Prettyman was forty-one years old, married, and the father of two children. The son of a prominent U.S. Court of Appeals judge, he had earned degrees from Yale and Virginia, and in 1961 his book *Death and the Supreme Court* had won the Mystery Writers of America Award for the best fact crime book of the year and the Scribes Award for the best explanation for the lay reader of the aims and purposes of the legal profession. He had been a special assistant to U.S. Attorney General Robert F. Kennedy and an aide to Presidents Kennedy and Johnson from 1963 to 1964. Since 1964 he had been a partner in the Washington law firm Hogan and Hartson. By the summer of 1967 he was "Barrett" to Katherine Anne after many occasions for friendly talk, usually over breakfast or lunch at her Spring Valley house. By the end of 1967 she was writing him love letters.

After her death he explained the love affair she manufactured as her tendency to "dramatize things" and the love letters as "just the kind of letters Katherine Anne wrote." Calling her "a great myth-maker" and "dissembler," he said that their relationship "was greatly embellished in her own mind, for her own purposes." Her own purposes had deep causes, which Isabel Bayley touched upon when she asked where Katherine Anne's creative energy might go when she had no more fiction to write.

It was psychologically crucial that she be the creator of the affair rather than the mere object of someone else's mythmaking, a requirement illustrated vividly in her relationship with Raymond Roseliep, a diocesan priest and poet, with whom she had corresponded since 1960. Roseliep was an English professor at Lorus College in Dubuque, Iowa, where David Locher was employed as head librarian, and when Roseliep learned that David was a friend of Katherine Anne's he began to write her letters. In Washington in the summer of 1964 as poet-in-residence at Georgetown University, he called on her at her Spring Valley mansion. She made a meal for him and served him bourbon, and when he expressed great admiration for her emerald ring, she insisted he wear it on his little finger throughout the evening. Afterward she began her letters to him "Dear Father Raymond," and he began his "Dear Katherine Anne." She signed hers, "Your friend, Katherine Anne." He signed his in various ways: "Devotedly, Raymond Roseliep," "Your loving friend, Fr. Raymond," "With my love, Fr. Raymond."

From the beginning there was an ambiguous eroticism in his letters and poems, which often conflated secular love and religious piety. In 1962 he sent her a poem he called "A Kind of Love Song," which ended "I love you on the fine earth/past death or Empedocles." As his elderly mother's health began to fail, he seemed to increase his devotion to Katherine Anne. On her part, Katherine Anne had no interest at all in participating in an amatory, epistolary affair with him. She was finding her own satisfaction in the myth she was weaving around Barrett Prettyman.

Prettyman respected her art and claimed to develop a friendly love for her. He eventually signed his social notes to her "Love, Barrett," and he wrote one letter to her in which he enumerated "all the wonderful things" he loved about her: her speech, her laugh, her intelligence and wit, her "passionate caring about things," her "romanticism," and "even your down moods when they must come." As he said, he was happy to go along with her charade "up to a point."

With her creative energy focused exclusively on Barrett, Katherine Anne, with Cyrilly Abels's help, was recycling previously written work, such as "A Christmas Story," which Seymour Lawrence published in 1967 as a small hardback gift book with illustrations by Ben Shahn. Mindful that Lawrence was waiting for the books she owed him, she promised to get to work. Before she could accomplish anything, however, she came down with an especially severe case of influenza and was hospitalized for nearly two months. She was released 5 January 1968, the day before her favorite holiday, Twelfth Night, which she was too weak to celebrate.

Through the winter and early spring of 1968 she did not go out often, and she entertained sparingly. She was as likely to call off engagements as fulfill them, and sometimes, after inviting a friend for a visit or a meal, she cancelled at the last minute, pleading illness or shattered nerves. Once Cleanth and Tinkum drove down from New Haven for a planned visit only to be met at the door by her maid, who told them, "Miss Porter apologizes, but she isn't up to seeing anybody today." When she did receive guests, she did so in style. Any event was likely to include a meal with very good champagne or wine from her "wine jail," as she called her little cellar, and she was always elegantly dressed, usually in white or emerald green, but sometimes in a glamorous black negligee.

Although having guests taxed her, she wouldn't consider reducing the amount of work for herself. Barbara Thompson came for a long weekend visit that she cut short when she became aware of Katherine Anne's painfully early rising each day to fix an elaborate breakfast and the subsequent hours spent preparing exquisite lunches and dinners. Owning no electrical appliances, she made everything from scratch, from special sausage to crusty loaves of bread, declaring that store-bought bread was fit only for feeding pigeons and even that was "cruelty to dumb animals." When Barbara concocted a ruse to leave early, Katherine Anne said she was "so sorry" but probably was relieved.

For the next two years, events in her life were an assortment of social pleasures, tragedies, and annoyances. Her greatest satisfaction derived from her relationship with the University of Maryland, where the Katherine Anne Porter Room was opened with a gala reception on her sixty-eighth birthday. Particularly irritating to her was the new generation of militant feminists, a group of whom crashed the Miss America pageant, tossing bras and stenographer notebooks into "freedom trash cans" and proclaiming "Women's Liberation." But even though she didn't consider herself one of "them," she vehemently deplored chauvinism wherever she encountered it, as she unexpectedly did at Harvard University in the fall. When she was asked to address the Signet Club, the all-male undergraduate literary society there, she thought it might be fun, especially since she would be the first woman to do so.

Escorted to the event by Seymour Lawrence, Katherine Anne entered the room carrying a nosegay of sweetheart roses sent by the literary society and wearing a white designer gown and her jewels (in addition to the emerald ring, she now owned an emerald and diamond pin and a double strand of pearls with an emerald and diamond clasp). She expected to impress the audience with her style and aged beauty and with what she had to say about the state of modern literature. She was offended, however, by the students' jocular attitude and their president's introduction that emphasized how honored she should feel for being there rather than how honored the students should feel by her presence. She interpreted the tone of the whole evening as sexist, and when it was her turn to speak, she told the young men that she wanted no part of the "man's world" they were entering and perpetuating. "You can have it," she said.

She had been ill off and on in the spring and summer, generally with colds and flu or simple exhaustion that seemed to come on the heels of tiring social events such as the evening at Harvard. In the last two months of the year, however, she was determined to reverse her physical decline and return to the entertaining she enjoyed. She cooked Thanksgiving dinner for a small group of family and friends, and early in December she planned a Twelfth Night party that she carried out with the help of Avignon Frères, her favorite Washington caterer. The Madrigal Singers from the university performed, and she directed the ritual burning of the Christmas wreaths.

Peter Taylor, one of her protégés, had flown to Washington especially for the party and reported that Katherine Anne had been in "fine fettle" throughout the dazzling evening. Taylor was one among a number of younger men who were captivated by Katherine Anne. When he met her in the spring of 1952 at a party after a forum in Chicago, he had been at the center of a group of admiring men who had clustered around her. Admitting that he probably had made a fool of himself, he had remained enthralled. When someone criticized her to him he replied, "But we all love her. She's our Cleopatra." Katherine Anne was hardly oblivious to the adulation of Taylor and others. She basked in it. She mentioned to her nephew Paul all the handsome young men who paid court to her and wished "this gang" had been around when she was twenty. It was altogether a different kind of adoration than the peculiar devotion of Raymond Roseliep.

That Twelfth Night party was almost the last good time Katherine Anne had in 1969, which she later referred to as a "calamitous" year. In March she was ill again with the flu and through the spring and summer seemed to spend more time in bed than out. She did receive occasional visitors, however, such as *Baltimore Sun* reporter John Dorsey. During the several-hours-long interview, in which they shared drinks while she talked about her whole life, she told Dorsey, "Writing is a dog's life." But as it had turned out, she said, she had been, like so few, the master of her fate. "And you know, in the very strangest kind of way, I can't explain this, but I have come as near as anybody I know in the world to getting just where I wanted. I wanted to be a good artist, and I wanted to be known as an honest artist, and they can say anything they want, but they can't say that I ever compromised on that one point. It took everything I had. It took a lifetime, and it took an enormous amount of suffering. But it was worth it. It was what I wanted."

All the verbs she used were past tense, and, without realizing it, she implied that her active artistic life was over. As far as writing either stories or novels, that was true. But her creative compulsion was far from dead, for her fantasy romance with Prettyman was more intense than ever. One of its most extraordinary expressions was her letter to him on his forty-fourth birthday, 1 June 1969, re-creating a fictional version of his birth:

> You were born today, on a Sunday again, I think you told me at 10:27 evening, so you are not really born yet, just trying hard, and no doubt your mother is good and tired of you, and will be very happy to get rid of you.
>
> But women are as much fools in their ways as men are in theirs—by 11:30 tonight she will have forgotten her pains in her joy at having brought forth a man-child. The old Hebrew Bible *says* so—and in too many cases in a year or two she will have forgotten the whole bloody mess, and will be in the same pickle again. Well, my love, happy birthday! Think of all the chances you had for not getting here at all! And thank your mother . . .

You know how I have the habit of celebrating my birthday not for myself, but for my mother and father, who were reckless enough to let me out into the daylight to take my luck. It has been pretty grimly horrible at times, painful beyond belief in others, but somehow brilliant and exciting beyond any expectation a great deal of the time, I endure the disappointments and disillusions a romantic beastie like me must face and live over. After the life I have lived through, it is plain I can take the rest without too much regret, and truly, my dear love, with all my heart I can say I wouldn't have missed a day of it! And I would not live a day of it again! I am glad to have lived, and I shall be glad to die—Happy birthday, my dear love, as many as you want! . . .

12 minutes to 1 p.m. you seem to be making very slow work of getting born. But boys are notorious for refusing to come out head first as they should, but often insist on doubling up, presenting breech first as if bent on proving their triumphant gender at first sight. Others settle for feet first, and often have to be hauled out by the legs by main force, with great bloodshed and lacerations . . .

. . . in 1925 . . . I was 35 years old that year, merry as a cricket, not dreaming that I should ever be old, imagine! . . . not dreaming that I should ever meet this infant, deploring his forty-first or second birthday, drowning in early-chosen marriage, politics, law, frustrated fatherhood, murdered friends—this infant I am fated to love dearly, to believe in, to hope for—at what I hope is—give or take a year or two—the end of my life. Nothing could be better, because I expect nothing, he asks for nothing, we spend our very few moments together happily—joyously, even frivolously and have found something charmingly new in the man-and-woman question—so often a bore, a curse, a pain, a disease, a nuisance—and then, something, unbelievably wonderful—once in a long lifetime, if ever . . .

10:27—So help us all, there he is, head first in the most polite fashion, a nicely shaped boy, if at the moment a little cheesy and bloody—but the doctor and nurse cut the string and the doctor picks him up by the heels and gives him a good flat handed smack on his little behind, at this first insult to his humanity he draws in his first breath and returns it in one hell of a furious yell—But it is established that he is alive, he is a man, he is going to be the joy and misery of his parents for years, of his society until he

dies—and a mystery to himself and all near him—especially those
unlucky enough to love—for a number of years—

Dear love—
This is the after-note of the birth
Keep all of this
Please
Yours,
K. A.
10:39—P.M.
1 June, Sunday 1969

Barrett Prettyman was one year younger than her male child stillborn in 1924, four years younger than the child she aborted in 1921,
and considerably younger than the child she presumably lost when
she was married to John Koontz. If love comes out of need, as she
told Herbert Schaumann in 1945, her love for Prettyman was created
as much out of her need to replace her lost children as it was her lifelong and unfulfilled yearning, as Cleanth Brooks pointed out, to find
a perfect lover or husband as well as a perfect home.

In April, with the encouragement of Robert (Bob) Beach, assistant to
the president for University Relations at the University of Maryland,
Katherine Anne decided to give up the Spring Valley house. Even with
domestic help, the twelve-room house was too much for her to manage. In the aftermath of a stretch in the hospital at the end of March, it
was clear that she was becoming frailer and needed to be closer to
people who could get to her quickly if she needed help. College Park
seemed the ideal place. English Department faculty, administrators,
and students were always happy to look after her, and the additional
benefit was that she would be closer to the Katherine Anne Porter
Room, which she could regularly visit to continue sorting her papers.
Beach found a seven-room townhouse on Westchester Drive that
seemed just right, and so she said an "endless farewell to romantic
49th Street," as she wrote her friends.

The move was exhausting, and 5 May she was admitted to the
Georgetown University Hospital for a complete checkup by six or
seven specialists, among them a young psychiatrist who recorded,
"Miss Porter suffers a good deal of anxiety and fears regarding death
and particularly suffering with illness and old age. She regrets very
much not being able to be young and carefree and to do somewhat
wreckless [sic] things." Katherine Anne claimed not to have known he

was a psychiatrist until she read the report—she thought him only a charming young man who stopped by to chat. "I've never talked to a psychiatrist and I didn't want to," she told an interviewer the following spring. "That's picking my pocket." She had insisted on speaking to the young psychiatrist again, and she told him, "Kid, there are rules in every game. What you did is like tapping a telephone or opening a private letter. I don't want you in my mind. I have little packages there, and they're not labeled, but I know what everything is for. I need every weapon I've got—my weaknesses as well as my strengths." As for his suggestion that she was an old woman frightened at age, she declared indignantly, "I was never afraid of growing old."

Through the summer Katherine Anne tried to gain strength and adjust to her new surroundings. In late September, however, while descending stairs to feed her four-month-old kittens, she took a bad fall that knocked her out for several hours and injured her head, vertebrae, ribs, right arm, left leg, and spine. She was in the hospital more than a month. While she was recovering, she had another fall that resulted in a torn tendon in her left knee.

The year ended on an even more grievous note. After several years of increasing dementia and failing health, her beloved sister Gay died on 28 December. In Katherine Anne's appointment calendar she made a note of Gay's death and her funeral on 31 December. "After long suffering," she wrote, "her death was a release for her, and for Ann and me." Her calendar for the previous January showed no acknowledgment of the death of her old friend Josie, but in a way the deaths were the bookends of a bad year.

Seymour Lawrence was determined that 1970 would be better for Katherine Anne, as well as for him, and in the midst of all the moving, illness, and relocation, he had been able to extract from her the necessary material for *The Collected Essays and Occasional Writings*, which he was bringing out under his new imprint, Seymour Lawrence/Delacorte. It was on his spring list, and he organized a publication gala the last week in March at the McKeldin Library. Among the many guests was her friend William Jay Smith, poet-in-residence at the Library of Congress, who recently had published *A Rose for Katherine Anne Porter*, a poem in her honor. Two reporters who covered the event for the *Baltimore Evening Sun* found their headline when someone lightheartedly asked Katherine Anne whether she was ready to join the Women's Liberation Movement. After laughing "uproariously," as they described her reaction, she declared, "Certainly not . . . I don't agree with them . . . I just can't read any more about them. I don't care what they do just so they don't do it in the streets and scare the horses. I felt that way, too, about Betty Friedan's book when it was sent me to read. While I was going through it, I thought, 'Oh, Betty, why don't you go and mix a good cocktail for your husband and yourself and forget about this business.'" When Rhea Johnson, her housemate on Q Street, jokingly explained his presence at the event as someone who once lived with Katherine Anne, she said, "If all the men I'm supposed to have lived with were crammed into this room we couldn't turn around."

Throughout the evening she was busy inscribing her guests' copies of the book and posing for photographs, in most of them flanked by Seymour Lawrence and Barrett Prettyman. The book was dedicated to Barrett:

> To E. Barrett Prettyman, Jr. Faithful friend, able and fearless counselor, gifted writer, and joyful company, who has guided me through a rain-forest in these past rather terrible years. Yet we can laugh together and we know what to laugh at.

At the party she inscribed Barrett's copy with an addendum, a paraphrase of a passage from Shakespeare's *Richard II*:

> *For God's sake, let us sit upon the ground*
> *And tell sad stories of the death of kings*
> *And old, unhappy far-off things*
> *And battles long ago.*

Three days after the McKeldin Library reception, Barrett and his wife, Evelyn, hosted a dinner at the F Street Club to honor Katherine Anne and to acknowledge the dedication of the book.

Although some reviews of *The Collected Essays* conveyed unmitigated praise, most of them were mixed, and a greater number than usual were outright negative. She hardly had time to think about them, however, for 9 April, exactly two weeks after the Prettymans' dinner, she fell and broke her left hip, "a classic Granny trick," she said. She underwent surgery the following evening at Holy Cross Hospital at Silver Spring, Maryland. On 13 April she was moved to Sligo Gardens, a convalescent home in Takoma Park, Maryland, for two months of rehabilitation.

On 15 May friends and family members converged in her room at the convalescent home for a birthday party. There were gifts and flowers galore, and everyone was served ice cream, cookies, angel food cake (her favorite dessert), and champagne (which was against the rules at the medical facility). In addition to her friends in and around Washington and College Park, Ann had come down from Connecticut, and Paul arrived from New York. She had not seen Paul for several years, after a silly tiff over a broken glass, during which they each took offense at the other's remarks. Both had wanted to make up for a long time, and when he heard about her accident, he wrote her an amusing note and sent a recording of Monteverdi's "L'Orfeo" and a poster of a kitten dangling from a branch with the caption "Hang in there, Baby!" Before his arrival, he asked Ann to warn her that he now had a beard. When he bent over to kiss Katherine Anne, she gently tugged his beard and said (nervously, he thought), "You may not believe it, but there's a good-looking man behind these whiskers." She then reached up and put her arms around his neck and hugged him. He felt, he said later, that he had reestablished his fifteen-year-old nephew role.

Katherine Anne's friends realized that she would have to move out of the townhouse, which, counting the basement, had three floors of stairs to negotiate. Bob Beach found an apartment that seemed ideal on the fifteenth floor of a high-rise building on Westchester Park Drive, not far from the townhouse. Actually, it was two apartments combined and comprised four bedrooms and four bathrooms, two kitchens, a dining room, a formal parlor, and an office. Katherine Anne was pleased that there would be plenty of room for guests and for all her remaining furniture and other treasures. She saw it for the first time on 15 June, when she was released from Sligo Gardens.

Around the time of the publication of *The Collected Essays*, she had given several interviews, and in each one she mentioned books she intended to finish and new pieces she expected to write. Because Cyrilly understood that she was not likely to write anything new in the immediate future, if ever, she continued to search the wicker baskets for publishable manuscripts. Before the holidays, she happened upon "The Spivvleton Mystery," which Katherine Anne had written in 1926, and the *Ladies Home Journal* accepted it for their January 1971 issue. The story was a farcical romp through her very bad feelings about Ernest Stock, represented in the story as "Deadly Ernest," who, after having been drowned in the bathtub by his wife, Ida Mae, comes back to haunt her. Artistically, it was inferior to her short stories that had established her reputation. But the *Ladies Home Journal* and their readers were delighted with it, and the Mystery Writers of America gave her an award for the best short mystery story of the year.

In January she had a cataract operation, after which she had to wear unsightly, thick-lensed glasses. But by spring, her season, she was getting out more and entertaining a little. In May she had a birthday party for herself and met with the Katherine Anne Porter Foundation, which she had formed to support young writers. Although she had to turn down Lawrence's yacht party for her dear friend John Malcolm Brinnin, she managed, with Bob Beach's careful arrangement, a trip to Michigan to speak to the American Association of University Women.

Before 1971 was out Katherine Anne was able to complete a piece *McCall's* commissioned for the Christmas issue. Supposedly a memoir and meditation, the essay contains fiction in the account of her childhood Christmases in which she has Alice present alongside Harrison and Cat. The piece seemed to illustrate John Prince's observation that Katherine Anne at times seemed unable to separate reality from imagination. That tendency, first noticeable in her fanciful love affairs after her divorce from Albert Erskine, was becoming increasingly apparent.

CHAPTER TWENTY-NINE

Return to Texas

January 1972–May 1976

I long to return to my homeland just once more before I return as dust.

"It has not been a time of parties and visitors and all such celebrations of the seasons," Katherine Anne wrote John Malcolm Brinnin, Twelfth Night 1972. "Tonight at midnight I shall turn out the lights on the two Christmas Trees . . . Blow out the candles and face another year." Despite the sound of lonely resignation in her tone, she was also gently hopeful. She was working on the manuscript of her Cotton Mather biography, and after she finished that she intended to keep on going. There were half-written essays she wanted to complete, and she had a sudden, new resolve to finish her French murder mystery. "*Then* [triple underlined]," she told Brinnin, "I shall be free, and hope to have a little time of sweet idleness, full of music and books and Friends and Conversation in some pleasant climate near the sea."

Although the writing was not completed, in the spring she began to treat herself to the idle pleasures she sketched to Brinnin. Friends came to visit: Red and Eleanor and their two children, Gabriel and her goddaughter, Rosanna; Cleanth and Tinkum; Ann and Walter with their sons, David and Donald; Monroe; Paul; new friends Fern and Bill Wilkins; and two attentive young professional men, Clark Dobson and Jack Horner, who frequently escorted her to area concerts.

In April she went to New York to accept an award from Brandeis University at the Whitney Museum of American Art, and she returned to the city in May for the joint meeting of the American Academy of Arts and Letters and the National Institute of Arts and Letters. She had become a member of the National Institute in 1942, and in 1950 was named one of two vice presidents, only the second woman to be elected to the board. She has resigned from the organization in 1943 in protest against the practice of the institute of identifying some candidates as "Negro." Having reinstated her membership before she was elected to the American Academy, an elite body culled from the members of the National Institute, she now felt more or less at home at the annual gatherings, basking in admiration and "deploying great charm," as Matthew Josephson had described her in 1928. She, in fact, encountered Josephson upon her arrival, and when he gallantly offered her his arm she accepted it with cool grace and entered the auditorium with him. If seeing him was a little bittersweet, she was truly happy to see others, such as Eudora, whom she considered one of her dearest friends. "Now honey," she asked Eudora in the presence of the *Times* reporter, "how long have we known each other—40 years?" She patted Eudora on the shoulder and told the reporter, "I love her and everything she ever wrote."

One of the newly elected members to the National Institute that spring was the poet and novelist James Dickey, whom Katherine Anne had known for well over a decade. In the 1950s, when he had been a graduate assistant to her old friend Andrew Lytle at the University of Florida, he had called on her once at her Georgetown house. She liked Dickey (although she didn't like his poetry), and she was always glad to see him—and to talk. She apparently tried to shock him with a genteelly bawdy joke or two, difficult to bring off since her vulgar vocabulary did not extend past "hell" and "damn." He remembered her willingness, even eagerness, to express her opinion, especially on what she did *not* like. In 1972 it was hippies and feminists.

Ever since her months at Pigeon Cove in 1961, she had wanted to spend more time near the sea. She suddenly decided that this year she would return to Bermuda. Her choice of destination was probably inspired by seeing Josephson again. After all, her broken affair with him had driven her to Bermuda in 1929, and she remembered her six months there as a time of renewal and productivity, "the best six months of my life," she told Barrett Prettyman.

Unlike the half-year sojourn of 1929, the visit in the summer of 1972 was only a couple of weeks. And because she was not so independent at age eighty-two as she had been at thirty-nine, she was accompanied by her nurse, Addie Hubbard. But the little vacation apparently fulfilled her anticipation. "I love this scattered treasure of islands unreasonably and joyously," she wrote Brinnin. "Do look!" she wrote Tinkum and Cleanth. "Would you believe that at last I got back to this place that I love first of three loved places. I wish I could be in all three at once—Bermuda, Taormina, Sicily, and Amecamecca, a village at the foot of Popocateptl, guess where. Well I am here and wish it could be for life." The three idealized places, selected from all those she had identified and imagined over the years, spanned her life from 1920 to 1962, her creative years.

After she returned from Bermuda she did not take up the writing she outlined in January. No one, however, was putting any pressure on her. She heard nothing these days from Lawrence, who was busy adding new authors to his list, but she was angry with him anyway ever since he had remaindered both her *Collected Essays* and *A Christmas Story*. She had always felt strongly about having her books in print through her lifetime, proof, as she saw it, that her art was enduring. "I shall never throw another book away on that firm," she told Barrett, with whom her relationship had returned to a mostly professional level.

She was also upset with Glenway over a collection of their letters, which he was editing and which Lawrence, expecting to publish it, had already announced as forthcoming. Because Glenway had not returned her original letters to her, as she had repeatedly asked, she imagined that he intended to slip in letters she had not authorized for publication. She asked Barrett to set up legal restrictions that would prevent such publication.

Once a prolific letter writer, she now relied on the telephone as her primary means of communication, and she spent many evenings in long conversations with relatives and friends, thinking nothing of calling Isabel Bayley in Toronto or Marcelle Sibon in Paris. She most often talked with Ann and Paul, and her phone conversations with Paul were especially wide-ranging and entertaining. He called her "Angel" and played to her vanity. They aired common complaints about ailments and intrusive people; they talked about literature, music, and dance; they shared recipes; they reminisced about cats they loved; they discussed photographs of Katherine Anne he had taken and she liked. "Don't let anyone take pictures of you except me," he told her. "I've known since I was fifteen that there was a particular way to photograph you." "Yes, yes, Honey," she said, "so many people go snap, snap and have no idea what they are doing." Shamelessly vain in her talk with Paul, she repeated compliments she received, telling him once about being accosted on the street by a man ("a thang") who told her, "Migod, you're gorgeous!" Katherine Anne and Paul always closed their conversations with endearments. "Bless your heart, Angel, I love you" was their common sign-off.

During these talks with Paul she sometimes was candid, telling him one of her greatest fears (blindness—but not her deeper fear of insanity) and of her worry about her heart condition, which apparently had worsened, several angina attacks having occurred in recent months. But she loved to entertain him, too, telling him stories that were a jumble of fact and fiction. In October of 1972 she delighted in telling him about a telephone call the night before. "It was *Playboy!*" she shouted with merriment. "You're not going to pose for the centerfold, are you?" he teased. As it turned out, she had received a call from a *Playboy* editor who invited her to go on a December cruise with other selected persons and to watch from the Caribbean the last Apollo moon shot of the twentieth century. She was to discuss space travel with other notable writers and scientists in shipboard seminars and write an article about it.

Katherine Anne never finished the article for *Playboy*, but she enjoyed most of the nine-day cruise on the SS *Statendam*. The event was covered by major newspapers and magazines, and the embarkation of the celebrities was broadcast on television. The cruise, called "Voyage beyond Apollo," was the inspiration of a CBS consultant and a physicist who hoped many people would want to pay $1,000 to watch the launching of the rocket and attend seminars with distinguished persons discussing mankind's future in space. In addition to Katherine Anne and a scattering of scientists and space engineers, other participants were Norman Mailer, Isaac Asimov, and Robert Heinlein. Hugh Downs of *The Today Show* was the moderator. From New York the ship cruised to Cape Kennedy, Florida, for a close-up view of the launching of Apollo 17 on 7 December. From there the ship proceeded to St. Thomas in the Virgin Islands, swung back to Puerto Rico, and returned to New York.

In practical ways the enterprise was a failure. Only one hundred people paid to take the cruise, and of them only forty paid an additional $400 to attend the seminars. The Holland-America cruise line lost $250,000. Neither did the seminars live up to most expectations. Meetings were called and cancelled, some of the panelists seemed unprepared, and some, such as the former astronaut Edgar D. Mitchell, the physicist Werner von Braun, and screenwriter Arthur Clarke (*2001: A Space Odyssey*), had not shown up on the ship at all. Norman Mailer, whom Katherine Anne once called "an adolescent," seemed to dominate the discussions.

Reporters on board the ship interviewed Katherine Anne repeatedly to get her reaction to the moon shot. "I had never seen an Apollo launching," she told the *New York Times* reporter. "It was rather glorious, not frightening at all. I was very exhilarated. I never saw a light that grew and grew and grew"—here she threw out her arms with what the reporter described as "the spontaneous enthusiasms of a child." "I never in my life expected to see anything like it," she told him. "We barely had gaslight in New Orleans when I was a girl. When I saw them take off I wanted with all my soul to be going with them." The young writer whom *Playboy* assigned to escort Katherine Anne thought she was "the most stimulating conversationalist" he had ever met. She even provided the punch line for the event. The in-joke on board the celebrity-laden ship, and repeated in almost all the newspaper accounts, was whether this ship constituted another "ship of fools."

Shortly after her return to College Park, she was asked by Bob Beach to give an informal lecture about the voyage to a group of students and faculty members in the Katherine Anne Porter Room at McKeldin Library. The talk proved to be a long, extemporaneous account of her philosophy and experiences interspersed with observations about the Apollo launch, all of it progressing by free association and tied together with a leitmotif of references to Breugel's *Fall of Icarus*, one of her favorite paintings, a copy of which hung in her apartment. She was still able to hold the interest of her audience despite her increasing digressions. "If I give myself a parenthesis, I'll go completely off the track," she told them. And she still knew how to get a laugh. Having circuitously arrived at the subject of dreams, she talked about having dreamed of flying. "I remember all I had to do was to spread my arms like this and take off" (she demonstrated). "It was wonderful . . . the perfectly innocent and natural and human aspiration, you know, to get into the great blue sky that's so much nicer than where we live." But Freud, she said, who interpreted a dream of flying as sexual frustration, "came along and messed it up with his dirty old mind."

She also wrung (or created) a couple of good stories out of the moon launch. She told of a young female scientist with whom she had become acquainted on board the ship. This dignified young woman with the trained mind, however, who watched the soaring rocket that looked to Katherine Anne like a great, magical French parrot with wings of fire, was able to say only, "Go, baby." "I think that's lovely," Katherine Anne told her laughing audience. "And just back of me there was a young boy standing, and he said, 'God, God, God!' And I turned around and looked at him and I said, 'That's just the word I was looking for.' It was a great moment. I wouldn't have missed it for anything." She told her audience that she not only expected to write an essay about it for *Playboy*, but also intended to write a short story about it. In a way, she already had.

When Katherine Anne looked back on 1972, the Apollo launch was the highlight of what she thought of as a pretty good year, despite certain sour notes, such as her failed relationship with Lawrence, her faltering friendship with Glenway, and dreary national and world events she tried to ignore. In 1968 she had mustered enough civic duty to register and vote against Richard Nixon and Spiro Agnew for president and vice president. She had not bothered to vote in 1972, when they were reelected. Her only real political action during the year had been her return of the National Institute's Emerson-Thoreau medal as a protest against the institute's refusal to ignore Ezra Pound's fascism in order to acclaim his poetry.

Her entry in *The Celebrity Register* of 1973 contained numerous errors, but she had stopped trying to respond to every biographical statement put out about her. Such irritations made her aware, however, of the need to set up a literary executor who would protect her life from every "hyena" who wanted to feast on it. She had hoped that one of her friends might perform that duty and also undertake writing her biography. In 1966 she had rescinded the designation of Glenway as her literary executor and recently had concluded that Hank Lopez was not sufficiently knowledgeable and trustworthy to produce a respectable biography. She had Barrett write him an official letter telling him she was withdrawing her support of the project.

For her literary executor she settled on M. M. Liberman, a professor at Grinnell College, in Iowa, whose 1971 book, *Katherine Anne Porter's Fiction*, had pleased her. She asked Barrett to extend the invitation and tell Liberman to come to Maryland as quickly as possible because her time was growing short. Surprised and flattered, Liberman accepted the task.

The weekend Liberman spent with her in College Park was a three-day social event rather than the organized and serious meeting he expected. Always dressed extravagantly in designer clothes and a profusion of emeralds, pearls, and diamonds, she cooked lavish meals for him, gossiped, and made outrageous statements: Nixon should be assassinated; John Peale Bishop, who once kissed her foot at the Museum of Modern Art, was the only man she ever loved; Faulkner sentimentalized his Negroes. Liberman went away puzzled that she had been more interested in entertaining him than taking care of business.

Perhaps because of all the time she was spending with Barrett setting her affairs in order, she had revived her fantasy love affair with
him. Having accepted a writer-in-residence position at Herbert H.
Lehman University in New York City for the spring semester, she
asked him to drop by for cocktails before she left. When Barrett arrived
on 19 January she had Mrs. Hubbard, as usual, take a photograph at
precisely the moment he delivered the requisite kiss to her cheek.
Mrs. Hubbard took several more photographs that evening, including
one of Barrett and Katherine Anne smiling and lifting champagne
glasses to Katherine Anne's usual Mexican toast that she translated,
"To many secret love affairs, and Time to enjoy them."

Photographs of her and Barrett nevertheless did not completely sat-
isfy her. Either they weren't flattering enough or they failed to convey
the intimacy she pretended existed. She cut apart several of the January
photographs, one that showed a smiling, happy Barrett and one that
showed her with an anguished look on her face. She combined the
pieces like a jigsaw puzzle that made it look as if she and Barrett were
standing with their arms around each other. She decided, however,
that she didn't like her face in the photograph, and she cut it out,
making herself headless. She sent the montage to Barrett with notes
of explanation scribbled around it. One note read: "This is neither
art nor photography, but it is full of a certain truth." She once told
Edward Schwartz, "Some things come from very deep down in the consciousness . . . we tap it no doubt intentionally, but we cannot always
foresee what will be brought up."

After she moved temporarily into a New York apartment at 400
West 119th Street and began her teaching duties at Lehman, she wrote
a letter to Barrett containing an admission about her relationship with
him but also further fantasizing: "Ah, well—look back over our career
of . . . inevitable long separations, irrevocable situations in life—vast
difference in age and vocations; unchangeable domestic states; and for
every sort of reason—or maybe just feelings, or God knows maybe a
deep down doubt or fear, disguised as a principal of human obligation
to our fearfully restrictive code of human conduct—what? What? Kept
us in that state of near-chastity where we never kissed on the lips and
never touched below the belt, and never on the bed together except
when visiting each other in the hospital—*yet* [three underlines] we
smile at each other over our breakfast of snails and champagne, saying
goodbye for another of our long absences from each other with a bliss
in each other not only when we are together . . . but in our being

together *now* in this world—my dear, my love, who would believe this? Who could know it but you and me? Who ever had a more delicious secret?" Barrett was busy and able to treat her mythmaking as he had treated it before (largely ignoring it), but he added kindly and indirect reminders that there were limitations on their friendship.

A week after her birthday in 1973, Katherine Anne finished the semester at Lehman and on the same day learned that Baby had died. She had never loved her younger sister very much, but Baby's death wiped out the last link to her immediate family and unexpectedly saddened her. Reminded that she was the only one of Harrison and Alice's children left, she wanted more than ever to settle her affairs— spiritual, financial, and personal.

For the past few years she had been giving more thought to her religious faith, or the limits of it, and since 1970 she had been closely communicating with nuns and priests she had met at the College of Notre Dame of Maryland. She had become especially close to Sister Kathleen Feeley, Sister Maura Eichner, and Father Joseph Gallagher. As for her finances, the few months of teaching had done nothing to put her in better fiscal shape since she spent more than she earned. On the personal front she put her relationship with Barrett on terms tolerable to both of them. She told him she accepted the "limitations," but she also said, "I adore you, really—Try not to mind. It will never harm you." She had one final task to complete the organization of her life at the end of 1973. After Baby's death in the spring she had begun looking for a coffin for herself.

She knew exactly what she wanted: a simple wooden coffin with rope handles, the kind of primitive box in which people in Mexico were buried. She finally found one advertised by a mail-order cabinet shop in Arizona and sent away for it. When it arrived, she discovered that it was awfully large, not exactly the way she had pictured it. But she had a wooden coffin. She told everybody she was pleased with it, and she laid inside it the linen winding-sheet she had bought in Belgium in 1954.

After an attack of diverticulitis, she was taken to Prince George Hospital the night of 22 May and spent more than a miserable week tolerating breathing and feeding tubes. After returning home, she was forced to stay in bed and limited to a liquid diet for several more weeks. "What a bore," she wrote in the calendar 9 June. "I read and write little notes to remind me of all I have meant to write all these deadly five years past. Silence, please." The illness was another painful reminder of her failing health and certain dissatisfactions, and before June was over she added a codicil to her will. She had decided to remove Liberman as literary trustee and put Isabel Bayley in his place.

Whenever she was up to social events, she happily received visitors and accepted invitations. She welcomed Carl Griffin, a young graduate student writing what she regarded as a brilliant analysis of *Ship of Fools*, and at the end of August her young friends Clark Dobson and Jack Horner accompanied her and Mrs. Hubbard to Wolf Trap Park to see Prokofiev's opera *War and Peace*. Katherine Anne, exquisitely dressed, was excited about the whole event. "She didn't miss anything," Clark said. At a certain point in the performance, she hit his arm and pointed up to the rafters of the theater, where many technicians were working so unobtrusively that Clark had not even noticed them. He thought it was the image that captivated her: the silhouette of the workers against a cobalt-blue sky the color of an "Evening in Paris" perfume bottle. He thought then that she probably had been cursed with the habit of storing up impressions like that for future use. "She just saw everything, and she saw it differently, certainly than I did, and, perhaps, than anyone I know."

The physical setbacks that began in the spring resumed in the fall. The evening of 9 October she experienced severe pain in her left arm, numbness, choking, nausea, and sweating. A similar attack three weeks later convinced her that she had had two mild heart attacks, and her personal physician, Dr. Lawrence Z. Satin, confirmed her diagnosis.

As 1975 began, aware of her failing health, she was working again on her writing—the French murder mystery and also, at Cyrilly's urging, a memoir of the Sacco-Vanzetti affair of 1927. She hired a young woman, Ginger Woolly, as a secretary. Cyrilly salvaged an autobiographical piece that had been titled "The Land That Is Nowhere" and, with only a little polishing by Katherine Anne, sold it to the *Atlantic Monthly* as "Notes on the Texas I Remember."

Katherine Anne had to confront the fact that she was going to be without the aid and friendship of Cyrilly, who had been diagnosed with terminal lung cancer. In October she made a special trip to New York to see her. When she returned home she wrote a letter with the farewell sentiments she had been unable to express in person: "I want to say to you what I have always felt and loved about you," she wrote, "and that is the incredible strength and beauty in your whole life as I have known it, your real understanding of love and somehow a depth of meaning which you surmised in human relationships, your genius for friendship and understanding of even the most complicated and hidden motives and sufferings and joys of the human beings near you. You are and have been a kind of exemplar of everything loving and admirable to your friends that I have known all these years, and I simply want to say to you now what I have felt about you and learned about love and a way of living from you all this time." Cyrilly died 8 November.

During Cyrilly's illness Katherine Anne tried to take on, with Barrett's help, the duties her friend had carried out. But she was intemperate in letters to Lawrence and in an interview with a *Washington Star* reporter in which she talked about exploitive editors who would "destroy" a writer's work. Barrett wrote a strong warning to her about making slanderous statements. His letter annoyed her, however, and in her reply she referred to her "blessed old friends" with whom she had "a lifetime of love and gentleness," indirectly pointing out to him that he was a more recent friend and therefore not so treasured. She said, "Don't call me. I *must* not be disturbed. I'm writing." There was no loving signature this time.

By the end of 1975 Katherine Anne was without an agent, editor, or publisher, and maybe without an attorney. She had no brothers or sisters alive, but she did have those old friends she mentioned to Barrett, and they were increasingly important to her. She was as delighted as a child when she received letters or gifts from them: special coffee from Isabel and Hew, a flower bulb for planting from Tinkum Brooks, photographs from Eudora. One of the best gifts she received in the last months of 1975 was sent by Dr. Roger L. Brooks, president of Howard Payne University, a small Baptist college in Brownwood, Texas, about twenty-five miles from Indian Creek. Brooks had made a rubbing of Alice Porter's tombstone for her. She was touched, and she was homesick for Texas. Brooks wanted to bring her to Brownwood the following spring to give her an honorary degree, and the correspondence that ensued as a result of his gift was full of talk about a homecoming.

Brooks planned a five-day itinerary to coincide with the week of her eighty-sixth birthday and the Howard Payne commencement. Her visit was to be capped with a birthday banquet at which she would give a talk. Katherine Anne told Brooks that she couldn't remember looking forward to anything with so much joy. Two weeks before her scheduled arrival, however, she sent him a telegram saying, "All of our beautiful plans must be set aside. The doctors have advised me that I am too ill to travel." Her change of mind occurred after she made a mid-April trip to Skidmore College, in Saratoga Springs, to deliver the annual Frances Steloff lecture and to receive an honorary doctor of letters degree. She was not satisfied, however, with her 14 April lecture. Critical of American en masse education, she praised Skidmore's small ratio of students to teachers and told the audience *not* to be afraid of asserting their "independence" and *not* to follow the current trend of "mocking the arts." But the audience seemed not in her control. She told about a person who objected to the "blasphemy" in the ending of "The Jilting of Granny Weatherall." "But it wasn't taking the Lord's name in vain," she said. "It was a person addressing God." She expected laughter instead of the loud silence. "Don't you think that's funny?" she asked. "Aren't you going to laugh?" There was a murmur of forced laughter. A student reporter covering the event said, "Most of us thought it was sad." When she returned to College Park, she felt physically unequal to a long trip to Texas and another round of exhausting, and perhaps disappointing, college events.

Roger Brooks quickly wrote her a carefully worded letter in which he enumerated the elaborate plans that had been made and told her that his personal physician, Dr. Seal Cutbirth, would attend her on every public occasion and be available to her throughout the visit. Contrite, Katherine Anne replied, because of all the preparations, "I cannot refuse you."

Brooks sent an alumnus and two young professors from the English Department, Charlotte Laughlin and Alta Ada Schoner, to Dallas–Fort Worth International Airport on 7 May to meet her arriving plane, present her with a bouquet of yellow roses, and drive her to Brownwood. During the car trip, which included an impromptu stop at the Ramada Inn in Stephenville for pecan pie, Katherine Anne entertained her three hosts with lively stories and praise of Texas food. "I haven't had a good sausage patty," she said, "since I left Texas." "It was performance, really," Charlotte Laughlin said. For all that, Katherine Anne's exuberance at being back in Texas was sincere.

On Saturday, a group of professors and a school nurse took her to the cemetery at Indian Creek to visit the grave of her mother. The group had a picnic in the cemetery, and Katherine Anne, after placing pink talisman roses on the grave, read aloud her poem "Anniversary in a Country Cemetery." According to her companions, she "talked to" her mother and became so overwrought they had to rush her back to her motel and call Dr. Cutbirth, who prescribed rest and quiet in the darkened room for the rest of the day.

She attended the commencement in the Brownwood Coliseum on Sunday, 9 May, when she was awarded an honorary degree, and Tuesday evening, 11 May, she addressed a banquet audience of six hundred. Part of her talk was similar to her December lecture at McKeldin in that she summarized her life and philosophy. Instead of the uniting references to the Apollo space lift and *The Fall of Icarus*, however, she anchored her May remarks in a motif of womb and tomb as she spoke of her birth in Indian Creek, her visit to her mother's grave, and her own desire to be buried in the Indian Creek cemetery.

Before her departure from Brownwood, Katherine Anne insisted on hosting a dinner to thank those of the Howard Payne staff who had been most deeply involved in planning and carrying out her visit. She chose one of the few area restaurants that served liquor, and she ordered champagne and escargot for everyone, ignoring the fact that many of her guests were Baptist teetotalers who had never eaten snails in their lives. Brooks had a hard time explaining the dinner to his board of trustees. "But by then," he recalled, "I had prepared them for Katherine Anne Porter, and I think they overlooked that and other things." "Other things" included her telling one group of startled listeners that she had had thirty-seven lovers and three husbands.

In an article for the *Brownwood Bulletin* Charlotte Laughlin disclosed that some of Katherine Anne's relatives on her mother's side had been invited to the banquet but had declined. Roscoe Jones of Brownwood and Hardin Jones of Goldthwaite, both sons of Katherine Anne's uncle George Melton Jones and his second wife, said they couldn't see paying $7.50 to see Katherine Anne. "We got along this long," Hardin said, "and I suppose we can go a lot longer." She wouldn't have wanted to see them either, continuing to fear a shattering of any part of her idealized image of her mother.

Her visit in the native land of her birth had been a good one. There in Brown County in the May light and sun-warmed air, among blooming wild flowers and live oaks in full leaf, she wanted to believe that she had finally found the ideal place she had sought much of her life.

CHAPTER THIRTY

The Last Candles

May 1976– September 1980

I'm busy dying; it's the hardest job I ever had.

When Katherine Anne returned from Texas, focused more than ever on organizing her life, she hired a new agent, Joan Daves, to oversee all her publishing affairs. "I couldn't wait to tell you all this," she wrote Barrett Prettyman, "because it must be good news to you to be free from all these complications so totally foreign to your legal field and activity and to be certain that I am in the best possible hands that I could ever wish to be." She asked him to rejoice with her. "I feel as if I am having a birthday to a new life now and the joyful festival at Indian Creek was just a preparation for my happiness."

Her letter to Barrett had been dictated to William (Bill) Wilkins, who started working as her assistant around the first of April. Bill and his wife, Fern, were already her friends, and when Bill, who was looking for interesting part-time work, was approached by Bob Beach, Fern's cousin, about becoming Katherine Anne's personal secretary, he readily accepted. Katherine Anne, pleased, remarked to Paul that Bill knew about human nature as well as literature. "Maturity," she added knowingly.

She told Bill, "This is a man-sized job. You're going to work your head off, and you're going to run this show." His first big task was to untangle the three different manuscripts of her memoir of the Sacco-Vanzetti affair. Within a few months he had put together what he considered the best version, which required only a little refining by her. At the end of the summer she set him to work on the Cotton Mather biography, thinking that he might make a miracle with another messy manuscript that dated from the 1920s. After that, who knew? Perhaps he could help her get the anthology of short stories together.

"He's wonderful," she told Paul. "He's the person I've needed for twenty-five years."

After only a few months she decided to end her association with Joan Daves, the result of her usual frustration with agents who did not produce income quickly. Recognizing that she needed an agent, however, she appealed to Red Warren, who quickly recommended his own agent, Owen Laster, a young man affiliated with the William Morris Agency. Letters were exchanged, and a two-year contract was signed. "I wish you luck," Katherine Anne wrote Laster. He recalled being "thrilled" to be her agent. He made a trip to College Park to meet her and discuss possible publications.

The last months of 1976 brought Katherine Anne satisfying resolutions to most of her affairs. She signed a codicil to her will that instructed Isabel Bayley to use the net income from the estate to support charitable, literary, and scientific causes, including the giving of grants and scholarships for the benefit of writers of literature; she gave a farewell reading at the Poetry Center; she invited an Englishwoman, Joan Givner, who had written an article on "Theft" that she liked, to be her biographer; and Laster sold *The Never-Ending Wrong* to Atlantic–Little, Brown. It was to be published in 1977, the fiftieth anniversary of the trials and executions of the two Italian immigrants, first in the *Atlantic Monthly* and then as a book by Little, Brown. "I am slowly finishing my life," she wrote David Locher, "but I have wonderful help in getting together work I need to finish, my mind works fairly, I don't suffer too much . . . Pray for me, dear David."

Her letter to Locher was written eleven days before she entered the Johns Hopkins Medical Center for a thorough physical examination. Like many of her hospital stays in the past, this one was designed to include seclusion and rest as well as a battery of tests and consultations that would define her condition and set forth a healthful regimen of medication and exercise. With Bill's help she sent letters and notes to many of her friends, telling them where she was but not to worry. "I really am wonderful," she said. When she was released after three weeks, she felt as if her health had been restored and asked Dr. Warren Summer, a pulmonary specialist, to record on her chart that she said, "I was born on Thursday May 15, 1890. Alleluia! Reborn on [Tuesday, 11 January] 1977."

On 18 February, however, she suffered a severe stroke and was quickly returned to Johns Hopkins. A second stroke soon followed, and it seemed as if she might not survive more than a few days.

Several newspapers began to draft her obituary, and her friends at Howard Payne University set up a committee to prepare for her burial at Indian Creek and for a memorial service on the campus.

Ann and Paul rushed to Baltimore, shocked to see her paralyzed, white, incoherent, disheveled, and attached to tubes and machines in the sterile surroundings of an intensive care unit. When a doctor with four or five students entered her room and asked Ann and Paul to step outside, Katherine Anne began crying hysterically, outraged at the indignity of having students standing around her bed staring at her while the doctor talked about her as if she were no more than a specimen under a microscope. She felt depersonalized, dehumanized, just as she did when agents and publishers referred to her as an "asset" or "property" or when she concluded a man loved the *idea* of her and not really *her*. Preferring for herself mature and courtly male physicians, she did not think well of medical students anyway. She had depicted them as callous, empty heads in *Ship of Fools*, and among her papers is a sketch, intended as a scene in an unfinished story, in which she has a medical student showing Miranda a handful of dead, green flesh and telling her it was a prostitute's pubic area harvested in a university's pathology laboratory.

Although doctors would give only a guarded prognosis, Katherine Anne survived the strokes, the result, Bill thought, of her being such a "fighter." But her right side was paralyzed, and the portion of her brain that controlled speech functions was impaired. Although she was generally aware of what she wanted to say, she was unable to summon the words and articulate her thoughts. Her doctors released her in early April after round-the-clock nursing care had been arranged. Bill Wilkins was to stay on managing the household staff, writing letters for her, and assisting in whatever way he could. He wrote to her friends that she still was *"very* ill, but trying very hard to get back in the world."

It was soon apparent that her speech and mobility were not all that was affected. Her reason and emotions had been jarred, and paranoia and rage took over for increasingly longer periods. For the next month her feelings toward Bill ricocheted between love and loathing. One day she would rationally discuss business affairs with him and dictate letters; the next day she would blame him for all her troubles, including her paralysis and her "imprisonment," and tell him she didn't trust him. Finally convinced that he no longer could perform his job as her helper, he stepped out of the picture.

When Paul came for a visit in late May, he talked to her about becoming her legal guardian. She seemed amenable to the idea. A week later she sent Paul's letter to Barrett, called her whole relationship with her nephew a "catastrophe," and asked Barrett to save her. It wasn't long, however, before she also turned on Barrett with a vengeance. To anyone who listened, she called Bill, Paul, and Barrett a "triumvirate of evil," a label she earlier had reserved for Darwin, Freud, and Nietzsche.

In June "The Never-Ending Wrong" was published in the *Atlantic Monthly*, and the book appeared in August. Secker and Warburg brought it out in England soon afterward. Like many of her other autobiographical essays and memoirs, it was a blend of fact and fiction. She had been in the 1920s, she said, simply a liberal humanitarian protesting the executions in Boston, and she had been shocked and disillusioned to discover that the affair was being exploited by hard-core Communists. In 1927, however, she really had not been so politically naïve as she said. Some of the Communists involved in the protest, such as Mike Gold, Genevieve Taggard, and Kenneth Durant, were her friends, and she was more involved with their activities than she wanted to remember. Although she admitted to being "a sympathizer with the new (to me) doctrines brought out of Russia from 1919 to 1920 onward by enthusiastic, sentimental, misguided men and women who were looking for a New Religion of Humanity," at one point she was assistant to Durant when he was the American editor of *Tass*.

Throughout the summer friends called or wrote to say how much they liked the memoir, and reviews of the book appeared in the major newspapers and magazines, attention ensured by her celebrity and age. Not many were favorable, for in 1977 attacking the left was not popular in liberal quarters. The few praising reviews appeared in the *New Yorker* ("She writes like an angel—a shining style, gleaming candor"), in *Publishers Weekly* ("It is, in the noblest sense, the memory-laden statement of one of the grand women of American letters"), and an especially admiring one by Eudora in the *New York Times Book Review*.

The publication of the book entered the chaos already in her mind, and she sometimes confused the events of 1927 with her present condition and failed to recognize persons she knew well. Her friend William Jay Smith showed up with an armload of white roses, and she had no idea who he was. But there were good days when people dropping in found her peaceful and alert, even chatty. Roger Brooks, who came to see her in July to talk about transporting to Brownwood items she had rashly promised to Howard Payne University, ignoring the fact that she had already bequeathed them to the University of Maryland, reported a good two-hour visit.

As a result of Brooks's visit, Katherine Anne became obsessed with the notion of moving to Texas. She talked about the good people there who would take care of her until she found a little house of her own. She even could teach there, she said, and then she could finish all her remaining work. In her irrationality she even thought that Brooks was a medical doctor who would cure her. Barrett and Paul considered the petition to make Paul her legal guardian now urgent, and Circuit Court Judge Ernest A. Loveless Jr. granted the request 28 September after two court-appointed psychiatrists confirmed that Katherine Anne was in a deteriorated mental state and unable to manage her business affairs.

The pattern of alternating lucidity and bewilderment, marked by emotional outbursts and wishes for death, was set. Paul settled into the task of managing her business, aware that most of the time she considered him a "traitor" and sometimes referred to him as her "idiot nephew." A significant part of his supervision was to pay the bills and be sure that nurses were retained for the twenty-four-hour care. Some quit after she threw objects at them or accused them of stealing from her, but some seemed to know just how to handle her on an "off" day. When she was rational, she was charming, intently interested in their personal lives, and receptive to their kindness and competent caretaking. She became especially attached to one of her nurses, Gloria Leet, who was soon to be married in Bermuda. Katherine Anne announced that she planned to attend the wedding, and Isabel Bayley thought she might really rise to the challenge and go.

Katherine Anne called Isabel on 3 November to ask her to please come see her. "I want to tell you goodbye," she said. It was an invitation hard to refuse, and Isabel, after weighing what she might spare herself by *not* going—being screamed at, insulted, turned against, as had happened to Bill Wilkins, Paul, Barrett, and Ann, whom Katherine Anne referred to as "that girl"—decided to risk disfavor on the chance that she might "ease, a bit," Katherine Anne's misery. When Isabel arrived in College Park and reached Katherine Anne's bedroom, she found her halfway sitting up, her right hand curled into a claw shape, the right side of her face a crevice that descended to her neck. Isabel thought that the left side of her face, however, was still astonishingly what it had always been, quite recognizably what the person in the exquisite photographs outside her door had become in eighty-seven years of life. Isabel's best moments with Katherine Anne were spent reminiscing about past good times together and discussing literature and music they both loved. There even were spells of merriment and laughter. Isabel quoted favorite sentences from Katherine Anne's essays and recited all of "Life That Is So Sweet," the medieval poem with which Katherine Anne often concluded her public talks. When Katherine Anne handed her a recent copy of the *Sewanee Review*, Isabel figured out by the impatient finger jabs and the word "doctor" that she wanted her to read an essay on Samuel Johnson, whom Katherine Anne had always referred to as "the divine doctor." The next morning, finding her alert and looking lovely in a blue dressing gown, Isabel read to her Johnson's "How to Die."

For the next two years change occurred slowly as her physical and mental conditions gradually worsened. Small seizures continued, disconnections in her mind increased, and the grasp on reality gradually became more tenuous. Nurses came and went. Paul, Ann, friends, and acquaintances fell in and out of favor from one day to the next. When nurses at her urgent request placed calls to old friends, Katherine Anne most often begged them to come see her and to spring her from her awful "prison." She dictated letters that, if they weren't diatribes, ranged from partly articulate messages of love and friendship to variations of a *cri de coeur*.

In the fall of 1978 Katherine Anne dictated a letter to Seymour Lawrence praising Tillie Olsen's *Silences*, which Lawrence had recently published. She had recommended Tillie to Lawrence some time back, and the publication pleased her. "I loved and enjoyed it," she said. "I am going to write her at once." Evoking "remembrance" of their old friendship, Katherine Anne told Lawrence, "I would give anything in the world to see you come here to see me." Having regretted the collapse of their relationship and being disturbed by the angry letters Katherine Anne had written him over the past half-dozen years, Lawrence made a trip to College Park to call upon her. The day of his visit, however, was not one of her better days. Barely coherent, she spent most of the time railing against persons she accused of "treachery." The only satisfying part of the visit was that she seemed to want a reconciliation with him. Throughout his hour-long stay, she repeated from time to time, "Angel, give me work. I still have another book to write." In recent months she seemed to be nearly obsessed with writing an essay on abortion.

On 9 February Allen Tate died in Nashville, and after the funeral Red and Eleanor returned through Maryland in order to see Katherine Anne. Rosanna was living in Washington at the time, and she went with her parents to call on her godmother. Red reported to Peter Davison that they found Katherine Anne weak but mostly bright and clear and much like herself. He and Eleanor were "deeply moved to see the genuine affection between Rosanna, her life before her, and her godmother, whose long life was approaching its end."

Paul arranged to have Katherine Anne transferred to Carriage Hill Nursing Home at the end of March 1980. He made sure that her copies of favorite paintings, *The Fall of Icarus*, by Pieter Brueghel, and *The Virgin and Child Surrounded by Flowers and Fruit*, by Rubens and Jan Brueghel, went with her, and to a long list of her friends he mailed change-of-address cards with her unlisted telephone number and a map to the nursing home. Some came, but many did not, for a variety of reasons, one of which, of course, was that they simply did not want to see her as she was.

In the spring Clark Dobson, Jack Horner, Jane DeMouy, a recent PhD from the University of Maryland who had met Katherine Anne and become devoted to her, and Ted Wojtasik, a young man Katherine Anne had talked to about editing her letters, planned her ninetieth birthday party. Many of her other friends sent cards and gifts, and Isabel decided to make the trip from Canada for what she suspected was Katherine Anne's last birthday party. On 15 May the five of them decorated her room with red and white balloons and roses, helped her open gifts, and took turns reading birthday greetings before the birthday cake, ice cream, and champagne were wheeled into her small room on a cart. Katherine Anne, however, was uninterested in the party food as she struggled to tell them something at which they could only guess. Isabel supposed that her "unordered sounds" were meant to be a "disavowal of the place" in which they found her. With her unparalyzed left hand she gestured an arc that took in the small room as if to encompass her diminished life. She seemed to be saying, "I have never lived this way and do not wish to do so now." She had refused to have the Brueghel and Rubens paintings hung, underscoring her resistance to call this place her "home."

Her birthday no longer was the haven-day of good omens, for she had nothing to which she could look forward. She seemed deflated for the first time, finally relinquishing any thought, really a fantasy since 1977, of writing again. She once had lifted her paralyzed right hand with her left and told Sister Kathleen Feeley, "My writing hand. It served me well. I still love it." Now, on her ninetieth birthday, the nurse who attended her during the party gave another name to the hand, more symbolic than she could have known. Placing it gently inside the bedcover, the nurse said, "Let's tuck the baby in." Writing finally was the only "child" she had.

After her birthday and through the summer Katherine Anne's increasing decline was visible to her friends and the nursing staff at Carriage Hill. On 18 September, a little after three o'clock in the afternoon, the director called Jane DeMouy, who lived nearby, to say that Katherine Anne had had a bad spell and that her pulse was very weak. Jane ran all the way to Carriage Hill to find Katherine Anne with unseeing eyes wide open, her breath uneven. A nurse, who was giving her oxygen, told Jane to talk to her, that Katherine Anne could hear her. Jane, who was a devout Catholic, held her hand, assured her that she was not alone, that the Lord was beside her, and that all she had to do was reach out her arms. There was no sign of recognition. Jane told her that she was leaving herself behind in her wonderful stories that gave her immortality. Jane sang what she could remember of the old spiritual "Pale Horse, Pale Rider" and told her she would finally be reunited with Alexander, the lover she lost in 1918. If Katherine Anne heard Jane at all, one wonders whether she had told the story about the mythical Alexander so often that she believed it herself.

At five o'clock her breath stopped.

Katherine Anne's body was bathed, wrapped in the Belgian linen, and sent to the mortuary for cremation, as she had specified. Paul was notified, and he in turn called the *New York Times* to tell them that Katherine Anne Porter had died. An obituary went out on the wire services and appeared the next day in newspapers across the country.

On 19 September a requiem mass was offered at the College of Notre Dame, and 19 October a Month's Mind Memorial Service was held in the same chapel. Students and nuns from the college sang songs accompanied by flute and guitar; Jane DeMouy read from Job and Revelation; Father Joseph Gallagher, who had given her last rites many times in the past year, delivered the homily. Katherine Anne's family and friends met in the social hall to reminisce and share good food and drink, a funeral festival Katherine Anne had requested. The celebration continued when Eudora softly suggested that they all move along in the drizzly evening to a favorite seafood restaurant in Baltimore. "I think that is what Katherine Anne would want us to do," she said.

On 3 April 1981, Paul flew to Austin with Katherine Anne's ashes. The next day he and his nephew Tom Parrish and Tom's wife, Karen, drove to Brownwood and then to the cemetery at Indian Creek, where they were met by a local priest. It was a bright, sunny day, cool and windy. In the cemetery, enclosed by a barbed wire fence and surrounded by vast fields of young grain plants, the priest repeated the ritual words. Paul, having decided against the wooden coffin, buried the box of ashes in the vacant plot beside Alice Porter's grave. Soon, over the burial place would stand the marble stone he designed, engraved with her epitaph:

In my end is my beginning.

ABBREVIATIONS

PERSONS

AHH	Ann Holloway Heintze
AJ	[Mary] Alice Jones [Porter]
ARE	Albert Russel Erskine III
AT	Allen Tate
BP	Elijah Barrett Prettyman Jr.
CASP	Catharine Ann Skaggs Porter
CB	Cleanth Brooks
CG	Caroline Gordon
DB	Donald Brace
DHU	Darlene Harbour Unrue
DL	David Locher
EAB	Edith Amy (Tinkum) Brooks
EDP	Eugene Dove Pressly
ES	Edward Schwartz
ESJ	Erna Schlemmer Johns
EW	Eudora Welty
GPH	Gay Porter Holloway
GW	Glenway Wescott
HBP	Harrison Boone Porter
HPP	Harrison Paul Porter Sr., Katherine Anne Porter's brother
IB	Isabel Bayley
JH	Josephine Herbst
KAP	Katherine Anne Porter
MAPH	Mary Alice Porter Hillendahl (Baby)
MCW	Marcella Comès Winslow
MJ	Matthew Josephson
MW	Monroe Wheeler
PP	Harrison Paul Porter Jr., Katherine Anne Porter's nephew

RPW	Robert Penn Warren
SL	Seymour Lawrence
WW	William Wilkins

COLLECTIONS

CU	Kroch Library, Cornell University
DHUC	Collection of the author
HRC	The Harry Ransom Humanities Research Center, University of Texas at Austin
K	The Kentucky Library, Western Kentucky State University, Bowling Green, Kentucky
MD	The University of Maryland, College Park, archives, currently in Hornbake Library. In addition to the Papers of KAP, a designation that includes photographs, furniture, memorabilia, and her personal collection of books, magazines, and audio recordings; the library also houses the associated Papers of Cyrilly Abels, E. Barrett Prettyman Jr., Mary Louis Doherty, Ann Holloway Heintze, Thomas Walsh, Toni Willison, Paul Porter, and a special collection of Seymour Lawrence related to Porter
N	The Newberry Library, Chicago
NYPL	New York Public Library
PPC	The personal collection of Harrison Paul Porter Jr., distinguished from the Paul Porter Papers at the University of Maryland
P	Princeton University Library; houses the Caroline Gordon and Allen Tate Papers; and the Sylvia Beach Papers
THC	The Texas History Center, University of Texas at Austin
Y	The Beinecke Rare Book and Manuscript Library at Yale University; houses the Cleanth Brooks and Edith Amy Brooks Papers; the Josephine Herbst Papers; the Robert Penn Warren and Eleanor Clark Papers; and the Robert McAlmon Papers

WORKS

CEOW	*The Collected Essays and Occasional Writings of Katherine Anne Porter*
CS	*The Collected Stories of Katherine Anne Porter*

I	*Katherine Anne Porter: Conversations* [Interviews], edited by Joan Givner
Letters	*Letters of Katherine Anne Porter*, edited by Isabel Bayley
Life	*Katherine Anne Porter: A Life*, by Joan Givner
Mexico	*Katherine Anne Porter and Mexico*, by Thomas F. Walsh
N-EW	*The Never-Ending Wrong*, by Katherine Anne Porter
Poetry	*Katherine Anne Porter's Poetry*
Refugee	*Conversations with Katherine Anne Porter: Refugee from Indian Creek*, by Enrique (Hank) Lopez
SOF	*Ship of Fools*, by Katherine Anne Porter
SW	*"This Strange, Old World" and Other Book Reviews by Katherine Anne Porter*
UEP	*Uncollected Early Prose of Katherine Anne Porter*

OTHER

AN	Autobiographical notes at MD; includes files under the labels "The Land That Is Nowhere," "The First Step," "Pull Dick, Pull Devil," "Legends of the Ancestors," "Mardi Gras," "Jane and Grandmother," "Essanay Studio," "Many Redeemers," and "Midway of This Mortal Life," many of which overlap
C	Copy, by KAP, at MD; either a carbon copy or a retyped copy; possibly in some instances a letter was unsent.
TI	Telephone interview
TTC	Taped telephone conversation

Unless otherwise indicated, all unpublished material is located at the University of Maryland.

NOTES

Introduction: Katherine Anne Porter and the Honest Biography

I was present for KAP's talk at Howard Payne University, but for her exact words I have relied on a transcript supplied by Charlotte Laughlin.

"Don't be afraid": KAP to EDP, December 1931, "Notes on Writing", CEOW, 443.

"incredible": KAP to PP, 20 June 1957.

"You haven't got a notion": KAP to ES, 1 July 1956.

"There are dozens": "St. Augustine and the Bullfight," CEOW, 93–94.

"real life": KAP to GW, 23 October 1954, Letters, 461.

"I'm a Southerner": Thompson, I, 78.

"We had no money": "Portrait: Old South," CEOW, 163.

"The search for factual material": Stalling, 17.

"sweet": GW, "KAP: The Making of a Novel," 44.

"girlish" and "breathless": Dorsey, I, 142.

"someone talking to a bird": Thompson, I, 78.

"a soda-water syphon": Janeway, I, 69.

"that flared like blown coals": Ruoff, I, 61.

"hell to live with": Eleanor Clark, "The Friendships of a Lifetime," 6.

"morally victious": Solotaroff, 277.

"tragic": CB, "The Woman and Artist I Knew," Machann and Clark, 16.

"simple decency": notes on privacy.

"all one thing": CS, vii.

"wangle the sprawling mess": "St. Augustine and the Bullfight," CEOW, 93.

"And then, Honey": KAP to PP, taped telephone conversation (TTC), 21 October 1975, PPC.

"He wanted a story": CS, 105.

"life's treasures" . . . "marrow": "Reflections on Willa Cather," CEOW, 34–35.

One: Indian Creek

General facts and details in this chapter have been gleaned from "The Porter Family History" and Porter family letters at MD; the Texas Bureau of Vital Statistics; deed and probate records in Guadalupe and Brown counties (TX); Harrison Porter's obituary ("H. B. Porter, 84"); the 1900 U.S. Census; tombstones in Lamar Churchyard at Indian Creek; and historical material, including maps, supplied to me by Walter Robertson.

"the sound of": KAP to Jordan Pecile, 9 March 1959, C.

"I was born": AN.

"I was bred": AN.

"somehow gay and spirited . . .": AN.

Coronal Institute: Pritchett; Stovall et al., 148–149; GPH to KAP, 8 April 1957.

"literary bent": KAP to HBP, 21 January 1933.

"Almost everyone approves": AJ to HBP, 31 December 1882.

"impish quality": Refugee, 6–7.

Caroline Jones's insanity: Gaver; HBP to KAP, n.d.; GPH to KAP, 26 February 1956.

"melancholia": KAP to GPH, 5–6 December 1955; IB Diary, 10 March 1971.

"the best man I ever knew": HBP to KAP, n.d.

Wedding of HBP and AJ: HBP to editor of *Houston Chronicle,* 18 April 1938.

Indian Creek in the 1880s: GPH to KAP, 14 December 1955, 26 February 1956.

Harry Ray Porter: born 2 February 1887; Ray was the maiden name of HBP's paternal grandmother.

Drought in Texas: HBP to KAP, 7 July 1929; Ferguson.

"invalid wife": HBP to KAP, 7 July 1929.

Family deaths at Indian Creek: John Jacob Myers to James F. Cahill, 26 September 1885; HBP to KAP and MAPH, 11 February 1934.

Death of Johnnie Porter: GPH to KAP, 26 February 1956.

"Do you want to see my little Tad": GPH to KAP, 14 December 1955.

William and Marinda Russell: Walter Robertson to DHU, 4, 12 February, 2 April 1998; 22 August 1999, DHUC; Laughlin, "Katherine Anne Porter's Brown County Connections"; William Russell was bondsman in HBP's 1893 petition for guardianship of his children after Alice's death in order to claim her share of John Jones's estate.

"Was she beautiful?": Refugee, 4.

"birth control": Refugee, 6.

"Five children in eight years": KAP to GPH, 5–6 December 1955.

"Dear Baby": KAP to MAPH, 24 January 1942.

"If your mother": Refugee, 4–5.

"She lost her life": AN.

"There was an auction": Willene Hendrick, "Indian Creek: A Sketch from Memory," Machann and Clark, 6.

"weeping like a soul in torment": GPH to KAP, 1 December 1955.

Death of Caroline Jones: 30 November 1914, "non compos mentis."

Caroline Jones's insanity: HBP to KAP, 7 July 1929.

Aunt Sallie Jones: GPH to KAP, 1 December 1955; KAP to GPH, 5–6 December 1955.

"mother's mother": KAP to GPH, 5–6 December 1955.

"jailor"; "fanged and clawed": KAP to GPH, 5–6 December 1955.

"the cult he built": AN.

"I wish you might have found": KAP to HBP, 22 March 1933.

Two: Catharine Ann Skaggs Porter

For the Skaggs family Kentucky history I have relied on works by Collins, Lancaster, and Pratt and the Family File at the Kentucky Library (K) as well as Warren County wills, marriage records, and census records of 1820, 1830, and 1840 and the slave census of 1850. I found significant information about Bowling Green in Baird et al. and Rodes. I drew facts of Texas history largely from Fehrenbach. Hays County, Texas, deed, probate, and tax records as well as the Texas Department of Vital Statistics confirmed additional legal details about the Porter family in this chapter as well as chapters 3 and 4.

"Grandmother was by nature": "Portrait: Old South," CEOW, 160.

"the real story": KAP to Cora Posey, 26 February 1956.

Family legends: HBP to KAP, 27 November 1932; Virginia Myers Cahill to KAP, 11 February 1939.

Abraham and Rhoda Skaggs: HBP to KAP, 27 November 1932; Gertrude Cahill Beitel to KAP, 11 January 1940.

"High-nosed old aristocrats": KAP to GPH, 6 December 1955.

"Merest surface ripples": "Portrait: Old South," CEOW, 161.

Asbury Porter and the Civil War: "Portrait: Old South," CEOW, 161.

"I am the grandchild of a lost war": "Portrait: Old South," CEOW, 160.

"social belles": Missy Myers Williams to GPH, 3 October 1936.

"sho 'nuff honest to God aristocrats": KAP to GPH, 8 April 1957.

"excellent advice": AJ to HBP, August twenty-something 1880.

CASP's purchase of Kyle house: Vliet, "Porter's House."

CASP and tenant farmers: GPH to KAP, 18 October 1961.

"The Cat Porter Branch": Stalling, 24.

"Aunt Cat was too exquisite": Gertrude Cahill Beitel to KAP, 14 January 1947.

"Lovely": Stalling, 25.

On CASP: "Grandmother," unpublished fragment; "Portrait: Old South," CEOW, 160–165.

"a devout lady": Stalling, 26.

"Skaggs pride": AN.

"great": AN.

"I was fed from birth": AN.

Three: The Fiery Furnace

"I have not much interest": "Reflections on Willa Cather," CEOW, 31.

"Our sainted grandmother": KAP to PP, 26 February 1975, TTC, PPC.

"the fiery furnace": "Reflections on Willa Cather," CEOW, 31.

The town of Kyle: Strom, 107; Stalling, 31–32.

"an old matriarch" . . . "became an elder child": AN.

"effective" . . . "systematically": AN.

"supernaturalism"; "wrath": AN.

"liberal-minded moralists": AN.

Kyle revival meeting: KAP, "Notes on the Texas I Remember, 102–103.

"Inappropriate conduct": "Portrait: Old South," CEOW, 164.

"She had vague stirrings": CS, 365

"children should be seen": Winston, I, 10

"Who are you?" AN.

"caused witches to be burned": Grumbach, I, 185.

"pale, gray-eyed" and "dyspeptic": AN.

"a long procession": AN.

"an accumulation of storied dust"; "tangled together": *Pale Horse, Pale Rider*, CS, 269.

"silence": manuscript of "Holiday" at HRC.

"If one pulled out": AN.

HBP reading Mark Twain to his children: GPH to KAP, 10 January 1959.

"pronounced 'Weeda'"; "trashy . . . grosser the better": AN.

"No one *acted* the part": Refugee, 15.

"A precocious child": AN.

"I remember you on a little foot stool": GPH to KAP, 25 July 1954.

"The yard would be full": Stalling, 35.

"awfully" and "ceremoniously": AN.

"A flame burned": ESJ to KAP, 13 April 1978.

"scenes": ESJ to KAP, 23 March 1937.

"Fairy": ESJ to KAP, 13 April 1978.

KAP's first attempt to write: Kunitz, 538.

"And so I put an old man there": Newquist, I, 105.

"they all laughed their heads off": AN.

"natural skeptic" . . . "She had no": AN.

"We saw and touched her gloves": AN.

"earthly hopes": HBP inscription on photograph of AJ.

"Since I was your bedfellow": GPH to KAP, 3 November 1962.

HBP's preference for gray: KAP to GPH, n.d. [after June 1928].

Beauty as curse: KAP to Margaret Marshall, 6 July 1970, Y.

"small voice of axiomatic morality": CS, 215.

"I remember all kinds of beautiful things": AN.

"hoverings of buzzards": "'Noon Wine': The Sources," CEOW, 470.

"It was late summer": "'Noon Wine': The Sources," CEOW, 474.

Ghost of little brother; awareness of mother's death: KAP, entry on questionnaire, 1971.

"unnaturally far-sighted . . . bearings": Kunitz, 538–539.

"such an ungrateful" . . . "something strange": AN.

CASP's last trip to Marfa: KAP, "Notes on the Texas I Remember," 104.

CASP's burial: "Mrs. C. A. Porter Buried [obituary]."

"Miranda could never find out": CS, 352.

"I do not believe that childhood"; "Remembering childhood": AN.

"forlorn" and "lonely": KAP to GPH, n.d. [mid-September 1919].

"So my horror and pain": KAP, marginalia in Grasset, 10.

"an awful child": KAP to Ione Funchess Porter, Spring, 1933.

"Alas myself?" That's me": KAP, marginalia in Grasset, 157.

"The extraordinary thing is": AN.

"the cheil among 'em": KAP to Jean Thompson, 18 July 1950, UCLA.

Four: Adolescence

"I was self-conscious": KAP, AN.

"Father was strange": AN.

"knew . . . though she could not say how": CS, 364–365.

Porter family departure from Kyle: KAP to PP, 12 July 1974, TTC, PPC.

"We were poor": AN.

Alpha Y. Porter: according to the San Antonio city directory, Alpha Porter was employed by Wells Fargo as a messenger.

Stay at the Thompson farm: KAP to GPH, 8 October 1956; "'Noon Wine': The Sources," CEOW, 467–482; Life, 74.

KAP's reading, 1902–1904: AN.

1890s depression: Green, 133.

Eugene Debs: Woodward; Green, 137–139.

"a tall, pale colored thin man": KAP to Kenneth Durant, 30 March 1936, NYPL.

Porters in San Antonio in 1903: KAP, AN.

St. Ann St. Ecole du Sacre Coeur: Reeves; KAP to PP, 26 February 1975, TTC, PPC; Schoettler, I, 175; Herbst, "A Year of Disgrace," 63; Sally Reeves to DHU, 23 May 2000, DHUC.

"immured": CS, 194.

"dull": KAP to PP, 26 February 1975, TTC, PPC.

"It doth make a difference": KAP, marginalia on title page of St. Augustine's *Confessions*. She improved on Pusey's translation, which was "it doth make a difference when a man's joy is" (VI:10).

"Nasty friend": KAP, marginalia in G. Hendrick (1965), 18.

"It was scant and fragmentary": Marshall, 473.

"Why don't you read this?": Thompson, I, 80.

The Thomas School: Allen, "The Thomas School."

Porter house near West End Lake: KAP, AN.

HBP's borrowing money for children's education: Life, 80.

"I know that we were at the end": AN.

KAP attendance at Thomas School: Whiteaker, I, 159; KAP, marginalia in Phelps and Deane, 15.

KAP reading William James: KAP, marginalia in Phelps and Deane, 8.

"flash the eyes up": Janeway, I, 70.

KAP's interest in boys: AN; Refugee, 31.

"Don't let me hear": AN.

KAP's first essay on women's rights: KAP, "Mr. George and the Woman Problem," SW, 35; no such essay has been discovered.

Thomas Gay: U.S. Census, 1900, Precinct 1, Menard County, Texas, 98.

"Lasca": McAlexander, 206.

Drama teacher elderly actress: KAP to PP, 12 July 1974, TTC, PPC.

Electric Park: Allen, "Flamboyant Park."

"Peck's Bad Boy": KAP to PP, 23 October 1974, TTC, PPC.

"owl service": PP to DHU, 25 July 1999, DHUC.

Victoria, Texas: Grimes.

Brontë Public Library: Charles Spurlin to DHU, 7 August 2000, DHUC.

"music, physical culture and dramatic reading": Life, 88.

"Dear little Sister": HPP to KAP, 6 December 1905.

KAP's quoting HPP's words back to him: PP to DHU, 21 August 2002, DHUC.

"When he saw me": Refugee, 32.

"The fact that I was": Refugee, 32.

Koontz family: Grimes; Life, 88–89.

John Koontz: Life, 89–91.

Five: Marriage

"My own experience": KAP, notes on *Old Mortality*, 24 June 1948.

"a mass of little frills": AN.

Wedding of KAP and John Koontz: *Victoria Advocate*, 27 June 1906; Life, 88–90.

"The trouble with me is": "Marriage Is Belonging," CEOW, 187.

HBP whipping Harry Ray: PP to DHU, 16 April 1997, telephone interview (TI).

"That makes you tight": KAP to PP, 12 July 1974, TTC, PPC.

"held out": KAP to IB, IB Diary.

"the wrong man": SOF, 29–30, 34–37, 61, 206–207, 444–445.

"I saw through my monster": KAP to PP, 20 June 1956.

"merciless revealer": "Marriage Is Belonging," CEOW, 188–189.

"good broad hips": AN.

KAP's fondness for Mary Lowry: Life, 96.

"douche with water": KAP to PP, 26 February 1975, TTC, PPC.

"one long orgy of reading . . . cold realism": KAP to CG, 24 September 1957, P.

Nietzsche and Freud "jags": KAP to GPH, 24 September 1957.

"I practiced writing": Whiteaker, I, 159.

J. H. Koontz and Koontz family: Grimes; Life, 91–93, 96–97; Houston City Directory, 1909–1911.

Laredo Bunton Humphris in Marfa: Humphris; Thompson, I, 266–267, 287, 300.

"consanguinity and affinity": AN.

Asbury Porter's arts-and-crafts-style house in Marfa: R. Smith.

J. H. Koontz's threats: KAP to IB, IB Diary.

KAP attitude toward Koontz family: Life, 94–95.

"Oh, that narrow-minded family": Whiteaker, I, 160.

"Between 1908 and 1910": KAP to GPH, 25 February 1931.

"Dear, why should you . . . other evils": HPP to KAP, 23 March 1909.

"Maria" and "Veronica": Life, 100; KAP, marginalia in G. Hendrick (1965), 18.

KAP "proselytized": Refugee, 21–23; GPH to KAP, 22 January 1962.

KAP fascinated by nuns of Gothic literature: ESJ to KAP, 3 May 1939.

"a vulgar handing over": "Marriage Is Belonging," CEOW, 189.

KAP in Corpus Christi, Texas: Corpus Christi City Directory, 1912; *Corpus Christi Caller Times*, 7 September 1941, 9 July 1950, 8 October 1960; KAP, marginalia in Phelps and Deane, 57.

KAP's discovery of Stein: KAP, "Reflections on Willa Cather," CEOW, 32.

"Texas: By the Gulf of Mexico": Poetry, 7, 9, 35, 55n.

Mary Alice Holloway: KAP to GPH, 4 July 1920.

"Tante Katherine": KAP to GPH, n.d. [mid-September 1919].

KAP's 1912–1913 surgery: Medical records.

"At the time . . . dangers": "Holiday," CS, 407.

Johnses' move to Corpus Christi: Johns, vol. 2, 93–97.

History of Schlemmer family: Johns, vol. 1.

Erna as straitlaced and conventional: Rita Johns to DHU, 29 October 1994, interview, Austin.

"preposterous marriage": KAP to PP, 20 June 1956.

"Marriage—that old fortress": Introduction to *What Price Marriage*, 11.

"one-man-one-woman-until-death": "Marriage Is Belonging," CEOW, 189.

Six: The Wild Dash from Texas

"She knew now why": on Miranda in *Old Mortality*, CS, 220.

"I got out of Texas": KAP to William Humphrey, 8 October 1950, HRC.

"wild dash": KAP to PP, 23 March 1963 ("Letters to a Nephew"), CEOW, 121.

"not thinking": KAP to CG, 6 January 1931, P.

"I had to leave Texas": Refugee, 39.

"girls whose fathers": KAP to GPH, 6 June 1933.

"lifted a hand": KAP to GPH, 10 October 1930.

KAP in Chicago: Dorsey, I, 144; Refugee, 40–42; Life, 105–106; Fernett.

"The city editor": KAP, "Essanay Studios," unpublished fragment.

The Song in the Dark: Reviewed in *Moving Picture World*, 6 June 1914, 1434.

From Out the Dregs: Reviewed in *Moving Picture World*, 13 June 1914, 1542.

"artistic experience": KAP, marginalia in Phelps and Deane, 54–57.

Breckenridge Porter: Breckenridge Porter Sr. to DHU, 28 January 1997, TI.

KAP in Gibsland: KAP to PP, 8 November 1951; KAP to PP, 27 March 1975, TTC, PPC.

KAP on lyceum circuit: KAP, marginalia in Child; KAP to PP, 27 March 1975, TTC, PPC.

"Oh when my apron strings was low . . . Honey": KAP to PP, 27 March 1975, TTC, PPC.

KAP in Dallas, 1915: Dallas City Directory, 1916; KAP to PP, 12 July 1974, TTC, PPC.

KAP divorce from J. H. Koontz: waiver signed by J. H. Koontz filed, 19 May 1915; Divorce judgment 19893-C, Dallas District Court, 68.

"It is famous": "Marriage Is Belonging," CEOW, 188.

KAP marriage to H. Otto Taskett: Marriage record 32423, Tarrant County, Texas; BP, notes on conversation with KAP.

"frigid as a cucumber": Refugee, 32.

KAP's employment at Neiman-Marcus: Dallas City Directory, 1916.

KAP's tuberculosis diagnosis: Medical records.

Background on tuberculosis: Rothman.

KAP at County Detention Home: KAP to Lon Tinkle, 19 August 1978.

KAP at J. B. McKnight Hospital: Jean Baldwin to DHU, 12 June 1997, TI; PP to DHU, 10 April 1994, DHUC; Havener.

"a fearful place": KAP to Lon Tinkle, 19 August 1978, C.

"a rather pleasant place" and "restless eyes": Refugee, 44.

"This is a land of hell-fire things": Life, 1.

Kitty and Garfield Crawford: Fort Worth Critic Archives, University of Texas at Arlington; Stalling, 29.

HPP adoption of Breckenridge [Townsend]: Breckenridge Porter Sr. to DHU, 28 January 1997, TI.

"Academy Oaks": KAP to Lon Tinkle, 19 August 1976, C; KAP to HBP, 21 December 1916; Shearer, I, 3.

"Darling Old Dear" . . . And then, Youngun": KAP to HBP, 21 December 1916.

"so you see": KAP to HBP, 21 December 1916.

KAP and Carl Von Pless marriage: Baton Rouge Parish, State of Louisiana, Conveyance Book 38, Entry 32, 78–80; "Von Pless [obituary]"

Von Pless Family: Genealogical records, Church of Jesus Christ of Latter Day Saints, Salt Lake City, Utah.

KAP on first three marriages: Winsten, I, 10; Allen, I, 165.

"a rich man": Allen, I, 165.

John Pleskett: KAP to IB, IB Diary.

"instant realization": Refugee, 32.

"I don't like to talk about it": Refugee, 32.

KAP in Fort Worth, 1917: Stalling, 71; Naylor; Life, 118–119; Kitty Barry Crawford to George Hendrick, 20 November 1961, DHUC.

"the exuberant young person": "Society Gossip of the Week," Fort Worth Critic, 15 September 1917.

Seven: Apocalypse in Denver

"In the old symbolism": KAP, marginalia in Deirdre C. Handy, "The Family Legend in the Stories of Katherine Anne Porter" (MA thesis, University of Oklahoma, 1953), HRC.

Jane Anderson: Myers, 292–309; 359–367, 369–372; Edwards; "Lady Haw-Haw."

"It is perhaps unforgiveable": Jane Anderson to KAP, 6 June 1918.

Cheyenne Mountain: KAP, daybooks 1920–1922; Life, 120–122; Kitty Barry Crawford to George Hendrick, 13 November 1961, DHUC; KAP, "St Augustine and the Bullfight," CEOW, 92.

KAP in Denver: Sexton; KAP to Margaret Harvey, 15 September 1964, C.

"the epitome of Southern femininity"; "the baby doll type": Sexton, 24.

"Some of us": KAP to CG, 10 June 1939, P.

"direly"; "the right attitude": KAP to CG, 10 June 1939, P.

KAP applying for Red Cross duty: Marcellus Foster to KAP, 7 October 1918; KAP to GPH, 5 March 1928.

Spanish influenza epidemic: Kolata.

Influenza in Denver: Rocky Mountain News, 2, 3, 13 October 1918; 21 January 1919.

KAP's influenza experience: Kitty Barry Crawford to George Hendrick, 13 November 1961, DHUC; KAP to HBP, 21 January 1933; GPH to KAP, 17 April 1947.

"a young boy": KAP to HBP, 21 January 1933.

"on the sidewalk" and "the plague": Kitty Barry Crawford to George Hendrick, 13 November 1961, DHUC.

"inexpressibly sad" . . . "Tell her Papa": HBP to GPH, 23 October 1918.

"What the Christians call": Thompson, I, 85.

"There it is": Pale Horse, Pale Rider, CS, 310.

"Virgin and Child Surrounded by Flowers and Fruit": WW to DHU, 20 April 1995, interview, College Park, MD.

"enthusiasm and gayety" . . . "asking a corner on no one": Lucille Clayton Robinson to KAP, 12 December 1930.

"in which the heroine": "Beauty Unadorned Attracts When War Hero Is Passed By," Rocky Mountain News, 4 May 1919, 11.

Park French: Life, 132; Lucille Clayton Robinson to KAP, 12 December 1930. French became a prominent Hollywood art director in the 1930s.

"from the skin out": Lucille Clayton Robinson to KAP, 12 December 1930.

Death of Mary Alice Holloway: Jules Von Hillendahl to KAP [July 1919]; KAP to GPH, 30 July 1919.

"shy soul" and "young years": KAP to GPH, 21 July 1924.

"newspaper woman": KAP, "You Are What You Read," 248.
"I never said anything": KAP to GPH, n.d. [mid-September 1919].
"I had to go to New York": Dorsey, I, 141.

Eight: Greenwich Village

For the history and background of Greenwich Village in the 1920s I have drawn on Aaron, Cowley, Dell, Humphrey, Edmiston and Cirino, and Morton.

"that after-war life": "My First Speech," CEOW, 436.
KAP arrival in New York, 1919: KAP, marginalia in Phelps and Deane, 79.
"Where is Greenwich Village?": Refugee, 48–49.
KAP at Arthur Kane Agency: KAP to GPH, n.d. [1919–1920].
"The wilder the place looks": KAP to Porter Family, 3 January 1920.
KAP meets Mexican musicians and artists: Refugee, 57.
"tinkling and rattling": KAP to Porter Family, 3 January 1920.
"Harold, a young editor": Refugee, 50–52.
"the city of opportunity": KAP to Porter Family, 3 January 1920.
"Mary Alice would love it": KAP to Porter Family [GPH], 3 January 1920.
Ballet Mexicana: KAP to Mitzi Berger Hamovitch, 1 July 1975, cited in Hamovitch, 133n.
"I seem to care for nothing but ballets": KAP to GPH, 13 February 1920.
"I love all of you": KAP to Porter Family, n.d. [1920].
"I wish you would say": KAP to GPH and HBP, 4 July 1920.
"a dozen things at once": KAP to GPH, n.d. [1920].
"What Happened to Hadji": Ramsay and McCullagh, 12–15.
"Nothing has happened in Spain": Refugee, 23.
"familiar country": KAP, "Why I Write about Mexico (a letter to the editor of The Century)," CEOW, 355.
KAP in Ann Arbor, Michigan: KAP to IB, IB Diary; KAP to Babette Deutsch, n.d. [after 4 September].
Mae Tiam Franking: Holly Franking, introduction to My Chinese Marriage.

Nine: Revolutionary Mexico

For history of the Mexican Revolution, I have drawn upon Dulles, Gruening, Hart, and Schmidt. For Katherine Anne Porter's activities in Mexico, I have relied heavily (in this chapter and the next) on KAP's own notes, her words to Hank Lopez (as reported in Refugee), and in particular the work of Thomas F. Walsh, not only his book Katherine Anne Porter and Mexico, but material in the Thomas F. Walsh Papers at MD, which includes Military Intelligence Files and transcriptions of interviews with Porter's friends, most notably, Mary Louis Doherty.

"I went running off": Thompson, I, 85.

"across the barren windswept desert": Refugee, 58.

"*Viva la Revolucion!*": Refugee, 59–60.

"ran smack into": Thompson, I, 86.

Thorberg and Roberto Haberman: MacKinnon and MacKinnon; M. R. Clark; Dulles; and "Roberto Haberman Dead at 79."

"Miss Katherine Anne Porter": *El Heraldo de México*, 9, 10 November 1920.

"they see the just thing": KAP, Mexico notes [1920].

"who for seven years": KAP, "The New Man and the New Order," UEP, 55.

"holders of the government reins": KAP to Porter Family, 31 December 1920.

"I expect to be connected": KAP to Porter Family, 31 December 1920.

KAP review of Ibañez book: UEP, 28–31.

"Long Live the Devil": Dulles, 121–122.

KAP's editorship of English-language section of *El Heraldo*: Mexico, 20.

"Why not story on impossibility": KAP, Mexico notes [1920].

"The non-politicals": Mexico notes [1920].

"Under a brilliant morning sky": "The Funeral of General Benjamin Hill," UEP, 43–44.

"She has that deadly female accuracy": UEP, 40; Mexico, 16.

"rich American oil magnates": KAP to Porter Family, 31 December 1920.

"Life here is a continual marvel": KAP to Porter Family, 31 December 1920.

"a welter": KAP to Porter Family, 31 December 1920.

Ten: Adventure and Betrayal in Mexico

"Adventure is something": KAP, "St. Augustine and the Bullfight," CEOW, 92.

"Most of her stories are about": EW in *Katherine Anne Porter: The Eye of Memory*.

"an enlightened human being": Mexico notes [1921].

Joseph Jerome Retinger: Retinger.

KAP and Gompers: Mexico, 26.

"there was enough political dynamite": "The Charmed Life," CEOW, 429.

Harry S. Bryan: "Assails Wilson Policy," Bryan's letter to the editor, *New York Times*, 30 September 1913; Walsh, 35–37.

"You have been told" Mexico notes [1921].

"Sidronio Mendez . . . plot": Mexico notes [1921].

"What's the life of one old man": Mexico notes [1921].

"especially in the pitiable trivialities": KAP to Paul Hanna, 19 April 1920, C.

"entertained"; "My friend R.": Mexico notes [1921].

Retinger's weak sexual drive: Life, 152.

"a complex and fascinating liar": Mexico notes [1921].

"intimate terms"; "personally known": copy of J. Edgar Hoover's MID report
    10058-0-79, 91 in Walsh Papers at MD; Mexico, 28.

Salomón de la Selva: White; Ureña.

Roberto Turnbull movie in Mexico: Refugee, 79–80.

"physical attributes" . . . "My God": KAP to IB, IB Diary.

Mexican Book: KAP notes from letter KAP to Freda Kirchwey, 8 September
    1921.

"Trinidad's Story": "Trinidad," UEP, 86–97.

KAP's 1921 pregnancy: Mary Doherty to Thomas F. Walsh (Mexico, 64); tran-
    scription of interview in Walsh Papers at MD.

"That house in Guanajuato": Mexico notes [1921].

"I am going": Mexico notes [1921].

"A woman is good for only one thing": Mexico notes [1921].

"Starvation is very hard": Mexico notes [1921].

"Five conspirators": Mexico notes [1921].

"I shall come back some day": Mexico notes [1921].

"Mexico . . . is a place": KAP to ES, 5 November 1955, C.

Eleven: Mexican Bounty

I am indebted primarily to Ruth M. Alvarez ("Katherine Anne Porter and
Mexican Art") for details of the popular arts exhibition in the United States.

"Here in Mexico": KAP, "The Mexican Trinity," CEOW, 401.

KAP in Fort Worth: Hicks; Naylor; Fort Worth Record, 19 November 1921;
    Kitty Barry Crawford to George Hendrick, 20 November 1921, DHUC.

"She always wore beautiful clothes": Life, 159.

"The Dove of Chapacalco": UEP, 107–108.

"I'll never get any writing done here": KAP to MAPH, n.d. [1921].

"GOVERNMENT APPOINTS": J. H. Retinger to KAP, 24 March 1922.

J. Alfred Prufrock [ring-tailed monkey]: Kitty Barry Crawford to George
    Hendrick, 13 November 1961, DHUC.

I read "in an immense hall": KAP to George Sill Leonard, UEP, 132.

"point of view"; "sympathies": Outline of Mexican Popular Arts and Crafts,
    UEP, 138.

"I was struck": KAP to George Sill Leonard, in Leonard, UEP, 133.

"little Cati": Refugee, 63–64.

"something about the nuns": Mexico notes [1922].

U.S. Exhibit of Mexican Popular Arts: In addition to Alvarez, also Roberto Turnbull to KAP, 10 October 1922; Louis Bouchee to KAP, 23 August 1922; KAP to HBP, 27 July 1922; Miguel Covarrubias to KAP, 4 October 1922; Xavier Guerrero to KAP, 27 January 1923.

"bitter as gaul": Lopez, I, 126–127.

"One evening": Newquist, I, 107–108.

William Niven: Wicks and Harrison.

Charles Sumner Williams: Life, 168, 172, 202; Charles Sumner Williams to KAP, n.d. [1922].

"wild man of Mexican art": KAP to Robert McAlmon, 5 February 1934, Y.

"really gorgeous record": Mexico notes [1922–1923].

"impish understanding"; "metaphysics": KAP, "Ay, Que Chamaco," SW, 40–41.

Carleton Beals: Britton; Beals.

Rivera's murals: Charlot; Marnham; Wolfe.

"Diego's monkeys"; "whitewash": Marnham, 165–166.

"the most illustrious": "The Martyr," CS.

"She-devil": "The Martyr," CS, 34.

"little tirade": KAP, notes on CS.

"The Lovely Legend": UEP, 204–217.

"endless tales": "The Lovely Legend," UEP, 205.

"I dedicate this story": KAP, notes on fragment of "The Lovely Legend."

"This Transfusion": Poetry, 71.

"Instead . . . eternal verities": "The Funeral of General Benjamin Hill," UEP, 196–197.

Twelve: Friends and Lovers in New York and Connecticut

"I have suffered": KAP to GPH, 21 July 1924.

KAP regarding Sumner Williams: KAP, marginalia on Sumner Williams to KAP, 25 June, 5 July, 25 October 1923.

Francisco Aguilera: "Francisco Aguilera Dies"; "Francisco Aguilera: Specialist in Hispanic Culture."

"unconditionally": Francisco Aguilera to KAP, n.d. [late fall 1923].

"enchanted medieval castle"; "paralyzed": Francisco Aguilera to KAP, n.d. [1924].

Aguilera credited with giving KAP name for Miranda: KAP to ES, Ash Wednesday 1958, C.

"You should come here": KAP to Francisco Aguilera, 1 March 1924, C.

"Write me": Francisco Aguilera to KAP, 31 March 1924.

"night of happiness": Alvaro Hinojosa to KAP, 22 April 1924.

"Señora Doña Catalina Bien-Querida": KAP to Francisco Aguilera, n.d. [late spring 1924], C.

"I love my birthday": KAP to Genevieve Taggard, 10 May 1924, NYPL.

KAP and Ignacius McGuire: David Locher to DHU, 6 June 1926; 1958 correspondence between KAP and McGuire.

"Miranda": KAP to Genevieve Taggard, 14 November 1924, NYPL.

"Miranda Aguilera": KAP marginalia on Francisco Aguilera to KAP, 3 November 1924.

"dancing": "Virgin Violeta," CS, 25.

"too long germinating": KAP to Genevieve Taggard, 31 October 1924, NYPL.

"watchdog"; "a 38 Colt revolver": KAP to Genevieve Taggard, 31 October 1924, NYPL.

"I feel sometimes": KAP to GPH, 21 July 1924.

"Dear darlin'": KAP to Genevieve Taggard, 14 November 1924, NYPL.

"I did think of killing myself": KAP to IB, telephone conversation, 2 March 1971, IB Diary.

"Holiday": drafts at HRC.

"Jedsie Darling—You're not to worry": KAP to Genevieve Taggard, 28 November 1924, NYPL.

"I should be happy to come up for Christmas": KAP to Genevieve Taggard, 18 December 1924, NYPL.

"Winter Burial": CEOW, 488; Poetry, 27, 82.

"November in Windham": CEOW, 490; Poetry, 81.

Malcolm Cowley: Cowley; Kempf.

Allen Tate and Caroline Gordon: Makowsky.

Josephine Herbst: Langer, *Josephine Herbst*.

"the talkingest women in New York": Langer, *Josephine Herbst*, 89.

Ernest Stock: JH, "A Year of Disgrace," in *The Starched Blue Sky of Spain*; Marlor, 523; Jewel; "Art Exhibitions of the Week."

"All that fullness of green": KAP to Genevieve Taggard, 3 June 1926, NYPL.

"As he ran around in his shorts" . . . "Deadly Ernest": JH, "A Year of Disgrace," in *The Starched Blue Sky of Spain*, 63.

"vanished with the mist": JH, "A Year of Disgrace," in *The Starched Blue Sky of Spain*, 65.

KAP's surgery in 1926: Medical records, Georgetown University Hospital.

"It was seven years": AN [1926–1927].

Thirteen: Boston and Salem

"I can't think": KAP to GPH, 5 March 1928.

"One of the important": N-EW, 4.

"caused witches to be burned": Grumbach, I, 185.

"unrelieved horror and fascination": Refugee, 116–117.

"portentously, as if pronouncing": N-EW, 54.

"where Voodoo doctors": KAP to Isidor Schneider, n.d. [1927], C.

"Calvinism"; "petty fundamentalists": KAP to GPH, n.d. [1927].

"don't really mind": CS, 51.

"Transplantation spoiled": AN [1927].

"a lady": Newquist, I, 109.

"burn this": KAP to JH, 14 May 1927, Y.

"aggressive writer": KAP to Kenneth Burke, 6 October 1930, Penn State.

"loll around": KAP to GPH and HBP, n.d. [winter 1927–1928].

"developed into a famous cook": KAP to GPH and HBP, n.d. [winter 1927–
    1928].

"I suppose my interest": KAP to HBP, 12 February 1928.

"Will write you soon again": William Doyle to KAP, 5 April 1928.

"She could not remember": "The Jilting of Granny Weatherall," CS, 89.

Fourteen: Escape to Bermuda

"I am, let me tell you": KAP to GPH and HBP, 16 June 1929.

William Doyle's *Carnival*: KAP to JH, 21 May 1929, Y.

"She oughta have nice things": CS, 65.

Matthew Josephson: Shi; MJ, *Life Among the Surrealists.*

"intelligence": MJ, unpublished memoir, Y.

"What does this mean?": Life, 202.

"First Episode": Poetry, 83–84.

"candour": KAP to MJ, 16 March 1929, Y.

"for the honour of the line": KAP to MJ, 17 March 1929, Y.

"the plan": KAP to Becky Crawford, 11 March 1929.

"All the passengers": KAP to Becky Crawford, 11 March 1929.

"I lie here": KAP to MJ, 19 March 1929, Y.

"I feel now like a Marathon runner": KAP to Becky Crawford, 1 May 1929.

"Once more": Horace Liveright to KAP, 14 June 1929; qtd. in Gilmer, 190.

"I wish Daddy": KAP to HBP, 16 June 1929.

"Night Blooming Cereus" and "West Indian Island": Poetry, 30–33, 166–168.

"familiar country": Poetry, 88.

"Yudico's story": KAP to Richard Blackmur, 29 November 1929; Hamovitch, 127–128.

"I was out on the corner": Thompson, I, 95.

"In that glimpse": KAP, "Why She Selected 'Flowering Judas,'" in *This Is My Best*, ed. Burnett, 539.

"murderer": CS, 102.

Fifteen: Relinquishing Mexico

Background and historical information is drawn from Wolfe, Dulles, Walsh (Mexico), and interviews in Mexico City with Winifred Hill, Paul O'Higgins, Juan O'Gorman, Edgar Skidmore, and Kathryn Blair.

"I don't feel strange": KAP to Kenneth Burke, 6 October 1930, Letters, 24.

"With the band playing": KAP to JH, 28 April 1930, Letters, 19–20.

"It is not death": KAP to GPH, 1 April 1930, Letters, 19.

"to keep out drunken Indians": Dorothy Day to CG, 31 May 1930, P.

"She was feeling her age": SOF, 247.

"where so much had happened"; "might have been a mistake": KAP to Delafield Day Spiers, 7 June 1930.

"It is just precisely": KAP to GPH, 30 May 1930, Letters, 21.

"It is a dramatic moment": Dawson.

"lovely reviews": KAP to GPH, 10 January 1931.

"This is all very well": KAP to Kenneth Burke, 10 October 1930, Penn State.

"all the other God-awful mediocrities": notes from letter KAP to Ernestine Evans, 3 October 1930.

"one of the main springs" . . . "that all art": Mexico notes [1930–1931].

"pathological cases": notes from letter KAP to CG, 13 August 1930.

"run from life": KAP to JH and John Herrmann, 20 February 1931, C.

"limp-haired boys"; "sleeping with his mozo": notes from letter KAP to Ernestine Evans, 3 October 1930.

"horrible, hopeless" . . . "but I know well": KAP to GPH, 10 October 1930.

"Plant a cape jessamine": KAP to CG, 13 August 1930, P.

"There a cabin on the river": KAP to CG, 28 January 1931, P.

"I have a new idea of hell": KAP to CG, 28 January 1931, P.

"twelve or so interconnected": KAP to HBP, 24 February 1931.

"with my old and wonderful friend": Crane, *Letters*, 367.

"Katherine Anne, you're a whore": Crane, *Letters*, 377.

"I have borne to the limit": KAP to Hart Crane, 22 June 1931, Letters, 45–46.

Visit to the Hacienda Tetlapayac: KAP to Malcolm Cowley, 22 July 1931, N.

"house-wrecking": KAP to CG, 27 August–24 September 1931, Letters, 46.

"I leave a troubled land": KAP to HBP, 25 August 1931.

Sixteen: The German Interval

"being on that ship": Ruoff, I, 67.

"I felt the very earth": KAP to SL, 2 May 1956, Letters, 504.

"to remember" . . . "Herr Doktors": KAP to CG, 28 August–24 September, Letters, 46.

"half of us" . . . "a very short short-story": KAP to CG, 28 August–24 September, Letters, 46–60.

"Praise God" . . . "but I don't know": KAP to CG, 28 August–24 September, Letters, 59.

"Why must you touch things": KAP, notes in response to essay by Kay Boyle on "The Leaning Tower."

"Bouquet for October": Poetry, 93–94.

"altogether sane" . . . "bawling like a calf": KAP to EDP, 3 November 1931.

"a set of pinkish wool": KAP to EDP, 3–5 November 1931.

Herbert Kline: "Kline, Herbert," Contemporary Authors; "Herbert Kline [obituary]," New York Times; "Herbert Kline," International Directory of Films and Filmmakers.

"You'll be pleased to learn": KAP to EDP, 18 November 1931.

"Went out with some comrades": KAP to Peggy Cowley, 9 December 1931, N.

Sigrid Schultz: Life, 260–262.

"morbidly anxious": Refugee, 175.

Hermann Göring: Manville and Fraenkel; Mosley; Overy.

"smack, smack": KAP to JH, 16 October 1933, C.

"We've got to restore": Dolan, I, 179.

"the only kind of woman" . . . "was probably": Refugee, 181.

"Why, hell yes": Refugee, 186.

"Mr. Von Gehring": 12:34 PM, 17 November 1931.

"like drunken bumble bees": KAP to Peggy Cowley, 9 December 1931, N.

"marching, almost walking": KAP, Berlin notes [1931–1932].

"I'm going to get up on a soap box"; "I'm going to fight for Russia"; "the famous Russian fanaticism": KAP to Peggy Cowley, 9 December 1931, N.

"Confused as the devil": KAP to EDP, 23 January 1932.

Seventeen: Paris, Madrid, Basel

"I have a feeling of continuity": KAP to HBP, 8 March 1932, Letters, 79.

"If I went to Paris": KAP to EDP, 1 December 1931.

"For me, this is such a good thing": KAP to GPH, 30 January 1932.

"Why are not you": KAP to William Harlan Hale, 14 February 1932, C.

"and drying up my tears": KAP to CG and AT, 6–13 March 1932, Letters, 73.

"Well, Miss Caroline": KAP to CG and AT, 6–13 March 1932, Letters, 73.

"after all these centuries" . . . "and I'll never live": KAP to HPP, 8 March 1932.

Harrison of Paris: Ford.

"One day it showers": KAP to Janice Biala, 11 April 1932, CU.

"Let's continue to be": KAP to William Harlan Hale, 11 May 1932, C.

"1932—or is it 1400?": KAP to EDP, 3 November 1932.

KAP's French Song Book: Poetry, 95–149.

William Harlan Hale: "William Hale, 63, an Editor, Dead."

"bill of particulars": KAP to William Harlan Hale, 8 July 1932, C.

"Go burn a candle": KAP to EDP, 28 November 1932.

"muggy piety" . . . "And a string of emeralds": KAP to EDP, 28 November 1932.

"personal scraps": KAP to EDP, 30 November 1932.

Eighteen: Paris

"I never saw such rainbows": Mrs. Treadwell, SOF, 209.

"well-known economic determinism": KAP to Peggy Cowley, 30 January 1933, N.

"arrangement": KAP to HBP, 2 March 1933, Letters, 92.

"I'm very settled": KAP to Robert McAlmon, 19 April 1933, Letters, 95.

"made their debut": KAP to Janice Biala, 9 June 1933, CU.

"Does Madame wish": Feeley; KAP to IB, IB Diary.

"Just keeping the house clean": KAP to Janice Biala, 26 June 1933, CU.

Barbara Harrison at Davos: Porhorilenko and Crump, 93.

"Katherine Anne Porter": "A Little Incident on the Rue de l'Odéon," CEOW, 105–106.

"too dull to be saleable": Raymond Everitt to KAP, 26 September 1933.

"fraternized like a house afire": KAP to Janice Biala, 15 November 1933, CU.

"battlefields": KAP to Porter Family, 22 March 1934.

"What a feller!": KAP to Janice Biala, 26 June 1933, CU.

"gloomily drinking by himself"; "very poor health": Pohorilenko and Crump, 93.

"rudeness and hatred and quarreling": KAP to EDP, 21 April 1934.

"shockingly cruel things"; "It terrifies me": KAP to EDP, 2 May 1934.

"rough edges": EDP to KAP, 11 May 1934.

"He had arms and legs": JH, "Man of Steel," in *The Starched Blue Sky of Spain*, 35.

"Myself, I never used anybody": KAP to JH, 3 August 1934, Letters, 109–110.

"I am overcome by that acedia": KAP to Robert McAlmon, 12 November 1934, Y.

"blupblupblup": KAP to CG, 19 December 1935, P.

"a smash-up": KAP to CG, 12 July 1935, P.

"the secret": Langer, *Josephine Herbst*, 127.

"exactly"; "physical comfort": Langer, *Josephine Herbst*, 195.

"You might try": EDP to KAP, n.d. [July 1935].

"women . . . so often lose": SOF, 247.

"God knows I shall be glad": KAP to JH, 23 October 1935, Y.

"You will notice": KAP to JH, 7 November 1936, Y.

"To give a true testimony": KAP, "My First Speech," CEOW, 433; original inscribed to Sylvia Beach in Beach Papers, P.

"rabbit stew": Beach, 207.

Nineteen: Going Home

"so my time": KAP, "'Noon Wine': The Sources," CEOW, 470.

"Jumbo": PP to DHU, 29 October 1994, interview, Austin.

"Well, what are you": KAP to EDP, 20 April 1936.

"It is there": KAP to EDP [May 1936].

"This time of year": KAP, summer 1936 journal; Poetry, 40, 41–43, 155, 170–172.

George Melton Jones at Ebony: Laughlin, "KAP's Brown County Connections."

"full tilt": KAP to EDP, 20 April 1936.

"it turned into a mud-lark": KAP to JH, 7 November 1936, Y.

"felt his arms": CS, 255–256.

"What is the truth?": CS, 222.

"She lives again": CS, 181.

"an old cemetery": KAP to MW, 6 December 1936, Letters, 147.

"little Miranda": ESJ to KAP, 3 May 1939.

"the assemblage of you stories": HBP to KAP, n.d. [mid-December 1936].

"Now let me": KAP to MAPH and Jules Hillendahl, 29 January 1937.

"Dinner last night": Wescott, *Continual Lessons*, 3.

"the littlest Porter girl" . . . "But I had": KAP to JH, 15 August 1937, Letters, 149.

KAP at Benfolly: CG to Sally Wood, 16 October 1937, Wood, Letters, 214.

"darling": CB to DHU, 22 December 1993, interview, New Haven.

"deluge": KAP to JH, 22 October 1937, Y.

"exhausted and cross": KAP to CG, 20 September 1937, P.

"My darling": KAP to ARE, 13 November 1937, C.

"olive and tan": CS, 278.

"Last time I saw": KAP to ARE, 18 October 1940, C.

"perhaps we'll have" . . . "the whole thing": KAP to ARE, 13–14 February 1938, C.

"My entire mind": KAP to ARE, 21 January 1938, C.

"something like the flu": KAP to ARE, 24 March 1938, C.

"it is astonishing": KAP to ARE, 13 February 1938, C.

". . . a small, silver-haired woman": PP, "Remembering Aunt Katherine," in Machann and Clark, 25–26.

"totally enchanted": PP, "Remembering Aunt Katherine," in Machann and Clark, 26.

"What was an alligator"; "If you feel you must": ARE to KAP, 14 February 1938.

"Bless you for your goodness": KAP to EDP, 11 January 1938.

"Let's talk about": KAP to ARE, 22 February 1938.

"In the good Catholic": KAP to CG, 11 April 1938, P.

"traumatic": PP to DHU, 8 December 1999, DHUC.

"Now you are safely": KAP to George Platt Lynes, 12 May 1938, Letters, 163.

Twenty: Transition from Marriage to Independence

"This is not the end": KAP to ARE, 18 June 1940, C.

"old bull-headed bore": KAP to PP, 23–24 March 1963, CEOW, 119.

"heavily on Henry James": KAP to ARE, 17 July 1938, C.

"No, I am sorry" . . . "Gret God": KAP to ARE, 25 July 1938, C.

"first choice": "Away from Near-War Consciousness," *Times Literary Supplement* (London), 27 May 1939, 311.

"a drawing card": KAP to ARE, 12 May 1939, C.

"Where shall I" . . . "I say it again": KAP to ARE, 15 May 1939, C.

"confiding": CB to DHU, 22 December 1993, interview, New Haven.

"She was just": Matthew Bruccoli to DHU, 31 March 1996, interview, Las Vegas.

"that quiet, tranquil": "Eudora Welty and *A Curtain of Green*," CEOW, 284.

"tongue-tied"; "an abstract memory": EW to DHU, 23 February 1994, interview, Jackson, MS.

"decayed Southern grandeur"; "friends for life": KAP to GW, 16 July 1939, Letters, 69–70.

"man of the world"; "rough diamond note": KAP to George Platt Lynes, 28 July 1938, Letters, 172.

"talking all the time": Delmore Schwartz to Mark Van Doren, 29 January 1940; qtd. in Atlas, 159.

"There is at the heart": "Notes on a Criticism of Thomas Hardy," CEOW, 7.

"Myself I think" . . . "At the risk": KAP to Lodwick Hartley, 4 May 1940,
    Letters, 176–178.
Yaddo: KAP, "Yaddo that Rhymes with Shadow," unpublished fragment;
    Shaynerson; Bongartz.
"Maybe I could": KAP to ARE, 4 June 1940, C.
"tiresome to what": KAP to ARE, 29 August 1940, C.
"I just sat"; "Prospects, which": KAP to CG, 19 November 1940, P.
"somehow enough": KAP to ARE, 7 January 1941, Letters, 186.
"probably not": KAP to Elizabeth Ames, 27 December 1940, Letters, 184.
"Oh how glad": KAP to ARE, 7 January 1941, C.

Twenty-one: "Ah, the House . . . the House"

My attempts to determine Katherine Anne's role, if any, in the investigation
of Josephine Herbst began in 1995 with my request under the Freedom of
Information and Privacy Act for Katherine Anne Porter's entire FBI file and
continued through 2000. With the intervention of Senator Harry Reid
(Nevada), I received the nine-page file, which includes three pages of summary and copies of news articles that mention her name in association with
Communist organizations or events, such as the Sacco-Vanzetti protest.
There is no evidence in the report of her participation in the Herbst investigation, and cross-reference numbers, attached to blacked-out, classified passages, are not links to Herbst's file. I persistently appealed, asking that
classified passages be declassified and that any participation by Katherine
Anne Porter in the Josephine Herbst investigation be verified since both
women are long dead. Friends in New York and South Caroline prevailed
upon Senator Alfonso D'Amato and Senator Strom Thurman to request the
same. The requests were consistently denied under exemption (b) (1), which
states that the passage in question "applies to material which is properly classified pursuant to an Executive order in the interest of national defense or foreign policy." Finally, after several appeals, two passages were declassified:

> A confidential informant who has furnished reliable informa-
> tion in the past advised that one Katherine Anne Porter was a
> sponsor of the Second Congress of American Writers held in New
> York City on June 4, 5, 6, 1937, under the auspices of the League
> of American Writers. (reference number 100-7322-23, p. 9)
>
> During December, 1945, a confidential informant who has
> furnished reliable information in the past reported that a Miss
> Katherine Anne Porter was a member of the Committee of

Women, National Council of American-Soviet Friendship. (reference number 100-146964-744, p. 67)

After I had sought still more information, I received in April of 2000 an unexpected letter from Kathryn I. Dyer, Information and Privacy Coordinator for the Central Intelligence Agency (CIA). She informed me that my appeal had been referred to her since it concerned CIA material. She denied my request not only by exemption (b) (1) but also (b) (3): "applies to the Director's statutory obligations to protect from disclosure intelligence sources and methods, as well as the organization, functions, names, official titles, salaries or numbers of personnel employed by the Agency, in accord with the National Security Act of 1947 and the CIA Act of 1949, respectively."

Finally, in response to my request, channeled through the Justice Department of the United States, to the Salt Lake City office of the FBI, for tapes, transcripts, or any other raw material from the 12 May 1942 FBI interview in Reno, Nevada, with Katherine Anne Porter, I received a letter saying no such material existed.

"Ah, the house": KAP to ARE, 25 February 1941, Letters, 193.
"the truth is": KAP to GW, 23 January 1941, Letters, 190.
"When that dope Goering": KAP to Donald Elder, 28 February 1942, Letters, 228.
"I do so like": KAP to ARE, 29 January 1941, Letters, 192.
"I have looked": KAP to GW, 23 January 1941, Letters, 191.
"And here I am": KAP to ARE, 29 January 1941, Letters, 192–193.
"regrets for not": KAP to JH, 16 February 1941, Y.
"Please, Katherine Anne"; "But I had": Carr, 155–156.
"You may read": EW, "My Introduction to Katherine Anne Porter," 22–24.
"from Piaf": EW, "My Introduction to Katherine Anne Porter," 22.
EW and KAP at Yaddo: EW, "My Introduction to Katherine Anne Porter,"
    and EW, remarks in Katherine Anne Porter: The Eye of Memory, a film.
"When I was your age": KAP to PP, 24 July 1941, Letters, 203–206.
"All her generosity": EW, "My Introduction to Katherine Anne Porter," 23–24.
Death of HBP: "H. B. Porter, 84, Last Survivor of Travis Rifles, Dies."
"After all the rage": KAP to HPP and GPH, 24 January 1942, unpublished
    letter at MD.
"I visited my house": KAP to John Peale Bishop, 22 February 1942, P.
"let the Gestapo": KAP to Donald Elder, 28 February 1942, Letters, 229.
Judge George A. Bartlett: "Reno Divorce Judge," "Judge Bartlett Dead,"
    Bartlett Papers at the University of Nevada, Reno.
"gambling hells": KAP to EAB, 3 June 1942, Y.

"to determine": Langer, *Josephine Herbst*, 248–249.

"has a violent temper": Langer, *Josephine Herbst*, 251–254.

"Informant I": Langer, *Josephine Herbst*, 355–356.

"a full-scale": Langer, *Josephine Herbst*, 249–251.

"[name excised]": Langer, *Josephine Herbst*, 355.

"tracked . . . down": KAP to Donald Elder, 14 June 1942, Letters, 240.

"I was really happy": KAP to Donald Elder, 14 June 1942, Letters, 240.

"FBI man"; "young": KAP to Donald Elder, 14 June 1942, Letters, 240.

"A confidential informant": KAP's FBI file, copy, DHUC.

"very dark place": KAP to EAB, 3 June 1942, Y.

"unwedding ceremony": KAP to George A. Bartlett, 26 June 1942, Bartlett Papers, University of Nevada, Reno.

"Which of us": KAP to EAB, 22 June 1942, Y.

"I want to know": KAP, marginalia in Woolf, 365.

"duty": KAP to PP, 27 March 1975, TTC.

"I'll tell you": KAP to PP, 30 September 1972, TTC.

"which I love"; "Can you": KAP to George A. Bartlett, 26 June 1942, Bartlett Papers, University of Nevada, Reno.

"pretty marvelous": KAP to EAB, 22 June 1942, Y.

"Have you ever" . . . "cold as": Refugee, 253.

"I was only half joking": KAP to Alfred Kinsey, qtd in Pomeroy, 193.

"Dear Katherine Anne"; "very considerable": Alfred Kinsey to KAP, qtd. in Pomeroy, 193.

"Good speed": Elizabeth Ames to KAP, 22 July 1942.

Twenty-two: South Hill and Washington, D.C.

"I make plans": KAP, daybooks, n.d. [1943].

"To see the new": KAP, South Hill Book, 12 September 1942.

"murderous cold"; "Well, of course": KAP to CG, 15 February 1943, P.

"just throwing a suitcase": KAP to CB and EAB, 23 September 1943, Y.

"People ask me": JH to KAP, 27 November [1943], Y.

"anyone in power": KAP to AT, 15 January 1944, P.

"KAP has pure white hair": Winslow, 43–44.

"madly in love": Winslow, 60.

"heretic": Winslow, 115–116.

"thank goodness": Winslow, 53.

Charles Shannon affair: KAP, chronology of Shannon affair.

"I have a charming": KAP to Barbara Wescott, 23 July 1944, Letters, 284–285.

"bad shape": Winslow, 73.

"wonderful": KAP to GPH, 9 October 1944.

"so far as I was able": KAP, chronology of Shannon affair.

"Deweyites and Nazis": KAP to JH, 14 October 1944, Y.

"a good, sound": KAP to GPH, 9 October 1944.

" I know about": KAP to JH, 14 October 1944, Y.

"get a little nest egg": KAP to GPH, 23 December 1944.

Twenty-three: California

"I remember": KAP to HBP, n.d. [1936].

"I have a prejudice": KAP to HBP, n.d. [1936].

"full of energy"; "falsified and romanticized": KAP to AT, 8 February 1945, P.

"amiable" . . . "Who ever said": KAP to Herbert Schaumann, 16 March 1945.

"Not a woman": KAP to CG, 6 October 1945, P.

"war work" . . . "that made possible": "They Lived with an Enemy in the House," SW, 124–125.

"I was reading again": KAP to Herbert Schaumann, n.d., fragment [ca. November 1945].

"Your little": KAP to Herbert Schaumann, 9 February 1946.

"incoherent babble": PP to DHU, 16 January 2001, DHUC.

"to rest": PP to DHU, 17 January 2002, DHUC.

"heavenly reunion" . . . "We look": KAP to MW, 13 June 1946, Letters, 325.

"I am already": KAP to ARE, 9 April 1946, Letters, 319.

"talking about everything": KAP to Herbert Schaumann, 5 April 1946.

"Who in the hell": PP, "Gertrude Stein and All That," unpublished paper, PPC.

Gertrude Stein and KAP: "Ole Woman River," CEOW, 272.

"The bitch": Christopher Blake to DHU, 9 May 2002, DHUC.

"Love me": KAP to Herbert Schaumann, 14 September 1946.

"My God": KAP to Russel Lynes, 27 October 1947, Y.

"I doubt the veracity": KAP to Lincoln Kirstein, 19 October 1933, in Hamovitch, 133.

"Much as I like": JH to KAP, 8 January [1948].

"Is there any relevance": JH, "Miss Porter and Miss Stein."

"I would have appreciated": JH to KAP, 8 January [1948].

"grandmotherly quality": Langer, *Josephine Herbst*, 262.

"I thought your picture": JH to KAP, 4 September 1947.

"it makes me feel": KAP to Wallace Stegner, 14 August 1948.

"ungracious": Richard Scowcroft to DHU, 9 July 1995, TI.

"Teep": KAP to MW, 6 July 1949, Letters, 375.

"costume": Janet Lewis Winters to DHU, 15 July 1994, interview, Palo Alto.

"Pound, in Mental Clinic"; "ruthless mockery": Qtd. in McGuire, 114–115.
"I am glad": KAP, "A Letter to the Editor of the Saturday Review," CEOW, 212.
"sadness and longing": Herbert Steiner to DHU, 10 July 2000, TI.

Twenty-four: New York City and France

"I know well": KAP to GPH, 17 December 1949.
"ghastly": KAP to Donald Brace, 12 September 1949, C.
"look well": KAP to AHH, 14 March 1949.
"as if she": Brinnin, 20.
"Mr. Goyen": "This Strange, Old World," SW, 131–132.
"great work"; "guiding principle": Goyen, 159.
"Please don't": William Goyen to KAP, 9 February 1951.
"lover or near-lover": Spender's afterward in Goyen, 412–413.
"What are you": EW to DHU, 28 February 1994, interview, Jackson, MS.
"my darling"; "my love"; "I hope": KAP to William Goyen, 14 July 1951.
"fine": KAP to EW, 15 April 1952, C.
CCF: Saunders.
"God knows": KAP to PP, 6 June 1952.
"Over and over": KAP to William Goyen, 11 June 1952, C.
"this delegation": KAP, "Opening Speech at the Paris Conference," CEOW, 216–219.
"furious": Blotner, Faulkner, 2:1422.
"a wonderful" . . . "he looked": KAP to PP, 6 June 1952.
"Already I am": KAP to William Goyen, 11 June 1952, HRC.
"All this whole collection": KAP to Catherine Carver, 3 June 1952, C.
"problems of existence": KAP to Eugene Reynal, 4 January 1952, C.
"I pulled myself": KAP to Catherine Carver, 21 June 1952, C.
"too special to be read": James Brown to KAP, 19 June 1952.
"I am still": KAP to James Brown, 24 June 1952, C.
"I did not know": KAP to James Brown, 12 July 1952, C.
"My mind is": KAP to Catherine Carver, 12 July 1952, C.
"tone": KAP to Catherine Carver, 27 July 1952, C.
"It had begun": KAP to Donald Brace, 27 July 1952, C.

Twenty-five: Michigan and Belgium

"My what a fuss": KAP to Andrew Lytle, 30 August 1933, Letters, 442.
"Reading these": Carlos Baker, "A Happy Harvest," New York Times Book Review, 1 November 1954, 4.
"For Ezra Pound": the inscribed book is in the Pound collection at Yale.

"led": KAP to Ezra Pound, 21 October 1952, Letters, 437–438.

"the monster": KAP, marginalia in Beauvoir, 345.

"Where he was": KAP to Thomas Carter, 9 March 1953, Washington and Lee Library.

"Although of an age": McGrory, I, 28.

"maul": McGrory, I, 29.

"permanent feature": "Poetry of Our Times," Variety, 29 April 1953, 39.

"Look who's landed": KAP to Lily Cahill, 4 May 1953.

KAP at the University of Michigan: Life, 389–391, 396; David Locher to DHU, 1990–2004; correspondence in KAP Papers and the University of Michigan between KAP and faculty and administrators at Michigan and between KAP and Mary Cooley.

"fervents": Life, 395.

"You're not Katherine Anne Porter": Rockwell.

"in her presence": David Locher to DHU, 12 August 1995, DHUC.

"pack up": KAP to CB and EAB, 6 March 1954, Y.

"about the size": KAP to MW, 1 April 1954, Letters, 455–456.

"Oh, I'm so sorry": David Locher to DHU, 21 November 1996, TI.

"SLOW DOWN!": KAP to Monroe Wheeler, 1 April 1954, Letters, 455–458.

"I am really": KAP to GW, 23 October 1954, Letters, 460.

"smilingly with": "A Defense of Circe," CEOW, 135.

"I am melancholy": KAP to GW, 23 October 1954, Letters, 461.

"I'm glad": KAP to GW, 27 December 1954, Letters, 469.

Twenty-six: *Ship of Fools*

"It is customary": KAP to RPW, 4 February 1955, Letters, 476.

Death of Lily Cahill: "Lily Cahill [obituary]."

Death of Adrienne Monnier: "A Letter to Sylvia Beach," CEOW, 107–108.

"were four": KAP to Gertrude Cahill Beitel, 20 September 1955, Letters, 487.

"determined": KAP to Felicia Geffen (American Academy of Arts and Letters), 16 October 1955, C.

"Now my days": KAP to GW, 4 August 1955, Letters, 485.

"I am now": KAP to William Jovanovich, 16 October 1955, C.

"inherited" ... "Well if my name": KAP to Donald Elder, 21 October 1955, C.

"My Lawrence, my dear friend": SL to DHU, 9 December 1992, DHUC.

"final": KAP to William Jovanovich, 2 November 1955, C.

"Katherine Anne": SL to KAP, 29 November 1955.

"Dear Seymour": KAP to SL, 12 December 1955.

"thoroughly vile"; "It *is* offensive": KAP to SL, 5 April 1956, Letters, 499.

"At the risk": KAP to SL, 2 May 1956, Letters, 503.

"an instrument": KAP to James F. Powers, 20 July 1956, Letters, 510–511.

"I am going": KAP to SL, 20 August 1958.

"protector": SL, remarks at KAP Centennial, 9 November 1990, Atlanta.

KAP at the University of Virginia: Jason.

"collateral": KAP to CB, 7 September 1958, Y.

"Yankees": KAP to ES, 23 February 1959, C.

KAP and the University of Texas: Holland.

"I look upon"" Bode, I, 35.

"I know Texas": Harry Ransom to KAP, 7 November 1958.

"Your decision": KAP to Harry Ransom, 16 November 1958, THC.

KAP at Washington and Lee: DHU interview with Rita Johns, 29 October 1994, Austin.

"I love this place": KAP to ES, 23 February 1959, C.

"golden glory": KAP to GW, 3 April 1959, Letters, 563.

"I don't want us": KAP to Jordan Pecile, 21 April 1959, C.

KAP in Georgetown: John Prince memoir and papers at MD.

David Locher's visit to Georgetown: DL to DHU, 26 October 1995.

"the gospel": KAP to CB and EAB, 9 June 1960, Y.

"I call that": Flannery O'Connor, 416.

"shout the good news": SL to KAP, 30 November 1960.

"Seymour darling": KAP to SL, 28 December 1960, Letters, 579–582.

"eagerness": SL to KAP, 16 January 1961.

"inertia"; "unbearable pressure"; "Don't call": KAP to SL, 4 February 1961.

"Nobody knows": KAP to Cyrilly Abels, 30 May 1961, C.

"The ship is in port": Mary McGinnis to SL, 30 June 1961.

"The midwife": SL to G. Royce Smith, 31 July 1961.

"mangled": KAP to SL, 18 August 1961.

Twenty-seven: Success and Failure in the Aftermath of a Novel

"Seymour, darling": KAP to SL, qtd. by SL to DHU, 9 December 1992, DHUC.

"All I want": KAP to CB, 18 July 1961, Y.

Katherine Anne Porter at Marshall University: "Author at MU Today," *Huntington Herald Dispatch*, 4 October 1961, sec. 2, 13; A. Mervyn Tyson to DHU, 17 July 1995, TI.

"Oh I wish": A. Mervyn Tyson to DHU, 17 July 1995, TI.

"For Seymour": SL to DHU, 17 November 1992.

"Believe me": Lefkowitz.

"the beau monde": William Maxwell to Frank O'Connor, 2 April 1962, in O'Connor and Maxwell, 172–173.

"This novel": Schorer, 1.

"These material pretties": KAP to Barbara Wescott, 3 May 1962, Letters, 591–592.

"See how publishers": SL to KAP, 18 April 1962.

"My God": Parker, 129.

"outstanding": Mortimer, "A Scathing Microcosm of Eternity," London Sunday Times Magazine, 28 October 1962, 31.

"a great universal": Sybille Bedford, "Voyage to Everywhere," Spectator 109 (16 November 1962): 763–764.

"snideness": Solotaroff.

"There is not only": JH to Alfred Kazin, qtd. in Langer, 312–313.

"moral attitudes": JH to Daniel Curley, 26 April 1962, Illinois.

"Even those": KAP to RPW, 22 July 1963, Letters, 615.

"I wrote"; "a passenger": KAP to CG, 28 April 1963, P.

"very good health": KAP to EAB, 7 October 1963, Y.

"I arrived home": KAP to RPW, 24 November 1963, Letters, 624.

"Honey, you know": John Prince memoir at MD.

"and all hopes": KAP to John Prince, 10 January 1964.

"dreadful the way": KAP to SL, 31 January 1964.

"skeptics": SL to KAP, 25 June 1964.

"Dear Seymour": KAP to SL, 30 June 1964.

"I am sorry": Arthur Thornhill Jr. to KAP, 8 July 1964.

"This talk": SL to KAP, 10 July 1964.

"for life": KAP to CG, 5 November 1964, P.

"unreasonable": "A House of My Own," CEOW, 175.

"My taste": KAP to CB and EAB, n.d. [1963], Y.

"I'll do anything": Refugee, xv.

"He was": Refugee, xiv–xv.

"to part is to die": CS, vi.

"aspects of Katherine Anne Porter": Spoto, 270.

"a dedicated": Gilroy.

"I should like to put": CB to Nobel Committee of the Swedish Academy, 15 December 1966, Y.

"the Nobel Prize and a Congressional Medal": KAP to Frances Hudspeth, 1 March 1958, THC.

Twenty-eight: Spring Valley and College Park

"Bobby Kennedy": KAP to IB, 15 January 1968, qtd in IB Diary.

"dramatize": BP, remarks at KAP Centennial, 7 November 1990, Atlanta.

"a great myth-makers" . . . "was greatly": BP to Joan Givner, 22 November 1982, carbon copy in Barrett Prettyman Papers at MD.

Raymond Roseliep: biographical information supplied by DL; Life, 448.

"I love you": Raymond Roseliep to KAP, 26 January 1962.

"all the wonderful": BP to KAP, 3 September 1968.

"up to a point": BP to Joan Givner, 22 November 1982, C.

"Miss Porter apologizes": CB to DHU, 20 December 1993, interview, New Haven.

"wine jail" WW to DHU, 27 May 1996, Baltimore.

"cruelty": PP, "In the Kitchen with Katherine Anne Porter" unpublished memoir, PPC.

"so sorry": Barbara Thompson Davis to DHU, 28 July 2001, DHUC.

"man's world": SL, remarks at KAP Centennial, 7 November 1990, Atlanta.

"fine fetter": McAlexander, 202.

"But we all": McAlexander, 219.

"this gang": KAP to PP, 16 November 1975, TTC, PPC.

"calamitous": KAP to DL, 23 December 1969.

"Writing is" . . . "It was what": Dorsey, I, 154.

"endless farewell": KAP to John Malcolm Brinnin, 18 May 1969, Delaware.

"Miss Porter": Georgetown University Hospital medical records.

"I've never": Schenker.

"after long suffering": KAP, appointment calendar, 1969–1970.

"uproariously": Novak and Chisholm, I, 155–157.

"classic Granny trick": KAP to Margaret Marshall, 6 July 1970, Y.

"You may believe": PP to DHU, 13 July 2001, DHUC.

Twenty-nine: Return to Texas

"I long to return": KAP to Roger L. Brooks, n.d. [before 1976].

"It has not been": KAP to John Malcolm Brinnin, 6 January 1972, C.

"Now honey": Corry.

"hell" and "damn": James Dickey to DHU, 25 September 1996, interview, Columbia, SC.

"the best six": KAP, inscription on photograph given to BP, dated 7 August 1972.

"I love this scattered": KAP to John Malcolm Brinnin, 28 August 1972, Delaware.

"Do look!": KAP to CB and EAB, 28 August 1972, Y.

"I shall never": KAP to BP, 23 November 1971.

"Don't let anyone"; "Yes, yes": KAP and PP, 15 October 1972, TTC, PPC.

"a thang"; "It was *Playboy!*": KAP to PP, 30 September 1972, TTC, PPC.

"adolescent": KAP, marginalia on newspaper clipping sent to BP.

"I had never": Corry.

"the most stimulating": Whiteaker, I, 158.

"If I give": KAP lecture, McKeldin Library, December 1972.

"This is neither": KAP to BP, 5 January 1973.

"Some things": KAP to ES, 23 February 1959, C.

"Ah well": KAP to BP, 13 February 1973.

"limitations" KAP to BP, 15 November 1973.

"She didn't": Dobson.

"I want to say": KAP to Cyrilly Abels, 22 October 1975.

"destroy": Dolan, I, 185.

"All our beautiful": KAP to Roger Brooks, n.d. [April 1976], C.

"independence": Booth.

"I cannot": KAP to Roger Brooks, 26 April 1976, C.

"I haven't had": Rodenberger, "The Prodigal Daughter Comes Home," in Busby and Heaberlin, 123.

"But by then": Roger Brooks, "Hosting Miss Porter," in Busby and Haeberlin, 116.

"We got along": Laughlin, "HPU Profesor Looks into Life of Author" and "Porter Anticipated Death."

Thirty: The Last Candles

"I'm busy dying": Gallagher.

"I couldn't wait": KAP to BP, 2 July 1976.

"Maturity" . . . "He's wonderful": KAP to PP, 20 April 1976, TTC, PPC.

"I wish you luck"; "thrilled": Owen Laster to DHU, 17 August 2000, TI.

"I am slowly": KAP to DL, 9 December 1976.

"I really": KAP to MW, 9 January 1977, C.

"I was born": Medical file, 11 January 1977.

"fighter": WW to Toni Willison, 22 February 1977.

"*very* ill": WW to Toni Willison, 9 April 1977.

"a sympathizer": KAP, N-EW, 14.

"She writes": Brooks, "Books: Briefly Noted," *New Yorker* 53 (29 August 1977): 87–88.

"It is": "The Never-Ending Wrong," *Publisher's Weekly* 211 (13 June 1977): 103.

"I want to tell you": KAP to IB, IB Diary.

"prison": EW to DHU, 23 February 1994, interview, Jackson, MS.

"I loved and enjoyed": KAP to SL, 28 August 1978.

"treachery"; "Angel": SL to William Humphrey, 19 June 1985, HRC.

"deeply moved": RPW to Peter Davison, 11 October 1979, qtd by Blotner, *Robert Penn Warren*, 457–458.

"unordered sounds" . . . "I have never": IB Diary.

"my writing hand": Feeley.

"Let's tuck": IB Diary.

Death of KAP: DeMouy; PP, Diary of KAP's illness.

"I think that's what": Robert Wilson to Hubert McAlexander, 12 September 1999, qtd in McAlexander, 242.

KAP's burial: PP to DHU, 10 March 2000, DHUC.

BIBLIOGRAPHY

Works by Katherine Anne Porter

"Adventures in Living." *Mademoiselle* 41 (July 1955): 28–34.

"The Adventures of Hadji: A Tale of a Turkish Coffee House." *Asia* 20 (August 1920): 683–684. Reprint, UEP, 22–27.

"And to the Living, Joy." *McCall's* 99 (December 1971): 76–77.

"Brother Spoiled a Romance." *Chicago Sunday Tribune*, 29 March 1914, sec. 6, 2.

"A Christmas Story." *Mademoiselle* 24 (December 1946): 155, 277–279. Reprinted as a separate publication by Seymour Lawrence/Delacorte, 1967.

The Collected Essays and Occasional Writings of Katherine Anne Porter. New York: Seymour Lawrence/Delacorte, 1970. Reprint, Boston: Houghton Mifflin/Seymour Lawrence, 1990.

The Collected Stories of Katherine Anne Porter. New York: Harcourt Brace Jovanovich, 1965.

The Days Before. New York: Harcourt Brace Jovanovich, 1952.

"The Faithful Princess." *Everyland* 2 (February 1920): 42–43. Reprint, UEP 15–18.

Flowering Judas. Limited ed. New York: Harcourt, Brace, 1930.

Flowering Judas and Other Stories. New York: Harcourt, Brace, 1935.

"The Gift of Woman." *Woman's Home Companion*, December 1956, 29–32, 56.

"Here Is My Home." *Perfect Home*, November 1954, 3.

Introduction. *What Price Marriage?* New York: J. H. Sears, 1927.

Katherine Anne Porter's French Song-Book. Paris: Harrison of Paris, 1933. Reprint, Poetry.

Katherine Anne Porter's Poetry. Edited by Darlene Harbour Unrue. Columbia: University of South Carolina Press, 1996.

The Leaning Tower and Other Stories. New York: Harcourt, Brace, 1944.

Letters of Katherine Anne Porter. Edited by Isabel Bayley. New York: Atlantic Monthly Press, 1990.

"The Magic Ear Ring." *Everyland* 2 (March 1920): 86–87. Reprint, UEP 18–21.

My Chinese Marriage, by M.T.F. New York: Duffield, 1921. Reprinted as *Mae Franking's My Chinese Marriage.* Edited by Holly Franking. Austin: University of Texas Press, 1991.

The Never-Ending Wrong. Boston: Atlantic–Little, Brown, 1977.

"Notes on the Texas I Remember." *Atlantic Monthly* 235 (March 1975): 102–106.

Outline of Mexican Popular Arts and Crafts. Los Angeles: Young and McCallister, 1922. Reprint, UEP 136–187.

Pale Horse, Pale Rider: Three Short Novels. New York: Harcourt, Brace, 1939.

"The Shattered Star." *Everyland* 2 (January 1920): 422–423. Reprint, UEP 12–15.

Ship of Fools. Boston: Atlantic–Little, Brown, 1962.

"The Spivvleton Mystery." *Ladies' Home Journal* 88 (August 1971): 74–75, 101.

"This Strange, Old World" and Other Book Reviews by Katherine Anne Porter. Edited by Darlene Harbour Unrue. Athens: University of Georgia Press, 1991.

Uncollected Early Prose of Katherine Anne Porter. Edited by Ruth M. Alvarez and Thomas F. Walsh. Austin: University of Texas Press, 1993.

"Why She Selected 'Flowering Judas.'" In *This Is My Best,* edited by Whit Burnett and Burton C. Hoffman, 539–540. New York: Dial, 1942.

"You Are What You Read." *Vogue* 164 (October 1974): 248, 250, 252.

Interviews

Allen, Henry. "Present at the Destruction." *Washington Post, Potomac Magazine,* 31 March 1974, 12–14. Reprinted as "Katherine Anne Porter: The Vanity of Excellence," I, 162–172.

Bode, Winston. "Miss Porter on Writers and Writing." *Texas Observer,* 31 October 1958. Reprint, I, 30–38.

Boutell, Clip. "Authors Are Like People: Short Story Secret—A Plea for Dueling." *New York Evening Post,* 21 September 1944, 23.

Crawford, Kitty Barry. "Miss Porter Heads Clinic Campaign." *Fort Worth Record,* September 1921. Reprint, I, 6–7.

Dolan, Mary Ann. "Almost Since Chaucer with Miss Porter," *Washington Star,* 11 May 1975, sec. 1, 1, 6. Reprint, I, 177–183.

Dorsey, John. "Katherine Anne Porter on: Truman Capote . . . Edith Sitwell . . . Ernest Hemingway . . . And on Her Life and Writing." *Baltimore Sun Magazine*, 26 October 1969, 16, 18–19, 21, 23, 40–41. Reprint, I, 139–154.

Foley, Eileen. "Katherine Anne Porter Gets a Gift, Day of Her Own at LaSalle College." *Philadelphia Evening Bulletin*, 27 October 1961, 19.

Givner, Joan, ed. *Katherine Anne Porter: Conversations.* Jackson: University Press of Mississippi, 1987.

Grumbach, Doris. "The Katherine Anne Porter Watch: After Sacco and Vanzetti, What? 'The Devil and Cotton Mather'?" *Village Voice*, 26 January 1976, 43–44. Reprint, I, 184–188.

Janeway, Elizabeth. "For Katherine Anne Porter, 'Ship of Fools' Was a Lively Twenty-Two Year Voyage." *New York Times Book Review*, 1 April 1962, 4–5. Reprint, I, 69–73.

Kernan, Michael. "It's Just Fine to Be 83." *Washington Post*, 30 March 1974, D3.

Lopez, Hank. "A Country and Some People I Love." *Harper's Magazine* 231 (September 1965): 58–68. Reprint, I, 120–134.

McCardle, Dorothy. "Author Abridged by Only One Word." *Washington Post*, 16 May 1968, E8.

McGrory, Mary. "Reading and Writing." *Washington Star*, 12 April 1953, E9. Reprint, I, 28–29.

Newquist, Roy. "An Interview with Katherine Anne Porter." *McCall's* 98 (August 1965): 87–89, 137–142. Reprint, I, 99–119.

Novak, Josephine, and Elise Chisholm. "Don't Scare the Horses, Miss Porter Tells Liberation Women." *Baltimore Evening Sun*, 25 March 1970. Reprint, I, 155–157.

Ruoff, James. "Katherine Anne Porter Comes to Kansas." *Midwest Quarterly* 4 (July 1963): 305–314. Reprint, I, 61–68.

Schenker, Israel. "Katherine Anne Porter Is 79 and Sovereign." *New York Times*, 3 April 1970, 39.

Schoettler, Carl. "Katherine Anne Porter Reigns for Students." *Baltimore Evening Sun*, 15 April 1974. Reprint, I, 173–176.

Shearer, Gordon K. "What One Woman Is Doing to Help Children." *Dallas Morning News*, 16 December 1916. Reprint, I, 3–5.

Thompson, Barbara. "Katherine Anne Porter: An Interview." *Paris Review* 8 (winter–spring 1963): 87–114. Reprint, I, 78–98.

Whitaker, Mildred. "Glimpses of San Antonio at Turn of the Century." *San Antonio Express and News*, 21 January 1973, sec. A, 2, 4. Reprint, I, 158–161.

Winston, Archer. "Presenting the Portrait of an Artist." *New York Post*, 6 May 1937, 17. Reprint, I, 8–13.

Bibliographies

Hilt, Kathryn, and Ruth M. Alvarez. *Katherine Anne Porter: An Annotated Bibliography*. New York: Garland, 1990.

Wade, Sally Dee. "'The Homeless One Home Again': A Texas Bibliography of Katherine Anne Porter." In Machann and Clark, 113–182.

Secondary

* Indicates a volume with marginalia in KAP's library at MD.

Aaron, Daniel. *Writers on the Left: Episodes in American Literary Communism*. New York: Harcourt, Brace and World, 1961.

"Aguilera, Francisco." *National Directory of Latin Americanists*. 2nd ed. Hispanic Foundation Bibliographical Series No. 12. Washington: Library of Congress, 1966.

Allen, Paula. "Flamboyant Park a Bright Light for Thrill-Seekers: A Look Back." *San Antonio Express-News*, 17 September 2000, 5G.

———. "The Thomas School." *San Antonio Express-News*, 24 April 1994.

Almon, Bert. *William Humphrey, Destroyer of Myths*. Denton: University of North Texas Press, 1998.

Alvarez, Ruth M. "Katherine Anne Porter and Mexican Art." PhD diss., University of Maryland, 1990.

"Art Exhibitions of the Week." *New York Times*, 2 March 1924, X10.

Atlas, James. *Delmore Schwartz: The Life of an American Poet*. New York: Farrar, Straus and Giroux, 1977.

*Augustine of Hippo, Saint. *The Confessions*. Translated by E. B. Pusey. London. J. M. Dent, 1932.

Austenfeld, Thomas Carl. *American Women Writers and the Nazis: Ethics and Politics in Boyle, Porter, Stafford, and Hellman*. Charlottesville: University Press of Virginia, 2001.

"Author at MU Today." *Huntington Herald Dispatch*, 4 October 1961, sec. 2, 13.

Baird, Nancy Disher, Carol Crowe-Carraco, and Michael L. Morse. *Bowling Green: A Pictorial History*. Norfolk, VA: Downing Co., 1983.

Baker, Carlos. "A Happy Harvest." *New York Times Book Review*, 1 November 1954, 4.

Beach, Sylvia. *Shakespeare and Company: The Story of an American Bookshop in Paris*. New York: Harcourt, Brace, 1956.

Beals, Carleton. *Glass Houses: Ten Years of Freelancing*. Philadelphia: J. B. Lippincott, 1938.

*Beauvoir, Simone de. *The Second Sex*. Translated by H. M. Parshley. New York: Knopf, 1953.

Bedford, Sybille. "Voyage to Everywhere." *Spectator* 109 (16 November 1962): 763–764.

Beer, Thomas. *The Mauve Decade*. New York: Knopf, 1926.

"Bessie Beatty, 61, Commentator Dies." *New York Times*, 7 April 1947, 23.

Blotner, Joseph. *Faulkner: A Biography*. 2 vols. New York: Random House, 1974.

———. *Robert Penn Warren*. New York: Random House, 1997.

Blum, John Morton. *V Was for Victory: Politics and American Culture during World War II*. New York: Harcourt Brace Jovanovich, 1977.

Bongartz, Roy. "Yaddo at 60." *Publishers Weekly*, 13 June 1987, 32–35.

Booth, C. Robie. "'Writer's Writer': Miss Porter a Skidmore Delight, D. Litt." *Entertainer*, 1 April 1976, 3.

Brackenridge, R. Douglas. *Voices in the Wilderness: A History of the Cumberland Presbyterian Church in Texas*. San Antonio: Trinity University Press, 1968.

Brinkmeyer, Robert H., Jr. *Katherine Anne Porter's Artistic Development: Primitivism, Traditionalism, and Totalitarianism*. Baton Rouge: Louisiana State University Press, 1993.

Brinnin, John Malcolm. *Dylan Thomas in America: An Intimate Journal*. Boston: Atlantic–Little, Brown, 1955.

Britton, John A. *Carleton Beals: A Radical Journalist in Latin America*. Albuquerque: University of New Mexico Press, 1987.

Brooks, Cleanth. "The Woman and Artist I Knew." In Machann and Clark, 13–24.

Brooks, Roger. "Hosting Miss Porter." In Machann and Clark, 110–121.

Buckley, Tom. "Caribbean Cruise Attempts to Seek Meaning of Apollo." *New York Times*, 12 December 1972, 49–53.

Busby, Mark, and Dick Heaberlin, eds. *From Texas to the World and Back: Essays on the Journeys of Katherine Ann Porter*. Fort Worth: Texas Christian University Press, 2001.

Carr, Virginia Spencer. *The Lonely Hunter: A Biography of Carson McCullers*. New York: Doubleday, 1975.

"Charles Shannon, An Art Instructor and Painter, 81 [obituary]." *New York Times*, 20 April 1996, 50.

Charlot, Jean. *The Mexican Mural Renaissance, 1920–1925*. New Haven: Yale University Press, 1963.

*Child, Francis James. *English and Scottish Popular Ballads*. 1904; reprint, Boston: Houghton Mifflin, 1932.

Churchill, Allen. *Over Here!* New York: Dodd, Mead, 1968.

Clark, Eleanor. "The Friendships of a Lifetime." *Washington Post Book World* 11 (26 July 1981): 1–2, 9–10.

Clark, Marjorie Ruth. *Organized Labor in Mexico*. New York: Russell and Russell, 1973.

Clark, Thomas D. *A History of Kentucky*. Ashland, KY: Jesse Stuart Foundation, 1988.

Collins, Lewis. *History of Kentucky*. 3 vols. Lexington, 1874.

Corry, John. "Intellectuals in Bloom at Spring Gathering." *New York Times*, 18 May 1972, 49, 63.

Cowley, Malcolm. *Exile's Return*. 1934; reprint (with subtitle, *A Literary Odyssey of the 1920s*). New York: Viking, 1951.

Crane, Hart. *The Letters of Hart Crane, 1916–1932*. Edited by Brom Weber. Berkeley: University of California Press, 1952.

Crume, Paul. "Pale Horse, Pale Rider, by Katherine Anne Porter." *Southwest Review* 25 (January 1940): 213–218.

"Cyrilly Abels [obituary]." *New York Times*, 9 November 1975, C9.

Dardis, Tom. *Firebrand: The Life of Horace Liveright*. New York: Random House, 1995.

Dawson, Margaret Cheney. "A Perfect Flowering." *New York Herald Tribune, Books*, 14 September 1930, 3–4.

De la Barca, Frances Inglis Calderón. *Life in Mexico*. New York: E. P. Dutton, 1913.

De la Selva, Salomón. *Tropical Town and Other Poems*. New York: John Lane, 1918.

Dell, Floyd. *Love in Greenwich Village*. New York: George H. Doran, 1926.

DeMouy, Jane Krause. "Elegy for Katherine Anne." *Virginia Quarterly Review* 75, no. 3 (summer 1999): 504–510.

———. *Katherine Anne Porter's Women: The Eye of Her Fiction*. Austin: University of Texas Press, 1983.

Dobson, Clark. "Clark Dobson and Kathleen Feeley Remember Katherine Anne Porter. *Newsletter of the Katherine Anne Porter Society* 4, no. 2 (November 1997): 1, 3–5.

*Drake, Daniel. *Pioneer Life in Kentucky, 1785–1800*. New York: Schuman, 1948.

Duffy, Bernard. *The Chicago Renaissance in American Letters*. East Lansing: Michigan State University Press, 1956.

Dulles, John F. W. *Yesterday in Mexico: A Chronicle of the Revolution, 1919–1936*. Austin: University of Texas Press, 1961.

Edmiston, Susan, and Linda Cirino. *Literary New York*. Boston: Houghton Mifflin, 1976.

Edwards, John. "Atlanta's Prodigal Daughter: The Turbulent Life of Jane Anderson as Expatriate and Nazi Propagandist." *Atlanta Historical Journal* 18 (1984): 23–42.

Enciso, Jorge. *Design Motifs of Ancient Mexico*. New York: Dover, 1953.

"Ernestine Evans, Editor-Critic 77 [obituary]." *New York Times*, 4 July 1967, 19.

Feeley, Sr. Kathleen. "Remembering Katherine Anne Porter." *Newsletter of the Katherine Ann Porter Society* 5, no. 1 (May 1998): 1–4.

Fehrenbach, T. R. *Lone Star: A History of Texas and the Texans*. New York: Macmillan, 1968.

Ferguson, Walter Keene. *Geology and Politics in Frontier Texas: 1845–1909*. Austin: University of Texas Press, 1969.

Fernett, Gene. "Essanay." *American Film Studios*. Jefferson, NC: McFarland and Co., 1988.

Fitch, Noel Riley. *Sylvia Beach and the Lost Generation: A History of Literary Paris in the Twenties and Thirties*. New York: W. W. Norton, 1983.

Ford, Hugh. *Published in Paris: American and British Writers, Printers, and Publishers in Paris, 1920–1939*. New York: Macmillan, 1975.

"Francisco Aguilera: Specialist in Hispanic Culture [obituary]." *Washington Post*, 14 June 1981.

"Francisco Aguilera Dies: LC Hispanic Specialist from 1944 to 1969." *Library of Congress Information Bulletin*, 19 June 1981, 216.

*Freud, Sigmund. *A General Introduction to Psychoanalysis*. Translated by Joan Rivere. Garden City, NY: Garden City Publishing, 1920.

Gallagher, Joseph. "Katherine Anne Porter: The Last Candle Is Out." *Baltimore Evening Sun*, 30 September 1980.

Gaver, Kenneth D. "Mental Illness and Mental Retardation: The History of State Care in Texas." *Impact* 5, no. 2 (July–August 1975).

Gebhard, Paul H., and Alan B. Johnson. *The Kinsey Data: Marginal Tabulations of the 1938–1963 Interviews Conducted by the Institute for Sex Research*. Philadelphia: W. B. Saunders, 1979.

Geduld, Harry M., and Ronald Gottesman. *Sergei Eisenstein and Upton Sinclair: The Making and Unmaking of "Que Viva Mexico!"* Bloomington: Indiana University Press, 1970.

Gilderhus, Mark T. "Senator Albert B. Fall and 'The Plot against Mexico.'" *New Mexico Historical Review* 48 (fall 1973): 304–305.

Gilmer, Walker. *Horace Liveright: Publisher of the Twenties*. New York: David Lewis, 1970.

Gilroy, Harry. "Book Awards Go to 4 U.S. Writers." *New York Times*, 16 March 1966, 42.

Ginger, Ray. *Age of Excess: The United States from 1877 to 1914*. New York: Macmillan, 1965.

Givner, Joan. *Katherine Anne Porter: A Life*. New York: Simon & Schuster, 1982. Revised, Athens: University of Georgia Press, 1991.

Goyen, William. *Selected Letters from a Writers Life*. Edited with an introduction by Robert Phillips. Austin: University of Texas Press, 1995.

*Grasset, Joseph. *The Semi-Insane and the Semi-Responsible*. Translated by Smith Ely Jelliff. New York: Funk and Wagnalls, 1907.

Green, James R. *Grass-Roots Socialism: Radical Movements in the Southwest, 1895–1943*. Baton Rouge: Louisiana State University Press, 1978.

Gretlund, Jan Nordby. "'The Man in the Tree': Katherine Anne Porter's Unfinished Lynching Story." *Southern Quarterly* 31 (1993): 7–16.

Grider, Sylvia. "Memories That Never Were: Katherine Anne Porter and the Family Saga." In Busby and Heaberlin, 225–237.

Grimes, Roy, ed. *300 Years in Victoria County*. Victoria, TX: Victoria Advocate, 1968.

Gruening, Ernest. *Mexico and Its Heritage*. New York: Appleton Century, 1936.

"H. B. Porter, 84, Last Survivor of Travis Rifles, Dies." *Houston Chronicle*, 24 January 1942.

Hale, William Harlan. *Challenge to Defeat: Modern Man in Goethe's World and Spengler's Century*. New York: Harcourt, Brace, 1932.

Halverson, John, and Ian Watt. "Notes on Jane Anderson." *Conradiana* 23 (1991): 59–87.

Hamilton, Ian. *Robert Lowell: A Biography*. New York: Random House, 1982.

Hamovitch, Mitzi Berger. *The Hound & Horn Letters*. Athens: University of Georgia Press, 1982.

Handy, Deirdre C. "The Family Legend in the Stories of Katherine Anne Porter." MA thesis, University of Oklahoma, 1953.

Hanna, Paul. "Mexico—1921: v. Relations with the United States." *Nation* 112, no. 2912 (27 April 1921): 614–617.

Hardwick, Elizabeth. "Katherine Anne." *Vanity Fair*, March 1984, 81–85.

Hart, John Mason. *Revolutionary Mexico: The Coming and Process of the Mexican Revolution*. Berkeley: University of California Press, 1987.

Havener, Sandra. "Unsung Native Daughter." *San Angelo Magazine*, April 1985, 13–18.

Havins, T. R. *Something about Brown: A History of Brown County, Texas*. Brownwood, TX: Banner, 1958.

*Hendrick, George. *Katherine Anne Porter*. New York: Twayne, 1965.

Hendrick, George, and Willene Hendrick. *Katherine Anne Porter*. Boston: Twayne/G. K. Hall, 1988. Revision of *Katherine Anne Porter*, by George Hendrick, 1965.

Hendrick, Willene. "Indian Creek: A Sketch from Memory." In Machann and Clark, 3–12.

"Herbert Kline." In *International Directory of Films and Filmmakers*. Chicago: St. James Press, 1984.

"Herbert Kline [obituary]." *New York Times*, 17 February 1989. C23.

Herbst, Josephine. "Miss Porter and Miss Stein." *Partisan Review* 15 (1948): 568–572.

———. *The Starched Blue Sky of Spain and Other Memoirs*. Introduction by Diane Johnson. New York: HarperCollins, 1992.

———. "A Year of Disgrace." *Noble Savage* 3 (1961): 128–160. Reprinted in Herbst, *The Starched Blue Sky of Spain and Other Memoirs*.

Hicks, Ida Belle. "Twenty Years Ago Today the Little Theater Got Its Start in Fort Worth." *Fort Worth Star-Telegram*, 12 October 1941, 10.

Holland, Richard. "Katherine Anne Porter and the University of Texas: A Map of Misunderstanding." In Busby and Heaberlin, 78–97.

Humphrey, Robert E. *Children of Fantasy: The First Rebels of Greenwich Village*. New York: John Wiley and Sons, 1978.

Humphris, Lady Bunton. "Life of Lady Bunton Humphris in Presidio County." Unpublished autobiography, 1959.

Irving, David John Cawdell. *Göring, a Biography*. New York: Morrow, 1989.

Jaeger, Art. "Celebrated Writer Assigned Guardian." *Prince Georges County Journal*, 5 October 1977, 1, 7.

Jason, Philip K. "The University as Patron of Literature: The Balch Program at Virginia." *Journal of General Education* 35, no. 3 (1983): 174–188.

Jewell, Edward Allen. "Three Phases of a Hardy Perennial [Ernest Stock]." *New York Times* 14 April 1935, X7.

Johns, Erna Schlemmer. *To Whom It May Concern*. 2 vols. Austin, TX: privately printed, 1977.

Jones, James H. *Alfred C. Kinsey: A Public/Private Life*. New York: W. W. Norton, 1997.

"Joseph Retinger, Polish Diplomat [obituary]." *New York Times*, 24 June 1960, 27.

"Josephine Herbst, Novelist and Social-Political Reporter, Dead." *New York Times*, 29 January 1969.

Josephson, Matthew. *Life Among the Surrealists*. New York: Holt Rinehart Winston, 1962.

*———. *Zola and His Time*. New York: Macaulay, 1928.

"Katherine A. Porter Gives Books, Grant to Md. U. Library." *Washington Post*, 21 December 1966, C3.

Katherine Anne Porter: The Eye of Memory. A film produced by Calvin Skaggs. Lumiere Productions, 1988.

Kempf, James Michael. *The Early Career of Malcolm Cowley: A Humanist among the Moderns*. Baton Rouge: Louisiana State University Press, 1981.

Kennedy, David M. *Over Here: The First World War and American Society*. Oxford: Oxford University Press, 1980.

"Klein, Herbert, 1909–1999." *Contemporary Authors*, vol. 184, 159. Detroit: Gale, 2000.

Kolata, Gina. *Flu: The Story of the Great Influenza Pandemic of 1918 and the Search for the Virus That Caused It*. New York: Farrar, Straus and Giroux, 1999.

Kunitz, Stanley, ed. *Authors Today and Yesterday*. New York: H. H. Wilson, 1933.

"Lady Haw-Haw." *Time* 39 (19 January 1942): 30.

Lancaster, Ida M. *The Long Hunter*. Amarillo, TX: privately published, 1995.
———. *Skaggs Carousel*. Amarillo, TX: privately published, 1994.

Langer, Elinor. *Josephine Herbst*. Boston: Little, Brown, 1984. Reprint, Boston: Northeastern University Press, 1994.
———. "The Measuring Stick." *Grand Street* 3 (summer 1984): 108–139.

Laskin, David. *Partisans: Marriage, Politics and Betrayal Among the New York Intellectuals*. New York: Simon & Schuster, 2000.

Laughlin, Charlotte. "HPU Professor Looks into Life of Author." *Brownwood Bulletin*, 21 September 1980, 1, 11–12.
———. "Katherine Anne Porter's Brown County Connections." Unpublished paper.
———. "Porter Anticipated Death." *Brownwood Bulletin*, 22 September 1980.

Lefkowitz, Bernard. "Author Finds Luxury Too Costly." *New York Post*, 5 March 1962, 34.

Leonard, George Sill. "A Letter from Mexico and the Gleam of Montezuma's Golden Roofs." *Christian Science Monitor*, 5 June 1921, 22. Incorporated letter from Katherine Anne Porter. Reprint, UEP.

Liberman, M. M. *Katherine Anne Porter's Fiction*. Detroit: Wayne State University Press, 1971.
———. "Meeting Miss Porter." *Georgia Review* 41 (summer 1987): 299–303.
———. "The Responsibility of the Novelist: The Critical Reception of *Ship of Fools*." *Criticism* (fall 1966): 377–388.

"Lily Cahill [obituary]." *New York Times*, 21 July 1955, 23.

Lopez, Enrique Hank. *Conversations with Katherine Anne Porter: Refugee from Indian Creek*. Boston: Little, Brown, 1981.

Lowell, Robert. "Visiting the Tates." *Sewanee Review* 67 (1959): 557–558.

Machann, Clinton, and William Bedford Clark, eds. *Katherine Anne Porter and Texas: An Uneasy Relationship*. College Station: Texas A & M University Press, 1990.

MacKinnon, Janice R., and Stephen R. MacKinnon. *Agnes Smedley: The Life and Times of an American Radical*. Berkeley: University of California Press, 1988.

Makowsky, Veronica A. *Caroline Gordon: A Biography*. New York: Oxford University Press, 1989.

Mallett, Daniel Trowbridge. "Ernest Stock." In *Mallett's Index of Artists: International—Biographical*, 811. New York: Peter Smith, 1948.

Manville, Roger, and Heinrich Fraenkel. *Hermann Göring*. New York: Simon and Schuster, 1962.

Marlor, Clark S. "Ernest Stock." In *The Society of Independent Artists: The Exhibition Record, 1917–1944*, 600. Park Ridge, NJ: Noyes Press, 1984.

Marnham, Patrick. *Dreaming with His Eyes Open: A Life of Diego Rivera*. New York: Alfred A. Knopf, 1998.

Marshall, Margaret. "Writers in the Wilderness: III: Katherine Anne Porter." *Nation* 150 (13 April 1940): 473–475.

McAlexander, Hubert H. *Peter Taylor: A Writer's Life*. Baton Rouge: Louisiana State University Press, 2001.

McGrory, Mary. "Reading and Writing." *Washington Star*, 12 April 1953, E9. Reprint, I, 28–29.

McGuire, William. *Poetry's Catbird Seat: The Consultantship in Poetry in the English Language at the Library of Congress, 1937–1987*. Washington, DC: Library of Congress, 1988.

Miller, William D. *Dorothy Day: A Biography*. New York: Harper and Row, 1982.

Mizener, Arthur. *The Saddest Story: A Biography of Ford Madox Ford*. New York: Carroll & Graf, 1971.

Mooney, Harry John, Jr. *The Fiction and Criticism of Katherine Anne Porter*. Pittsburgh: University of Pittsburgh Press, 1957.

Morris, Leopold. *Pictorial History of Victoria and Victoria County*. San Antonio: Clemens Printing Co., 1953.

Morton, Marian J. *Emma Goldman and the American Left: Nowhere at Home*. New York: St. Martin's, 1991.

Mosley, Leonard. *The Reich Marshall*. Garden City, NY: Doubleday, 1974.

"Move to Kaffie Building Marks New Chapter for Firm." *Corpus Christie Caller-Times*, 9 July 1950.

"Mrs. C. A. Porter Buried." *San Antonio Daily Express*, 6 October 1901.

Myers, Jeffrey. *Joseph Conrad: A Biography*. New York: Charles Scribner's Sons, 1991.

Nance, William Leslie, S. J. *Katherine Anne Porter and the Art of Rejection*. Chapel Hill: University of North Carolina Press, 1964.

Naylor, Pauline. "Early Porter Tales Written Here." *Fort Worth Star-Telegram*, 17 April 1966, sec. 5, 16.

———. "Katherine Anne Porter's Fort Worth Days Recalled." *Fort Worth Star-Telegram*, 10 April 1966, sec. 5, 1.

O'Connor, Flannery. *The Habit of Being: Letters*. Edited with an introduction by Sally Fitzgerald. New York: Farrar, Straus and Giroux, 1979.

O'Connor, Frank, and William Maxwell. *The Happiness of Getting It Right: Letters of Frank O'Connor and William Maxwell, 1945–1966*. Edited by Michael Steinman. New York: Alfred A. Knopf, 1996.

Olsen, Tillie. *Silences*. New York: Delacorte/Seymour Lawrence, 1970.

Overy, R. J. *Goering, the Iron Man*. London: Routledge and Kegan Paul, 1984.

Parker, Dorothy. Book review. *Esquire* 58 (July 1962): 129.

Payton, Green. *San Antonio: City in the Sun*. New York: McGraw-Hill, 1946.

Pells, Richard H. *Radical Visions & American Dreams: Culture and Social Thought in the Depression Years*. Middletown, CT: Wesleyan University Press, 1973.

*Phelps, Robert, and Peter Deane. *The Literary Life: A Scrapbook Almanac of the Anglo-America Literary Scene from 1900 to 1950*. NewYork: Farrar, Straus and Giroux, 1968.

"Pioneer Merchant Gunst Will Close Book on Firm." *Corpus Christi Caller-Times*, 8 October 1960.

"Poetry of Our Times." *Variety*, 29 April 1953, 39.

Pohorilenko, Anatole, and James Crum. *When We Were Three: The Travel Albums of George Platt Lynes, Monroe Wheeler, and Glenway Wescott, 1925–1935*. New York: Arena, 1998.

Pomeroy, Wardell B. *Dr. Kinsey and the Institute for Sex Research*. New York: Harper and Row, 1972.

Porter, Paul. "Remembering Aunt Katherine." In Machann and Clark, 25–37.

Pratt, David H. *The Skaggs Story, 1763–1979: Southern Revolutionary War Soldier to Western Entrepreneur*. Provo, UT: Brigham Young University Press, 1979.

Pritchett, Roberta Belvin. "Coronal Institute: 1866–1918." *Kyle News*, 20 April 1928.

Ralph, Stephen C., ed. *The Correspondence of Flannery O'Connor and the Braiaerd Cheneys.* Jackson: University Press of Mississippi, 1986.

Reeves, Sally Kittredge. *Legacy of a Century: Academy of the Sacred Heart in New Orleans.* New Orleans: Archdiocese of New Orleans, 1987.

Retinger, Joseph Jerome. *Memoirs of an Eminence Grise.* Edited by John Pomian. Foreword by H. R. H. Prince Bernhard of the Netherlands. Sussex, England: University Press, 1972.

"Retreat for the Demented." *San Antonio Daily Express,* 26 August 1894.

"Roberto Haberman Dead at 79: Founder of Mexican Labor Unit." *New York Times,* 5 March 1962, 23.

Rockwell, Jeanne. "The Magic Cloak: On Meeting Katherine Anne Porter." *Michigan Quarterly Review* 5 (fall 1966): 283–284.

Rodes, John Barrett. "The Story of Bowling Green, Kentucky, and the First Presbyterian Church." Maunscript at the Kentucky Library (K).

Rosenfeld, Megan. "The Glory Wall," *Washington Post,* 4 June 2000, F1, 4.

Rothman, Sheila M. *Living in the Shadow of Death: Tuberculosis and the Social Experience of Illness in American History.* New York: HarperCollins, 1994.

Rueckert, William H. *Glenway Wescott.* New York: Twayne, 1965.

Saunders, Frances Stonor. *Who Paid the Piper? The CIA and the Cultural Cold War.* London: Granta, 1999.

Schmidt, Henry C. *The Roots of lo Mexicano: Self and Society in Mexican Thought, 1900–1934.* College Station: Texas A & M University Press, 1978.

Schorer, Mark. "We're All on the Passenger List." *New York Times Book Review,* 1 April 1962, 1, 5.

Seton, Marie. *Sergei M. Eisenstein: A Biography.* London: Bodley Head Press, 1952. Revised, London: Dennis Dobson, 1978.

Sexton, Kathryn Adams. "Katherine Anne Porter's Years in Denver." MA thesis, University of Colorado, 1961.

Shaynerson, Michael. "One Hundred Years of Attitude." *Vanity Fair,* July 2000, 88–102.

Shi, David E. *Matthew Josephson, Bourgeois Bohemian.* New Haven: Yale University Press, 1981.

Smith, Roberta. "A World According to Judd." *New York Times,* 26 February 1995, B31.

Smith, Tevis Clyde. "The Reverend Noah T. Byars—Figures in Texas History." *Pecan Valley News,* 22 December 1976.

Socher, June. *The New Woman: Feminism in Greenwich Village, 1910–1920.* New York: Quadrangle Books, 1972.

Solomon, Barbara. *Emma Goldman*. Boston: Twayne, 1987.

Solotaroff, Theodore. "'Ship of Fools' and the Critics." *Commentary* 34 (October 1962): 277–286.

"Some Important Writers Speak for Themselves—Katherine Anne Porter." *New York Herald Tribune Book Review*, 12 October 1952, 8.

"Song in the Dark." *Moving Picture World*, 6 June 1914, 1434.

Spoto, Donald. *Stanley Kramer: Film Maker*. New York: G. Putnam's Sons, 1978.

Spraker, Hazel Atterbury. *The Boone Family: A Genealogical History of the Descendants of George and Mary Boone Who Came to American in 1717*. 1922. Reprint, Baltimore: Genealogical Publishing Co., 1974.

Spratling, William. *File on Spratling: An Autobiography*. Introduction by Budd Schulberg. Boston: Little, Brown, 1967.

Stalling, Donald. "Katherine Anne Porter: Life and the Literary Mirror." MA thesis, Texas Christian University, 1951.

Stout, Janis. *Katherine Anne Porter: A Sense of the Times*. Charlottesville: University Press of Virginia, 1995.

Stovall, Francis, Maxine Storm, Louise Simon, Gene Johnson, Dorothy Schwartz, Dorothy Wuinberley Kerbox, and Cindy McCoy. *Clear Springs and Limestone Ledges, A History of San Marcos and Hays County: For the Texas Sesquicentennial*. San Marcos: Hays County Historical Commission, 1986.

Strom, Ann Miller. *The Prairie City: A History of Kyle, Texas, 1890–1980*. Burnet, TX: Nortex, 1981.

"This Book Mart Grew with the City." *Corpus Christi Caller-Times*, 7 September 1941.

Thompson, Cecilia. *History of Marfa and Presidio County, Texas, 1535–1946*. 2 vols. Austin: Nortex, 1985.

"Travis Guards and Rifles." *Handbook of Texas*. Austin: Texas State Historical Association, 1952.

Tytell, John. *Ezra Pound: The Solitary Volcano*. New York: Doubleday, 1987.

Unrue, Darlene Harbour. "The Game Players: Katherine Anne Porter and William Goyen." *Mississippi Quarterly* 49, no. 1 (winter 1995–1996): 119–126.

———. *Truth and Vision in Katherine Anne Porter's Fiction*. Athens: University of Georgia Press, 1985.

———. *Understanding Katherine Anne Porter*. Columbia: University of South Carolina Press, 1988.

———, ed. *Critical Essays on Katherine Anne Porter*. New York: G. K. Hall, 1997.

Updike, John, ed. *A Century of Arts & Letters*. New York: Columbia University Press, 1998.

Ureña, Pedro Henriquez. *Honenaje a Salomón de la Selva: 1959–1969*. León, Nicaragua: Cuadeemos Universitarios, 1969.

Vann, William H. *The Texas Institute of Letters, 1936–1966*. Austin: Encino Press, 1967.

Vliet, Vida Ann Rutherford. "Porter's House Eyed for Preservation." *San Antonio Sunday Express-News*, 20 May 1988.

———. "The Shape of Meaning: A Study of the Development of Katherine Anne Porter's Fictional Form." PhD diss., Pennsylvania State University, 1968.

"Von Pless [obituary]." *Buffalo (NY) Evening News*, 29 March 1954, 23.

Waldron, Ann. *Eudora: A Writer's Life*. New York: Doubleday, 1998.

Walsh, Thomas F. *Katherine Anne Porter and Mexico: The Illusion of Eden*. Austin: University of Texas Press 1992.

Welty, Eudora. *A Curtain of Green and Other Stories*. New York: Doubleday, Doran 1941.

———. "My Introduction to Katherine Anne Porter." *Georgia Review* 44, nos. 1–2 (spring–summer 1990): 13–27.

Wescott, Glenway. *Continual Lessons: The Journals of Glenway Wescott, 1937–1955*. Edited by Robert Phelps with Jerry Rosco. New York: Farrar, Straus and Giroux, 1990.

———. "Katherine Anne Porter." *Book-of-the-Month Club News*, March 1962, 5–7.

———. "Katherine Anne Porter: The Making of a Novel." *Atlantic Monthly* 209 (April 1962): 43–49.

"What Happened to Hadji." In *Tales from Turkey*, translated by Allan Ramsay and Francis McCullagh, 12–15. London: Simpkin, Marshall, Hamilton, Kent, 1914.

White, Stephen F. *Modern Nicaraguan Poetry: Dialogues with France and the United States*. Lewisburg, PA: Bucknell University Press, 1993.

Wicks, Robert S., and Roland H. Harrison. *Buried Cities, Forgotten Gods: William Niven's Life of Discovery and Revolution in Mexico and the American Southwest*. Lubbock: Texas Tech University Press, 1999.

"William Hale, 63, an Editor, Dead." *New York Times*, 1 July 1974, 32.

Winslow, Marcella Comès. *Brushes with the Literary: Letters of a Washington Artist, 1943–1959*. Baton Rouge: Louisiana State University Press, 1993.

Wolfe, Bertram D. "Art and Revolution in Mexico." *Nation* 119 (27 August 1924): 207–208.

———. *The Fabulous Life of Diego Rivera*. New York: Stein and Day, 1963.

Womack, John, Jr. *Zapata and the Mexican Revolution*. New York: Alfred A. Knopf, 1969.

Wood, Sally, ed. *The Southern Mandarins: Letters of Caroline Gordon to Sally Wood, 1924–1937*. Baton Rouge: Louisiana State University Press, 1984.

Woodward, C. Vann. *Origins of the New South, 1877–1913*. Baton Rouge: Louisiana State University Press, 1951.

*Woolf, Virginia: *A Writer's Diary: Being Extracts from the Diary of Virginia Woolf*. Edited by Leonard Woolf. London: Hogarth Press, 1953.

Young, Thomas, and John J. Hindle, eds. *The Republic of Letters in America: The Correspondence of John Peale Bishop and Allen Tate*. Lexington: University of Kentucky Press, 1981.

Young, Thomas, John J. Hindle, and Elizabeth Sarcone, eds. *The Lytle-Tate Letters*. Jackson: University Press of Mississippi, 1987.

INDEX